UNIVERSITY OF NORTH CAROLINA
STUDIES IN COMPARATIVE LITERATURE

NUMBER 46

RUSSIAN STUDIES
OF AMERICAN LITERATURE

UNIVERSITY OF NORTH CAROLINA
STUDIES IN COMPARATIVE LITERATURE

Founded by Werner P. Friederich

For Reprints from this Series see page 218.

RUSSIAN STUDIES
OF AMERICAN LITERATURE

A Bibliography

Compiled by **Valentina A. Libman**

(Gorky Institute)

Translated by **Robert V. Allen**

(Library of Congress)

Edited by **Clarence Gohdes**

(Duke University)

CHAPEL HILL
UNIVERSITY OF NORTH CAROLINA PRESS
1969

Printed in the Netherlands by Royal VanGorcum Ltd., Assen

CONTENTS

PREFACE

The bibliography which appears in translation and transliteration in this book is the most important tool for the general study of Russian comment on the literature of the United States. It covers a period of more than a hundred and fifty years prior to 1964 and is divided into two parts: a section listing works on separate periods and general topics, and a much longer division concerned with the criticism of individual American authors, from the time of Benjamin Franklin to the present day — one hundred and forty-eight all told. The check list was compiled by Mrs. Valentina A. Libman, head bibliographer of the Library of Social Sciences of the Academy of Sciences of the USSR. Her work was originally published in a volume whose title may be translated *Problems of the History of the Literature of the U.S.A.* (Moscow: Publishing House Science, 1964, pp. 373-475). Through the kindness of W. Shcherbina, Assistant Director, permission to translate has been secured from the Gorky Institute of World Literature, which originally sponsored the check list.

It will be of interest to all students of American-Russian cultural relations and of particular service to scholars working in the field of American literature, who may now isolate items bearing on the authors or topics with which they are especially concerned and have them translated.

By merely glancing through the contents of this book a reader may see something of the general contours of the shifts in the Russian view of our literature — from the repercussions of Longfellow, Cooper, Mrs. Stowe *et al.* in the Czarist era and the considerable interest in American authors during the early years of the Revolution of 1917, through the concentration on proletarian literature of the late 1920's and early 1930's, to the barrage against our writers as minions of imperialism in the late Stalin era, to a selective willingness to give them more serious attention after 1953. The relative insignificance of authors like Henry James and the prominence of those like Albert Malz will come as no surprise to readers who are even slightly familiar with the permutations of "socialist realism" — the general critical gospel that has long prevailed behind the Iron Curtain. In a number of the items of most recent date there are, however, indications of what has been called a thaw in the permafrost of rigid doctrine. The ideology reflected in the criticism seems less official, and the authors discussed appear to have been less tendentiously selected. Patience, which is the best armanent for humanists in a cold war, may at last be rewarded. The fact that Vernon Parrington's *Main Currents in American Thought* has been recently translated in Russia may seem to those acquainted with its strong Jeffersonian bias like the admittance of a Homeric wooden horse behind erstwhile barriers of exclusion.

Readers of Mrs. Libman's bibliography may, perhaps, be disturbed in noting the changes of the titles of many of the American works translated. For example, O. Henry's novel *Cabbages and Kings* appears in Russian as *Kings and Cabbage*. But the Russians are by no means unusual in this respect. Even in England such changes have been fairly common. More surprising are the several booklets which celebrate various anniversaries of our authors. The forty-fifth anniversary of Jack London's death marked an occasion in Russia, but not in the United States. Of course, Afro-American writers have been steadily written about by Soviet critics, and even Richard Hildreth's *Archy Moore* (1836), sometimes called the "first" antislavery novel printed in the United States, was given renewed life behind the Iron Curtain in 1950. The comments of Marx and Engels on Fenimore Cooper and Harriet Beecher Stowe head the lists of criticisms of those two Americans. Lenin, too, belongs to the roster of Soviet commentators on American literature, with his remarks on Jack Reed. And a marginal note by Lenin in a pamphlet by Jack London has not remained hidden from the critics.

Among the *curiosa*, so to speak, one may note that our "comics" have been discussed as a "contagious disease," and that the "Angry Young Men," the "Hipsters," and the "Beatniks" have not passed unobserved. There is even a sober treatise on the prose of *Time* magazine. An especially ironic circumstance is evident in the fact that Russian criticism of American literature apparently began with a favorable reaction to Benjamin Franklin's *Poor Richard*—a bourgeois work *par excellence*.

The Libman bibliography fills a lacuna in the recording of research and discussion concerned with the reception of the national letters abroad, for *American Literature*, the research journal sponsored by the American Literature Section of the Modern Language Association, has not been able to list material from Russia in its quarterly department "Articles on American Literature Appearing in Current Periodicals." A partial record of Russian translations of both English and American authors appeared in Moscow in 1942 and 1945; and in this country Glenora W. Brown and Deming B. Brown have provided *A Guide to Soviet Translations of American Literature* (New York, 1954), based necessarily on incomplete sources. Their preliminary survey of the vogue of various American authors is of inestimable value. No earlier counterpart to Mrs. Libman's work exists, though we have had a few very helpful studies such as Deming B. Brown, *Soviet Attitudes Toward American Writing* (Princeton, N.J., 1962), which affords more or less extensive treatment of John Dos Passos, Upton Sinclair, Jack London, O. Henry, Sinclair Lewis, Theodore Dreiser, Howard Fast, and Ernest Hemingway.

Financial aid in the preparation of this translation has been supplied by Duke University, with funds from a grant made by the Ford Foundation for the support of international studies and dispensed upon the advice of the University's Provost, R. Taylor Cole. The project was sanctioned at its initial stage by a special committee on the History and the Comparative Study of Ideas, consisting of Craufurd Goodwin (chairman), John H. Hallowell, Irving B. Holley, and Lionel Stevenson. Advice and assistance have also been received from John S. Curtiss, Warren Lerner, Bronislas Jeziersky, and George Williams, likewise members of the faculty of Duke University, from John Broderick, of the Library of Congress, and from Edward J. Meyers, of the Duke University Library.

This bibliography was initially suggested by A. N. Nicolyukin, who also edited and helped to organize the Russian edition. In order to accommodate the non-Russian reader, Mrs. Libman has kindly provided several improvements and additions as an aid to Mr. Allen and myself in our effort to clarify titles of works referred to, etc. To these two scholars across the seas I wish to express my heartfelt thanks.

Robert V. Allen, the translator, is Area Specialist (USSR) of the Slavic and Central European Division of the Library of Congress, a position which he has held since 1960. He was the assistant editor of, as well as a contributor to, *Basic Russian Publications: A Selected and Annotated Bibliography on Russia and the Soviet Union*, edited by Paul L. Horecky and published by the University of Chicago Press in 1962. He contributed also to Mr. Horecky's *Russia and the Soviet Union: A Bibliographic Guide to Western Language Publications* (University of Chicago Press, 1965). He compiles for *The American Historical Review* lists of references to material on Russian history and has published a number of articles surveying the publications relating to Russia and the Soviet Union housed in the Library of Congress. An historian by training, Mr. Allen has taught in Southern Illinois University, the University of Toronto, American University, and George Washington University.

CLARENCE GOHDES

TRANSLATOR'S NOTE

There are in the original Soviet edition of this bibliography some 100 pages almost as closely packed with small grey type as ingenious editors and printers can manage. As a rule entries are separated only by semicolons, and references to Russian books and journals are given in the form of cryptic abbreviations scarcely known outside the Soviet Union. Furthermore, American literary works are cited under the titles of their Russian translations and not of their first-born versions. These factors imposed a special responsibility upon the translator, who has had to seek ways of bringing clarity and accuracy to a most difficult and recalcitrant text. It is hoped that his labors have somehow come close to this goal, and that the reader will meet with no special difficulties beyond those inherent in any translated bibliography. Still, some words of special explanation are necessary.

All titles of books and articles in the Russian language have been given both in transliterated and in translated form. The transliteration system followed is that of the Library of Congress, omitting, as is a usual practice, the ligatures which show that two or more letters of the Latin alphabet represent a single letter of the Cyrillic one. Furthermore, the transliteration follows the version of a title given in the present orthography of the Russian language. The translations which are offered are intended only as a guide to the titles and not as any full-fledged rendering of the artistic or philosophical concepts involved.

There are no translations of the titles of journals or newspapers which are cited in the bibliography as containing material of interest. All that has been done is to expand, for example *Rus. obozr.* to *Russkoe obozrenie*, according to the present orthography and overlooking the fact that a strict adherence to pre-1918 standards would make that *Russkoe obozrienie*. The user in need of such publications needs only to remember the common pitfall of the, now abolished, letter "iat'" and that the Library of Congress, or *Union List of Serials*, will enter a pre-Revolutionary journal such as that listed in Soviet bibliographies as *Severnyi vestnik* under the form *Sievernyi viestnik*, since the second letter of both words is, by the old standards, a "iat'" which is transliterated as "ie" and not "e."

In all but a handful of cases the original American title has been supplied when reference is made to Russian translations of American works to which variant titles have been given. This is in addition to the transliteration and translation of the Russian title, and is done especially so that users may be able to locate possible copies of these editions in the catalogs of libraries following the *Anglo-American Cataloging Rules*. When no such original title could be determined a notation is supplied to that effect.

Special reference is also made, by means of footnotes, to English language publications issued in the Soviet Union which are mentioned in this bibliography. The translator's experience with Soviet bookstores and libraries indicates that, for many Soviet readers, such editions may comprise almost the only literature in English which is available to them, cut off as they often are from printed matter from outside their own borders.

Within each section the order of entries is that of the original text. In some cases, especially in relation to authors about whom little has been written, this reflects merely a chronological arrangement, but in others, let us say for Mark Twain, in which entries are grouped by years, the sequence within each year is that of the Cyrillic alphabet.

Even without reference to the material represented by these entries it is possible to discern in this bibliography a reflection of Russian and Soviet attitudes toward American writing, ranging from the distant and peripheral concern of the nineteenth century to a growing acquaintance in the first two decades of the twentieth and on into the varying assessments of the Soviet period. One may note, for instance, the shift in the view of Upton Sinclair in the years from 1948 through 1949 and 1950, or the fact that nothing is entered relating to John Reed for the years between 1935 and 1955. A similar silence toward Hemingway is observable in the years 1939 to 1955. Furthermore, it is possible to note what seem at first to be surprising gaps in Russian and Soviet attention to American literature. Some authors, little regarded as major writers by American critics, are the subject of extensive Soviet examination, and others are almost entirely neglected. Finally, the reader may be struck by the comparative neglect of American poetry. This is perhaps understandable when one considers how perishable a commodity poetry in translation is, and when this translator remembers some of the Russian failures to capture even a flicker of the nature of American verse. The chief exception to this seems, according to good report, to be Ivan Bunin's translation of Longfellow's *Hiawatha*, which is praised as better than the original.

Since the translator is neither Bunin nor Longfellow, and since the text with which he deals is not poetry, it is his only hope that he has managed to present a clear and useful version of a major work of bibliographical scholarship, adapted insofar as possible to the practices of American libraries, which others can rely upon as a guide to the study of one great aspect of Russian and American relations.

ROBERT V. ALLEN

I. WORKS ON SEPARATE PERIODS AND PROBLEMS OF THE LITERATURE OF THE UNITED STATES

1829 Cooper, J. F. Vzgliad na sostoianie literatury i prosveshcheniia v Amerikanskikh Soedinennykh Shtatakh [A view of the condition of literature and education in the American United States]. Moskovskii telegraf, 1829, t. 28, no. 16, p. 387-417. (Letter XXIII of Cooper's *Notions of the Americans*).

1837 Slovesnost' v Severo-Amerikanskikh Shtatakh [Literature in the North American States]. Zhurnal Ministerstva narodnogo proveshcheniia, 1837, no. 10, p. 480-482.

1839 Literaturnye novosti v Anglii—O zhenshchinakh-pisatel'nitskah v Severo-Amerikanskikh Shtatakh [Literary news in England—Concerning female writers in the North American States]. Biblioteka dlia chteniia, 1839, t. 33, otd. VII, p. 70-71.

1841 Literatura i literatory v Amerikanskikh Shtatakh [Literature and writers in the American States]. Severnaia pchela, December 8, 9, 1841.

1850 Iskusstvo i literatura v Severo-Amerikanskikh Shtatakh [Art and literature in the North American States]. Panteon, 1850, no. 11, otd. III, p. 1-6.

   Sakharov, G. A. O sovremennom napravlenii poezii v Soedinennykh Shtatakh Severnoi Ameriki [Concerning the contemporary trend of poetry in the United States of North America]. Zhurnal Ministerstva narodnogo proveshcheniia, 1850, ch. 66, no. 4, p. 72-74. (Signed: G. S.)

1851 Montegiu [Montague?], E. O zhenshchinakh poetakh v Severnoi Amerike [Concerning female poets in North America]. Biblioteka dlia chteniia, 1851, t. 108, otd. VII, p. 124-133.

1855 Poety Severo-Amerikanskikh Soedinennykh Shtatov [The poets of the North American United States]. Biblioteka dlia chteniia, 1855, t. 132, otd. VII, p. 18-38.

   T. Amerikanskaia literatura [American literature]. Biblioteka dlia chteniia, 1855, t. 130, otd. III-IV, p. 164-204.

1857 Serakovskii, S. I. Zhurnalistika v Soedinennykh Shtatakh [Journalism in the United States]. Sovremennik, 1857, no. 7, otd. V, p. 119-127.

1879 Frank, L. Teatr v Amerike [The theater in America]. Ezhenedel'noe novoe vremia, 1879, t. II, no. 17, cols. 235-245.

1881 Udberri [Woodberry?], G. E. Literatura v Severo-Amerikanskikh

Soedinennykh Shtatakh [Literature in the North American United States]. Literaturnyi zhurnal, 1881, no. 8, cols. 857-868.

1882 Zotov, V. Velikobritaniia i Severo-Amerikanskie Shtaty. Angliiskaia literatura [Great Britain and the North American States. English literature]. *In*: Zotov, V. Istoriia vsemirnoi literatury [History of world literature]. St. Petersburg, Moscow, 1882. v. IV, p. 349-638.

Siuinton, Dzh. [Swinton, J.?]. Amerikanskaia literatura [American literature]. Zagranichnyi vestnik, 1882, no. 6, p. 596-605.

1885 Chuiko, V. Amerikanskie belletristy [American writers]. Zhivopisnoe obozrenie, 1885, t. II, no. 40, p. 215-218; no. 41, p. 232-235; no. 42, p. 251-254; no. 45, p. 295-298; no. 47, p. 330-334.

Shtern, A. Nachatki severno-amerikanskoi literatury [The origins of North American literature]. *In:* Shtern, A. Vseobshchaia istoriia literatury [General history of literature]. St. Petersburg, 1885, p. 462-464.

1886 Amerikanskie poety i iumoristy [American poets and humorists]. Nedelia, 1886, August 10.

Koropchevskii, D. A. Sovremennaia belletristika v Amerike [Contemporary writing in America]. Nov', 1886, no. 20, p. 278-282; no. 21, p. 54-60; no. 22, p. 130-135.

1891 Iz literaturnogo mira. Amerikanskii zakon o literaturnoi sobstvennosti [From the literary world. The American law on copyright]. Knizhki nedeli, 1891, no. 4, p. 258-260.

P. M. Roman i romanisty Novogo sveta [The novel and novelists of the New World]. Knizhki nedeli, 1891, no. 12, p. 7-23.

1892 Borzenko, A. Literaturnaia sobstvennost' v Severo-Amerikanskikh Soedinennykh Shtatakh [Copyright in the North American United States]. Russkoe obozrenie, 1892, no. 10, p. 310-313.

1895 Nechto ob amerikanskoi belletristike [Something about American literature]. Russkii vestnik, 1895, no. 10, p. 310-313.

Tverskoi, P. Sovremennaia belletristika v amerikanskoi periodicheskoi pechati [Contemporary literature in the American periodical press]. Vestnik Evropy, 1895, no. 8, p. 515-543.

1898 Sherr, I. Severnaia Amerika [North America]. *In:* Sherr, I. Illiustrirovannaia vseobshchaia istoriia literatury [Illustrated general history of literature]. Moscow, 1898. v. 2, p. 134-147.

1900 Mizhuev, P. E. Literaturnye faktory amerikanskoi revoliutsii [Literary factors in the American Revolution]. Russkoe bogatstvo, 1900, no. 5, p. 65-102; no. 6, p. 51-88; no. 7, p. 25-62; no. 8, p. 82-116. *See also:* Velikii raskol anglo-saksonskoi rasy. Amerikanskaia revoliutsiia — preimushchestvenno s tochki zreniia literaturnykh faktorov [The great schism of the Anglo-Saxon race. The American Revolution — primarily from the point of view of literature]. *An abridged translation of:* Tyler, M. C. *The Literary History of the American Revolution.* St. Petersburg, 1891. 252 p.

1902 Rubinov, I. Amerikanskie "bessmertnye" [American "immortals"]. Obrazovanie, 1902, no. 10, otd. III, p. 16-33.

1904 Veselovskii, Iu. Chto novogo v inostrannykh literaturakh? Angliiskaia i amerikanskaia literatury [What is new in foreign literature? English and American literatures]. Vestnik i biblioteka samoobrazovaniia, 1904, no. 32, cols. 1231-1235.

Gart [Hart?], Iu. Proiskhozhdenie severo-amerikanskoi-angliiskoi literatury. Severo-amerikanskaia literatura [The origin of English-language literature in North America. North American literature]. *In:* Gart, Iu. Istoriia zapadnoi literatury XIX stoletiia [The history of Western literature in the 19th century]. St. Petersburg, 1904, p. 43-45, 90-91.

1906 Po, E. [Poe, E. A.]. Poeticheskii printsip. Amerikanskaia literature. Natsional'nost'. [The poetic principle. American literature. Nationality]. *In:* Poe, E. Sobranie sochinenii [Collected works]. Moscow, 1906. v. 2, p. 150-153, 193-196.

1908 Gamsun, K. [Hamsun, K.]. Dukhovnaia zhizn' sovremennoi Ameriki. III. Literatura. IV. Poeziia i pisateli [Spiritual life of contemporary America. III, Literature; IV, Poetry and writers]. *In:* Hamsun, K. Polnoe sobranie sochinenii [Complete collected works]. Moscow, 1908. v. 12, p. 88-191.

1909 Tverskoi, P. A. Novoe techenie v amerikanskoi belletristike [A new tendency in American belles-lettres]. Vestnik Evropy, 1909, no. 8, p. 671-678.

1910 Zakon ob avtorskom prave v Amerike [The copyright law in America]. Teatr i iskusstvo, 1910, no. 1, p. 3.

1914 Bekk [Bucke], R. M. Uot Uitman — Ral'f Uol'do Emerson — Genri Devid Toro [Walt Whitman — Ralph Waldo Emerson — Henry David Thoreau]. *In:* Bekk [Bucke], R. M. Kosmicheskoe soznanie [Cosmic awareness]. Petrograd, 1914, p. 229-248, 295-296, 299-302.

Vengerova, Z. Amerikanskaia literatura [American literature]. *In:* Istoriia zapadnoi literatury [History of Western literature]. v. 3. Moscow, 1914. p. 288-327.

Vol'skii, S. Dva priatiia mira (Uitmen, London, O. Genri) [Two forms of perceiving the world (Whitman, London, O. Henry)]. Zavety, 1914, no. 4, otd. II, p. 63-78.

Tolstoi, L. Pis'mo L. P. Nikiforovu ot 21-22 iiulia 1890 g. Ob Uitmene, Gouelse, Gotorne [Letter to L. P. Nikiforov, July 21-22, 1890. On Whitman, Howells, Hawthorne]. Ezhemesiachnyi zhurnal, 1914, no. 1, p. 87. *See also:* Tolstoi, L. Polnoe sobranie sochinenii [Complete collected works]. v. 65. Moscow, 1953. p. 130.

Trent, W. and Erskin, Dzh. [Erskine, J.]. Velikie amerikanskie pisateli [Great American writers]. Translated from the English. St. Petersburg, P. I. Pevin, 1914. 144 p. (*Contents:* Ch. 1. Franklin, Brockden

3

Brown, and Irving; Ch. 2. William Cullen Bryant; Ch. 3. James Fenimore Cooper; Ch. 4. Nathaniel Hawthorne; Ch. 5. Edgar Allan Poe; Ch. 6. The Transcendentalists Emerson, Thoreau, Fuller; Ch. 7. The Poets of New England; Ch. 8. Harriet Beecher Stowe; Ch. 9. Walt Whitman; Ch. 10. Bret Harte and Mark Twain).

1921 Shchepkina-Kupernik, T. Sovremennye amerikanskie p'esy [Contemporary American plays]. Kul'tura teatra, 1921, no. 7-8, p. 56-59.

1922 Krymov. Vl. Amerikanskie vpechatleniia. I. Ob amerikanskoi literature [American impressions. I. Concerning American literature]. *In:* Zapad [The West]. vyp. 4. Moscow, 1922. p. 28-31.

1923 Aksenov, I. A. Review of: Amerikanskaia novella [The American short story]. Petrograd, 1923. Pechat' i revoliutsiia, 1923, no. 5, p. 302-303.

Levman, S. Rabochii v zapadnoi literature. Amerikanskii rabochii [The working man in Western literature. The American working man]. Na postu, 1923, no. 2-3, p. 162-175.

Onegin, V. Literatura N'iu-iorkskogo getto [The literature of the New York ghetto]. *In:* Petrograd. Almanakh. Moscow, Petrograd, 1923. p. 117-119.

Efros, N. E. Teatr negrov [The Negro theater]. Sovremennyi zapad, 1923, no. 3, p. 223-224. (Signed: N. E.)

1924 Iz zhizni amerikanskoi literatury (nachala XX v.) [From American literary life (of the beginning of the twentieth century)]. *In:* Zapadnye sborniki [Western notebooks]. vyp. 2. Moscow, 1924. p. 211-213.

Klark [Clark?], B. Literatura Soedinennykh Shtatov Ameriki [The literature of the United States]. Beseda (Berlin), 1924, no. 4, p. 251-279.

1925 Urazov, I. Amerikanskie pisateli. Dzhek London. O. Genri. Upton Sinkler [American writers. Jack London. O. Henry. Upton Sinclair]. *In:* Amerikanskie pisateli [American writers]. Khar'kov, 1925. p. 3-8.

Friche, V. Tri amerikantsa (Sinkler—Genri—Dzh. London) [Three Americans (Sinclair—Henry—J. London)]. Novyi mir, 1925, no. 5, p. 119-129.

1926 Dinamov, S. Literaturnoe vozrozhdenie v Amerike [The literary renaissance in America]. (C. E. Bechofer. *The Literary Renaissance in America*). Knigonosha, 1926, no. 1, p. 14-16.

Dinamov, S. Sovremennaia amerikanskaia literatura [Contemporary American literature]. Krasnoe studenchestvo, 1926, no. 3, p. 85-88.

Dinamov, S. Tri amerikanskikh pisatelia. Sinkler L'iuis—Shervud Anderson—Dzhozef Gerzhkheimer [Three American writers. Sinclair Lewis—Sherwood Anderson—Joseph Hergesheimer]. Knigonosha, 1926, no. 44-45, p. 14-17.

Kashkin, I. Angliia i Amerika. Obzor literatury [England and America. A survey of literature]. Zapad i vostok. kn. 1-2. Moscow, 1926. p. 155-164.

Kulle, R. O sovremennoi amerikanskoi literature [On contemporary American literature]. Zvezda, 1926, no. 6, p. 230-243.

Menken, G. L. [Mencken, H. L.]. Literatura po-amerikanski [Literature American-style]. Zhurnalist, 1926, no. 8-9, p. 68-69.

N'iumen [Newman?], F. Amerikanskii "korotkii rasskaz" v pervoe 25-letie XX veka [The American "short story" in the first quarter of the twentieth century]. Novyi mir, 1926, no. 7, p. 159-163.

Sinkler [Sinclair], U. Iskusstvo Mammony. Opyt ekonomicheskogo issledovaniia [The art of Mammon—i.e. *Mammonart*. An essay in economic research]. Leningrad, "Priboi," 1926. 278 p. *Reviews:* Frid, Ia. Novyi mir, 1926, no. 1, p. 191; Friche, V. Iskusstvo Mammony [The art of Mammon]. Novyi mir, 1927, no. 2, p. 202-205.

Sinkler, E. [Sinclair, U.]. Moi sobrat'ia po peru [My brothers of the the pen]. *In:* Sinkler, E. [Sinclair, U.]. Sobranie sochinenii [Collected works]. v. 7. Moscow, Leningrad, 1926. p. 411-478. (Emerson, Longfellow, Whittier, Hawthorne, Poe, Whitman, Twain, Howells, Bierce, R. H. Davis, Crane, Frank Norris, David Graham Philips, O. Henry, London). 2nd ed., 1927.

Tsingovatov, A. Novinki amerikanskoi literatury [New features in American literature]. Molodaia gvardiia, 1926, no. 7, p. 166-171.

1927 Aleksandrov, V. Amerikanskoe. (Obzor sovremennoi literatury) [American. (A survey of contemporary literature)]. Na pod"eme (Rostov-na Donu), 1927, no. 7, p. 38-40.

Lann, E. Standartnyi ianki (v literature SShA) [The standard Yankee (in the literature of the US)]. Krasnaia nov', 1927, no. 1, p. 245-254.

Frimen, Dzh. [Freeman, J.]. Literatura sovremennoi Ameriki [The literature of contemporary America]. Na literaturnom postu, 1927, no. 17-18, p. 66-71.

1928 Anderson, Sh. Dzhaz-Band kul'tury i pisatel' [The jazz band of culture and the writer]. Vestnik inostrannoi literatury, 1928, no. 10, p. 116-118.

Borrouz [Burroughs?], L. Negritianskaia kul'tura v Amerike [Negro culture in America]. Vestnik inostrannoi literatury, 1928, no. 10, p. 146-149.

Vil'son, U. [Wilson, W.?]. Sovremennye negritianskie poety [Contemporary Negro poets]. Vestnik inostrannoi literatury, 1928, no. 6, p. 146-148.

Gold, M. Tri shkoly amerikanskoi literatury. Konets literaturnogo Renessansa. "Transition" — "Perekhod." Pisateli-kommunisty [Three schools of American literature. The end of the literary renaissance. "Transition" "Communist writers"]. Vestnik inostrannoi literatury, 1928, no. 11, p. 121-125.

Danilin, Iu. I. Novye amerikanskie perevody [New American translations]. Na literaturnom postu, 1928, no. 13-14, p. 110-114. (Signed: Diar.)

Dinamov, S. Literatura amerikanskikh brodiag. (Sotsial'no-literaturnyi ocherk) [Literature of American vagabonds. (Socio-literary essay)]. Vestnik inostrannoi literatury, 1928, no. 8, p. 116-126.

Dinamov, S. Tri amerikantsa. (Vudvord—L'iuis—Dell) [Three Americans. (Woodward—Lewis—Dell)]. Vestnik inostrannoi literatury, 1928, no. 2, p. 151-154.

I. S. Zarozhdenie proletarskoi dramy i rabochego teatra v Amerike [The origin of proletarian drama and the workers' theater in America]. Revoliutsiia i kul'tura, 1928, no. 6, p. 69-70.

Kashkin, I. Novoe v negritianskoi literature [New features in Negro literature]. Vestnik inostrannoi literatury, 1928, no. 10, p. 143-146. (Signed: I. K-n.)

Literaturnaia Amerika. (Po dokladu S. Dinamova o literature SShA nachala XX veka) [Literary America. (On the report of S. Dinamov on the literature of the USA of the beginning of the twentieth century)]. Chitatel' i pisatel', December 23, 1928.

N. Negritianskaia literatura v Amerike [Negro literature in America]. Na literaturnom postu, 1928, no. 13-14, p. 79-80.

Novye tendentsii v amerikanskoi literature [New tendencies in American literature]. Vestnik inostrannoi literatury, 1928, no. 7, p. 153-155.

Sinkler, E. [Sinclair, U]. Den'gi pishut! Etiud o vlianii ekonomiki na literaturu [Money writes! A study of the influence of economics on literature]. Translated by B. Ia. Zhukovetskii. Foreword and comments by S. Dinamov. Moscow, Leningrad, Gosizdat, 1928. 296 p. *Reviews:* A. O. Kak karasiu stat' shchukoi [How the carp can become a pike]. Zhurnalist, 1928, no. 12, p. 53-54; Messer, R. Literaturno-khudozhestvennyi sbornik "Krasnoi panoramy," 1928, no. 12, p. 60-61; Novyi pamflet E. Sinklera [A new pamphlet by U. Sinclair]. Revoliutsiia i kul'tura, 1928, no. 6, p. 68-69; Ryklin, G. *In:* Novyi mir, 1928, no. 11, p. 251-254; M. F. Na pod"eme (Rostov-na-Donu), 1929, no. 4, p. 77.

Sinkler, E. [Sinclair, U.]. Pisateli novoi Ameriki [The writers of new America]. Na literaturnom postu, 1928, no. 19, p. 57-63.

Tolkachev, E. Predislovie [Foreword]. *In:* Sem' amerkanskikh iumoristov [Seven American humorists]. Khar'kov, 1928. p. 3-5. (Signed: Sostavitel'.)

Uol'f [Wolf], R. Amerikanskaia poeziia [American poetry]. Vestnik inostrannoi literatury, 1928, no. 5, p. 133-140. *Review:* Dinamov, S. Ob amerikanskoi proletarskoi i revoliutsionnoi poezii. (Neskol'ko zamechanii o stat'e Rob. Uol'fa) [On American proletarian and revolutionary poetry. (Some remarks on the article of Rob. Wolf)]. Vestnik inostrannoi literatury, 1928, no. 5, p. 141-143.

Fainberg, D. Real'nye geroi amerikanskikh romanov [The real heroes of American novels]. Vestnik inostrannoi literatury, 1928, no. 8, p. 145-146. (Signed: D. F.)

Frimen, Dzh. [Freeman, J.]. Amerikanskie zametki. (Sovremennaia literatura SShA) [American notes. (Contemporary literature of the US)]. Vestnik inostrannoi literatury, 1928, no. 7, p. 127-139.

Frimen, Dzh. [Freeman, J.]. Amerikantsy i Tolstoi [Americans and Tolstoi]. Vestnik inostrannoi literatury, 1928, no. 10, p. 137-141.

1929 Angliia i Amerika. Literatura (1929 g.) [England and America. Literature (in 1929)]. Pechat' i revoliutsiia, 1929, no. 12, p. 110, 112; 1930, no. 1, p. 91-92.

Voker [Walker?], Ch. Standartnaia devushka amerikanskoi belletristiki [The standard young woman of American belles-lettres]. Vestnik inostrannoi literatury, 1929, no. 1, p. 226-229.

Gold, M. Sakko i Vantsetti v amerikanskoi literature [Sacco and Vanzetti in American literature]. Vestnik inostrannoi literatury, 1929, no. 3, p. 247-248.

Dzhekson, Dzh. [Jackson, J.]. Perspektivy amerikanskoi literatury [The prospects for American literature]. Literaturnaia gazeta, June 17, 1929.

Dzhekson, Dzh. [Jackson, J.]. Pochemu mirovaia voina tak malo otrazhena v amerikanskoi literature? [Why is the World War so little shown in American literature?]. Vestnik inostrannoi literatury, 1929, no. 4, p. 223-224.

Dinamov, S. Literatura sovremennoi Ameriki [The literature of contemporary America]. Narodnyi uchitel', 1929, no. 12, p. 132-141; 1930, no. 1, p. 106-109.

Kulle, R. O sovremennoi amerikanskoi proze [Concerning contemporary American prose]. Oktiabr', 1929, no. 9, p. 142-156.

Kulle, R. Realisty sovremennoi amerikanskoi prozy [Realists of contemporary American prose]. Sibirskie ogni (Novosibirsk), 1929, no. 3, p. 148-165.

Literaturnye novinki Ameriki [New appearances in American literature]. Pechat' i revoliutsiia, 1929, no. 6, p. 122-125.

Misho [Michaud?], R. Noveishie techeniia v amerikanskoi literature [The most recent tendencies in American literature]. Na literaturnom postu, 1929, no. 8, p. 52-56.

Poletika, Iu. Ocherki sovremennoi amerikanskoi literatury. Literaturnaia reforma [Sketches of contemporary American literature. A literary reform]. Leningrad, "Krasnaia gazeta," 1929. 48 p.

Rashkovskaia, A. Literatura sovremennoi Ameriki [The literature of contemporary America]. Zhizn' iskusstva, 1929, no. 3, p. 15.

Frid, Ia. Amerikantsky. Obzor (sovremennoi literatury) [Americans. A survey (of contemporary literature)]. Plamia, 1929, no. 9, p. 19.

Cherniak, Ia. Chto chitaet Amerika [What America is reading]. Tridtsat' dnei, 1929, no. 2, p. 74-77.

Eishiskina, N. Osnovnye tendentsii sovremennoi kritiki v Soedinennykh shtatakh [The basic tendencies of contemporary criticism in the United States]. Pechat' i revoliutsiia, 1929, no. 11, p. 88-95.

1930 Dinamov, S. Amerikanskaia proletarskaia poeziia [American proletarian poetry]. Literatura i iskusstvo, 1930, no. 1, p. 91-112.

Dinamov, S. Tvorcheskii opyt amerikanskoi poezii. (K plenumu MBRL) [The creative experience of American poetry. (On the occasion of the plenum of the Mezhdunarodnoe biuro revoliutsionnoi literatury — International Bureau of Revolutionary Literature)]. Literaturnaia gazeta, September 29, 1930.

Dinamov, S. Chto chitaet Amerika [What America is reading]. Tridtsat' dnei, 1930, no. 1, p. 78-80.

Kal'verton [Calverton], V. F. Gumanizm v amerikanskoi literature [Humanism in American literature]. Literaturnaia gazeta, December 19, 1930.

Lann, E. Probeg po sovremennoi amerikanskoi literature [A survey of contemporary American literature]. Novyi mir, 1930, no. 10, p. 198-202.

Levit, T. Proletliteratura SASSh [Proletarian literature of the US]. Vestnik inostrannoi literatury, 1930, no. 6, p. 74-98.

M. P. Poety-buntovshchiki. (Ob"edinenie amerikanskikh revoliutsion-nykh poetov "Rebel Poets, an Internationale of Song") [Poet rebels. (Association of American Revolutionary Poets. "Rebel Poets, an Internationale of Song")]. Vestnik inostrannoi literatury, 1930, no. 4, p. 152-153.

O putiakh amerikanskoi proletliteratury [Concerning the paths of American proletarian literature]. Vestnik inostrannoi literatury, 1930, no. 5, p. 180-184.

Frimen, Dzh. [Freeman, J.]. Sotsial'nye rassloeniia v amerikanskoi literature [Social cleavages in American literature]. Vestnik inostran-noi literatury, 1930, no. 6, p. 174-183.

1931 Gold, M. Krizis amerikanskoi literatury [The crisis of American litera-ture]. Inostrannaia kniga, literaturno-khudozhestvennaia seriia, 1931, no. 1, p. 1-3.

Gold, M. Literatura sovremennoi Ameriki [The literature of contempo-rary America]. Literatura mirovoi revoliutsii, 1931, no. 1, p. 84-91.

Dinamov, S. Amerikanskii fashizm i literatura [American fascism and literature]. Literatura i iskusstvo, 1931, no. 4, p. 79-87.

Dinamov, S. Tema rabstva negrov v amerikanskoi literature [The theme of Negro slavery in American literature]. In: Litso kapitalisticheskogo rabstva v inostrannoi khudozhestvennoi literature [The face of capita-list slavery in foreign fiction]. Moscow, Leningrad, 1931. p. 52-65.

8

Elistratova, A. Literaturnyi fashizm v Amerike [Literary fascism in America]. RAPP, 1931, no. 1, p. 213-217.

Elistratova, A. Review of: *An Anthology of American Negro Literature.* Inostrannaia kniga, literaturno-khudozhestvennaia seriia, 1931, no. 1, p. 5-6.

Zenkevich, M. O novinkakh angliiskoi i amerikanskoi literatury [Concerning new features of English and American literature]. Novyi mir, 1931, no. 12, p. 163-176.

Kal'verton [Calverton], V. F. Spory o literature i deistvitel'nosti v Amerike [Controversies about literature and reality in America]. Literaturnaia gazeta, May 20, 1931.

L'iuis [Lewis], S. Amerika i literatura. (Rech', proiznesennaia posle vrucheniia Nobelevskoi premii) [America and literature. (Speech delivered upon receipt of the Nobel Prize)]. Literaturnaia gazeta, January 19, 1931.

Rezoliutsiia amerikanskoi delegatsii po voprosu proletarskoi i revoliutsionnoi literatury v Amerike [Resolution of the American delegation on the problem of proletarian and revolutionary literature in America]. *In:* 2-ia—i.e. Vtoraia—Mezhdunarodnaia konferentsiia revoliutsionnykh pisatelei, Khar'kov, 1930. Doklady, rezoliutsii, preniia [Second International Conference of Revolutionary Writers, Khar'kov, 1930. Reports, resolutions, debates]. Moscow, 1931. p. 122-123.

Startsev, A. New Masses. Novye massy—organ amerikanskogo proletliteraturnogo dvizheniia [The *New Masses*—the organ of the American proletarian literary movement]. Na literaturnom postu, 1931, no. 10, p. 6-12.

Startsev, A. Perevodnaia belletristika. 5. Pisatel' proletarskoi Ameriki. (Maikl Gold). 6. Pasynki zemli (Edit Kelli "Sornaia trava." Egnis Smedli "Doch' zemli"). 7. "V Garlem, v Garlem!" (Klod Makkei "Domoi v Garlem") [Fiction in translation. 5. A writer of proletarian America (Michael Gold). 6. Stepsons of the land (Edith Kelley. "Weeds." Agnes Smedley. "Daughter of earth"). 7. "To Harlem, to Harlem!" (Claude McKay. "Home to Harlem")]. Oktiabr', 1931, no. 4-5, p. 234-236.

1932 Gold, M. Proletarskaia i revoliutsionnaia literatura Ameriki. (Iz stenogrammy II konferentsii revoliutsionnykh pisatelei mira) [Proletarian and revolutionary literature of America. (From the stenographic report of the 2nd Conference of Revolutionary Writers of the World)]. *In:* Literatura mirovoi revoliutsii [Literature of the world revolution]. Moscow, Leningrad, 1932. p. 170-171.

Elistratova, A. "New Masses" (in 1931). Literatura mirovoi revoliutsii, 1932, no. 2, p. 89-95.

Elistratova, A. "Novye massy"—zhurnal amerikanskoi sektsii MORP

[*New Masses*—the journal of the American section of MORP—Mezhdunarodnoe ob"edinenie revoliutsionnykh pisatelei—International Alliance of Revolutionary Writers]. Marksistsko-leninskoe iskusstvoznanie, 1932, no. 5-6, p. 202-212. (Signed: A. Matveeva.)

Elistratova, A. Review of: *Left*, 1931, no. 2. Literatura mirovoi revoliutsii, 1932, no. 6, p. 115-122.

Kak my prishli k kommunizmu. (U. Frenk, Sh. Anderson, M. Gold, E. Sinkler i dr.) [How we came to communism. (W. Frank, Sh. Anderson, M. Gold, U. Sinclair, and others)]. Literatura mirovoi revoliutsii, 1932, no. 9-10, p. 127-134.

Karmon, U. [Carmon, W.]. Literaturnyi N'iu-Iork. 1. Grinvich Villedzh. 2. V Dzhonrid-klube. 3. Po zhurnalam i gazetam. 4. N'iu-Iorkskie izdateli. 5. Izdatel'stva i krizis. [Literary New York. 1. Greenwich Village. 2. In the John Reed Club. 3. Among the magazines and newspapers. 4. New York publishers. 5. Publishing houses and the depression]. Literaturnaia gazeta, November 11-29, December 5, 1932.

Lann, E. Amerikanskaia literatura v 1931 godu [American literature in 1931]. Proletarskii avangard, 1932, no. 5-6, p. 234-244.

"N'iu Messes" na puti perestroiki [*New Masses* on the way to reorganization]. Literatura mirovoi revoliutsii, 1932, no. 1, p. 112-113.

Siver, E. Literatura na perekrestke [Literature at the crossroads]. Literaturnaia gazeta, July 11, 1932.

Startsev, A. Vseobshchii krizis kapitalizma i novaia volna soiuznikov proletariata v literature Ameriki [The general capitalist depression and the new wave of allies of the proletariat in the literature of America]. Marksistsko-leninskoe iskusstvoznanie, 1932, no. 5-6, p. 39-62.

Startsev, A. Krizis i revoliutsionnaia literatura Ameriki [The depression and revolutionary literature of America]. Literaturnaia gazeta, July 11, 1932.

Startsev, A. Literaturnyi manifest o krizise amerikanskogo kapitalizma (*Behold America!* 1931) [A literary manifesto on the crisis of American capitalism (*Behold America!* 1931)]. Marksistsko-leninskoe iskusstvoznanie, 1932, no. 2, p. 105-107.

1933 Dinamov, S. Kuda idet peredovaia intelligentsiia Ameriki [The goal toward which the progressive intelligentsia of America is moving]. Izvestiia, February 25, 1933.

Draizer [Dreiser], T. Velikii amerikanskii roman. (S primechaniiami redaktora) [The great American novel. (With editorial remarks)]. Internatsional'naia literatura, 1933, no. 2, p. 112-115. *See also:* Draizer [Dreiser], T. Polnoe sobranie sochinenii [Complete collected works]. v. 11. Moscow, 1954. p. 549-556.

Dymshits, A. Obzor zhurnala "N'iu messiz" [A review of the magazine *New Masses*. Zalp, 1933, no. 7-8, p. 77-78.

Ellistratova, A. Literatura SASSh [The literature of the US]. Literaturnaia gazeta, November 29, 1933.

Elistratova, A. Literatura sovremennoi Ameriki [The literature of contemporary America]. Internatsional'naia literatura, 1933, no. 5, p. 99-112.

Elistratova, A. Novye iavleniia v literature Ameriki [New features of the literature of America]. Kniga i proletarskaia revoliutsiia, 1933, no. 11, p. 116-124.

Karmon, U. [Carmon, W.]. Posledniaia literaturnaia "sensatsiia N'iu-Iorka" [The latest literary "sensation of New York"]. Literaturnaia gazeta, January 5, 1933.

Miller, L. Predislovie [Foreword]. In: Afrika v Amerike [Africa in America]. Moscow, 1933. p. 3-11.

Nemerovskaia, O. Proletarskaia literatura sovremennoi Ameriki [Proletarian literature of contemporary America]. Literaturnaia ucheba, 1933, no. 10, p. 61-79.

Peredovaia o literature SShA [Leading article on literature in the US]. Internatsional'naia literatura, 1933, no. 5, p. 3-4.

Startsev, A. I. Krizis kapitalizma i differentsiatsiia melkoburzhuaznoi literatury v Amerike [The capitalist depression and the differentiation of petty bourgeois literature in America]. In: Krizis kapitalizma i soiuzniki proletariata v literature Zapada [The capitalist depression and allies of the proletariat in the literature of the West]. Sb. 1. Moscow, Leningrad, 1933. p. 36-63.

Startsev, A. Literatura i klassovaia bor'ba v SASSh [Literature and the class struggle in the US]. Literaturnaia gazeta, November 29, 1933.

Khiks [Hicks], G. O soiuznikakh revoliutsii v amerikanskoi literature [Concerning the allies of the revolution in American literature]. Internatsional'naia literatura, 1933, no. 5, p. 116-118.

1934 Abramov, A. Litso literaturnogo N'iu-Iorka. (*The New York Times Book Review*) [The face of literary New York. (*The New York Times Book Review*)]. Literaturnaia gazeta, February 6, 1934.

Balashov, P. Amerikanskaia dramaturgiia. O sovremennom krizise, rasovoi probleme i voine. [American dramaturgy. On the contemporary crisis, the race problem, and war]. Inostrannaia kniga, 1934, no. 4, p. 36-40.

Vstupitel'nye zametki k publikatsiiam proizvedenii S. Krena, G. Dzheimsa, A. Birsa, Dzh. Londona, O. Genri, R. Lardnera, Dzh. Rida, Sh. Anderson, E. Khemingueia, U. Folknera, E. Kolduella, Dzh. Milberna, A. Smedli, L. Kh'iuza, M. Golda [Introductory remarks on the publication of works of S. Crane, H. James, A. Bierce, J. London, O. Henry, R. Lardner, J. Reed, S. Anderson, E. Hemingway, W. Faulkner, E. Caldwell, J. Milburn, A. Smedley, L. Hughes, M. Gold]. In: Amerikanskaia novella XX veka [The American short story of the 20th century]. Moscow, 1934.

11

Gal'perin, S. Begstvo ot zhizni. Upadok realizma v amerikanskom teatre. Ot "segodniashnego dnia" k "istorii." "Obrashchenie" O'Neilia. Na mezhdunarodnoi teatral'noi vystavke v N'iu-Iorke [A flight from life. The decline of realism in the American theater. From "today" to "history." O'Neill's "transformation." At the international theatrical exposition in New York]. Sovetskoe iskusstvo, February 28, 1934.

Gessner, R. Amerikanskaia revoliutsionnaia literatura. Rech' (na Vsesoiuznom s"ezde sovetskikh pisatelei) [American revolutionary literature. A speech (at the All-Union Congress of Soviet Writers)]. Literaturnaia gazeta, August 29, 1934.

Gordon, Iu. Negritianskaia literatura v Amerike [Negro literature in America]. Internatsional'naia literatura, 1934, no. 1, p. 94-97.

Dinamov, S. O realizme v amerikanskoi literature [On realism in American literature]. Pravda, June 3, 1934.

Karmon, U. [Carmon, W.]. "N'iu-messes"—amerikanskii revoliutsionnyi zhurnal [New Masses—an American revolutionary journal]. Internatsional'naia literatura, 1934, no. 6, p. 107-109.

Karmon, U. [Carmon, W.]. Rost amerikanskoi revoliutsionnoi literatury [The growth of American revolutionary literature]. Internatsional'naia literatura, 1934, no. 3-4, p. 228-232.

Miller-Budnitskaia, R. Otvet tov. Lenskomu (o sovremennoi literature SShA) [An answer to com. Lenskii (about contemporary literature in the US)]. Literaturnaia ucheba, 1934, no. 7, p. 132-134.

Ol'gin, M. Teodor Draizer o pisateliakh i literature [Theodore Dreiser on writers and literature]. Pravda, June 5, 1934.

Startsev, A. Ot "Masses" k "N'iu Masses." (Kratkii ocherk razvitiia revoliutsionnogo literaturnogo dvizheniia v SShA) [From Masses to New Masses. (A short outline of the development of the revolutionary literary movement in the US)]. Inostrannaia kniga, 1934, no. 6, p. 8-12.

Khiks [Hicks], G. Dva puti. (Otryvki iz knigi "Velikaia traditsiia") [Two paths. (Selections from the book "The great tradition")]. Internatsional'naia literatura, 1934, no. 3-4, p. 214-227.

1935 Abramov, A. Molodost' veka [The youth of the century]. Internatsional'naia literatura, 1935, no. 6, p. 141-143.

Gordon, Iu. Znachenie kongressa amerikanskikh pisatelei [The significance of the Congress of American Writers]. Internatsional'naia literatura, 1935, no. 8, p. 176-177.

Grits, T. Sovremennaia amerikanskaia novella [The contemporary American short story]. (A review of: Amerikanskaia novella XX veka [The American short story of the 20th century]. Moscow, 1934.) Literaturnyi kritik, 1935, no. 3, p. 220-222.

Dinamov, S. Pisatel' i revoliutsiia. (I-i s"ezd revoliutsionnykh pisatelei

SShA.) [The writer and the revolution. (First congress of revolutionary writers of the US)]. Izvestiia, June 8, 1935.

Kalmer, A. S"ezd revoliutsionnykh pisatelei Ameriki. (N'iu-York, 1935) [The congress of revolutionary writers of America. (New York, 1935)]. Internatsional'naia literatura, 1935, no. 7, p. 121-124.

Klei, Iu. [Clay, E.?]. Negritianskie pisateli Ameriki [Negro writers of America]. Internatsional'naia literatura, 1935, no. 11, p. 66-70.

Nemerovskaia, O. Review of: Amerikanskaia novella XX veka [The American short story of the 20th century]. Moscow, 1934. Zvezda, 1935, no. 5, p. 230-232.

Nemerovskaia, O. Sud'ba amerikanskoi novelly [The fate of the American short story]. Literaturnaia ucheba, 1935, no. 5, p. 72-108.

Rollan, R. [Rolland, Romain]. Pisateliam Ameriki. Svobodnye golosa Ameriki [To the writers of America. The free voices of America]. *In:* Rolland, R. Sobranie sochinenii [Collected works]. v. 18. Leningrad, 1935. p. 131-143.

Shiller, F. Severoamerikanskaia literatura pervoi poloviny XIX veka. Severoamerikanskaia literatura vtoroi poloviny XIX veka. Kriticheskii realizm i severo-amerikanskaia literatura nachala XX veka [North American literature of the first half of the 19th century. North American literature of the second half of the 19th century. Critical realism and North American literature of the beginning of the 20th century]. *In:* Shiller, F. Istoriia zapadnoevropeiskoi literatury novogo vremeni [A history of Western European literature of the modern period]. v. 1. Moscow, 1935. p. 343-360; v. 2. Moscow, 1937. p. 226-252; v. 3. Moscow, 1937. p. 380-424.

Eishiskina, N. Dovoennaia literatura SShA [The pre-War literature of the US]. *In:* Gal'perina, E., Zaprovskaia, A. and Eishiskina, N. Kurs zapadnoi literatury XX veka [A course in Western literature of the 20th century]. Moscow, 1935. p. 283-343.

1936 Abol'nikov, S. Negritianskaia poeziia. (Antologiia negritianskoi poezii. Moscow, 1936) [Negro poetry. (Anthology of Negro poetry. Moscow, 1936)]. Literaturnaia gazeta, September 1, 1936.

Kashkin, I. Tri amerikanskikh poeta. Archibal'd Mak-Lish. Karl Sendberg. Vechel Lindzi. [Three American poets. Archibald MacLeish. Carl Sandburg. Vachel Lindsay]. Znamia, 1936, no. 8, p. 125-135.

Konferentsiia pisatelei zapadnykh shtatov Ameriki. (Chikago, 1936 g.) [Conference of writers of the Western states of America. (Chicago, 1936)]. Internatsional'naia literatura, 1936, no. 9, p. 177-180.

Nemerovskaia, O. Sovremennaia amerikanskaia literatura [Contemporary American literature]. Sovetskoe studenchestvo, 1936, no. 6, p. 81-85.

Pel'son, E. V. Rollins v Moskve. Avtor romana "Ten' vperedi" o novoi amerikanskoi literature [W. Rollins in Moscow. The author of the novel "The shadow before" on recent American literature]. Literaturnaia gazeta, August 1, 1936.

Tagger, Dzh. [Taggard, G.]. Po sledam Uota Uitmena. Pis'mo iz N'iu-Iorka. (Literatura SShA XX v.) [On the traces of Walt Whitman. A letter from New York. (Literature of the US in the 20th century)]. Literaturnyi Leningrad, August 23, 1936.

U Dzhona Dos-Passosa. (Dos-Passos o sovremennoi literature SShA) [With John Dos Passos. (Dos Passos on contemporary literature of the US)]. Literaturnaia gazeta, October 10, 1936.

U Teodora Draizera. (Draizer o sovremennoi literature SShA) [With Theodore Dreiser. (Dreiser on contemporary literature of the US)]. Literaturnaia gazeta, October 10, 1936.

1937 A. S. "Dusha Dzhona Brauna." (Grazhdanskaia voina 60-kh godov i sovremennyi amerikanskii istoricheskii roman) ["The soul of John Brown." (The Civil War of the '60's and the contemporary American historical novel)]. Internatsional'naia literatura, 1937, no. 9, p. 216-218.

Antifashistskie pisateli mira. SShA. Teodor Draizer. Ernest Kheminguei. Shervud Anderson. Malkolm Kauli. Erskin Kolduell. Maikl Gold. Lengston Kh'iuz. Grenvill Khiks. Dzhosefina Kherbst. Pol' de Kraif. Archibal'd Mak Lish. Epton Sinkler. Karl Sendberg. [Antifascist writers of the world. USA. Theodore Dreiser. Ernest Hemingway. Sherwood Anderson. Malcolm Cowley. Erskine Caldwell. Michael Gold. Langston Hughes. Granville Hicks. Josephine Herbst. Paul de Kruif. Archibald MacLeish. Upton Sinclair. Carl Sandburg]. Internatsional'naia literatura, 1937, no. 11, p. 208-216.

Antifashistskie pisateli mira. SShA. Van Uik Bruks. Meri Khiton Vors. Robert Gerrik. Dzhosefin Dzhonson. Dzhoshua K'iunits. L'iuis Memford. Dzhenev'ev Teggard. Al'bert Khalper. Fanni Kherst. Aisidor Shneider. [Antifascist writers of the world. USA. Van Wyck Brooks. Mary Heaton Vorse. Robert Herrick. Josephine Johnson. Joshua Kunitz. Lewis Mumford. Genevieve Taggard. Albert Halper. Fannie Hurst. Isidore Schneider.]. Internatsional'naia literatura, 1937, no. 12, p. 130-134.

Karmon, U. [Carmon, W.]. (Pis'ma iz N'iu-Iorka o sovremennoi literaturnoi zhizni SShA i uchastii pisatelei v bor'be respublikanskoi Ispanii) [(Letters from New York about contemporary literary life in the US and the participation of writers in the struggle of Republican Spain)]. Internatsional'naia literatura, 1937, no. 4, p. 235-236; no. 5, p. 232-235; no. 6, p. 232-236; no. 7, p. 220-224.

Karmon, U. [Carmon, W.]. S"ezd amerikanskikh pisatelei, iiun' 1937. (Pis'mo iz N'iu-Iorka) [The congress of American writers, June 1937. (Letter from New York)]. Internatsional'naia literatura, 1937, no. 8, p. 213-216.

Kashkin, I. Mezhdu voinoi i krizisom. (Amerikanskie poety desiatykh i dvadtsatykh godov XX veka) [Between war and depression. (American poets of the 1910's and 1920's)]. Literaturnyi kritik, 1937, no. 3, p. 97-120.

Kashkin, I. Pesni i ballady amerikanskikh poetov XX veka. (S publikatsiei tekstov) [Songs and ballads of American poets of the 20th century. (With texts)]. Internatsional'naia literatura, 1937, no. 4, p. 125-134.

Kashkin, I. Tvorchestvo amerikanskikh poetov-imazhistov [The work of the American imagist poets]. Internatsional'naia literatura, 1937, no. 2, p. 210-220.

Frimen, Dzh. [Freeman, J.]. Zavet amerikantsa [The behest of an American]. Internatsional'naia literatura, 1937, no. 1, p. 176-182; no. 2, p. 140-152; no. 3, p. 156-174.

Etingin, B. Velikoe i maloe. (Chaplinskie motivy i temy v literature XX veka) [The great and the small. (Chaplinesque motifs and themes in the literature of the 20th century)]. Internatsional'naia literatura, 1937, no. 8, p. 189-202.

1938 Elistratova, A. Vtoroi kongress amerikanskikh pisatelei. (Iiun', 1937. Po sborniku materialov kongressa "The Writer in a Changing World") [The second Congress of American Writers. (June, 1937. A consideration of the volume of materials of the congress "The writer in a changing world")]. Internatsional'naia literatura, 1938, no. 2-3, p. 358-362.

Startsev, A. Amerika i Staryi svet. O sotsial'nom kharaktere amerikanskoi literatury XIX veka [America and the Old World. On the social character of American literature of the 19th century]. Internatsional'naia literatura, 1938, no. 8, p. 180-202.

Teggard, Dzh. [Taggard, G.]. Liga amerikanskikh pisatelei [The League of American Writers]. Literaturnaia gazeta, October 15, 1938.

Khenter, E. [Hunter, E.]. Negry v amerikanskoi literature. (Pis'mo iz SShA) [Negroes in American literature. (Letter from the US)]. Internatsional'naia literatura, 1938, no. 4, p. 201-202.

Khiks [Hicks], G. Literaturnye zametki (o Lige amerikanskikh pisatelei) [Literary notes (on the League of American Writers)]. Internatsional'naia literatura, 1938, no. 6, p. 220-221.

Khiks [Hicks], G. Novosti literatury i teatra v SShA [News of literature and the theater in the US]. Internatsional'naia literatura, 1938, no. 2-3, p. 382-384.

Khiks [Hicks], G. Novyi proletarskii roman [The new proletarian novel]. Internatsional'naia literatura, 1938, no. 7, p. 203-205.

Khiks [Hicks], G. Pis'mo iz Ameriki (o literaturnoi zhizni SShA) [A letter from America (on literary life in the US)]. Internatsional'naia literatura, 1938, no. 4, p. 194-196.

Shneider, A. [Schneider, I.?]. Amerikanskie pisateli i bor'ba ispanskogo naroda [American writers and the struggle of the Spanish people]. Internatsional'naia literatura, 1938, no. 8, p. 233-234.

1939 Abramov, A. Geroi antifashistskoi dramaturgii [The hero in antifascist dramaturgy]. Sovetskoe iskusstvo, February 23, 1939.

Abramov, A. "Negritianskaia tema" v amerikanskoi literature [The "Negro theme" in American literature]. Internatsional'naia literatura, 1939, no. 7-8 (first printing), p. 360-362. (Signed: A. Terekhov) *See also: idem* (second printing), p. 269-271.

Abramov, A. Novoe v amerikanskoi dramaturgii [New features of American dramaturgy]. Teatr, 1939, no. 2-3, p. 39-50.

Abramov, A. Peredovaia literatura sovremennoi Ameriki [Progressive literature of contemporary America]. Internatsional'naia literatura, 1939, no. 7-8 (first printing), p. 272-283.

Vishnevskii, V. Primite nashe rukopozhatie [Accept our handshake]. Internatsional'naia literatura, 1939, no. 7-8 (first printing), p. 216.

Gladkov, F. Nashi druz'ia i soratniki [Our friends and comrades in arms]. Internatsional'naia literatura, 1939, no. 7-8 (first printing), p. 367-368.

Graf, O. M. Dva kongressa. (Kongress Penkluba. N'iu-Iork, mai 1939 g. i Kongress Ligi amerikanskikh pisatelei. N'iu-Iork, iiun' 1939 g.) [Two congresses. (The Congress of PEN, New York, May 1939, and the Congress of the League of American Writers, New York, June 1939)]. Internatsional'naia literatura, 1939, no. 7-8 (first printing), p. 429-430.

Grou, M. S"ezd amerikanskikh pisatelei (2 iiunia 1939) [The congress of American writers (June 2, 1939)]. Literaturnaia gazeta, July 5, 1939.

Zenkevich, M. and I. Kashkin. Vstupitel'nye zametki k publikatsiiam E. A. Robinsona, K. Sendberga, V. Lindzi, R. Frosta, E. L. Mastersa, A. Mak-Lisha, E. Khemingueia, M. Golda, Dzh. Khilla, L. Kh'iuza i dr. [Introductory remarks to works of E. A. Robinson, C. Sandburg, V. Lindsay, R. Frost, E. L. Masters, A. MacLeish, E. Hemingway, M. Gold, J. Hill (i.e. Joe Hill), L. Hughes and others]. *In:* Zenkevich, M. and I. Kashkin. Poety Ameriki. XX vek. [The poets of America. The 20th century]. Moscow, 1939.

Kauli [Cowley], M. Liga amerikanskikh pisatelei [The League of American Writers]. Internatsional'naia literatura, 1939, no. 7-8 (first printing), p. 369-370.

Koonen, A. Amerikanskaia dramaturgiia [American dramaturgy]. Internatsional'naia literatura, 1939, no. 7-8 (first printing), p. 312-313.

Korneichuk, A. Literatura velikogo amerikanskogo naroda [The literature of the great American people]. Internatsional'naia literatura, 1939, no. 7-8 (first printing), p. 236.

Kupala, Ia. Moi liubimye pisateli [My favorite writers]. Internatsional'-naia literatura, 1939, no. 7-8 (first printing), p. 288.

Lebedev-Kumach, V. Moi luchshie druz'ia s detstva [My best friends from childhood]. Internatsional'naia literatura, 1939, no. 7-8 (first printing), p. 341-342.

Lige amerikanskikh pisatelei. (Privetstvie Soiuza sovetskikh pisatelei Kongressu. Iiun', 1939) [To the League of American Writers. (Greetings of the Union of Soviet Writers to the Congress. June, 1939)]. Internatsional'naia literatura, 1939, no. 7-8 (first printing), p. 269.

Lidin, V. Kogda okean predstavliaetsia rechkoi [When the ocean is presented as a small river]. Internatsional'naia literatura, 1939, no. 7-8 (first printing), p. 342-343.

Manevich, D. Review of: Zenkevich, M. and I. Kashkin. Poety Ameriki. XX veka [The poets of America. 20th century]. Moscow, 1939. Molodaia gvardiia, 1939, no. 8, p. 189-190.

Novikov-Priboi, A. Moi liubimye pisateli [My favorite writers]. Internatsional'naia literatura, 1939, no. 7-8 (first printing), p. 312.

Norov, V. Review of: *Theatre Arts Monthly*, New York, nos. 1-4, 1939. Internatsional'naia literatura, no. 7-8 (first printing), p. 362-364.

Paustovskii, K. Novoe pokolenie amerikanskikh pisatelei [The new generation of American writers]. Internatsional'naia literatura, 1939, no. 7-8 (first printing), p. 311.

Petrov, E. Iskliuchitel'no talantlivyi narod [An exceptionally talented people]. Internatsional'naia literatura, 1939, no. 7-8 (first printing), p. 216.

Rapoport, I. Romantika i realizm v amerikanskoi literature [Romance and realism in American literature]. Internatsional'naia literatura, 1939, no. 7-8 (first printing), p. 286-287.

Rubin, V. "N'iu messes" v 1939 godu [*New Masses* in 1939]. Internatsional'naia literatura, 1939, no. 7-8 (first printing), p. 335-360. *Also, abridged, in:* Internatsional'naia literatura, 1939, no. 7-8 (second printing), p. 266-269.

Sovetskie chitateli ob amerikanskoi literature [Soviet readers on American writing]. Internatsional'naia literatura, 1939, no. 7-8 (first printing), p. 401-404.

Startsev, A. Amerika i russkoe obshchestvo [America and Russian society]. Internatsional'naia literatura, 1939, no. 7-8 (first printing), p. 289-309. *Also, with changes, in:* Internatsional'naia literatura, 1941, no. 9-10, p. 208-222. *Separately published:* Moscow, Academy of Sciences of the USSR, 1942. 31 p. Revised and enlarged ed. Tashkent, 1942. 39 p.

Startsev, A. Poety Ameriki [Poets of America]. (Review of: Zenkevich, M. and I. Kashkin. Poety Ameriki. XX v. [The poets of America.

20th century]. Moscow, 1939). Literaturnoi obozrenie, 1939, no. 23, p. 31-38.

3-i—i.e. Tret'ii—kongress Ligi amerikanskikh pisatelei (Iiun', 1939) [Third Congress of the League of American Writers (June, 1939)]. Internatsional'naia literatura, 1939, no. 7-8 (first printing), p. 428.

Tret'emu Kongressu Ligi amerikanskikh pisatelei. (Privetstvie redaktsii "Internatsional'noi literatury") [To the Third Congress of the League of American Writers. (Greetings of the editorial board of "Internatsional'naia literatura")]. Internatsional'naia literatura, 1939, no. 7-8, p. 270-271.

Teggard, Zh. [Taggard, G.]. Amerikanskaia literatura i narod [American literature and the people]. Literaturnaia gazeta, April 5, 1939.

Uze, B. Pis'mo s Kongressa (Ligi amerikanskikh pisatelei. Iiun', 1939) [A letter from the Congress (of the League of American Writers. June, 1939)]. Internatsional'naia literatura, 1939, no. 7-8 (first printing), p. 430-432.

Khenter [Hunter], E. V teatrakh N'iu-Iorka [In the theaters of New York]. Internatsional'naia literatura, 1939, no. 2, p. 211-215.

Shneider [Schneider?], I. Pis'mo iz SShA (o literaturnoi zhizni) [Letter from the US (about literary life)]. Internatsional'naia literatura, 1939, no. 7-8 (first printing), p. 376-378. *Also, abridged, in:* Internatsional'naia literatura, 1939, no. 7-8 (second printing), p. 279-281.

1940 Abramov, A. Amerikanskaia odnoaktnaia p'esa [The American one-act play]. Internatsional'naia literatura, 1940, no. 2, p. 181-184.

Aleksandrov, V. Poety Ameriki. XX vek [The poets of America. 20th century]. (Review of: Zenkevich, M. and I. Kashkin. Poety Ameriki. XX v. [The poets of America. 20th century]. Moscow, 1939). Literaturnyi kritik, 1940, no. 2, p. 188-192.

Amerikanskaia literatura [American literature]. (Summary of report by A. Startsev, "American literature today"). Literaturnaia gazeta, November 12, 1940.

Vystuplenie Teodora Draizera (protiv zakrytiia "New Masses") [A speech of Theodore Dreiser's (against the suspension of *New Masses*)]. Literaturnaia gazeta, April 26, 1940.

Gan, Z. Review of: *The Best Short Stories*, 1939. Internatsional'naia literatura, 1940, no. 9-10, p. 248-249.

Grits, T. Novaia amerikanskaia poeziia [New American poetry]. (Review of: Zenkevich, M. and I. Kashkin. Poety Ameriki. XX v. [The poets of America. 20th century]. Moscow, 1939). Leningrad, 1940, no. 5, p. 20-21.

Karmon, U. [Carmon, W.]. Zametki o literaturnoi zhizni SShA [Notes on the literary life of the US]. Internatsional'naia literatura, 1940, no. 2, p. 194-197.

18

Mansoni, A.-K. Negry v amerikanskoi poezii [Negroes in American poetry]. Internatsional'naia literatura, 1940, no. 7-8, p. 270-273.

Mendel'son, M. Tridtsatye gody v Amerike [The Thirties in America]. Literaturnaia gazeta, August 11, 1940.

Rubin, V. Review of: *American Stuff. Anthology of Prose and Verse.* New York, 1937. Internatsional'naia literatura, 1940, no. 9-10, p. 243-244.

Smirnov, Iu. Molodye revoliutsionnye pisateli SShA [The young revolutionary writers of the US]. Molodaia gvardiia, 1940, no. 9, p. 149-152.

Startsev, A. Amerikanskaia voina za nezavisimost' v russkoi pechati kontsa XVIII veka [The American War for Independence in the Russian press of the end of the 18th century]. Istoricheskaia literatura, 1940, no. 5-6, p. 175-177.

Khenter [Hunter], E. "Sukhie polia i zelenye pastbishcha." (Negritianskaia literatura 1939-1940 gg.) ["Dry fields and green pastures." (Negro literature of 1939-1940)]. Internatsional'naia literatura, 1940, no. 7-8, p. 315-317.

Shneider [Schneider?], I. Voina i pisateli [The war and writers]. Internatsional'naia literatura, 1940, no. 9-10, p. 252-254.

Shneider [Schneider?], I. Novosti literatury i iskusstva v SShA [News of literature and art in the US]. Internatsional'naia literatura, 1940, no. 7-8, p. 302-304.

1941 Abramov, A. Amerikanskaia iumoristicheskaia novella [The American humorous short story]. Literaturnaia gazeta, March 2, 1941.

Abramov, Al. Amerikanskie mastera kul'tury v bor'be s fashizmom [American cultural leaders in the struggle with fascism]. Internatsional'naia literatura, 1941, no. 9-10, p. 223-226.

Andreev, K. Amerikanskaia nauchnaia fantastika [American science fiction]. Literaturnaia gazeta, June 1, 1941.

Gold, M. V boiakh za peredovuiu literaturu SShA [In the battle for a progressive literature in the US]. Internatsional'naia literatura, 1941, no. 6, p. 142-157.

Zenkevich, M. "Poetri" v 1940 godu [*Poetry* in 1940]. Internatsional'naia literatura, 1941, no. 1, p. 173-175.

Karmon, U. [Carmon, W.]. Novinki literaturnogo sezona [News of the literary season]. Internatsional'naia literatura, 1941, no. 11-12, p. 310-311.

Malkin, M. M. Chernyshevskii i zaatlanticheskaia respublika (SShA) [Chernyshevskii and the trans-Atlantic republic (US)]. *In:* N. G. Chernyshevskii (1889-1939). Leningrad, 1941. p. 319-337.

Rid [Reed?], M. Novinki amerikanskogo knizhnogo rynka [New features of the American book market]. Internatsional'naia literatura, 1941, no. 5, p. 232-233.

19

Roktov, T. Anglo-amerikanskaia voennaia novella [The Anglo-American war short story]. Internatsional'naia literatura, 1941, no. 11-12, p. 116-117.

Sovetskie pisateli ob angliiskoi i amerikanskoi literature. Shaginian, M., Vstrecha anglo-amerikanskoi i sovetskoi literatur. Chukovskii, K., Kak ia poliubil anglo-amerikanskuiu literaturu. Novikov-Priboi, A., Chem ia obiazan Bicher-Stou. Antokol'skii, P., Moi druz'ia za okeanom. Sel'vinskii, I., Obrazy Ameriki. Pogodin, N., Nasha volia dolzhna byt' edina. Kirpotin, V., Nashi simpatii k amerikanskoi literature. Argo, Blizhe poznakomimsia s amerikanskim iskusstvom [Soviet writers on English and American literature. Shaginian, M., The meeting point of Anglo-American and Soviet literatures. Chukovskii, K., How I came to love Anglo-American literature. Novikov-Priboi, A., What I owe to (Harriet) Beecher Stowe. Antokol'skii, P., My friends beyond the ocean. Sel'vinskii, I., Images of America. Pogodin, N., Our wills should be united. Kirpotin, V., Our sympathies for American literature. Ergo, let us become more closely acquainted with American art]. Internatsional'naia literatura, 1941, no. 9-10, p. 230-242.

Khenter [Hunter], E. Amerikanskaia detektivnaia p'esa [The American detective play]. Internatsional'naia literatura, 1941, no. 6, p. 194-196.

Khenter [Hunter], E. "Zemlia obetovannaia" (Amerikanskie romany o Gollivude) [The "Promised Land" (American novels about Hollywood)]. Internatsional'naia literatura, 1941, no. 1, p. 187-189.

Sneider [Schneider?], I. Pis'mo iz SShA [A letter from the US]. Internatsional'naia literatura, 1941, no. 2, p. 228-229.

1942 Abramov, A. Anglo-amerikanskiia voennyi roman [The Anglo-American war novel]. Znamia, 1942, no. 7, p. 147-154.

Zenkevich, M. Na perelome (Angliiskaia i amerikanskaia voennaia poeziia) [At the point of separation (English and American war poetry)]. Internatsional'naia literatura, 1942, no. 8-9, p. 152-153.

Zenkevich, M. O stikhakh anglo-amerikanskikh poetov (v zhurnale "Poetry" 1941 g.) [Concerning the verse of Anglo-American poets (in the magazine *Poetry* in 1941)]. Internatsional'naia literatura, 1942, no. 1-2, p. 209-210.

Luchshie predstaviteli angliiskoi i amerikanskoi literatury. Bibliograficheskii ukazatel' perevodov i kriticheskoi literatury na russkom iazyke [The best representatives of English and American literature. Bibliographic guide to translations and critical literature in the Russian language]. Moscow, Gos. bibl.-bibliogrf. izd-vo, 1942. 49 p.

T. R. Angliiskaia i amerikanskaia literatura v dni voiny [English and American literature in war time]. Propagandist, 1942, no. 9, p. 59-64.

Khenter [Hunter], E. Poslednie novinki amerikanskoi literatury [The most recent items of American literature]. Internatsional'naia literatura, 1942, no. 6, p. 150-153.

1944 Motyleva, T. Angliiskie i amerikanskie romany o voine [English and American novels about the war]. Oktiabr', 1944, no. 1-2, p. 159-164.

Rubin, V. Voennaia tema v amerikanskoi literature [The subject of the war in American literature]. Znamia, 1944, no. 4, p. 156-159.

1945 Zhantieva, D. G. and M. S. Morshchiner. Sovremennye angliiskie i amerikanskie pisateli. Bibliograficheskii ukazatel' osnovnykh proizvedenii i kriticheskoi literatury na russkom iazyke [Contemporary English and American writers. A bibliographic guide to the basic works and to critical literature in the Russian language]. Moscow, Gos. bibl.-bibliogr. izd-vo, 1945. 56 p.

Zenkevich, M. Zametki poeta. Po stranitsam "Poetry" [The remarks of a poet. In the pages of *Poetry*]. Literaturnaia gazeta, February 23, 1945.

Rubin, V. and N. Karintsev. Obzor sovremennoi amerikanskoi i angliiskoi dramaturgii [A survey of contemporary American and English dramaturgy]. Novyi mir, 1945, no. 7, p. 109-117.

Startsev, A. Literaturnye spory v SShA (o sotsial'nom romane 20-kh — 30-kh gg.) [Literary controversies in the US (on the social novel of the '20's and '30's)]. Literaturnaia gazeta, August 11, 1945.

1946 Makogonenko, G. P. Rossiia i amerikanskaia revoliutsiia [Russia and the American Revolution]. Nauchnyi biulleten' Leningradskogo Gosudarstvennogo Universiteta, 1946, no. 8, p. 14-19.

Mendel'son, M. Amerikanskie romany o dniakh voiny [American novels about the war period]. Znamia, 1946, no. 4, p. 174-182.

Mendel'son, M. Maiakovskii ob Amerike [Maiakovskii about America]. Znamia, 1946, no. 5-6, p. 164-171.

Rubin, V. Nishcheta ideinaia i khudozhestvennaia. O "voennoi poezii" v Anglii i SShA [Poverty — ideological and artistic. Concerning "war poetry" in England and the US]. Literaturnaia gazeta, December 21, 1946.

Startsev, A. Amerikanskaia novella i razvitie amerikanskoi literatury v XIX veke. Primechaniia. [The American short story and the development of American literature in the 19th century. Notes]. *In:* Amerikanskaia novella XIX veka [The American short story of the 19th century]. Moscow, 1946. p. 3-11, 449-476.

1947 Istoriia amerikanskoi literatury [History of American literature]. v. 1. Moscow-Leningrad, Izd-vo Akademii nauk SSSR, 1947. 343 p. (Sponsored by Academy of Sciences of the USSR, Institute of World Literature named for A. M. Gor'kii). *See review:* Leites, A. Ob odnoi antinauchnoi kontseptsii. (Pervyi tom "Istoriia amerikanskoi literatury") [Concerning an unscholarly concept. (The first volume of "Istoriia amerikanskoi literatury")]. Kul'tura i zhizn', September 21, 1947.

Leites, A. M. Literatura sovremennogo amerikanskogo imperializma. Stenogramma publichnoi lektsii [The literature of contemporary American imperialism. Stenographic report of a public lecture]. Moscow, 1947. 24 p.

Mendel'son, M. Amerikanskaia literatura v poiskakh obraza nastoiashchego cheloveka [American literature in search of the image of a real person]. Znamia, 1947, no. 3, p. 156-178.

Mendel'son, M. Gideon Dzhekson i drugie. (Rasovaia diskriminatsiia i amerikanskaia literatura poslednikh let) [Gideon Jackson and others. (Race discrimination and American literature of recent years)]. Novyi mir, 1947, no. 5, p. 150-167.

Mendel'son, M. Peredovye pisateli SShA [Progressive writers of the US]. Literaturnaia gazeta, December 10, 1947.

Mendel'son, M. O. Sovremennaia amerikanskaia literatura. Stenogramma publichnoi lektsii. [Contemporary American literature. Stenographic report of a public lecture]. Moscow, "Pravda," 1947. 31 p.

Orlova, R. Sud'ba "glavnykh myslei." Zametki ob amerikanskoi literature. [The fate of the "main ideas." Remarks on American literature]. Molodoi bol'shevik, 1947, no. 5, p. 61-63.

S kem vy, amerikanskie mastera kul'tury? Otkrytoe pis'mo (gruppy sovetskikh pisatelei s prizyvom k bor'be protiv ugrozy fashizma i voiny) [Whose side are you on, leaders of American culture? Open letter (of a group of Soviet writers with an appeal to join the struggle against the threat of fascism and war)]. Literaturnaia gazeta, September 20, 1947.

Suchkov, B. Raby dollara. Zametki ob amerikanskoi burzhuaznoi literature [Slaves of the dollar. Remarks on American bourgeois literature]. Kul'tura i zhizn', July 10, 1947.

1948 Alekseev, M. P. Amerikano-russkie literaturnye zametki [Americo-Russian literary remarks]. Nauchnyi biulleten' Leningradskogo gosudarstvennogo universiteta, 1948, no. 8, p. 22-27.

Gal'perina, E. Vo vlasti strakha. (O sbornikakh "Cross Section," 1944, 1945, 1947 i 1948 gg) [In the grip of fear. (Concerning the collection "Cross Section," 1944, 1945, 1947 and 1948)]. Literaturnaia gazeta, August 4, 1948.

Mendel'son, M. Amerikanskie smertiashkiny [The death-ridden Americans]. Novyi mir, 1948, no. 12, p. 205-221.

Mendel'son, M. Sila pravdy. K voprosu o vlianii klassicheskoi russkoi i sovetskoi literatury na amerikanskuiu [The force of truth. On the problem of the influence of Russian classical and Soviet literature on America]. Znamia, 1948, no. 1, p. 149-174.

Mendel'son, M. Sud'ba amerikanskogo pisatelia (v XIX i XX vv.) [The fate of the American writer (in the 19th and 20th centuries)]. Literaturnaia gazeta, January 3, 1948.

Orlova, R. Vospitanie landsknekhtov. Vtoraia mirovaia voina i amerikanskaia literatura [The indoctrination of mercenaries. The Second
World War and American literature]. Novyi mir, 1948, no. 3, p. 201-
215.

Rubin, V. Krizis sovremennoi amerikanskoi literatury [The crisis of
contemporary American literature]. Zvezda, 1948, no. 8, p. 190-201.

Startsev, A. Iz istorii literatury amerikanskogo imperializma [From the
history of the literature of American imperialism]. Znamia, 1948,
no. 7, p. 179-192.

Startsev, A. Imperialisticheskaia agressiia i sovremennaia amerikanskaia
literatura [Imperialist aggression and contemporary American
literature]. Znamia, 1948, no. 11, p. 124-141.

Startsev, A. Imperialisticheskaia propaganda i literatura v SShA [Im-
perialist propaganda and literature in the US]. Pravda, June 23,
1948.

Chernyi, K. Negritianskii vopros v amerikanskoi literature [The Negro
question in American literature]. In: Delo Eiba Letema, negra [The
case of Abe Latham, Negro]. Stavropol', 1948. p. 3-17.

Ianovskii, Iu. Glubokie korni. (Negritianskaia tema v sovremennoi
amerikanskoi literature) [Deep roots. (The Negro question in contemporary American literature)]. Don (Rostov-na-Donu), 1948,
no. 12, p. 187-199.

1949 Mendel'son, M. Amerikanskaia progressivnaia literatura poslednikh let
[American progressive literature of recent years]. Zvezda, 1949,
no. 11, p. 167-182.

Orlova, R. Volny t'my. (Zametki o poslevoennoi amerikanskoi literature) [Waves of darkness. (Notes on post-War American literature)].
Molodoi bol'shevik, 1949, no. 3, p. 74-79.

Teatr na sluzhbe reaktsii [The theater in the service of reaction]. Pravda,
September 6, 1949.

Chukovskii, K. Vospitanie gangsterov. (Zametki ob amerikanskoi
literature dlia detei) [Rearing gangsters. (Remarks on American
literature for children)]. Znamia, 1949, no. 8, p. 185-192.

1950 Lavrenev, B. Svidetel' iz svoego doma [A witness from his own house].
(Review of: Rasskazy ob Amerike [Tales about America]. Moscow,
1950). Pravda, April 10, 1950.

Orlova, R. D. Obraz kommunista v progressivnoi literature SShA (1946-
1949) [The image of the Communist in the progressive literature of
the US, 1946-1949]. Abstract of dissertation presented for the degree
of Candidate of Philological Sciences. Moscow, 1950. 19 p.

Orlova, R. Predislovie [Foreword]. In: Rasskazy ob Amerike [Tales
about America]. Moscow, 1950. p. 5-18.

Sovremennaia amerikanskaia literatura. Sbornik statei [Contemporary
American literature. A collection of articles]. Moscow, Goslitizdat,

1950. 239 p. (Issued under auspices of Institute of World Literature named for A. M. Gor'kii of the Academy of Sciences of the USSR.) *Reviewed in:* Kondrashev, G. Leningradskaia pravda, February 11, 1951; Nikolaev, V. Dva lageria v sovremennoi amerikanskoi literature [Two camps in contemporary American literature]. Bol'shevik, 1951, no. 6, p. 68-73; Romanova, E. O literature segodniashnei Ameriki [Concerning the literature of today's America]. Novyi mir, 1951, no. 4, p. 241-243.

1951 Bekker, M. Negritianskaia literatura SShA v bor'be protiv rabstva, reaktsii i imperializma [Negro literature of the US in the struggle against slavery, reaction and imperialism]. Zvezda, 1951, no. 1, p. 94-100.

Borovoi, L. Dve Ameriki. (Posleslovie) [Two Americas. (Afterword)]. *In:* Rasskazy ob Amerike [Tales about America]. Moscow, 1951. p. 100-104.

Elistratova, A. Na sluzhbe agressivnoi politiki. Zametki ob amerikanskoi burzhuaznoi literature [In the service of an aggressive policy. Notes on American bourgeois literature]. Pravda, June 5, 1951.

Petelin, G. S. Dve Ameriki — dve literatury [Two Americas — two literatures]. *In:* Amerika kak ona est' [America as it is]. Rostov-Na-Donu, 1951. p. 3-13.

Romanova, E. Teoriia i praktika literaturnykh biznesmenov. ("Saturday Review of Literature") [The theory and practice of literary businessmen. (*Saturday Review of Literature*)]. Novyi mir, 1951, no. 11, p. 268-274.

1952 Dubashinskii, I. A. Razoblachenie amerikanskogo imperializma v progressivnoi literature SShA (1946-1951 gg) [The unmasking of American imperialism in the progressive literature of the US, 1946-1951]. Abstract of dissertation presented for the degree of Candidate of Philological Sciences. Moscow, 1952. 15 p.

Maslova, I. and V. Glunin. Reaktsionnaia literaturnaia kritika na sluzhbe podzhigatelei voiny [Reactionary literary criticism in the service of the warmongers]. Znamia, 1952, no. 10, p. 185-192.

Orlova, R. D. Zhurnal "Messes end meinstrim" [The magazine *Masses and Mainstream*]. *In:* Progressivnaia literatura stran kapitalizma v bor'be za mir [The progressive literature of the countries of capitalism in the struggle for peace]. Moscow, 1952. p. 327-351.

1953 Bekker, M. I. Progressivnaia negritianskaia literatura SShA v bor'be protiv rabstva i imperialisticheskoi reaktsii [Progressive Negro literature of the US in the struggle against slavery and imperialist reaction]. Abstract of dissertation presented for the degree of Candidate of Philological Sciences. Leningrad, 1953. 18 p.

Gold, M. Mysli ob amerikanskikh pisateliakh [Thoughts about American writers]. Literaturnaia gazeta, July 2, 1953.

Elistratova, A. Propaganda beznadezhnosti. Zametki o sovremennykh amerikanskikh burzhuaznykh p'esakh [The propaganda of hopelessness. Remarks on contemporary American bourgeois plays]. Pravda, May 24, 1953.

Zhulanov, N. Progressivnye pevtsy Ameriki [Progressive singers of America]. Zabaikal'e (Almanakh), 1953, no. 6, p. 218-231.

Romanova, E. Golos pravdy. Po stranitsam progressivnoi periodiki SShA [The voice of truth. In the pages of the progressive periodicals of the US]. Literaturnaia gazeta, November 12, 1953.

Tikhomirova, I. V bor'be protiv reaktsionnogo mrakobesiia, za mir, demokratiiu i sotsializm. (Zametki o sovremennoi progressivnoi amerikanskoi literature) [In the struggle against reactionary obscurantism, for peace, democracy and socialism. (Remarks about contemporary progressive American literature)]. Zvezda, 1953, no. 11, p. 161-172.

Trofimov, P. S. Sovremennaia reaktsionnaia amerikano-angliiskaia burzhuaznaia estetika na sluzhbe monopolii SShA [Contemporary reactionary Anglo-American bourgeois esthetics in the service of the monopolies of the US]. Voprosy filosofii, 1953, no. 2, p. 183-200.

1954 Bel'skii, A. Amerikanskaia progressivnaia literatura v bor'be za mir [American progressive literature in the struggle for peace]. *In:* Sovremennaia progressivnaia literatura zarubezhnykh stran v bor'be za mir [Contemporary progressive literature of foreign countries in the struggle for peace]. Moscow, 1954. p. 154-180.

Samokhvalov, N. Predislovie [Foreword]. *In:* Rasskazy amerikanskikh pisatelei [Tales of American writers]. Moscow, 1954. p. 3-14.

Sillen, S. Moral'noe razlozhenie amerikanskoi burzhuaznoi literatury [The moral decay of American bourgeois literature]. Pravda, January 11, 1954.

Ustenko, G. A. Bor'ba protiv rasovoi diskriminatsii v progressivnoi amerikanskoi literature 30 - 60-kh gg. XIX st. [The struggle against race discrimination in progressive American literature of the '30's to '60's of the 19th century]. Abstract of dissertation presented for the degree of Candidate of Philological Sciences. Kiev, 1954. 16 p.

Chaplygin, Iu. V tupike. (Zametki ob amerikanskom rasskaze) [In a dead end. (Remarks about the American short story)]. (Review of: *The Best American Short Stories*. Boston, 1952). Oktiabr', 1954, no. 4, p. 182-185.

1955 Baskin, M. P. Filosofiia amerikanskogo prosveshcheniia [The philosophy of American education]. Moscow, Izd-vo Moskovskogo universiteta, 1955. 27 p.

Gold, M. Pisatel' v Amerike [The writer in America]. *In:* Progressivnye deiateli SShA v bor'be za peredovuiu ideologiiu [Progressive figures of the US in the struggle for a progressive ideology]. Moscow, 1955. p. 309-316.

25

Lavrenev, B. Perelistyvaia stranitsy istorii ... (Russko-amerikanskie otnosheniia) [Turning the pages of history ... (Russian-American relations)]. Literaturnaia gazeta, July 23, 1955.

Orlova, R. D. Obraz kommunista v amerikanskoi literature 30-kh godov [The image of the Communist in American literature of the 1930's]. Uchenye zapiski Moskovskogo oblastnogo pedagogicheskogo instituta, 1955, t. 34. Trudy kafedry zarubezhnoi literatury, vyp. 2, p. 43-66.

Razgovorov, N. Lozhnaia panorama [A false panorama]. (Review of: Brown, J. Panorama de la littérature contemporaine aux États-Unis. Paris, 1954). Literaturnaia gazeta, March 19, 1955.

Rozanov, B. Velikie traditsii. ("Masses and Mainstream," 1955, no. 1) [Great traditions. (*Masses and Mainstream*, 1955, no. 1)]. Novyi mir, 1955, no. 5, p. 190-194.

Rozanov, B. ... Vperedi—ogni! ("Masses and Mainstream") [... Ahead there are lights! (*Masses and Mainstream*)]. Novyi mir, 1955, no. 3, p. 198-200.

Romanova, E. Zametki o novykh tipakh amerikanskikh pisatelei [Remarks about new types of American writers]. Literaturnaia gazeta, September 3, 1955.

Romanova, E. Mrachnye perspektivy. ("Perspectives USA." Obzor zhurnala) [Gloomy prospects. (*Perspectives USA*. A review of the journal)]. Novyi mir, 1955, no. 3, p. 200-204.

Romanova, E. O nekotorykh iavleniiakh v poslevoennoi literature SShA [Concerning some phenomena of postwar literature of the US]. Inostrannaia literatura, 1955, no. 1, p. 191-197.

Rubin, V. Dlia chitatelia—druga. ("Contemporary Reader," 1955, no. 1) [For a reader and a friend. (*Contemporary Reader*, 1955, no. 1)]. Novyi mir, 1955, no. 7, p. 228-231.

Samokhvalov, N. I. Iz istorii bor'by za realizm v amerikanskoi literature kontsa XIX veka [From the history of the struggle for realism in American literature of the end of the 19th century]. Uchenye zapiski Krasnodarskogo pedagogischeskogo instituta, 1955, vyp. 13, filologiia, p. 88-116.

Timofeev, T. Amerika smotrit v budushchee [America looks to the future]. Literaturnaia gazeta, March 26, 1955.

Uitmen, U. [Whitman, W.]. Iz stat'i "Poezii v sovremennoi Amerike — Shekspir — Budushchee" [From the article "Poetry in contemporary America — Shakespeare — The Future"]. Inostrannaia literatura, 1955, no. 1, p. 162-164.

Kholendro, D. Mnogoetazhnaia Amerika. ("Rasskazy amerikanskikh pisatelei." Moskva, 1955) [Multistory America. ("Tales of American writers." Moscow, 1955)]. Literaturnaia gazeta, April 7, 1955.

1956 Baskin, M. P. and M. S. Ivanov. Po povodu odnoi kontseptsii o vzaimo-otnoshenii russkoi i amerikanskoi kul'tur v XIX veke [Concerning one concept as to the interrelation of Russian and American culture in the 19th century]. Voprosy filosofii, 1956, no. 4, p. 56-64.

Zhuravlev, I. K. Voprosy khudozhestvennoi literatury na stranitsakh peredovoi pressy SShA posle vtoroi mirovoi voiny. (Na materiale "Deili Uorker," i "Messis end Meinstrim") [Problems of literature in the pages of the progressive press of the US after the Second World War. (On the basis of *Daily Worker* and *Masses and Mainstream*)]. Abstract of dissertation presented for the degree of Candidate of Philological Sciences. Moscow, 1956. 16 p.

Literatura Soedinennykh Shtatov Ameriki, 1870-1917 gg. [The literature of the United States of America, 1870-1917]. *In:* Kurs lektsii po istorii zarubezhnykh literatur XX veka [Course of lectures in the history of foreign literatures of the 20th century]. v. 1. Moscow, 1956. p. 417-520.

Romanova, E. Antologiia (sovremennykh amerikanskikh rasskazov) [An anthology (of contemporary American short stories)]. Literaturnaia gazeta, July 17, 1956.

Finkel'stain, S. Realizm i demokraticheskaia bor'ba v iskusstve Soedinennykh Shtatov [Realism and the democratic struggle in the art of the United States]. *In:* Finkel'stain, S. Realizm v iskusstve [Realism in art]. Moscow, 1956. p. 217-258.

1957 Bekker, M. I. Progressivnaia negritianskaia literatura SShA [Progressive Negro literature in the US]. Leningrad, 1957. 235 p. *Reviewed in:* Levidova, I. Kniga o progressivnoi negritianskoi literature SShA [A book about progressive Negro literature in the US]. Voprosy literatury, 1958, no. 7, p. 225-230.

Belogolovova, K. D. Teatr Severo-Amerikanskikh soedinennykh shtatov (v XVIII v.) [The theater of the North American United States (in the 18th century)]. *In:* Istoriia zapadnoevropeiskogo teatra [History of the Western European theater]. v. 2. Moscow, 1957. p. 829-860.

Bogoslovskii, V. N. Amerikanskaia literatura v kontse XIX veka [American literature at the end of the 19th century]. Uchenye zapiski Moskovskogo oblastnogo pedagogischeskogo instituta, 1955, t. 55. Trudy kafedry zarubezhnoi literatury, vyp. 5, p. 3-40.

Gorokhov, V. "Kol'ers" (1888-1957) [*Collier's*, 1888-1957]. Znamia, 1957. no. 3, p. 182-184.

D'iakonova, N. Tsennyi filologischeskii zhurnal [A valuable philological journal]. (*Zeitschrift für Anglistik und Amerikanistik.* Berlin). Voprosy literatury, 1957, no. 5, p. 211-215.

Zhuravlev, I. K voprosu o razvitii kriticheskogo realizma v amerikanskoi literature XX veka [On the problem of the development of critical realism in American literature of the 20th century]. Uchenye zapiski Dagestanskogo universiteta, 1957, vyp. 1, p. 65-81.

Zlobin, G. Spravochnik po amerikanskomu teatru [A handbook for the

American theater]. (*The Best Plays of 1955-56*. New York, 1956). Inostrannaia literatura, 1957, no. 10, p. 265-266.

Kanevskii, B. P. Velikaia Oktiabr'skaia sotsialisticheskaia revoliutsiia v osveshchenii Dzhona Rida, Al'berta Risa Vil'iamsa i Linkol'na Steffensa [The Great October Socialist Revolution as seen by John Reed, Albert Rhys Williams and Lincoln Steffens]. Istoriia SSSR, 1957, no. 4, p. 181-189.

Krugleevskaia, V. V. Vliianie Velikoi Oktiabr'skoi sotsialisticheskoi revoliutsii na razvitie progressivnoi literatury SShA [The influence of the Great October Socialist Revolution on the development of progressive literature of the US]. Uchenye zapiski Severo-Osetinsko-go pedagogicheskogo instituta, 1957, t. 22, vyp. 3. Seriia obshchest-vennykh nauk, p. 239-260.

Mikhal'skaia, N. P. Amerikanskii romantizm. Fenimor Kuper. Edgar Po; Amerikanskaia literatura. Garriet Bicher-Stou. Uolt Uitmen [American romanticism. Fenimore Cooper. Edgar Poe; American literature. Harriet Beecher Stowe. Walt Whitman]. *In:* Elizarova, M. E. and others. Istoriia zarubezhnoi literatury XIX veka [History of American literature of the 19th century]. Moscow, 1957. p. 204-219, 512-520.

"Natsional'naia assembleia" amerikanskikh pisatelei. (Mai, 1957) ["The National Assembly" of American writers. (May, 1957)]. Literatur-naia gazeta, May 11, 1957.

Orlova, R. D. Sovremennaia khudozhestvennaia literatura SShA [Contemporary literature of the US]. Moscow, 1957. 28 p.

Razumnikova, I. Ia. N. G. Chernyshevskii o grazhdanskoi voine v Soedinennykh Shtatakh Ameriki 1860-1865 godov [N. G. Chernyshevskii on the Civil War in the United States of America, 1860-1865]. Trudy Voronezhskogo universiteta, 1957, t. XLVIII, p. 34-55.

Romanova, E. Zametki o sovremennom amerikanskom romane [Remarks on the contemporary American novel]. Inostrannaia litera-tura, 1957, no. 12, p. 210-216.

1958 Gilenson, B. Fakty i ikh osveshchenie [Facts and their explanation]. (*American Literature*, 1951-1957). Voprosy literatury, 1958, no. 6, p. 195-202.

Gorbunov, A. and M. Davydova. Khudozhestvennaia literatura Ameriki... (Obzor izdanii 1956-1957 godov) [American literature... (Survey of the publications of 1956-1957)]. Bibliotekar', 1958, no. 3, p. 24-27.

Gurko, L. Krizis amerikanskogo dukha [Crisis of the American spirit[1]]. Abridged translation from the English by I. S. Tikhomirova. Moscow, Izd-vo inostrannoi literatury, 1958. 310 p.

---

[1] *Crisis of the American Mind*, originally entitled *Heroes, Highbrows and the Popular Mind*.

Efimov, A. V. Fol'klor i literatura 18-19 vv. [Folklore and literature of the 18th and 19th centuries]. *In:* Efimov, A. V. Ocherki istorii SShA [Outlines of the history of the US]. 2nd ed. Moscow, 1958. p. 395-410.

Koen [Cohen], M. R. Literaturnaia kritika [Literary criticism]. *In:* Koen [Cohen], M. R. Amerikanskaia mysl' [American thought]. Moscow, 1958. p. 261-274.

Kto oni—"serditye?" "poverzhennye?" "zlye?" [Who are they—The "angry?" The "afflicted?" The "evil?"]. (The "angry young men" and the "hipsters"). Inostrannaia literatura, 1958, no. 11, p. 240-234.

Melent'ev, Iu. S. Kritika N. G. Chernyshevskim burzhuaznoi demokratii SShA [Criticism by N. G. Chernyshevskii of bourgeois democracy in the US]. Uchenye zapiski Ural'skogo universiteta, 1958, vyp. 24, p. 203-215.

Startsev, A. Novella v amerikanskoi literature XIX-XX vv.—Kommentarii. [The short story in American literature of the 19th and 20th centuries.—Commentary]. *In:* Amerikanskaia novella XIX veka [The American short story of the 19th century]. v. 1. Moscow, 1958. p. 3-38, 657-675. v. 2: Amerikanskaia novella XX veka [The American short story of the 20th century]. Commentary, p. 519-532.

Tugusheva, M. "Razbitoe pokolenie" Ameriki [The "beat generation" of America]. Literaturnaia gazeta, December 20, 1958.

1959 Amerikanskaia dramaturgiia i ee perspektivy [American dramaturgy and its prospects]. Inostrannaia literatura, 1959, no. 11, p. 206-207.

B'iukenen, T. Dzh. [Buchanan, T. J.]. Amerikanskaia nauchnaia fantastika [American science fiction]. V zashchitu mira, 1959, no. 97, p. 49-55.

Vil'iams [Williams], A. R. Pionery vzaimoponimaniia. (Dzh. Rid, L. Braiant, L. Steffens i dr.) [Pioneers in mutual understanding. (J. Reed, L. Bryant, L. Steffens and others)]. Literaturnaia gazeta, November 7, 1959.

Gilenson, B. V zamknutom krugu modernistskoi estetiki [In the closed circle of modernist esthetics]. (*Journal of Aesthetics and Art Criticism*, 1957-1959). Voprosy literatury, 1959, no. 9, p. 168-179.

Gilenson, B. V iskazhennom rakurse [In a distorted foreshortening]. (Hoffman, F. *The Modern Novel in America.* Chicago, 1956). Voprosy literatury, 1959, no. 5, p. 236-240.

Gilenson, B. Literatura v svete "Psikhoanaliza." (Kratkii obzor rabot amerikanskikh freidistov) [Literature in the light of "psychoanalysis." (A short survey of the works of American followers of Freud)]. Voprosy literatury, 1959, no. 1, p. 184-194.

Gilenson, B. Starye priemy "novoi kritiki" [Old methods of the "new criticism"]. Inostrannaia literatura, 1959, no. 11, p. 177-184.

Elistratova, A. Dvukhtomnik amerikanskoi novelly [The two-volume collection of the American short story]. (Amerikanskaia novella. Moscow, 1958. 2v.). Voprosy literatury, 1959, no. 3, p. 233-237.

Zasurskii, Ia. Vozrazheniia Al'fredu Keizinu [A reply to Alfred Kazin]. Inostrannaia literatura, 1959, no. 11, p. 241-246.

Zasurskii, Ia. N. Freidizm i literaturnaia bor'ba v SShA [Freudianism and the literary struggle in the US]. Vestnik Moskovskogo universiteta, Istoriko-filologicheskaia seriia, 1959, no. 4, p. 139-148.

Zemlianova, L. Retsepty "ul'trachistoi" poezii [Recipes for "ultra-pure" poetry]. (Ciardi, J. "Dialogue with the Audience." *Saturday Review.* November 22, 1958). Inostrannaia literatura, 1959, no. 7, p. 269-270.

Zemlianova, L. M. Noveishie idealisticheskie teorii v sovremennoi amerikanskoi estetike [The most recent idealist theories in contemporary American esthetics]. Voprosy filosofii, 1959, no. 4, p. 85-92.

Zlobin, G. Knigi v zashchitu demokratii [Books in defense of democracy]. Inostrannaia literatura, 1959, no. 12, p. 206-210.

Levidova, I. Trudnye sud'by [Difficult destinies]. (Purdy, J. *The Color of Darkness.* New York, 1957; Swados, H. *On the Line.* Boston, 1957; Clayton, J. B. *The Strangers Were There.* New York, 1957). Literaturnaia gazeta, December 5, 1959.

Neuteshitel'nye vyvody. (Obzor sovremennoi amerikanskoi kritiki) [Unreassuring conclusions. (Survey of contemporary American criticism)]. Literaturnaia gazeta, March 26, 1959.

Orlova, R. Vlastiteli dollara i pokolenie bes molodosti [The rulers of the dollar and the generation without youth]. Molodoi kommunist, 1959, no. 4, p. 89-92.

Orlova, R. Davaite razberemsia. Chto nam dorogo v amerikanskoi literature [Let's settle the matter. What is dear to us in American literature]. Literatura i zhizn', September 11, 1959.

Samokhvalov, N. I. Amerikanskii neoromantizm i agressiia amerikanskogo imperializma v kontse XIX veka [American neo-romanticism and the aggression of American imperialism at the end of the 19th century]. Uchenye zapiski Krasnodarskogo pedagogicheskogo instituta, 1959, vyp. 2. Istoriia, pedagogika, psikhologiia, literaturovedenie, p. 159-186.

Tugusheva, M. "Obosoblenie" ot realizma. (Sovremennyi roman v SShA) ["Isolation" from realism. (The contemporary novel in the US)]. Literaturnaia gazeta, November 19, 1959.

Usenko, L. Antologiia amerikanskoi novelly [An anthology of the American short story]. (Amerikanskaia novella XIX-XX vv. Moscow, 1958. 2 v.) Don, 1959, no. 11, p. 163-165.

Kheminguei [Hemingway], E. Zelenye kholmy Afriki. (O literature Ameriki) [The green hills of Africa. (About the literature of America)]. Inostrannaia literatura, 1959, no. 7, p. 169-173.

1960 Alekseev, M. P. K istorii poniatiia "angliiskaia literatura." (V chastnosti, o termine "amerikanskaia literatura") [On the history of the concept "English literature." (In particular, about the term "American literature")]. *In:* Alekseev, M. P. Iz istorii angliiskoi literatury [From the history of English literature]. Moscow, Leningrad, 1960. p. 453-473. *See also:* Nauchnyi biulleten' Leningradskogo universiteta, 1946, no. 8, p. 39-43.

Anikst, A. A. Ocherk razvitiia literatury SShA (ot vozniknoveniia do nachala XX v.) [Outline of the development of the literature of the US (from its origins to the beginning of the 20th century]. *In:* Ocherki novoi i noveishei istorii SShA [Outlines of the modern and recent history of the US]. v. 1. Moscow, 1960. p. 487-523.

Beliaev, V.Novye izdaniia amerikanskikh knig [New editions of American books]. Inostrannaia literatura, 1960, no. 1, p. 247-248.

Gilenson, B. V zashchitu progressivnogo naslediia [In defense of a progressive heritage]. (Bonosky, Ph. "The 'Thirties' in American Culture." *Political Affairs*, 1959, no. 5). Voprosy literatury, 1960, no. 3, p. 105-109.

Gilenson, B. Golosa poetov Ameriki [The voices of the poets of America]. (Slyshu poet Amerika. Poety SShA. [I hear America singing. The poets of the US]. Moscow, 1960). Inostrannaia literatura, 1960, no. 8, p. 256-257.

Gold, Kh. [H.] Mrachnye prognozy Kherberta Golda. (Stat'ia iz zhurnala "Atlantic" o sovremennoi literature SShA) [The gloomy prophecies of Herbert Gold. (An article from the *Atlantic* about the contemporary literature of the US)]. Literaturnaia gazeta, October 4, 1960.

Gor'kii i amerikanskie pisateli. (S publikatsiei pisem) [Gor'kii and American writers. (With letters)]. *In:* Perepiska A. M. Gor'kogo s zarubezhnymi literatorami [The correspondence of A. M. Gor'kii with foreign literary figures]. Moscow, 1960. p. 302-328.

Zhukov, D. Bunt bez tseli. (Zametki o literature "razbitogo pokoleniia" Ameriki) [Rebellion without a goal. (Remarks on the literature of the "beat generation" of America)]. Molodaia gvardiia, 1960, no. 11, p. 200-205.

Zhuravlev, I. K. Voprosy khudzhostvennoi literatury na stranitsakh peredovoi pressy SShA (1917-1956 gg.) [Problems of literature in the pages of the progressive press of the US, 1917-1956]. Abstract of dissertation presented for the degree of Candidate of Philological Sciences. Moscow, 1960. 18 p.

Zhuravlev, I. K. Iz istorii bor'by marksistskoi kritiki SShA za literaturu sotsialisticheskogo realizma (20-e gody veka) [From the history of the struggle of Marxist criticism in the US for a literature of socialist realism in the 1920's]. Vestnik Moskovskogo universiteta, 1960. Filologiia, zhurnalistika, no. 5, p. 44-56.

Zasurskii, Ia. N. Literatura SShA v noveishee vremia [The literature of the US in recent times]. *In:* Ocherki novoi i noveishei istorii SShA [Outlines of the modern and recent history of the US]. v. 2. Moscow, 1960. p. 487-530.

Zasurskii, Ia. Predislovie [Foreword]. *In: Modern American Short Stories.*[1] S kritiko-biograficheskimi spravkami o pisateliakh. (Draizer. Rid. Anderson. L'iuis. Lardner. Gold. Kheminguei. Folkner. Vulf. Parker. Benet. Steinbek. Kh'iuz. Kiun. Kolduell. O'Khara. Saroian. Lesur. Mal'ts) [With critical-biographic notes about the writers. (Dreiser. Reed. Anderson. Lewis. Lardner. Gold. Hemingway. Faulkner. Wolfe. Parker. Benét. Steinbeck. Hughes. Quin. Caldwell. O'Hara. Saroyan. Le Sueur. Maltz)]. Moscow, 1960; 2nd ed. Moscow, 1963.

Zasurskii, Ia. N. Tvorchestvo amerikanskikh progressivnykh pisatelei glazami burzhuaznogo kritika [The work of American progressive writers in the eyes of a bourgeois critic]. (Rideout, W. B. *The Radical Novel in the United States, 1900-1954*). Vestnik Moskovskogo universiteta. Filologiia, zhurnalistika, 1960, no. 2, p. 82-85.

Zlobin, G. V poiskakh chelovechnosti. Zametki o novykh p'esakh amerikanskikh dramaturgov [In search of humane qualities. Remarks about the new plays of American dramatists]. Literaturnaia gazeta, March 17, 1960.

Istiny i zabluzhdeniia "razbitogo pokoleniia." [The truths and errors of the "beat generation"]. Inostrannaia literatura, 1960, no. 1, p. 211.

Kazantsev, A. Predislovie [Foreword]. *In:* Nauchno-fantasticheskie rasskazy amerikanskikh pisatelei [Science-fiction stories of American writers]. Moscow, 1960. p. 5-24.

Levidova, I. Neprikaiannye dushi. (Geroi knig Dzhek Keruaka, Dzheimsa Selindzhera, Trumena Kapote i Ivena Konnella) [Uneasy spirits. (The heroes of the books of Jack Kerouac, James Salinger, Truman Capote and Evan Connell)]. Voprosy literatury, 1960, no. 10, p. 108-131.

Levidova, I. M. Khudozhestvennaia literatura SShA. Obzor knig 1958-1960 gg., poluchennykh VGBIL [The literature of the US. A survey of the books of 1958-1960 received by the All-Union State Library of Foreign Literature]. Moscow, 1960. 60 p.

Luri [Lourie], S. Amerikanskii teatr segodnia. Pis'mo iz N'iu-Iorka [The American theater today. Letter from New York]. Sovetskaia kul'tura, May 31, 1960.

Luri [Lourie], S. Brodvei: ogni i sumerki. Pis'mo iz N'iu-Iorka [Broadway: footlights and shadows. Letter from New York]. (Theatrical survey of 1960). Literaturnaia gazeta, June 25, 1960.

---

[1] A work in the English language published in the Soviet Union.

L'iuis [Lewis], S. Pis'mo v komitet po pulittserovskim premiiam; Strakh amerikantsev pered literaturoi; Roman i sotsial'ny nedugi naskikh dnei (zakat kapitalzma) [Letter to the Pulitzer Prize Committee; The Americans' fear of literature; The novel and the social ills of our time (the twilight of capitalism)]. *In:* L'iuis [Lewis], S. Kingsblad, potomok korolei. Rasskazy. Stat'i. Ocherki. [Kingsblood Royal. Stories. Articles. Essays]. Leningrad, 1960. p. 693-711, 731-745.

Mendel'son, M. Voinstvuiushchii psevdorealizm [Militant pseudo-realism]. Inostrannaia literatura, 1960, no. 8, p. 190-199.

Mendel'son, M. Literatura dukhovnogo krizisa. O nekotorykh iavle-niiakh sovremennoi amerikanskoi literatury. Spinoi k svetu (Warren, R. P. *The Cave.* New York, 1959). "Sny bez kontsa" (Wright, R. *The Long Dream.* New York, 1958). Roman ob amerikanskoi voenshchine (Jones, J. *From Here to Eternity.* New York, 1953). "Tiazheloi, zloveshchee, groznoe oshchushchenie" (Jones, J. *Some Came Running.* New York, 1957). Skovannoe darovanie (T. Uil'iams). "Bitnik" i ego geroi (Dzh. Keruak). Olgren i drugie. Nekotorye itogi. [Literature of a spirital crisis. Concerning some phenomena of contemporary American literature. With the back turned to the light (Warren, R. P. *The Cave.* New York, 1959). "Dreams without end" (Wright, R. *The Long Dream.* New York, 1958). A novel about the American military (Jones, J. *From Here to Eternity.* New York, 1953). "A heavy, ominous, threatening sensation" (Jones, J. *Some Came Running.* New York, 1957). A fettered talent (T. Williams). The "beatnik" and his heroes (J. Kerouac). Algren and others. Some remarks in conclusion]. Literatura i zhizn', October 12, 19, 26; November 11, 16; December 2, 7, 11, 21, 1960.

Nikoliukin, A. Kongress komparativistov v Amerike (sept., 1958). [The congress of comparativists in America, September, 1958]. Voprosy literatury, 1960, no. 10, p. 219-224.

Nort, Dzh. [North, J.]. Chto chitaiut v SShA [What they are reading in the US]. Literaturnaia gazeta, July 23, 1960.

Orlova, R. V poiskakh znameni [In search of a banner]. (*Saturday Review*, 1959-1960). Novyi mir, 1960, no. 4, p. 218-223.

Orlova, R. Malen'kie liudi na bol'shoi voine. (Voennaia tema v sovre-mennom amerikanskom romane) [Little people in a big war. (The war theme in the contemporary American novel)]. Voprosy litera-tury, 1960, no. 6, p. 100-119.

Orlova, R. and L. Kopelev. Ot illiuzii—k pravde. (O sovremennoi amerikanskoi dramaturgii) [From illusion—to truth. (Concerning contemporary American dramaturgy)]. Teatr, 1960, no. 6, p. 169-181.

Orlova, R. Ot Toma Soiera do rybaka Sant'iago. (Literatura SShA v SSSR) [From Tom Sawyer to the fisherman Santiago. (The literature of the US in the USSR)]. Kul'tura i zhizn', 1960, no. 6, p. 42-46.

33

Orlova, R. Tragicheskii stoitsizm ili bor'ba? Otkrytoe pis'mo professoru Maksainu Grinu [Tragic stoicism or struggle? An open letter to Professor Maxine Green]. Inostrannaia literatura, 1960, no. 1, p. 218-222.

1961 Beliaev, A. Beskrylaia iunost' [Youth without wings]. Molodoi kommunist, 1961, no. 4, p. 124-128.

Elistratova, A. Review of: *A Casebook of the Beat.* Edited by Th. Parkinson. 1961. Sovremennaia khudozhestvennaia literatura za rubezhom, 1961, no. 3, p. 100-102.

Elistratova, A. Tragediia molodogo pokoleniia. (Molodezh' v amerikanskom romane). [The tragedy of the young generation. (Youth in the American novel)]. Novyi mir, 1961, no. 10, p. 246-256.

Zhukov, D. Poeziia na rasput'e. (Poeziia "razbitogo pokoleniia") [Poetry at the fork in the road. (The poetry of the "beat generation")]. Literaturnaia gazeta, January 31, 1961.

Zlobin, G. Chem nedovolen Uil'iam Barret. (O sovremennom politicheskom romane v SShA) [What William Barrett is upset about. (On the contemporary political novel in the US)]. Literaturnaia gazeta, March 18, 1961.

Kashkin, I. Review of: Rozenthal, M. L. *The Modern Poets.* New York, 1960. Sovremennaia khudozhestvennaia literatura za rubezhom, 1961, no. 3, p. 106-108.

L. I. Problemy literatury sovremennoi Ameriki [Problems of the literature of contemporary America]. Voprosy literatury, 1961, no. 11, p. 244-247.

Landor, M. Proshlo li vremia buntarei? (O sovremennoi literature SShA) [Has the time for rebels passed? (Concerning the contemporary literature of the US)]. Literaturnaia gazeta, April 11, 1961.

Landor, M. "Chuzhie" (Znachenie pisatelia v SShA) ["Aliens" (on the significance of the writer in the US)]. Voprosy literatury, 1961, no. 3, p. 155-160.

Luri [Lourie], S. Na oblozhke 1961 god [The date 1961 is on the cover]. Literaturnaia gazeta, May 27, 1961.

Mendel'son, M. O. Russko-amerikanskie literaturnye sviazi kontsa XIX v. [Russian-American literary relationships of the end of the 19th century]. *In:* Vzaimosviazi i vzaimodeistvie natsional'nykh literatur [Interrelationships and interaction of national literatures]. Moscow, 1961. p. 390-395.

Morev, V. Zarisovki s natury. (Sovremennaia literatura SShA) [Sketches from life. (Contemporary literature of the US)]. Literatura i zhizn', August 4, 6, 1961.

Nedelin, V. "Vozliubivshie voinu" i ikh zhertvy [The "war lovers" and their victims]. Inostrannaia literatura, 1961, no. 7, p. 171-184.

Nikoliukin, A. N. Ob osobennostiakh vzaimosviazei angliiskoi, ameri-

34

kanskoi, i frantsuzskoi literatur v period burzhuaznykh revoliutsii kontsa XVIII v. [Concerning the specific nature of the interrelationships of English, American and French literatures in the period of the bourgeois revolutions of the end of the 18th century]. *In:* Vzaimosviazi i vzaimodeistvie natsional'nykh literatur [Interrelationships and interaction of national literatures]. Moscow, 1961. p. 395-398.

Nikoliukin, A. Review of: Howard, L. *Literature and the American Tradition.* New York, 1960. Sovremennaia khudozhestvennaia literatura zarubezhom, 1961, no. 1, p. 119-121.

Orlova, R. Vnuki diadi Toma boriutsia [The grandchildren of Uncle Tom are fighting]. Molodoi kommunist, 1961, no. 5, p. 121-126.

Orlova, R. "Korenitsia v samoi chelovechnosti..." (O putiakh razvitiia amerikanskogo romana) ["It is rooted in the very quality of being human..." (On the course of development of the American novel)]. Voprosy literatury, 1961, no. 8, p. 97-122.

Rasiaev, V. V. Amerikanskaia literatura 20-kh godov i ee sovremennye amerikanskie kritiki [American literature of the 1920's and its contemporary American critics]. Uchenye zapiski Azerbaidzhanskogo gosudarstvennogo universiteta, 1961, Seriia obshchestvennykh nauk, no. 5, p. 85-98.

Romanova, E. Liudi i knigi Ameriki (1960 g.) [People and books in America, 1960]. Literaturnaia gazeta, April 18; May 18, 1961.

Sagan, F. Zaraznaia bolezn'. (Ob amerikanskikh komiksakh) [A contagious disease. (About American "comics")]. Literaturnaia gazeta, February 21, 1961.

Samokhvalov, N. I. Vozniknovenie kriticheskogo realizma v literature SShA (1830-1885) [The origins of critical realism in the literature of the US, 1830-1885]. Krasnodar, 1961. 458 p.

Tugusheva, M. Amerikanskaia tragediia 1960 goda [An American tragedy of 1960]. Voprosy literatury, 1961, no. 6, p. 195-200.

Tugusheva, M. Nechistye ustremleniia "chistoi" kritiki [The impure tendencies of "pure" criticism]. Literaturnaia gazeta, December 19 1961.

Urnov, M. Review of: Bowden, E. T. *The Dungeon of the Heart. Human Isolation and the American Novel.* New York, 1961. Sovremennaia khudozhestvennaia literatura za rubezhom, 1961, no. 3, p. 104-106.

Sheval'e, Kh. [Chevalier, H.]. Razdum'ia o dolge pisatelia [Thoughts on the duty of a writer]. Literaturnaia gazeta, February 16, 1961.

1962 Anikst, A. Review of: Steiner, G. *The Death of Tragedy.* New York, 1961. Sovremennaia khudozhestvennaia literatura za rubezhom, 1962, no. 4-5, p. 111-113.

Anisimov, I. Seredina veka. (Problemy sovremennoi literatury SShA v

35

otsenke amerikanskogo literaturovedeniia) [Mid-century. (The problems of the contemporary literature of the US as evaluated by American literary scholarship)]. (Brooks, V. W. *The Writer in America*, 1953; Thorp, W. *American Writing in the Twentieth Century*, 1960; Geismar, M. *American Moderns. From Rebellion to Conformity*, 1962). Inostrannaia literatura, 1962, no. 7, p. 178-188.

Boiadzhiev, G. Po teatram Ameriki [In the theaters of America]. Don, 1962, no. 8, p. 182-192.

Zhuravlev, G. Review of: *The Best Short Plays, 1959-1960*. Boston, 1960. Sovremennaia khudozhestvennaia literatura za rubezhom, 1962, no. 1, p. 70-72.

Zemlianova, L. M. Sovremennaia estetika v SShA [Contemporary esthetics in the US]. Moscow, Gospolitizdat, 1962. 160 p.

Zlobin, G. Byt' ili ne byt' realizmu na teatre? [Realism in the theater — To be or not to be?]. Voprosy literatury, 1962, no. 3, p. 127-130.

Kliuger, R. Na knizhnom rynke 1962 goda. Kratkii obzor amerikanskoi literatury [In the book marts of 1962. A short survey of American literature]. Za rubezhom, 1962, no. 52, p. 30.

Landor, M. "Mrachnoe i koliuchee iskusstvo." (Sovremennaia literatura SShA) ["A gloomy and thorny art." (Contemporary literature of the US)]. Voprosy literatury, 1962, no. 5, p. 143-147.

Louson, D. G. [Lawson, J. H.]. Sovremennaia dramaturgiia SShA [Contemporary drama of the US]. Inostrannaia literatura, 1962, no. 8, p. 186-196.

Louson, D. G. [Lawson, J. H.]. Tupiki i perspektivy. Zametki ob amerikanskoi kul'ture. [Dead ends and prospects. Remarks on American culture]. Literaturnaia gazeta, April 14, 17, 1962.

Marzani, K. [C]. Literatura otchaianiia [The literature of despair]. Literaturnaia gazeta, March 8, 1962.

Mendel'son, M. Poeziia Grazhdanskoi voiny v SShA [The poetry of the Civil War in the US]. Voprosy literatury, 1962, no. 2, p. 155-169.

Miller, A. Chto podryvaet nash prestizh [What undermines our prestige]. Literaturnaia gazeta, September 4, 1962.

Mints, N. Stanislavskii i amerikanskii teatr [Stanislavskii and the American theater]. Teatr, 1962, no. 12, p. 101-106.

Nedelin, V. Review of: Freedman, M. *Confessions of a Conformist*. New York, 1961. Sovremennaia kudozhestvennaia literatura za rubezhom, 1962, no. 1, p. 73-74.

Nikoliukin, A. N. Nekotorye osobennosti vzaimosviazei literatur v period burzhuaznykh revoliutsii kontsa XVIII veka. (Na materiale amerikanskoi i angliiskoi massovoi poezii) [Some traits of the interrelationships of literature in the period of the bourgeois revolutions of the end of the 18th century. (Based on American and English mass poetry)]. *In:* Iz istorii literaturnykh sviazei XIX veka [From the history of literary relationships of the 19th century]. Moscow, 1962. p. 15-36.

Orlova, R. D. Vnuki diadi Toma boriutsia. (Osvoboditel'naia bor'ba amerikanskikh negrov i sovremennaia literatura) [The grandsons of Uncle Tom are fighting. (The struggle for liberation of American Negroes and contemporary literature)]. Moscow, "Znanie," 1962. 32p.

Orlova, R. Review of: Hassan, I. *Radical Innocence. Studies in the Contemporary American Novel*, 1961. Sovremennaia khudozhestvennaia literatura za rubezhom, 1962, no. 9-10, p. 114-117.

Parrington, V. L. Osnovnye techeniia amerikanskoi mysli. Amerikanskaia literatura so vremeni ee vozniknoveniia do 1920 goda [Main currents of American thought.[1] American literature from its origins until 1920]. 3 v. Translated by V. Voronina and V. Tarkhova. *Introductory articles:* v. 1, R. Samarin; v. 3, E. Kh. Eibi. Moscow, Inostrannaia literatura, 1962-1963.

Sovremennaia literatura SShA [Contemporary literature of the US]. Moscow, Izd-vo Akademii nauk SSSR, 1962. 228 p. *Contents:* Anisimov, I. I. Seredina veka [Mid-Century]; Elistratova, A. A. Dukhovnyi krizis molodezhi SShA v amerikanskom romane [The spiritual crisis of the youth of the US in the American novel]; Mendel'son, M. O. "Sil'nyi chelovek" v sovremennoi literature SShA [The "strong man" in the contemporary literature of the US]; Balashov, P. S. Progressivnye tendentsii v poslevoennoi amerikanskoi literature [Progressive tendencies in postwar American literature]; Mendel'son, M. O. Tragediia Khemingueia [The tragedy of Hemingway]; Neupokoeva, I. G. Ideia "denatsionalizatsii" literatury v komparativistike SShA [The idea of the "denationalization" of literature in comparative literary studies in the US]; Zasurskii, Ia. N. Problema kriticheskogo realizma v sovremennom amerikanskom literaturovedenii [The problem of critical realism in contemporary American literary scholarship]; Beliaev, A. A. Realisticheskaia literatura SShA 30-kh godov v otsenke amerikanskoi kritiki [The literature of the US in the 1930's as evaluated by American critics]. Samarin, R. M. Iskazhenie istorii sovetskoi literatury v literaturovedenii SShA [The distortion of the history of Soviet literature in the study of literature in the US].

Steinbek, Dzh. [Steinbeck, J.]. V poiskakh Ameriki [In search of America]. (*Travels with Charley*). Zvezda, 1962, no. 4, p. 100-121.

Tugusheva, M. Dver' nastezh'—stuchat' ne nado. (O sovremennoi literature SShA) [The door is ajar—there's no need to knock. (About contemporary literature in the US)]. Literaturnaia gazeta, November 22, 1962.

[1] *Main Currents in American Thought* first appeared in New York, 1927-1930.

1963 Anikst, A. A. and G. N. Boiadzhiev. 6—i.e. Shest'—rasskazov ob amerikanskom teatre [Six tales about the American theater]. Moscow,
"Iskusstvo," 1963. 151 p. *Review:* Astakhov, I. V chem "sut' pred-
meta?" [What is "the core of the matter?"]. Oktiabr', 1963, no. 12,
p. 173-175.

Aptrek, G. Traditsii i bestsellery [Tradition and bestsellers]. Literaturnaia gazeta, February 7, 1963.

Beliaev, A. Apologiia imperializma v literature SShA [The apology for
imperialism in the literature of the US]. Kommunist, 1963, no. 13,
p. 109-116.

Beliaev, A. A. Progressivnaia literatura SShA 30-kh godov i sovremennaia amerikanskaia kritika [The progressive literature of the US of
the 'thirties and contemporary American criticism]. Abstract of
dissertation presented for the degree of Candidate of Philological
Sciences. Moscow, 1963. 15 p.

Bessi [Bessie], A. Novye amerikanskie romany. (Pis'mo iz San-Frantsis-
ko) [New American novels. (A letter from San Francisco)]. Inostrannaia literatura, 1963, no. 5, p. 202-204.

Dangulov, S. V mesto predisloviia [In place of a foreword]. (On the
publication of the testimony of A. R. Williams, J. Reed and others
to an American Senate committee on a visit to Soviet Russia in 1919).
Inostrannaia literatura, 1963, no. 4, p. 224-228.

Elistratova, A. "Igra idei" professora Brauna [The "play of ideas" of
Professor Brown]. (Brown, D. *Soviet Attitudes Toward American
Writing*. 1962). Literaturnaia gazeta, September 26, 1963.

Elistratova, A. Starye strakhi i novye mify. (Polemika so stat'ei M. Kauli
ob istorii amerikanskoi literatury) [Old fears and new myths. (A
polemic with the article by M. Cowley on the history of American
literature)]. Literaturnaia gazeta, March 16, 1963.

Zhuravlev, I. K. Ocherki po istorii marksistskoi literaturnoi kritiki SShA
(1900-1956) [Outlines of the history of Marxist literary criticism in
the US, 1909-1956)]. Saratov, 1963. 155 p.

Zhuravlev, G. Review of: *Beyond the Blues. New Poems by American
Negroes.* Selected and introducted by R. E. Pool. London, 1962.
Sovremennaia khudozhestvennaia literatura za rubezhom, 1963,
no. 6, p. 44-47.

Zelinskii, B. Est' li nasledniki u Khemingueia i Folknera? [Are there
heirs to Hemingway and Faulkner?]. Za rubezhom, 1963, no. 8, p. 30.

Izakov, B. Golos Kassandry. (Opisanie uzhasov vozmozhnoi voiny vo
sovremennoi amerikanskoi literature) [The voice of Cassandra. (The
description of the horrors of a possible war in American literature)].
Novoe vremia, 1963, no. 2, p. 30-32.

Kolombo, F. Pisateli chernoi Ameriki [The writers of black America].
Za rubezhom, 1963, no. 38, p. 31.

Landor, M. Konformizm i traditsiia. (O poslevoennoi amerikanskoi proze) [Conformism and tradition. (Concerning postwar American prose)]. Voprosy literatury, 1963, no. 3, p. 130-145.

Lorens [Lawrence], L. Iskusstvo prodavat'sia. (O polozhenii deiatelei literatury i iskusstva v SShA) [The art of selling oneself. (On the position of writers and artists in the US)]. Literaturnaia gazeta, June 18, 1963.

Luri [Lourie], S. Griaz' na podmostkakh. (Khellman, Uil'iams, Elbi) [Dirt on the stage (Hellman, Williams, Albee]. Izvestiia, May 30, 1963. (Moscow evening edition).

Marzani, K. [C.]. Kvadratnyi fut... literatury. (Polozhenie na knizhnom rynke SShA) [A square foot of... literature. (The situation in the book trade of the US)]. Sovetskaia kul'tura, September 25, 1963.

Nedelin, V. V sumerkakh psikhoanaliza [In the twilight of psychoanalysis]. Inostrannaia literatura, 1963, no. 10, p. 196-216.

Nikoliukin, A. Psikhografiia—"novyi metod" v literaturovedenii SShA [Psychography—a "new method" in literary scholarship in the US]. Voprosy literatury, 1963, no. 9, p. 126-128.

Orlova, R. Chto znachit zhit' v shestidesiaty gody? (Sovremennaia proza SShA v Zhurnal "Time" 1963, fevr.-mart) [What does it mean to live in the 'sixties? (Contemporary prose of the US in *Time* of February-March, 1963)]. Novyi mir, 1963, no. 5, p. 230-234.

Rasiaev, V. V. Problemy kriticheskogo realizma v literature SShA 20-kh godov i sovremennaia amerikanskaia kritika [The problems of critical realism in the literature of the US of the 1920's and contemporary American criticism]. Abstract of dissertation presented for the degree of Candidate of Philological Sciences. Moscow, 1963. 15 p.

Romanova, E. Posleslovie [Afterword]. *In:* Sovremennaia amerikanskaia novella [The contemporary American short story]. Moscow, 1963. p. 446-460.

Rubin, V. Amerikanskii roman i atomnaia ugroza [The American novel and the threat of the atom]. Voprosy literatury, 1963, no. 12, p. 113-116.

Rubin, V. Iskusstvo pisateli ili lovkost' biznesmena? (Zhurnal "Writer," 1963, no. 1-4) [The art of the writer or the cleverness of a businessman? (*Writer*, 1963, nos. 1-4)]. Voprosy literatury, 1963, no. 11, p. 177-180.

Samokhvalov, N. I. O sootnoshenii realizma s naturalizmom v literature SShA kontsa XIX veka [On the relationship between realism and naturalism in the literature of the US of the end of the 19th century]. Trudy Krasnodarskogo pedagogicheskogo instituta, 1963, vyp. 36. Voprosy russkoi i zarubezhnoi literatury, p. 183-198.

II. WORKS DEVOTED TO THE WRITINGS OF INDIVIDUAL AUTHORS

ADAMS Semuel' Gopkins   ADAMS Samuel Hopkins

1928 Bogoslovskii, N. Review of: Razgul [Revelry]. Moscow, Leningrad, 1928. Kniga i profsoiuzy, 1928, no. 5-6, p. 43.

Boss, A. G. Predislovie [Foreword]. *In:* Adams, S. H. Razgul [Revelry]. Moscow, Leningrad, 1928. p. 5-18.

Danilin, Iu. Review of: Razgul [Revelry]. Na literaturnom postu, 1928, no. 13-14, p. 110-114. (Signed: Diar.)

Lann, E. Review of: Razgul [Revelry]. Pechat' i revoliutsiia, 1928, no. 4, p. 214-215.

Polonskaia, L. Review of: Razgul [Revelry]. Krasnaia nov', 1928, no. 7, p. 239-242.

Sablin, I. Review of: Razgul [Revelry]. Chitatel' i pisatel', May 12, 1928.

1949 Zhantieva, D. Vashington bez maski [Washington without a mask]. (*Plunder*). Literaturnaia gazeta, February 2, 1949.

OLDRICH Tomas B.   ALDRICH Thomas Bailey

1934 Inozemtsev, I. Avtobiograficheskaia povest' Oldricha [The autobiographical tale by Aldrich]. ("Vospominaniia amerikanskogo shkol'nika" ["The memories of an American schoolboy"—i.e. *The Story of a Bad Boy*]. Leningrad, 1934). Detskaia i iunosheskaia literatura, 1934, no. 10, p. 13-15.

Stoletov, A. Review of: Vospominaniia amerikanskogo shkol'nika [The memories of an American schoolboy—i.e. *The Story of a Bad Boy*]. Leningrad, 1934. Pod"em (Voronezh), 1934, no. 7-8, p. 133-134.

1961 Tven, M. [Mark Twain]. Pominki po Oldrichu [A wake for Aldrich]. *In:* Mark Twain, Sobranie sochinenii [Collected works]. v. 12. Moscow, 1961. p. 446-459.

ANDERSON Shervud   ANDERSON Sherwood

1923 Okrimenko, P. Predislovie k rasskazu "Dver' lovushki" [Foreword to the tale "The door of the trap"]. Sovremennyi "Zapad," 1923, no. 3, p. 96. (Signed: P. O.)

1924 Dinamov, S. Review of: Uainsburg, Ogaio [Winesburg, Ohio]. Moscow, Leningrad, 1924. Knigonosha, 1924, no. 22-23, p. 10.

Levidov, M. Predislovie [Foreword]; Boid [Boyd?], E. Vvedenie [Introduction]. *In:* Anderson, Sh. Uainsburg, Ogaio [Winesburg, Ohio]. Moscow, Leningrad, 1924. p. 5-12.

Poletika, Iu. Review of: Uainsburg, Ogaio [Winesburg, Ohio]. Russkii sovremennik, 1924, no. 3, p. 283.

1925 Introduction to: Anderson, Sh. Sobranie sochinenii [Collected works]. v. 2: Uainsburg, Ogaio [Winesburg, Ohio]. Moscow, Leningrad, 1925. p. 5-10.

Dinamov, S. Review of: Torzhestvo iaitsa [The triumph of the egg]. Moscow, 1925. Knigonosha, 1925, no. 10, p. 18.

Levidov, M. Predislovie [Foreword]; Rozenfel'd, P. Kriticheskii ocherk [Critical essay]. *In:* Anderson, Sh. Torzhestvo iaitsa [The triumph of the egg]. Moscow, 1925. p. 3-19.

Ramm, E. Review of: Torzhestvo iaitsa [The triumph of the egg]. Moscow, 1925. Novyi mir, 1925, no. 8, p. 155-156.

Shervud Anderson. (Vmesto predisloviia) [Sherwood Anderson. (In place of a foreword)]. *In:* Novinki Zapada [Novelties from the West]. No. 1. Moscow, Leningrad, 1925. p. 95. (Signed: Red.)

1926 Rozental', N. Review of: Uainsburg, Ogaio [Winesburg, Ohio]. Pechat' i revoliutsiia, 1926, no. 1, p. 242-243.

1927 B. D. P. Review of: Loshadi i liudi [Horses and people—i.e. *Horses and Men*]. Moscow, 1927. Chitatel' i pisatel', December 1, 1927.

Lavretskii, V. Predislovie [Foreword]. *In:* Anderson, Sh. V nogu [In step—i.e. *Marching Men*]. Leningrad, 1927. p. 7-11.

1928 Shervud Anderson—provintsial'nyi redaktor [Sherwood Anderson—country editor]. Vestnik inostrannoi literatury, 1928, no. 2, p. 155-156.

1932 Shervud Anderson o svoem novom romane ("Po tu storonu zhelaniia"). K priezdu v SSSR [Sherwood Anderson about his new novel ("Beyond desire"). On his coming to the USSR]. Literaturnaia gazeta, October 23, 1932.

1933 Dinamov, S. O tvorchestve Shervuda Andersona [On the work of Sherwood Anderson]. *In:* Anderson, Sh. Po tu storonu zhelaniia [Beyond desire]. Moscow, 1933. p. 3-22. *See also:* Dinamov, S. Zarubezhnaia literatura [Foreign literature]. Moscow, 1960. p. 367-387.

Dinamov, S. O tvorchestve Shervuda Andersona [On the work of Sherwood Anderson]. Literaturnaia gazeta, September 29, 1933.

1934 Elistratova, A. Review of: Po tu storonu zhelaniia [Beyond desire]. Internatsional'naia literatura, 1934, no. 2, p. 115-119.

Levidov, M. Review of: Po tu storonu zhelaniia [Beyond desire]. Literaturnaia gazeta, February 18, 1934. (Signed: M. L.)

Mingulina, A. Review of: Po tu storonu zhelaniia [Beyond desire]. Khudozhestvennaia literatura, 1934, no. 5, p. 7-9.

Nemerovskaia, O. Novyi roman Shervuda Andersona (Po tu storonu zhelaniia) [A new novel of Sherwood Anderson (Beyond desire)]. Literaturnyi kritik, 1934, no. 4, p. 199-203.

Startsev, A. Po tu storony barrikad (Po tu storonu zhelaniia) [On the other side of the barricades (Beyond desire)]. Khudozhestvennaia literatura, 1934, no. 1, p. 34-37.

Stoletov, A. Review of: Po tu storonu zhelaniia [Beyond desire]. Pod"em (Voronezh), 1934, no. 4-5, p. 165-166.

1935 Dinamov, S. Zhiznennyi put' Shervuda Andersona [Sherwood Anderson's path through life]. Internatsional'naia literatura, 1935, no. 11, p. 115-118.

Dinamov,S. Predislovie [Foreword]. In: Anderson,Sh. Istoriia rasskazchika [A storyteller's story]. Moscow, 1935. p. iii-x. See also: Dinamov, S. Zarubezhnaia literatura [Foreign literature]. Moscow,1960. p.388-395.

Dinamov, S. Tvorcheskie priznaniia Shervuda Andersona [The creative avowals of Sherwood Anderson]. Internatsional'naia literatura, 1935, no. 10, p. 129-136.

1936 Khmel'nitskaia, T. Review of: Istoriia rasskazchika [A storyteller's story]. Literaturnyi sovremennik, 1936, no. 9, p. 213-215.

Khokhlov, G. Review of: Istoriia rasskazchika [A storyteller's story]. Literaturnoe obozrenie, 1936, no. 3, p. 23-24.

Shervud Anderson [Sherwood Anderson]. Literaturnaia gazeta, September 26, 1936.

Eishiskina, N. Stranstviia v mire fantazii i faktov. (Istoriia rasskazchika) [Wanderings in a world of fantasy and facts. (A storyteller's story)]. Literaturnaia gazeta, May 10, 1936.

1937 Anderson, Sh. Shervud Anderson o svoem tvorchestve [Sherwood Anderson about his writings]. Internatsional'naia literatura, 1937, no. 3, p. 229-230.

Filips, U. [Philips, W.?]. "Kit Brendon" Shervuda Andersona ["Kit Brandon" by Sherwood Anderson]. Internatsional'naia literatura, 1937, no. 1, p. 211-212.

1941 Abramov, A. Smert' Shervuda Andersona [The death of Sherwood Anderson]. Internatsional'naia literatura, 1941, no. 3, p. 186. (Signed: Al. A-v.)

1959 Kandel', B. Shervud Anderson [Sherwood Anderson]. In: Anderson, Sh. Rasskazy [Tales]. Moscow, Leningrad, 1959. p. 3-18.

APPEL BENDZHAMIN   APPEL BENJAMIN

1938 Startsev, A. Review of: Runaround. New York, 1937. Internatsional'naia literatura, 1938, no. 9, p. 210-202.

1940 Abramov, A. Review of: *The Power-House*. New York, 1939. Internatsional'naia literatura, 1940, no. 1, p. 183-184.

Ivanov, A. Review of: *The People Talk*. New York, 1940. Internatsional'naia literatura, 1940, no. 11-12, p. 313-314.

1948 Pagirev, B. Kuda ukhodit Met'iu Uells? [Where is Matthew Wells going?]. (*But Not Yet Slain*. 1947). Novyi mir, 1948, no. 10, p. 322-324.

1960 Vasil'ev, N. Stranitsa geroicheskogo proshlogo filippinskogo naroda [A page from the heroic past of the Philippine people]. *In:* Appel, B. Krepost' sredi risovykh polei [A fortress amidst the rice fields]. Moscow, 1960. p. 525-531.

1961 Drunina, Iu. Filippiny v ogne ("Krepost' sredi risovykh polei") [The Philippines ablaze ("A fortress amidst the rice fields")]. Inostrannaia literatura, 1961, no. 6, p. 253-254.

Orlova, R. Review of: *A Big Man, A Fast Man*. New York, 1961. Sovremennaia khudozhestvennaia literatura za rubezhom, 1961, no. 1, p. 79-81.

1962 Gorelov, G. Filippiny v ogne ("Krepost' sredi risovykh polei") [The Philippines ablaze ("A fortress amidst the rice fields")]. Dal'nyi Vostok (Khabarovsk), 1962, no. 1, p. 183-185.

Nedelin, V. Ispoved' Uil'iama Lloida [The confession of William Lloyd]. (*A Big Man, A Fast Man*. New York, 1961). Inostrannaia literatura, 1962, no. 8, p. 254-256.

1963 Elistratova, A. Review of: *A Time of Fortune*. New York, 1963. Sovremennaia khudozhestvennaia literatura za rubezhom, 1963, no. 9, p. 52-55.

ASH NATAN   ASCH NATHAN

1927 Ar—skii, M. Review of: Kontora [The office]. Moscow, 1927. Kniga i profsoiuza, 1927, no. 9, p. 44-45.

Grigor'ev, Ia. Review of: Kontora [The office]. Moscow, 1927. Na literaturnom postu, 1927, no. 19, p. 80-81.

Kashkin, I. Predislovie [Foreword]. *In:* Ash [Asch], N. Kontora [The office]. Moscow, 1927. p. 5-12.

1937 Elistratova, A. Review of: *The Road. In Search of America*. New York, 1937. Internatsional'naia literatura, 1937, no. 7, p. 215. (Signed: A. E.)

1938 Borisova, Iu. V poiskakh Ameriki [In search of America]. (*The Road. In Search of America*. New York, 1937). Literaturnaia gazeta, November 15, 1938.

1939 Nemerovskaia, O. "Doroga" Natana Asha ["The road" of Nathan Asch]. Literaturnyi sovremennik, 1939, no. 5-6, p. 298-299.

1962 Orlova, R. Skol'ko zhe pravdy mozhno sterpet'? [How much truth can be borne?]. Voprosy literaturg, 1962, no. 10, p. 164-170.
1963 Orlova, R. V poslednem krugu ada [In the last circle of Hades]. (*Another Country*. New York, 1962; *The Fire Next Time*. New York, 1963). Inostrannaia literatura, 1963, no. 12, p. 261-264.

Orlova, R. Review of: *The Fire Next Time*. Sovremennaia khudozhestvennaia literatura za rubezhom, 1963, no. 9, p. 49-52.

BELLAMI Edvard   BELLAMY Edward

1890 Review of: Cherez sto let [After a century—i.e. *Looking Backward*]. St. Petersburg, 1891. Russkoe ˌbogatstvo, 1890, no. 12, p. 175-176.

Review of: Cherez sto let [After a century—i.e. *Looking Backward*]. St. Petersburg, 1891. Severnyi vestnik, 1890, no. 12, otd. II, p. 115-118.

Ianzhul, I. Budushchii vek. Novaia fantaziia na staruiu temu [The coming century. A new fantasy on an old theme]. (Cherez sto let [After a century—i.e. *Looking Backward*]. St. Petersburg, 1891). Vestnik Evropy, 1890, no. 4, p. 553-589; no. 5, p. 173-203. *See also:* Ianzhul, I. V poiskakh luchshego budushchego [In search of a better future]. St. Petersburg, 1908. p. 103-180.

1891 Review of: Budushchii vek [The coming century—i.e. *Looking Backward*]. St. Petersburg, 1891. Zhivopisnoe obozrenie, 1891, no. 7, p. 126. [A second translation, differing from "Cherez sto let" listed above].

Review of: Budushchii vek [The coming century—i.e. *Looking Backward*]. Nabliudatel', 1891, no. 4, otd. II, p. 18-21.

Cheshikhin, V. E. Roman Bellami "Looking Backward" i koe-chto o sotsial'nom dvizhenii v Soedinennykh Shtatakh Sev. Ameriki [Bellamy's novel "Looking Backward" and something about the social movement in the United States]. Rizhskii vestnik, February 19, 1891. (Signed: Sozertsatel'.)

1892 Golovin, K. Sotsializm kak polozhitel'noe uchenie [Socialism as a positive doctrine]. St. Petersburg, 1892. 246 p.; 2nd ed. 1894. *Review:* Sementkovskii, R. Istoricheskii vestnik, 1892, no. 9, p. 727-731; Severnyi vestnik, 1894, no. 9, otd. II, p. 65-68.

1897 Novye utopicheskie grezy [New utopian day-dreams]. Novyi zhurnal inostrannoi literatury, 1897, no. 5, p. 235-239.

1898 Eduard Bellami. Nekrologi [Edward Bellamy. Obituaries]. Vsemirnaia illiustratsiia, 1898, no. 25, p. 544-565; Zhivopisnoe obozrenie, 1898, no. 25, p. 508; Knizhki nedeli, 1898, no. 6, p. 215-216; Literaturnye semeinye vechera, 1898, no. 7, p. 450-451.

1902 Kirkhengeim, A. Nekotorye drugie noveishie proizvedeniia (Bellami)

[Some other recent productions (Bellamy)]. *In:* Kirkhengeim, A. Vechnaia utopia [The eternal utopia]. St. Petersburg, 1902. p. 263-284.

1907 Nikitin, A. N. Noveishie utopii. (Po romanam Bellami) [The most recent utopias. (According to Bellamy's novels)]. Novyi zhurnal literatury, iskusstva i nauka, 1907, no. 10, p. 4-26; no. 11, p. 100-126.

1910 Sementkovskii, R. Vstuplenie [Introduction]. *In:* Buazhil'ber [Bois-gilbert?], E. Krushenie tsivilizatsii [The destruction of civilization]. St. Petersburg, 1910. p. i-xiv.

1931 Krupskaia, N. K. Po Bellami [According to Bellamy]. Narodnyi uchitel', 1931, no. 3, p. 79. *See also:* Krupskaia, N. K. Pedago-gicheskie sochineniia [Pedagogical works]. Moscow, 1959. v. 4, p. 410-411.

BENET Stiven Vincent   BENÉT Stephen Vincent

1941 Evgen'eva, Z. Review of: *Tales Before Midnight.* New York, 1939. Internatsional'naia literatura, 1941, no. 1, p. 177-179.

1945 Zenkevich, M. Epopeia pervykh amerikantsev [The epic of the first Americans]. (*Western Star.* 1945). Literaturnaia gazeta, August 25, 1945.

Panov, N. Foreword to the tale "D'iavol i Dan Uebster" ["The Devil and Daniel Webster"]. Leningrad, 1945, no. 23-24, p. 19.

BESSI Al'va   BESSIE Alvah Cecil

1957 Maikl Gold o romane A. Bessi "Antiamerikantsy" [Michael Gold about A. Bessie's novel "The anti-Americans"—i.e. *The Un-Americans*]. Inostrannaia literatura, 1957, no. 11, p. 284.

1958 Rapoport, S. Roman ob amerikanskom kommuniste [A novel about an American Communist]. (*The Un-Americans.* New York, 1957.) Inostrannaia literatura, 1958, no. 7, p. 261-262.

1961 Sablin, N. and I. Viduetskaia. Foreword to: Bessie, A. Antiamerikantsy [The anti-Americans—i.e. *The Un-Americans*]. Moscow, 1961. p. 5-15.

BIRS Ambroz   BIERCE Ambrose

1926 Azov, V. Foreword to the Russian edition. *In:* Bierce, A. Nastoiashchee chudovishche [A veritable monster—i.e. *In the Midst of Life*]. Leningrad, 1926, p. 304.

Anisimov, I. Review of: Bierce, A. Nastoiashchee chudovishche [A veritable monster—i.e. *In the Midst of Life*]. Pechat' i revoliutsiia, 1926, no. 5, p. 218-219.

45

Dinamov, S. Review of: Bierce, A. Nastoiashchee chudovishche [A veritable monster—i.e. *In the Midst of Life*]. Knigonosha, 1926, no. 11, p. 32. (Signed: S. D.)

1938 Elistratova, A. Foreword to: Bierce, A. Rasskazy [Stories]. Moscow, 1938. p. 3-10.

Oborin, A. Rasskazy Ambroza Birsa [The stories of Ambrose Bierce]. Knizhnye novosti, 1938, no. 24, p. 21.

1939 Kashkin, I. Ambroz Birs [Ambrose Bierce]. Literaturnyi kritik, 1939, no. 2, p. 42-64.

Levidov, M. Rasskazy Ambroza Birsa [The stories of Ambrose Bierce]. Literaturnoe obozrenie, 1939, no. 7, p. 41-43.

Nikulin, L. Ambroz Birs [Ambrose Bierce]. Internatsional'naia literatura, 1939, no. 7-8 (first printing), p. 313.

Solov'ev, B. Master novelly, zagadok i tain [The master of the short story, of riddles, and of mysteries]. Literaturnyi sovremennik, 1939, no. 7-8, p. 278-279.

BONOSSKII Filipp   BONOSKY Phillip

1954 Balashov, P. Sila zhiznennoi pravdy [The strength of a vital truth]. (*Burning Valley*. New York, 1953). Slaviane, 1954, no. 9, p. 59-61.

1961 Balashov, P. Deistvennaia sila mechty [The active force of a dream]. *In:* Bonosskii, P. Volshebnyi paporotnik [The magic fern]. Moscow, 1961. p. 5-12.

Balashov, P. Filipp Bonosskii [Phillip Bonosky]. *In:* Bonosky, P. Dolina v ogne [Burning valley]. Moscow, 1961. p. 5-12.

Elistratova, A. Operatsiia "Terpen" poluchaet oglasku [Operation "Terpen" is made public]. (Volshebnyi paporotnik [The magic fern]). Literaturnaia gazeta, September 7, 1961.

1962 Geevskii, I. "Ia veriu v svoi rabochii klass" ["I believe in my working class"]. (Dolina v ogne. Volshebnyi paporotnik. [Burning valley. The magic fern]). Inostrannaia literatura, 1962, no. 6, p. 274-276.

BORN Randol'f   BOURNE Randolph Silliman

1962 Zasurskii, Ia. Review of: Brooks, V. W. *Fenollosa and His Circle*. Sovremennaia khudozhestvennaia literatura za rubezhom, 1962, no. 12, p. 141-144.

BOID Tomas   BOYD Thomas

1940 Khmel'nitskaia, T. Amerikanskie budni [Every-day America]. *In:* Boyd, T. V mirnoe vremia [In time of peace]. Leningrad, 1940. p. 3-14.

46

1941 Nemerovskaia, O. Review of: V mirnoe vremia [In time of peace]. Zvezda, 1941, no. 6, p. 204-205.
Sil'man, T. Review of: V mirnoe vremia [In time of peace]. Literaturnoe obozrenie, 1941, no. 10, p. 67-70.

BREDBERI Rei   BRADBURY Ray

1954 Romanova, E. "451 gradusa po Farengeitu." Nauchno-fantasticheskaia povest' Reia Bredberi ["451 degrees Fahrenheit." A science-fiction tale of Ray Bradbury.] Sovetskaia kul'tura, November 20, 1954.
1956 Kazantsev, A. Foreword to: Bradbury, R. 451° po Farengeitu [Fahrenheit 451°]. Moscow, 1956. p. 3-10.
1957 Asmolova, N. Review of: 451° po Farengeitu [Fahrenheit 451°]. Znamia, 1957, no. 1, p. 219-220.
Berzerak, I. Temperatura, pri kotoroi goriat knigi [The temperature at which books burn]. (451° po Farengeitu. Moscow, 1956). Neva, 1957, no. 3, p. 206-207.
1958 Romanova, E. V strane, ne vidiashchei solntsa [In a country which does not see the sun]. (The October Country. New York, 1956). Inostrannaia literatura, 1958, no. 7, p. 266-267.
1963 Andreev, K. Foreword to: Bradbury, R. Fantastika Reia Bredberi [The fantasy of Ray Bradbury]. Moscow, 1963. p. 5-24.

BROMFILD Lui   BROMFIELD Louis

1940 Stakhova, N. Roman ob Indii [A novel about India]. (The Rains Came. New York, 1939). Literaturnaia gazeta, January 10, 1940.
1941 Abramova, A. Sekrety uspekha Liuisa Bromfil'da [The secrets of the success of Louis Bromfield]. (It Takes All Kinds). Internatsional'naia literatura, 1941, no. 2, p. 215-217.
1955 Zhukov, V. Narody dolzhny zhit' v mire [The nations must live in peace]. (A New Pattern for a Tired World. New York, 1954). Mezhdunarodnaia zhizn', 1955, no. 11, p. 138-140.

BRUKS Van Vik   BROOKS Van Wyck

1942 Startsev, A. O sovremennoi amerikanskoi literature. Po povudu knigi Van Vik Bruksa [Concerning contemporary American literature. On the subject of Van Wyck Brooks's book]. (On Literature Today. New York, 1941). Internatsional'naia literatura, 1942, no. 10, p. 115-118.
1957 Trevoga amerikanskogo kritika [The uneasiness of an American critic]. Literaturnaia gazeta, July 11, 1957.
1958 Startsev, A. Vospominaniia Van Vik Bruksa [The reminiscences of Van

Wyck Brooks]. (*Days of the Phoenix*). Voprosy literatury, 1958, no. 7, p. 234-239.
1962 Kashkin, I. Review of: Brooks, Van Wyck. *From the Shadow of the Mountain. My Post-Meridian Years.* New York, 1961. Sovremennaia khudozhestvennaia literatura za rubezhom, 1962, no. 4-5, p. 114-116.

BRAUN Lloid   BROWN Lloyd

1952 Dubashinskii, I. Istoriia Lonni Dzheimsa [The history of Lonnie James]. (*Iron City*). Literaturnaia gazeta, April 17, 1952.
1953 Elistratova, A. Foreword to: Brown, L. Zheleznyi gorod [Iron city]. Moscow, 1953. p. 3-8.
   Lukin, Iu. Review of: Zheleznyi gorod [Iron city]. Pravda, January 29, 1953.
   Maslova, I. Liudi, kotorym prinadlezhit budushchee [The people to whom the future belongs]. (Zheleznyi gorod [Iron city]. Moscow, 1953). Znamia, 1953, no. 3, p. 188-192.
   Toper, P. "Zheleznyi gorod" Lloida Brauna ["Iron city" of Lloyd Brown]. Novyi mir, 1953, no. 6, p. 269-272.

BRAIENT Vil'iam Kellen   BRYANT William Cullen

1849 Danilevskii. O sovremennom napravlenii poezii v Soedinennykh Shtatakh Severnoi Ameriki. (Braient) [Concerning the contemporary course of poetry in the United States. (Bryant)]. Sanktpeterburgskie vedomosti, November 18, 1849.
1875 Gerbel', N. Vill'iam Braint [William Bryant]. *In:* Gerbel', N. Angliiskie poety v biografiiakh i obraztsakh [English poets in biographies and excerpts]. St. Petersburg, 1875. p. 362.

BAK Perl   BUCK Pearl

1934 Alekseev, V. Amerikanskii roman o kitaiskoi derevne [An American novel about a Chinese village]. (*The Good Earth.* 1931). Bibliografiia Vostoka, 1934, no. 5-6, p. 137-143.
   Elistratova, A. Talantlivaia apologetika kulatskikh illiuzii [A talented apology for "kulak" illusions]. ("Zemlia" ["The earth"—i.e. *The Good Earth*]. Moscow, Leningrad, 1934). Khudozhestvennaia literatura, 1934, no. 6, p. 32-36.
   Krupskaia, N. Review of: Zemlia [The earth—i.e. *The Good Earth*]. Moscow, Leningrad, 1934. Krasnyi bibliotekar', 1934, no. 11, p. 9-12.
   Selivanovskii, A. Realizm i tendentsioznost' [Realism and tendentiousness]. (Zemlia [The earth—i.e. *The Good Earth*]. Moscow, Leningrad, 1934). Literaturnaia gazeta, June 2, 1934.

Semashko, N. Raby zemli [Slaves of the earth]. (Zemlia [The earth—i.e. *The Good Earth*]. Moscow, Leningrad, 1934). Literaturnaia gazeta, September 6, 1934.

Tret'iakov, S. O "Zemle" Perl' Bak [Concerning "The earth" of Pearl Buck]. Internatsional'naia literatura, 1934, no. 2, p. 99-102.

Tret'iakov, S. Razgovor s chitatelem [A conversation with the reader]. *In:* Bak [Buck], P. Zemlia [The earth—i.e. *The Good Earth*]. Moscow, Leningrad, 1934. p. 3-12.

1935 G. S. O "Zemle" Perl Bak [Concerning "The earth"—i.e. *The Good Earth*—by Pearl Buck]. Povolzh'e, 1935, no. 6-7, p. 111-112.

Gorelova, M. Kitaiskaia deistvitel'nost' i propoved' mira [Chinese reality and the preaching of peace]. Nastuplenie (Smolensk), 1935, no. 8, p. 103-106.

Elistratova, A. Kitai vne istorii [China outside history]. (Synov'ia [Sons]). Khudozhestvennaia literatura, 1935, no. 9, p. 41-43.

Konstantinov, N. Chuvstvo zemli pod nogami [The feeling of ground under one's feet]. (Zemlia [The earth—i.e. *The Good Earth*]. Moscow, Leningrad, 1934). Literaturnyi sovremennik, 1935, no. 2, p. 222-224.

Levidov, M. Vidimost' i realnost'. (Trilogiia Perl Bak) [Appearance and reality. (The trilogy of Pearl Buck)]. Znamia, 1935, no. 12, p. 237-250.

Munblit, G. Zametki o "Zemle" Perl Bak [Remarks about "The earth" of Pearl Buck]. Znamia, 1935, no. 4, p. 171-179.

1936 Bak [Buck], P. Dolg Dikkensu [A debt to Dickens]. Internatsional'naia literatura, 1936, no. 9, p. 172-174.

Elistratova, A. Review of: Mat' [The mother]. Moscow, 1936. Internatsional'naia literatura, 1936, no. 9, p. 158-160.

Kolesnikova, G. Propoved' vozrashcheniia [The preaching of a return]. Internatsional'naia literatura, 1936, no. 1, p. 120-127.

Startsev, A. Review of: Mat' [The mother]. Moscow, 1936. Izvestiia, August 6, 1936.

Strong, L. Review of: *The Exile.* 1936. Internatsional'naia literatura, 1936, no. 7, p. 195-196.

1937 Karmon, U. [Carmon, W.]. Beseda s Perl Bak [A conversation with Pearl Buck]. Literaturnaia gazeta, March 30, 1937.

Karmon, U. [Carmon, W.]. Review of: *Fighting Angel.* 1936. Internatsional'naia literatura, 1937, no. 2, p. 234-235.

Fish, G. Review of: Mat' [The mother]. Moscow, 1936. Literaturnoe obozrenie, 1937, no. 4, p. 26-28.

1942 Avarin, V. Review of: *Dragon Seed.* New York, 1942. Internatsional'naia literatura, 1942, no. 12, p. 124-126.

1950 Sergeeva, N. Bankrotstvo odnogo "znatoka Kitaia" [The bankruptcy of one "Old China hand"]. (*Kinfolk.* New York, 1949). Novoe vremia, 1950, no. 11, p. 27-31.

1956 Sergeeva, N. Net, revoliutsiiu ne eksportiruiut [No, revolution is not exported]. Sovetskaia zhenshchina, 1956, no. 6, p. 30.
1958 Zanegin, B. N. and V. V. Kunin. Review of: *The Man Who Changed China*. New York, 1953. Sovetskoe kitaevedenie, 1958, no. 3, p. 183-189.
1960 Eishiskina, N. Mirnyi li atom? [Is the atom peaceful?]. (*Command the Morning*. New York, 1959). Inostrannaia literatura, 1960, no. 6, p. 268-269.

KEIBL Dzhordzh Vashington   CABLE George Washington

1883 K. M. Moe znakomstvo s Keblem. Iz nedavnei poezdki v Ameriku [My acquaintance with Cable. From a recent trip to America]. Vestnik Evropy, 1883, no. 5, p. 313-323.

KOLDUELL Erskin   CALDWELL Erskine

1934 Kashkin, I. Erskin Kolduell [Erskine Caldwell]. Krasnaia nov', 1934, no. 10, p. 208-209.
T. U. Master korotkogo rasskaza [A master of the short story]. (*We Are the Living*. New York, 1933). Literaturnaia gazeta, February 12, 1934.
1936 Dinamov, S. Vozrozhdenie amerikanskoi novelly [A rebirth of the American short story]. Pravda, October 25, 1936.
Kashkin, I. Ne ta Amerika [Not that America]. Internatsional'naia literatura, 1936, no. 4, p. 137-141. *See also:* Caldwell, E. Amerikanskie rasskazy [American tales]. Moscow, 1936. p. 5-13.
1937 Aleksander, G. Review of: Amerikanskie rasskazy [American tales]. Moscow, 1936. Za rubezhom, 1937, no. 19, p. 434.
Nemerovskaia, O. Review of: Amerikanskie rasskazy [American tales]. Moscow, 1936. Literaturnyi sovremennik, 1937, no. 3, p. 278-280.
Sil'man, T. Review of: Amerikanskie rasskazy [American tales]. Moscow, 1936. Zvezda, 1937, no. 2, p. 294-297.
Frid, Ia. Review of: Amerikanskie rasskazy [American tales]. Moscow, 1936. Literaturnoe obozrenie, 1937, no. 4, p. 29-33.
Shtein, R. Rasskazy iz amerikanskoi zhizni [Stories from American life]. (Amerikanskie rasskazy [American tales]. Moscow, 1936). Chto chitat', 1937, no. 5, p. 68-70.
Erskin Kolduell [Erskine Caldwell]. Internatsional'naia literatura, 1937, no. 11, p. 211.
1938 A. O. Roman o sotsial'noi obrechennosti [A novel about social doom]. (Tabachnaia doroga [Tobacco road]. Leningrad, 1938). Knizhnye novosti, 1938, no. 8, p. 20-21.
Nemerovskaia, O. Review of: Tabachnaia doroga [Tobacco road].

Leningrad, 1938. Literaturnyi sovremennik, 1938, no. 9, p. 217-219.

Rukova, N. Predislovie [Foreword]. *In:* Caldwell, E. Tabachnaia doroga [Tobacco road]. Leningrad, 1938. p. 3-8.

1939 Borovoi, L. Review of: *Journeyman.* New York, 1938. Internatsional'-naia literatura, 1939, no. 7-8 (first printing), p. 348-349. *See also:* Internatsional'naia literatura, 1939, no. 7-8 (second printing), p. 274-276.

Zvavich, I. Review of: Caldwell, E. and M. Bourke-White. *North of the Danube.* New York, 1939. Internatsional'naia literatura, 1939, no. 7-8 (first printing), p. 351-353.

1940 Balashov, P. Udacha Erskina Kolduella [Erskine Caldwell's success]. (*Trouble in July.* New York, 1940). Literaturnaia gazeta, August 18, 1940.

Nemerovskaia, O. Kniga o liubvi i nenavisti [A book about love and hate]. (Tabachnaia doroga [Tobacco road]. Zvezda, 1940, no. 8-9, p. 271-277.

1941 Abramov, A. Amerika Erskina Kolduella [The America of Erskine Caldwell]. Literaturnaia gazeta, May 25, 1941.

Kashkin, I. Kolduell—novellist [Caldwell as a writer of short stories]. Internatsional'naia literatura, 1941, no. 5, p. 172-176.

Levidov, M. Review of: *Trouble in July.* New York, 1940. Literaturnoe obozrenie, 1941, no. 1, p. 54-56.

1942 Rokotov, T. Review of: *All Out on the Road to Smolensk.* New York, 1942. Internatsional'naia literatura, 1942, no. 10, p. 129-131.

Rokotov, T. Chto videl Kolduell v SSSR [What Caldwell saw in the USSR]. (*All Out on the Road to Smolensk.* New York, 1942). Ogonek, 1942, no. 49, p. 14.

1945 Smirnova, V. Posleslovie [Afterword]. *In:* Caldwell, E. Mal'chik iz Dzhordzhii [A boy from Georgia—i.e. *Georgia Boy*]. Moscow, 1945. p. 123-126.

1946 Romanova, E. Glazami mal'chika iz Dzhordzhii [With the eyes of a boy from Georgia]. (Mal'chik iz Dzhordzhii [A boy from Georgia—i.e. *Georgia Boy*]. Moscow, 1945). Literaturnaia gazets, April 27, 1946.

1948 Elistratova, A. Tletvornoe vliianie dekadansa [The baneful effect of decadence]. (*The Sure Hand of God.* New York, 1947). Literaturnaia gazeta, June 26, 1948.

Orlova, R. Tragicheskaia zemlia [Tragic ground]. (*Tragic Ground*). Znamia, 1948, no. 2, p. 168-171.

1956 Kashkin, I. Erskin Kolduell [Erskine Caldwell]. *In:* Caldwell, E. Povesti i rasskazy [Tales and stories]. Moscow, 1956. p. 5-15.

Nol'man, M. Erskin Kolduell [Erskine Caldwell]. *In:* Caldwell, E. Mal'chik iz Dzhordzhii [A boy from Georgia—i.e. *Georgia Boy*]. Moscow, 1956, p. 5-11.

1957 Baruk, A. Kniga gneva i oblicheniia [A book of anger and accusation].

51

(Povest' i rasskazy [A tale and stories]. Moscow, 1956). Moskva, 1957, no. 7, p. 207-209.

Romanova, E. "Rasskazy s poberezh'ia" Erskin Kolduella ["Tales from the shore"—*Gulf Coast Stories?*—of Erskine Caldwell]. Inostrannaia literatura, 1957, no. 6, p. 268-270.

1959 Gavrilov, Iu. and M. Tugusheva. Erskin Kolduell v "Literaturnoi gazete" [Erskine Caldwell in "Literaturnaia gazeta"]. Literaturnaia gazeta, October 31, 1959.

Gorokhov, V. Kazhdoe slovo Kolduella [Each of Caldwell's words]. Literatura i zhizn', November 20, 1959.

1960 Gruzinskaia, N. Novellistika E. Kolduella [The short story writing of E. Caldwell]. Sbornik studencheskikh nauchnykh rabot po gumanitarnomu tsiklu, Moskovskii gosudarstvennyi oblastnyi pedagogicheskii institut, 1960, no. 4, p. 137-157.

Krolik, I. and L. Nikol'skaia. "Vse brosheno na Smolensk" Erskina Kolduella ["Everything is flung at Smolensk"—i.e. *All-out on the Road to Smolensk*—of Erskine Caldwell]. *In:* V bol'shoe sem'e. Proza. Stikhi. Literaturnaia kritika [In a large family. Prose. Verse. Literary criticism]. Smolensk, 1960. p. 254-260.

M. B. Vstrecha s Erskinom Kolduellom [A meeting with Erskine Caldwell]. Voprosy literatury, 1960, no. 2, p. 254-255.

Erskin Kolduell [Erskine Caldwell]. Inostrannaia literatura, 1960, no. 2, p. 225-228.

1961 Kolduell [Caldwell], E. Nazovite eto opytom [Call it experience]. Voprosy literatury, 1961, no. 7, p. 180-185.

1962 Elistratova, A. "Vremena izmenilis'..." O poslednikh romanakh Kolduella ["Times have changed..." Concerning the recent novels of Caldwell]. Inostrannaia literatura, 1962, no. 12, p. 196-204.

Elistratova, A. Review of: Close to Home. New York, 1962. Sovremennaia khudozhestvennaia literatura za rubezhom, 1962, no. 7, p. 52-54.

1963 Dolgova, V. Razvenchannoe khanzhestvo [Bigotry dethroned]. Nauka i religiia, 1963, no. 6, p. 92-93.

Romanova, E. Ne otvodia glaz [Not turning aside the eyes]. Literaturnaia gazeta, December 26, 1963.

Romanova, E. Erskin Kolduell i ego novye knigi [Erskine Caldwell and his new books]. *In:* Caldwell, E. Dzhenni. Blizhe k domu. [Jenny. Close to home]. Moscow, 1963. p. 296-311.

Tugusheva, M. Erskin Kolduell v "Literaturnoi gazete" [Erskine Caldwell visits "Literaturnaia gazeta"]. Literaturnaia gazeta, October 31, 1963.

KONROI Dzhek   CONROY Jack

1934 Elistratova, A. Dzhek Konroi. ("Obezdolennyi"). [Jack Conroy. ("The disinherited")]. Internatsional'naia literatura, 1934, no. 1, p. 88-91.

1935 Balashov, P. Review of: *A World to Win*. New York, 1935. Za rubezhom, 1935, no. 31, p. 698.

Elistratova, A. Predislovie [Foreword]. *In:* Conroy, J. Obezdolennyi [The disinherited]. Moscow, 1935. p. 3-6.

1936 Nemerovskaia, O. Review of: Obezdolennyi [The disinherited]. Moscow, 1935. Zvezda, 1936, no. 3, p. 203-205.

KUPER Dzheims Fenimor   COOPER James Fenimore

Marks [Marx], K. and F. Engel's [Engels]. Kuper [Cooper]. *In:* K. Marks i F. Engel's ob iskusstve [K. Marx and F. Engels on art]. v. 1. Moscow, 1957. p. 575-576.

1825 Review of: Shpion [The spy]. Moscow, 1825. Moskovskii telegraf, 1825, no. 7, p. 254-255.

1829 Review of: Amerikanskie stepi [The American steppes—i.e. *The Prairie*]. Translated from the French. Moscow, 1829. Moskovskii telegraf, 1829, no. 16, p. 489-490.

1831 Dzhems Fenimor Kuper [James Fenimore Cooper]. Teleskop, 1831, ch. 4, no. 14, p. 192-214.

1832 Review of: Lotsman [The pilot]. Translated from the French. St. Petersburg, 1832. Moskovskii telegraf, 1832, no. 23, p. 400-403.

1835 Vol'f, D. Kuper [Cooper]. *In:* Vol'f, D. Chteniia o noveishei iziashchnoi slovesnosti [Readings in recent literature]. Moscow, 1835. p. 226-229.

Review of: Monikiny [The monikins]. Biblioteka dlia chteniia, 1835, t. 13, otd. VII, p. 66.

Review of: Monikiny [The monikins]. Moskovskii nabliudatel', 1835, ch. III, (kn. 9-12), p. 301-302.

1836 "Monikiny." Novoe sochinenie Kupera]"The monikins." A new work by Cooper]. Biblioteka dlia chteniia, 1836, t. 14, otd. II, p. 203-232.

1837 Vstrechi g. Kupera s Val'terom Skottom [Mr. Cooper's meetings with Walter Scott]. Biblioteka dlia chteniia, 1837, t. 21, otd. VII, p. 33-40.

Fenimor-Kuper i Sir Val'ter-Skott v Parizhe [Fenimore Cooper and Sir Walter Scott in Paris]. Literaturnye pribavleniia k Russkomu invalidu, 1837, no. 21, p. 203-204.

1839 Belinskii, V. G. Review of: Bravo, ili Venetsianskii bandit [The bravo, or, the Venetian bandit]. St. Petersburg, 1839. Moskovskii nabliudatel', 1839, ch. II, no. 4, otd. IV, p. 87-91. (Unsigned.) *See also:* Belinskii, V. G. Polnoe sobranie sochinenii [Complete collected works]. v. 3. Moscow, 1953. p. 158-160.

Review of: Bravo, ili Venetsianskii bandit [The bravo, or, The Venetian bandit]. St. Petersburg, 1839. Biblioteka dlia chteniia, 1839, t. 33, otd. VI, p. 3-4.

Review of: Bravo, ili Venetsianskii bandit [The bravo, or, The Venetian bandit]. St. Petersburg, 1838. Literaturnye pribavleniia k Russkomu invalidu, 1839, no. 6, p. 129-130.

Review of: Bravo, ili Venetsianskii bandit [The bravo, or, The Venetian bandit]. St. Petersburg, 1838. Otechestvennye zapiski 1839, no. 2, otd. VII, p. 28-31.

Review of: Bravo, ili Venetsianskii bandit [The bravo, or, The Venetian bandit]. St. Petersburg, 1839. Syn otechestva, 1839, no. 2, otd. IV, p. 128.

1841 Belinskii, V. G. Putevoditel' v pustyne ili Ozero-more [The guide in the desert, or, the great lake—i.e. *The Pathfinder*]. St. Petersburg, 1841. Otechestvennye zapiski, 1841, no. 1, otd. VI, p. 8-9. *See also:* Belinskii, V. G. Polnoe sobranie sochinenii [Complete collected works]. v. 4. Moscow, 1954, p. 457-460.

Noveishii roman Kupera [Cooper's most recent novel]. (Zveroboi [The killer of animals—i.e. *The deerslayer*]). Literaturnaia gazeta, October 4, 1841.

Review of: Otkrytie Ameriki [The discovery of America]. (Mersedes de Kastil'ia [Mercedes of Castile]). Literaturnaia gazeta, February 1, 1841.

1843 Angliiskaia literatura. "Bludiashchii ogon'," roman Kupera [English literature. "The will o' the wisp"—i.e. *The Wing-and-Wing, or, Le Feu-follet*—a novel by Cooper]. Otechestvennye zapiski, 1843, no. 3-4, otd. VII, p. 22-25.

1846 Review of: *Satanstoe*. Otechestvennye zapiski, 1846, no. 2, otd. VII, p. 48-49.

1847 Review of: Ravensnest, ili Krasnokozhie [Ravensnest, or, The Redskins— i.e. *The Redskins, or, Indian and Injin*]. Otechestvennye zapiski, 1847, no. 2, otd. VII, p. 40-43.

1848 Druzhinin, A. V. Dzhems Fenimor Kuper [James Fenimore Cooper]. Sovremennik, 1848, no. 7, otd. III, p. 1-20.

Review of: Dva admirala [The two admirals]. St. Petersburg, 1848. Biblioteka dlia chteniia, 1848, t. 9 0, otd. VI, p. 30-31.

Review of: Dva admirala [The two admirals]. St. Petersburg, 1848. Otechestvennye zapiski, 1848, no. 10, otd. VI, p. 45-48.

Review of: Dva admirala [The two admirals]. St. Petersburg, 1848. Sovremennik, 1848, no. 6, otd. III, p. 131.

Rozen. Review of: Dva admirala [The two admirals]. St. Petersburg, 1848. Syn otechestva, 1848, no. 12, otd. VI, p. 1-13.

Review of: Markova skala, ili Krater [Mark's cliff, or, The Crater—i.e. *The Crater*]. Otechestvennya zapiski, 1848, no. 1, otd. VII, p. 13-14.

1851 Dzhems Fenimor Kuper [James Fenimore Cooper]. Panteon, 1851, no. 11, otd. VII. p. 45-48.

Kuper. Biograficheskii ocherk [Cooper. A biographical sketch]. Sovremennik, 1851, no. 11, otd. VI, p. 42-46.

Fenimor Kuper. Nekrolog [Fenimore Cooper. An obituary]. Moskvitianin, 1851, ch. VI, no. 21, kn. 1 (second pagination), p. 1-5.

1853 Druzhinin, A. V. Review of: Morskie l'vy, ili Korablekrushenie okhotnikov za tiuleniami [The sea lions, or, the shipwreck of the seal hunters]. Moscow, 1853. Sovremennik, 1853, no. 11, otd. IV, p. 1-9.

Review of: Miss Anna ("Satanstoe"). St. Petersburg, 1853. Panteon, 1853, no. 11, p. 12-15.

1854 Review of: Miss Anna ("Satanstoe"). St. Petersburg, 1853. Biblioteka dlia chteniia, 1854, t. 123, otd. VI, p. 31-33.

1856 Sand, Zh. [G.] Fenimor Kuper [Fenimore Cooper]. Syn otechestva, 1856, no. 38, p. 258-260.

1857 Literaturnye siluety. 1. Fenimor Kuper [Literary silhouettes. 1. Fenimore Cooper]. Russkii invalid, April 19, 1857.

1859 Fenimor Kuper [Fenimore Cooper]. Zhivopisnaia russkaia biblioteka, 1859, t. IV, no. 29, p. 225-227.

1861 Linnichenko, A. Angliiskii epos ... Kuper [The English epic ... Cooper]. *In:* Linnichenko, A. Kurs istorii poezii dlia vospitannits zhenskikh institutov [A course in the history of poetry for students of female institutes]. 2nd ed. Kiev, 1861. p. 101-102.

Fenimor Kuper. (Biograficheskii ocherk) [Fenimore Cooper. (Biographical sketch)]. Kaleidoskop, 1861, no. 26, p. 202-204.

1884 Bulgakov, F. Istoricheskii roman na Zapade. Kuper i Vashington Irving [The historical novel in the West. Cooper and Washington Irving]. Istoricheskii vestnik, 1884, no. 8, p. 392-398.

1900 Bërne [Börne], L. Romany Kupera [Cooper's novels]. *In:* Bërne [Börne], L. Polnoe sobranie sochinenii [Complete collected works]. v. 2. St. Petersburg, 1900. p. 275-278.

1901 Dzhems Fenimor Kuper [James Fenimore Cooper]. Novyi zhurnal inostrannoi literatury, 1901, no. 11, p. 353-355.

50—i.e. Piatidesiati—letie so dnia smerti Fenimora Kupera [The fiftieth anniversary of the death of Fenimore Cooper]. Vskhody, 1901, no. 19, p. 865.

1912 Bykov, V. Fenimor Kuper. Kriticheskaia zametka [Fenimore Cooper. A critical note]. Priroda i liudi, 1912, no. 52, p. 818-821.

1913 Bykov, V. Predislovie k russkomu izdaniiu. Zhizn' i tvorchestvo Fenimora Kupera [Foreword to the Russian edition. The life and work of Fenimore Cooper]. *In:* Cooper, J. F. Shpion [The spy]. St. Petersburg, 1913. p. 3-21.

1923 Gor'kii, M. O romanakh Fenimora Kupera [Concerning the novels of Fenimore Cooper]. *In:* Cooper, J. F. Sledopyt [The pathfinder]. Petrograd, Moscow, Berlin, 1923. p. 6-8. *See also:* Gor'kii, M. Sobranie sochinenii [Collected works]. v. 24, Moscow, 1953. p. 225-227.

1927 Cooper, J. F. Polnoe sobranie romanov [Complete collection of novels].

Moscow, Leningrad, "ZIF," 1927-1928. 2nd ed. 1929-1930.
Contents: v. 1: Shpion [The spy]. Moguchii, N. Fenimor Kuper
[Fenimore Cooper]. p. 5-9. Predislovie [Foreword] p. 13-15.
v. 2: Penitel' moria. Khizhina na kholme [(The water-witch). The
hut on the hill—i.e. *Wyandotté, or The Hutted Knoll*].
Moguchii, N. Predislovie k romanu "Khizhina na kholme"
[Foreword to the novel "The hut on the hill"]. p. 187-188.
v. 3: Zveroboi [The deerslayer]. Moguchii, N. Predislovie [Fore-
word]. p. 5-10.
v. 4: Sledopyt [The pathfinder]. Predislovie [Foreword]. p. 5-8.
v. 5: Poslednii iz Mogikan [The last of the Mohicans]. Predislovie
[Foreword]. p. 7-9.
v. 6: Pionery [The pioneers]. Predislovie [Foreword]. p. 7-9.
v. 7: Preriia [The prairie]. Dinamov, S. Predislovie [Foreword].
p. 7-12.
v. 8: Krasnyi korsar. Dva admirala [The red corsair—i.e. *The Red
Rover.* The two admirals]. Predislovie [Foreword]. p. 7-8.
v. 9: Lotsman. Osada Bostona [The pilot. The siege of Boston—
i.e. *Lionel Lincoln, or, The Leaguer of Boston*]. Predislovie [Fore-
word]. p. 7-8.
v. 10: V Venetsii. Satanstoe [In Venice. Satanstoe]. Predislovie
[Foreword]. p. 7-9.
v. 11: Mersedes iz Kastilii [Mercedes of Castile]. S. D. Predislovie
[Foreword]. p. 7-8.
v. 12: Bluzhdaiushchaia iskra [The vagrant spark—i.e. *The Wing-
and-Wing, or, Le Feu-follet*]. Predislovie [Foreword]. p. 7-8.
v. 13: Koloniia na kratere [The colony in the crater]. A. Z.
Predislovie [Foreword]. p. 7-8.
1936 Zhelobovski, I. Fenimor Kuper. Tvorchestvo pisatelia i ego mesto v detskoi
literature [Fenimore Cooper. The author's works and his place in
literature for children]. Detskaia literatura, 1936, no. 12, p. 40-42.
1937 Vinogradov, A. Review of: Poslednii iz mogikan [The last of the Mohi-
cans]. Moscow, Leningrad, 1936. Kniga i proletarskaia revoliutsiia,
1937, no. 4, p. 164-165.
1938 Kononov, A. Vozvrashchenie Kupera. (Po povodu novogo izdaniia romana "Sledopyt") [The return of Cooper. (On the occasion of a new
edition of the novel "The pathfinder")]. Detskaia literatura, 1938,
no. 13, p. 24-27.
1939 Zhantieva, D. Dzhems Fenimor Kuper [James Fenimore Cooper].
Literaturnaia gazeta, September 15, 1939.
Startsev, A. Kozhanyi chulok. (K 150-letiiu so dnia rozhdeniia Fenimora
Kupera) [Leather stocking. (On the 150th anniversary of the birth of
Fenimore Cooper)]. Internatsional'naia literatura, 1939, no. 7-8
(second printing), p. 261-265.

1941 Bal'zak, O. [Balzac, H.]. Kuper [Cooper]. *In:* Bal'zak ob iskusstve [Balzac on art]. Moscow, Leningrad, 1941. p. 86-92.

1953 Soboleva, A. and Iu. Kovalev. Roman F. Kupera "Monikiny" [F. Cooper's novel "The monikins"]. *In:* Cooper, F. Monikiny [The monikins]. Moscow, 1953. p. v-xvi.

Sokolova, L. A. Kritika amerikanskogo burzhuaznogo obshchestva v tvorchestve Fenimora Kupera [Criticism of American bourgeois society in the work of Fenimore Cooper]. Abstract of dissertation presented for the degree of Candidate of Philological Sciences. Moscow, 1953. 16 p.

1958 Mlechin, V. Fenimor Kuper i "Preriia" [Fenimore Cooper and "The prairie"]. *In:* Cooper, F. Preriia [The prairie]. Kishinev, 1958, p. 3-8.

1959 Vainshtok, V. Velikii pioner amerikanskoi literatury [The great pioneer of American literature]. *In:* Cooper, F. Poslednii iz mogikan [The last of the Mohicans]. Moscow, 1959. p. 363-374.

Kovalev, Iu. Predislovie [Foreword]. *In:* Cooper, J. F. *The Last of the Mohicans.*[1] Moscow, 1959. p. 5-18.

Narkevich, A. "Lotsman" Fenimora Kupera ["The pilot" of Fenimore Cooper]. *In:* Cooper, J. F. Lotsman [The pilot]. Moscow, 1959. p. 402-420.

1960 Alekseev, M. P. Fenimor Kuper. (S publikatsiei pisem) [Fenimore Cooper. (With publication of letters)]. *In:* Neizdannye pis'ma inostrannykh pisatelei XVIII-XIX vekov iz leningradskikh rukopisnykh sobranii [Unpublished letters of foreign writers of the 18th and 19th centuries in Leningrad manuscript collections]. Moscow, Leningrad, 1960. p. 265-276.

1961 Cooper, J. F. Izbrannye sochineniia v 6 tomakh [Selected works in 6 volumes]. Moscow, Detgiz, 1961-1963.

Contents: v. 1: Zveroboi. Poslednii iz mogikan [The deerslayer. The last of the Mohicans]. Elistratova, A. Dzheims Fenimor Kuper [James Fenimore Cooper]. p. 5-16; Eishiskina, N. Posleslovie k romanam "Zveroboi" i "Poslednii iz mogikan" [Afterword to the novels "The deerslayer" and "The last of the Mohicans"]. p. 841-846.

v. 2: Sledopyt. Pionery [The pathfinder. The pioneers]. Eishiskina, N. Posleslovie k romanam "Sledopyt" i "Pionery" [Afterword to the novels "The pathfinder" and "The pioneers"]. p. 892-898.

v. 3: Preriia. Shpion [The prairie. The spy]. Eishiskina, N. Posleslovie k romanu "Preriia" [Afterword to the novel "The prairie"]. p. 807-810. Anikst, A. Posleslovie k romanu "Shpion" [Afterword to the novel "The spy"]. p. 810-814.

[1] A book in the English language published in the Soviet Union.

v. 4: Osada Bostona. Lotsman [The siege of Boston. The pilot]. Kovalev, Iu. Posleslovie k romanu "Osada Bostona, ili Laionel Linkol'n" [Afterword to the novel "The siege of Boston, or, Lionel Lincoln"]. p. 795-803. Narkevich, A. Lotsman Fenimora Kupera ["The pilot" of Fenimore Cooper]. p. 803-814.

v. 5: Bravo. Morskaia volshebnitsa [The bravo. The sea witch—i.e. *The Water-Witch*]. Anikst, A. Posleslovie k romanu "Bravo" [Afterword to the novel "The bravo"]. p. 800-811. Narkevich, A. Posleslovie k romanu "Morskaia volshebnitsa" [Afterword to the novel "The sea witch"]. p. 812-818.

v. 6: Mersedes i Kastilii. Krasnyi Korsar [Mercedes of Castile. The red corsair—i.e. *The Red Rover*]. Svet, Ia. Posleslovie k romanu "Mersedes iz Kastilii, ili Puteshestvie v Katai [Afterword to the novel "Mercedes of Castile, or, a voyage to Cathay"]. p. 836-846; Maizel's, S. "Krasnyi korsar" i ego mesto sredi morskikh romanov Kupera "The red rover" and its place among Cooper's novels of the sea]. p. 847-854.

1963 Nikoliukin, A. Review of: Ringe, D. *James Fenimore Cooper.* New York, 1962. Sovremennaia khudozhestvennaia literatura za rubezhom, 1963, no. 10, p. 97-99.

KAULI Malkolm   COWLEY Malcolm

1923 Levidov, M. Amerikanskii tragifars. ("Leiendekerovskii portret") [An American tragifarce. ("The Leyendecker portrait")]. Lef, 1923, no. 2, p. 45-46.

KREIN Stiven   CRANE Stephen

1929 Kennel' [Kennell], R. Predislovie [Foreword]. *In:* Crane, S. Beg iunosti [The pace of youth—original title not determined]. Moscow, 1929, p. 3-4.

1930 Gurvich, V. Review of: Alyi znak doblesti [The red badge of courage]. Leningrad, Moscow, 1930. Kniga i revoliutsiia, 1930, no. 17, p. 28.

Lann, E. Stiven Kren [Stephen Crane]; Konrad, Dzh. [Conrad, J.] Ego kniga o voine [His book about war]. *In:* Crane, S. Alyi znak doblesti [The red badge of courage]. Moscow, Leningrad, 1930. p. 3-19.

Frid, Ia. Review of: Alyi znak doblesti [The red badge of courage]. Leningrad, Moscow, 1930. Novyi mir, 1930, no. 11, p. 207.

1936 Startsev, A. Review of: Alyi znak doblesti [The red badge of courage]. Moscow, 1935. Literaturnoe obozrenie, 1936, no. 1, p. 32-33.

1959 Landor, M. Oblik Stivena Kreina [The face of Stephen Crane]. (Linson, C. K. *My Stephen Crane.* 1958). Voprosy literatury, 1959, no. 8, p. 228-233.

Landor, M. Stiven Krein i universitetskaia nauka [Stephen Crane and university scholarship]. Inostrannaia literatura, 1959, no. 6, p. 267-268.

1962 Smirnov, B. Stiven Krein [Stephen Crane]. *In:* Crane, S. Alyi znak doblesti [The red badge of courage]. Moscow, Leningrad, 1962. p. 3-20.

KROFORD Frensis Merion   CRAWFORD Francis Marion

1909 Marion Kroford. Nekrolog [Marion Crawford. An obituary]. Istoricheskii vestnik, 1909, no. 7, p. 358.

DAIS Dzhei   DEISS Jay

1951 Vetoshkina, N. Vashingtonskaia istoriia [A Washington story]. Novyi mir, 1951, no. 3, p. 213-215.
1958 Zorin, V. Pravdivaia istoriia [A truthful story]. *In:* Deiss, Jay. Vashingtonskaia istoriia [A Washington story]. Moscow, 1958. p. 3-6.
1959 Lerner, G. Review of: Vashingtonskaia istoriia [A Washington story]. Literatura i zhizn', June 19, 1959.
1960 Poletika, Iu. Konets doktora Uinslou. ("Krupnaia igra") [The end of Dr. Winslow. ("A game for high stakes"—i.e. *The Blue Chips*)]. Novyi mir, 1960, no. 8, p. 264-268.
1961 Cheprakov, V. Aktsii i uchenyi. ("Krupnaia igra") [Shares of stock and a scholar. ("A game for high stakes"—i.e. *The Blue Chips*)]. Literatura i zhizn', August 18, 1961.

KRIUI Pol' de [KRAIF P. de]   DE KRUIF Paul

1928 Ot redaktsii [From the editors]. *In:* Kruif, P. de. Okhotniki za mikrobami [Microbe hunters]. Moscow, Leningrad, 1928. p. 5.
1935 Kol'tsov, N. K. Predislovie [Foreword]. *In:* Kruif, P. de. Okhotniki za mikrobami [Microbe hunters]. Moscow, 1935. p. 3-5. *See also:* (another ed.), Moscow, 1935. p. 3-8; Moscow, 1940. p. 5-9.
1936 Urnov, M. Review of: Zachem im zhit'? [Why should they live?—i.e. *Why Keep Them Alive?*]. Literaturnaia gazeta, May 10, 1936.
    Iugov, A. Okhotniki za mikrobami [Microbe hunters]. Detskaia literatura, 1936, no. 21, p. 11-17.
1937 German, Iu. Bor'ba so smert'iu [The fight against death]. Literaturnyi sovremennik, 1937, no. 2, p. 236-240.
    Elistratova, A. Review of: Stoit li im zhit'? [Is it worthwhile for them to live?—i.e. *Why Keep Them Alive?*]. Internatsional'naia literatura, 1937, no. 7, p. 213-214. (Signed: A.E.)
    Krymov, A. Review of: Stoit li im zhit'? [Is it worthwhile for them to

live?—i.e. *Why Keep Them Alive?*]. Literaturnoe obozrenie, 1937, no. 23, p. 41-43.

Menken [Mencken?], R. Zachem podderzhivat' ikh zhizn'? [Why prolong their lives?]. (Stoit li im zhit'? [Is it worthwhile for them to live?—i.e. *Why Keep Them Alive?*]). Za rubezhom, 1937, no. 13, p. 270.

Iakimov, V. Review of: Okhotniki za mikrobami. Bor'ba so smert'iu. [Microbe hunters. The fight against death—i.e. *Men Against Death*]. Moscow, 1936. Priroda, 1937, no. 7, p. 142-144.

1938 Zalkind, S. Ia. Ob iskusstve khudozhestvennoi nauchno-populiarnoi knigi [On the art of the semi-fictional book of popular science]. Kniga i proletarskaia revoliutsiia, 1938, no. 10-11, p. 177-180.

Ivich, A. Review of: Bortsy s golodom [Hunger fighters]. 1937. Literaturnoe obozrenie, 1938, no. 8, p. 46-50.

Kandyba, F. Bortsy s golodom [Hunger fighters]. Detskaia literatura, 1938, no. 7, p. 27-29.

L. P. Review of: Stoit li im zhit'? [Is it worthwhile for them to live?—i.e. *Why Keep Them Alive?*]. Moscow, 1937. Kniga i proletarskaia revoliutsiia, 1938, no. 3, p. 150-152.

Storozhenko, N. Review of: Stoit li im zhit'? [Is it worthwhile for them to live?—i.e. *Why Keep Them Alive?*]. Moscow, 1937. Internatsional molodezhi, 1938, no. 1, p. 32-33.

Shif, A. Review of: Stoit li im zhit'? [Is it worthwhile for them to live? —i.e. *Why Keep Them Alive?*]. Internatsional molodezhi, 1938, no. 1, p. 32-33.

1939 Kruif, P. de. Chuvstva i plany [Feelings and plans]. Literaturnaia gazeta, May 1, 1939.

1941 Pisarzhevskii, O. Review of: Okhotniki za mikrobami [Microbe hunters] Moscow, Leningrad, 1940. Detskaia literatura, 1941, no. 3, p. 56.

Rokotov, T. Pol' de Kraif i ego poslednie knigi [Paul de Kruif and his latest books]. Internatsional'naia literatura, 1941, no. 9-10, p. 120-121.

1958 Navashin, S. Novaia kniga Polia de Kraifa [The new book by Paul de Kruif]. (Bor'ba s bezumiem [The struggle against insanity—i.e. *A Man Against Insanity*]. Inostrannaia literatura, 1958, no. 3, p. 247-249.

1960 Zinov'ev, P. M. Predislovie [Foreword]. *In:* Kruif, P. de. Bor'ba s bezumiem [The struggle against insanity—i.e. *A Man Against Insanity*]. Moscow, 1960. p. 5-7.

1963 Gilenson, B. Memuary Polia de Kriui [The memoirs of Paul de Kruif]. (*The Sweeping Wind*. New York, 1962). Inostrannaia literatura, 1963, no. 6, p. 266-267.

Gilenson, B. Review of: *The Sweeping Wind*. New York, 1962. Sovremennaia khudozhestvennaia literatura za rubezhom, 1963, no. 1, p. 46-48.

1928 Danilin, Iu. Review of: Prichudy starika [The whims of an old man—i.e. *An Old Man's Folly*]. Moscow, Leningrad, 1927. Oktiabr', 1928, no. 1, p. 243-244.

Dinamov, S. Review of: Prichudy starika [The whims of an old man—i.e. *An Old Man's Folly*]. Moscow, Leningrad, 1927. Pechat' i revoliutsiia, 1928, no. 2, p. 203-204.

1930 Gurvich, V. Review of: Chudak [The odd one—i.e. *Moon-Calf*]. Moscow, Leningrad, 1930. Kniga i revoliutsiia, 1930, no. 26, p. 43-44.

Kennel', R. Predislovie [Foreword]. *In:* Dell, F. Chudak [The odd one—i.e. *Moon-Calf*]. Moscow, Leningrad, 1930. p. 3-5.

DODD MARTA   DODD MARTHA E.

1941 Abramov, A. Predislovie (k publikatsii reportazha Marty Dodd "Iz okna posol'stva") [Foreword (to the publication of Martha Dodd's report "From the window of the embassy"—i.e. *Through Embassy Eyes*)]. Internatsional'naia literatura, 1941, no. 9-10, p. 147-148.

Kler [Clair?], S. Review of: *Through Embassy Eyes.* New York, 1939. Kommunisticheskii internatsional, 1941, no. 8, p. 74-80.

1942 Rokotov, T. Pravdivoe svidetel'stvo ochevidtsa [The trustworthy testimony of an eyewitness]. *In:* Dodd, M. Iz okna posol'stva [From the window of the embassy—i.e. *Through Embassy Eyes*]. Moscow, 1942. p. 3-8.

Rokotov, T. Strashnaia pravda o gitlerovskoi Germanii ("Iz okna posol'stva") [The awful truth about Hitlerite Germany ("From the window of the embassy"—i.e. *Through Embassy Eyes*]. Komsomol'skaia pravda, March 24, 1942.

1955 Orlova, R. Luchom prozhektora [In the rays of a searchlight]. (*The Searching Light.* New York, 1954). Inostrannaia literatura, 1955, no. 4, p. 229-321.

1958 Ermashev, I. Posleslovie [Afterword]. *In:* Dodd, M. Pod luchom prozhektora [Under the light of a searchlight—i.e. *The Searching Light*]. Moscow, 1958, p. 362-367.

1959 Polevoi, B. Neskol'ko slov ob etoi knige i ee avtore [A few words about this book and its author]. *In:* Dodd, M. Poseesh' veter [You sow the wind—i.e. *Sowing the Wind*]. Moscow, 1959. p. 5-11.

DOS PASSOS DZHON   DOS PASSOS JOHN

1924 Dinamov, S. Review of: Tri soldata [Three soldiers]. Leningrad, 1924. Knigonosha, 1924, no. 36, p. 8.

Poletika, Iu. Review of: Tri soldata [Three soldiers]. Leningrad, 1924. Russkii sovremennik, 1924, no. 4, p. 270.

1927 Veisenberg, L. Predislovie [Foreword]. *In:* Dos Passos, J. Mankhetten [Manhattan—i.e. *Manhattan Transfer*]. Leningrad, 1927, p. 5-12.

Tsingovatov, A. Review of: Mankhetten [Manhattan—i.e. *Manhattan Transfer*]. Leningrad, 1927. Kniga i profsoiuzy, 1927, no. 9, p. 45-46. (Signed: A. I.)

Tsingovatov, A. Review of: Mankhetten [Manhattan—i.e. *Manhattan Transfer*]. Leningrad, 1927. Molodaia gvardiia, 1927, no.12, p. 221-222.

1928 Dos Passos, Dzh [J.]. Moia zhizn' [My life]. Vestnik inostrannoi literatury, 1928, no. 9, p. 131-133.

Nemerovskaia, O. Roman kino-lenta. (O "Mankhettene" Dos Passosa) [A novel on film. (About "Manhattan"—i.e. *Manhattan Transfer*—of Dos Passos)]. Na literaturnom postu, 1928, no. 2, p. 26-32.

1930 Levit, T. Dos Passos. Literatura i iskusstvo, 1930, no. 3-4, p. 208-218.

Levit, T. 42—i.e. Sorok vtoraia—parallel' S. Sh. [The forty-second parallel of the US]. Vestnik inostrannoi literatury, 1930, no. 3, p. 206-209. (Signed: T.L.)

Sinkler, E. [Sinclair, U.]. Dzhon Dos Passos—amerikanskii pisatel' [John Dos Passos—an American writer]. Vestnik inostrannoi literatury, 1930, no. 4, p. 148-150. *Another translation appeared as:* O Dzhone Dos Passose [On John Dos Passos]. Literaturnaia gazeta, August 5, 1932.

1932 Anderson, Sh. Pobol'she by nam "prestupnogo sindikalizma" [We need more "criminal syndicalism"]. Literatura morovoi revoliutsii, 1932, no. 3, p. 78-81.

Elistratova, A. Pervaia kniga Dzhona Dos Passosa ("Posviashchenie odnogo cheloveka—1917 goda") [The first book of John Dos Passos ("The dedication of a man, 1917—i.e. *One Man's Initiation—1917*)]. Literatura mirovoi revoliutsii, 1932, no. 9-10, p. 122-126.

Zelinskii, K. Na shirote bur' ("42-ia—i.e. Sorok vtoraia—parallel'") [In the latitude of storms ("42d parallel")]. Literaturnaia gazeta, February 11, 1932. *See also:* Zelinskii, K. Kriticheskie pis'ma [Critical letters]. v. 1. Moscow, 1932. p. 157-167. v. 2. Moscow, 1934. p. 113-120.

Zelinskii, K. and P. Pavlenko. Pis'mo Dzhonu Dos Passosu [A letter to John Dos Passos]. Literatura mirovoi revoliutsii, 1932, no. 4, p. 77-78. *See also:* Literaturnaia gazeta, March 23, 1932.

Karmon, U. [Carmon, W.]. Dos Passos v Amerike [Dos Passos in America]. Literaturnaia gazeta, December 17, 1932.

Kuandro, M. O novom roman Dos Passosa ("1919") [Concerning Dos Passos' new novel ("1919")]. Literaturnaia gazeta, August 23, 1932.

Miller-Budnitskaia, R. O patsifizme v tvorchestve Dos Passosa ("Tri soldata" i "Menkhetten") [Concerning pacifism in Dos Passos' writing ("Three soldiers" and "Manhattan Transfer")]. Literaturnaia ucheba, 1932, no. 9-10, p. 76-88.

Miller-Budnitskaia, R. Tvorcheskii put' Dos Passosa [Dos Passos' creative course]. Literaturnaia ucheba, 1932, no. 9-10, p. 76-88.

Rusakova, E. Dos Passos i voina [Dos Passos and war]. LOKAF, 1932, no. 12, p. 165-183.

S-v, A. Review of: 42-ia—i.e. Sorok vtoraia—parallel' [42d parallel]. Moscow, 1931. Pod"em, 1932, no. 8-9, p. 141-142.

Sel'tser, F. Ot buntarstva—k proletarskoi revoliutsii. O tvorchestve Dzhona Dos Passosa [From a state of riot—to the proletarian revolution. Concerning the writing of John Dos Passos]. Rezets, 1932, no. 7, p. 11-14.

Startsev, A. Review of: *1919*. Inostrannaia kniga, 1932, no. 8, p. 68-70.

Chukovskii, K. Dos Passos u nas [Dos Passos among us]. Literaturnaia gazeta, December 17, 1932.

1933 Zelinskii, K. Dnevnik proisshestvii [A diary of events]. Literaturnyi kritik, 1933, no. 3, p. 87-99.

Miller-Budnitskaia, R. Kniga velikoi nenavisti. ("Menkhetten," "42-ia— i.e. Sorok vtoraia—parallel'," i "1919") [A book of great scorn. ("Manhattan"—i.e. *Manhattan Transfer*, "42d parallel," and "1919")]. Zalp, 1933, no. 5, p. 64-71.

Mirskii, D. Dzhon Dos Passos ("1919." Leningrad, 1933) [John Dos Passos "1919"]. Khudozhestvennaia literatura, 1933, no. 10, p. 5-7.

Mirskii, D. Dos Passos, sovetskaia literatura i Zapad [Dos Passos, Soviet literature and the West]. Literaturnyi kritik, 1933, no. 1, p. 111-126.

Nikolai, V. Review of the play: Vershiny schast'ia [The heights of happiness—i.e. *Fortune Heights*]. Literaturnyi Leningrad, September 17, 1933.

Otten, N. Dos Passos v gostiakh u Chekhova. ("Aktsionernaia kompaniia Vozdukh-Put'") [Dos Passos as a follower of Chekhov. ("Airways, Incorporated")]. Internatsional'naia literatura, 1933, no. 2, p. 119-121.

Pertsov, V. U kogo uchit'sia? [From whom can one learn?]. Oktiabr', 1933, no. 6, p. 187-189.

Sovetskaia literatura i Dos Passos. (Diskussiia) [Soviet literature and Dos Passos. (A discussion)]. Znamia, 1933, no. 5, p. 147-178; no. 6, p. 142-169.

Contents: A. Leites, Put' Dos Passosa [Dos Passos' course]; Vs. Vishnevskii, Chto khorosho u Dos Passosa? [What is good about Dos Passos?]; V. Kirpotin, Tendentsii rozhdeniia novogo stilia [Tendencies toward creation of a new style]; A. Fadeev, Pomen'she literaturshchina [Less literariness]; I. Makar'ev, Za literaturu "tipichnykh kharakterov" i "tipichnykh obstoiatel'stv" [For a literature of "typical characters" and "typical circumstances"]; V. Stenich, Kak rabotaet Dos Passos [How Dos Passos works]; I. Sel'vinskii, Novatorstvo ili "n'iumenstvo?" [Innovation or "a new stage of humanity?"]; V. Pertsov, Litsom k deistvitel'nosti [Facing reality]; A. Leites, Dos Passosa — v sferu vliianiia sovetskoi literatury [Dos Passos — in the sphere of influence of Soviet literature]. *Revised and issued as:* Tvorcheskii put' Dos Passosa [Dos Passos' record of creativity]. *In:* Leites, A. Literatura dvukh mirov [The literature of two worlds]. Moscow, 1934. p. 95-133.

Stenich, V. Rech' o Dos Passose [A speech about Dos Passos]. Zvezda, 1933, no. 8, p. 161-165.

Izaykov, Ia. "Mir bol'she ne shutka." (O novoi p'ese Dos Passosa. "Vershiny schast'ia") ["The world is no longer a joke." (On Dos Passos' new play, "The heights of happiness" — i.e. *Fortune Heights*]. Literaturnaia gazeta, October 29, 1933.

1934 Bobrova, M. Dzhon Dos Passos i kapitalizm [John Dos Passos and capitalism]. Budushchaia Sibir', 1934, no. 6, p. 88-99.

Borovoi, L. Dos Passos — dramaturg [Dos Passos as playwright]. Literaturnaia gazeta, April 16, 1934.

Dzhon Dos Passos [John Dos Passos]. Za rubezhom, 1934, no. 18, p. 8.

Dinamov, S. Dzhon Dos Passos i ego p'esa ("Vershiny schast'ia") [John Dos Passos and his play ("The heights of happiness" — i.e. *Fortune Heights*)]. Teatral'naia dekada, 1934, no. 12-13, p. 3. (Signed: S. D-ov.)

Dinamov, S. Review of the play: Vershiny schast'ia [The heights of happiness — i.e. *Fortune Heights*]. Izvestiia, April 18, 1934.

Zelinskii, K. Dnevnik proisshestvii [A diary of events]. *In:* Zelinskii, K. Kriticheskie pis'ma [Critical letters]. v. 2. Moscow, 1934. p. 121-140.

Mirskii, D. Dva spektaklia. ("Vershiny schast'ia") [Two plays. ("The heights of happiness" — i.e. *Fortune Heights*)]. Literaturnaia gazeta, May 12, 1934.

Startsev, A. Dzhon Dos Passos [John Dos Passos]. Moscow, 1934. 152 p. (Issued under the sponsorship of: Kommunisticheskaia akademiia pri TsIK SSSR. Institut literatury i iskusstva.) *Reviews:* Gerbstman, A. Literaturnyi Leningrad, November 14, 1934; Mingulina, A. K sporam o Dos Passose [On the subject of the controversies over Dos Passos]. Znamia, 1934, no. 11, p. 250-255; Nemerovskaia, O. Zvezda, 1934, no. 12, p. 180-182; Vaks, I. and V. Sablin. Literaturnaia ucheba, 1935, no. 1, p. 178; Leites, A. Vynuzhdennaia replika [A forced reply]. Znamia, 1935, no. 2, p. 253-255.

Startsev, A. Napadki na Dos Passosa [Attacks on Dos Passos]. Literaturnaia gazeta, July 18, 1934.

Urnov, [M. V.]. Dos Passos — ocherkist [Dos Passos the essayist]. (*In All Countries*). Literaturnaia gazeta, May 20, 1934.

1935 Zelinskii, K. Dzhon Dos Passos [John Dos Passos]. Pravda, September 10, 1935.

Miller-Budnitskaia, R. Dzhon Dos Passos [John Dos Passos]. Rezets, 1935, no. 21, p. 23-24.

1936 Aseev, N. Dos Passos. Literaturnaia gazeta, January 15, 1936.

Kashkin, I. Vdol' 42-i paralleli. V mesto putevoditelia [Along the forty-second parallel. In place of a guidebook]. *In:* Dos Passos, J. 42 — i.e. Sorok vtoraia — parallel' [42d parallel]. Moscow, 1936. p. 460-510.

Matsuev, N. Dos Passos. (Bio-bibliograficheskaia spravka) [Dos Passos. (A bio-bibliographical note)]. Knizhnye novosti, 1936, no. 34, p. 22.

Startsev, A. O novoi knige Dos Passosa [Concerning Dos Passos' new book]. (*The Big Money*). Internatsional'naia literatura, 1936, no. 10, p. 145-146.

1957 Gerasimov, G. Gde Dos Passos ishchet svobodu [Where Dos Passos is seeking freedom]. (*The Theme Is Freedom*. New York, 1956). Znamia, 1957, no. 4, p. 216-217.

1959 Komarov, S. Velikie sobytiia i nizkie mysli [Great events and petty thoughts]. (*The Great Days*. New York, 1958). Inostrannaia literatura, 1959, no. 4, p. 266-268.

1961 Orlova, R. Review of: *Midcentury*. Boston, 1961. Sovremennaia khudozhestvennaia literatura za rubezhom, 1961, no. 2, p. 58-60.

1963 Zatonskii, D. Iskusy lukavogo besa [The lures of a sly demon]. (*Midcentury*. Boston, 1961). Literaturnaia gazeta, June 6, 1963.

DRAIZER Teodor   DREISER Theodore

1925 [Dinamov, S.]. Review of: Sud Lincha i drugie rasskazy [Lynch law and other tales]. Moscow, 1925. Knigonosha, 1925, no. 25, p. 15. (Signed: S. Din.)

1926 Dinamov, S. Teodor Draizer [Theodore Dreiser]. Knigonosha, 1926, no. 33, p. 10-11.

1927 Anderson, Sh. Draizer [Dreiser]. *In:* Dreiser, T. Sestra Kerry [Sister Carrie]. Leningrad, 1927. p. 3-4.

Kulle, R. Predislovie [Foreword]. *In:* Dreiser, T. Dzhenni Gergardt [Jennie Gerhardt]. Leningrad, 1927. p. 5-16.

F. A. Review of: Dzhenni Gergardt [Jennie Gerhardt]. Moscow, 1927. Kniga i profsoiuzy, 1927, no. 9, p. 45.

1928 Draizer, T. Sobranie sochinenii [Collected works]. Edited by S. Dinamov. Moscow, Leningrad, "ZIF," 1928-1930. 2nd ed., 1929-1933.

v. 2.: Finansist [The financier]. Preface by S Dinamov, p. 7-12. Notes by S. Dinamov, p. 644-648. R. Misho [Michaud?], Lichnost' i vzgliady Draizera [Dreiser's personality and views], p. 649-655.

v. 3: Titan [The titan]. Foreword by S. Dinamov, p. 7-12. S. Saigel', Amerikanskaia deistvitel'nost' i "Trilogiia zhelaniia"

[American reality and the "Trilogy of longing"], p. 682-694.
v. 4: Genii [The "genius"]. Foreword by S. Dinamov, p. 7-10.
U. Sinclair, Amerikanskaia pobeda [The American victory], p. 705-
709. Kak byl zapreshchen "Genii" [How "The 'genius'" was
banned], p. 709-712.
v. 5: Osvobozhdenie [Free]. B. Rasko [Rascoe], Teodor Draizer
[Theodore Dreiser], p. 268-293.
v. 6: Amerikanskaia tragediia [An American tragedy]. Foreword
by S. Dinamov, p. 7-9. D. K. Pouis [J. C. Powys], Draizer i ego
tvorchestvo [Dreiser and his work], p. 827-831.
v. 7: Tsepi [Chains]. Foreword by R. Kennel [Kennell], p. 7-12.
R. D'iuffus [Duffus], Put' Draizera [Dreiser's path], 335-343.
v. 10: Dvenadtsat' amerikantsev [Twelve Americans—i.e. *Twelve
Men*]. Foreword by S. Dinamov, p. 7-12. K. Van-Doren [C. Van
Doren], Teodor Draizer [Theodore Dreiser], p. 430-434.
v. 11: Sestra Kerri [Sister Carrie]. Foreword by I. Anisimov,
p. 7-16. Ch. Uoker [Walker?], Ot "Sestry Kerri" k "Amerikanskoi
tragedii" [From "Sister Carrie" to "An American tragedy"], p. 643-
646. G. Menson [Munson?], Draizer—amerikanskii pisatel'
[Dreiser, an American writer], p. 646-647. E. Mak-Donal'd
[McDonald], Draizer do "Sestry Kerri" [Dreiser before "Sister
Carrie"], p. 647-653.
v. 12: Dzhenni Gergard [Jenny Gerhardt]. Foreword by I. Anisimov, p. 7-15. P. Bointon [Boynton], Teodore Draizer [Theodore
Dreiser], p. 491-494. E. Boid [Boyd], Vstrechi s Teodorom Draizerom [Meetings with Theodore Dreiser], p. 494-495.
S. Dinamov's forewords, abridged, in: S. Dinamov. Zarubezhnaia
literatura [Foreign literature]. Moscow, 1960, p. 300-328.

Anisimov, I. Perevody. ... Draizer. "Finansist" [Translations. ...
Dreiser. "The financier"]. Vestnik inostrannoi literatury, 1928, no. 5,
p. 162-163.

Benni, Ia. O romanakh Teodora Draizera [Concerning the novels of
Theodore Dreiser]. Novyi mir, 1928, no. 9, p. 240-241.

Vladko. Teodor Draizer [Theodore Dreiser]. Krasnoe slovo (Khar'kov),
1928, no. 8, p. 183-185.

Golovin, M. Review of: Finansist [The financier]. (v. 2. of: Sobranie
sochinenii [Collected works]. Moscow, Leningrad, 1928). Chitatel'
i pisatel', July 7, 1928.

Danilin, Iu. Review of: Amerikanskaia tragediia [An American tragedy]
Moscow, Leningrad, 1928. Na literaturnom postu, 1928, no. 13-14,
p. 110-114. (Signed, Diar.)

Danilin, Iu. Review of: Amerikanskaia tragediia [An American tragedy];
Finansist [The financier]. Moscow, Leningrad, 1928. Oktiabr', 1928,
no. 8, p. 210-212.

Danilin, Iu. Review of: N'iu-Iork [New York[1]]. Moscow, Leningrad, 1927. Oktiabr', 1928, no. 1, p. 242-244.

Dinamov, S. Review of: N'iu-Iork [New York]. Moscow, Leningrad, 1927. Neobyknovennaia istoriia i drugie rasskazy [An unusual history and other tales]. Leningrad, 1927. Pechat' i revoliutsiia, 1928, no. 2, p. 205-206.

Zhits, F. Review of: Finansist [The financier]. (v. 2 of: Sobranie sochinenii [Collected works]. Moscow, Leningrad, 1928). Kniga i profsoiuzy, 1928, no. 5-6, p. 44.

Istomina, E. Review of: Tsepi [Chains]. Moscow, 1928. Chitatel' i pisatel', August 18, 1928.

K. S. Review of: Finansist [The financier]. (v. 2. of: Sobranie sochinenii [Collected works]. Moscow, Leningrad, 1928). Izvestiia, November 2, 1928.

Lopashov, S. Amerikanskii Zolia. Teodor Draizer [An American Zola. Theodore Dreiser]. Chitatel' i pisatel', September 29, 1928.

F. A. Review of: Amerikanskaia tragediia [An American tragedy]. Moscow, Leningrad, 1928. Kniga i profsoiuzy, 1928, no. 7, p. 36-37.

F. A. Review of: N'iu-Iork [New York]. Moscow, Leningrad, 1927. Neobyknovennaia istoriia i drugie rasskazy [An unusual story and other tales]. Leningrad, 1927. Kniga i profsoiuzy, 1928, no. 3, p. 31-32.

1929 B. Ia-n. Review of: Dvenadtsat' amerikantsev [Twelve Americans—i.e. Twelve Men]. Na pod"eme, 1929, no. 11, p. 107.

Kenel' [Kennell], R. Draizer o Sovetskoi Rossii [Dreiser on Soviet Russia]. Vestnik inostrannoi literatury, 1929, no. 1, p. 219-221.

Kireev, B. Review of: Titan [The titan]. (v. 3 of: Sobranie sochinenii [Collected works]. Moscow, Leningrad, 1928). Kniga i profsoiuzy, 1929, no. 1, p. 42-43.

Sokolov, V. Review of: Titan [The titan]. (v. 3 of: Sobranie sochinenii [Collected works]. Moscow, Leningrad, 1928). Izvestiia, March 24, 1929.

1930 Gurvich, V. Omary i karakatitsy [Lobsters and cuttlefish]. (Concerning: Sobranie sochinenii [Collected works]. Moscow, Leningrad, 1928-1929). Kniga i revoliutsiia, 1930, no. 9, p. 17-18.

Krasovskii, Iu. Review of: Genii [The "genius"]. (v. 4 of: Sobranie sochinenii [Collected works]. Moscow, Leningrad, 1930). Na literaturnom postu, 1930, no. 11, p. 71-73.

Levit, T. Ot Draizera do Uellsa [From Dreiser to Wells]. Vestnik inostrannoi literatury, 1930, no. 6, p. 183-186.

Nemerovskaia, O. Review of: Sobranie sochinenii [Collected works]. Moscow, Leningrad, 1928-1929. Zvezda, 1930, no. 12, p. 209-212.

Stepanov, A. S togo berega. (T. Draizer. "N'iu-Iork") [From the other

---

[1] Original English title not known.

shore. (T. Dreiser. "New York")]. Rost (Sverdlovsk), 1930, no. 1-2, p. 133-135.

Eishiskina, N. Sinkler L'iuis i Teodor Draizer [Sinclair Lewis and Theodore Dreiser]. Russkii iazyk v sovetskoi shkole, 1930, no. 1, p. 177-180.

1931 Abramov, Al. Vtoraia "amerikanskaia tragediia" Draizera [The second "American tragedy" of Theodore Dreiser]. Literaturnaia gazeta, September 20, 1931.

Amerika k 60-letiiu Draizera: A. B. Magil [Magill?]. Staryi i novyi Draizer; M. Umanskaia. Teodor Draizer protiv Dzhessi Laski [America on Dreiser's sixtieth anniversary: A. B. Magil [Magill?]. The old and new Dreiser; M. Umanskaia. Theodore Dreiser against Jesse Lasky]. Literatura mirovoi revoliutsii, 1931, no. 8-9, p. 203-208.

Dinamov, S. Privet nashemu Amerikanskomu drugu! [Greetings to our American friend!]. Literaturnaia gazeta, August 25, 1931.

Dinamov, S. Teodor Draizer idet k nam [Theodore Dreiser is coming to us]. Literatura mirovoi revoliutsii, 1931, no. 10, p. 97-103.

Dinamov, S. Travlia Teodora Draizera nachalas' [The slandering of Theodore Dreiser has begun]. Literaturnaia gazeta, October 27, 1931.

1932 Anderson, Sh. Pobol'she by nam "prestupnogo sindikalizma" [We need more "criminal syndicalism"]. Literatura mirovoi revoliutsii, 1932. no. 3, p. 78-81.

Dinamov, S. Teodor Draizer prodolzhaet bor'bu [Theodore Dreiser continues the struggle]. Marksistsko-leninskoe iskusstvoznanie, 1932, no. 5-6, p. 135-138.

Elistratova, A. Review of: *Tragic America*. New York, 1931. Inostrannaia kniga, 1932, no. 4, p. 98-99.

Elistratova, A. Teodor Draizer na revoliutsionnom puti [Theodore Dreiser on the path of revolution]. Na literaturnom postu, 1932, no. 11, p. 39-41.

Khell [Hall, Hull?], A. Teodor Draizer i Tom Muni [Theodore Dreiser and Tom Mooney]. Internatsional'nyi maiak, 1932, no. 34, p. 7.

1933 Vygodskii, D. Review of: Gallereia zhenshchin [A gallery of women]. Moscow, Leningrad, 1933. Zvezda, 1933, no. 12, p. 193-195.

Dinamov, S. Teodor Draizer i revoliutsiia [Theodore Dreiser and revolution]. *In:* Krizis kapitalizma i soiuzniki proletariata v literature Zapada [The crisis of capitalism and the allies of the proletariat in the literature of the West]. v. 1. Moscow, Leningrad, 1933. p. 64-97. *Also, abridged, in:* Dreiser, T. Gallereia zhenshchin [A gallery of women]. Moscow, Leningrad, 1933. p. 5-23. *And in:* Dinamov, S. Zarubezhnaia literatura [Foreign literature]. Moscow, 1960. p. 329-366.

Elistratova, A. Amerikanskie zametki [American notes]. Literaturnaia gazeta, September 23, 1933.

Elistratova, A. Predislovie [Foreword]. *In:* Dreiser, T. Amerikanskaia tragediia [An American tragedy]. Moscow, 1933. p. 3-13.

Kennel' [Kennell], R. "Gallereia zhenshchin" Teodora Draizera ("A gallery of women" by Theodore Dreiser]; A. B. Magil [Magill?]. Teodor Draizer prezhnii i novyi [Theodore Dreiser, formerly and now]; G. Menken [H. Mencken]. Amerikanskii roman [The American novel]. *In:* Dreiser, T. Gallereia zhenshchin [A gallery of women]. Moscow, Leningrad, 1933, p. 287-307.

Oborin, A. Review of: Gallereia zhenshchin [A gallery of women]. Moscow, Leningrad, 1933. Oktiabr', 1933, no. 7, p. 208-210.

Startsev, A. Gallereia bessil'nykh ("Gallereia zhenshchin") [A gallery of the powerless ("A gallery of women")]. Khudozhestvennaia literatura, 1933, no. 9, p. 36-38.

Eishiskina, N. Ob "Amerikanskoi tragedii" [Concerning "An American tragedy"]. Literaturnaia gazeta, November 29, 1933.

Eishiskina, N. Tragediia srednego amerikantsa. ("Amerikanskaia tragediia." Moscow, 1933) [The tragedy of an average American. ("An American tragedy." Moscow, 1933)]. Khudozhestvennaia literatura, 1933, no. 11, p. 41-43.

1934 Kouen [Cowen?], L. Teodor Draizer na barrikadakh bor'by [Theodore Dreiser on the barricades of the struggle]. Internatsional'naia literatura, 1934, no. 5, p. 91-107.

Mikhailov, L. Review of: Amerikanskaia tragediia [An American tragedy]. Moscow, 1933. Zvezda Severa (Arkhangel'sk), 1934, no. 6, p. 77-78.

Rovda, K. Filosofskie iskaniia Teodora Draizera [The philosophical searchings of Theodore Dreiser]. Literaturnyi Leningrad, May 14, 1934.

Iuzovskii, Iu. O Draizere i zanimatel'nosti. ("Zakon Likurga") [Concerning Dreiser and the reader's interest. ("The law of Lycurgus"[1])]. Literaturnaia gazeta, February 16, 1934.

1935 Dreiser, T. Kniga o (samom) sebe [A book about myself]. Internatsional'naia literatura, 1935, no. 2, p. 104-110; no. 3, p. 67-72; no. 4, p. 77-87; no. 5, p. 83-98; no. 6, p. 88-95; no. 7, p. 76-86; no. 8, p. 120-125; no. 9, p. 65-72; no. 10, p. 99-106; no. 11, p. 79-84; no. 12, p. 61-68.

1936 Dreiser, T. Chetyre instsenirovki "Dela Klaida Griffits" [Four dramatizations of "The case of Clyde Griffiths"]. Internatsional'naia literatura, 1936, no. 6, p. 173-174. *Also in:* Dreiser, T. Polnoe sobranie sochinenii [Complete collected works]. v. 12. Moscow, 1955. p. 260-263.

Karmon, U. [Carmon, W.]. Teodor Draizer ob Ispanii. Interv'iu dlia "Literaturnoi gazety" [Theodore Dreiser on Spain. An interview for

---

[1] Presumably *An American Tragedy.*

"Literaturnaia gazeta"]. Literaturnaia gazeta, November 6, 1936.

Matsuev, N. Teodor Draizer. (Bio-bibliograficheskaia spravka) [Theodore Dreiser. (Bio-bibliographical note)]. Knizhnye novosti, 1936, no. 24, p. 22-23.

Nemerovskaia, O. Draizer-romanist [Dreiser the novelist]. *In:* Dreiser, T. Amerikanskaia tragediia [An American tragedy]. v. 1. Leningrad, 1936. p. 3-24. *Also in:* Literaturnaia ucheba, 1936, no. 9, p. 89-107.

1937 Garin, N. Sud'ba talanta. (Posleslovie) [The fate of talent. (An afterword)]. *In:* Dreiser, T. Genii [The "genius"]. Moscow, 1937. p. 779-783.

Startsev, A. Review of: Amerikanskaia tragediia [An American tragedy]. Leningrad, 1936. Literaturnoe obozrenie, 1937, no. 5, p. 29-33.

1940 Nemerovskaia, O. Teodor Draizer i amerikanskii realizm. [Theodore Dreiser and American realism]. Abstract of dissertation presented for the degree of Candidate of Philological Sciences]. Leningrad, 1940. 4 p.

1941 Gan, Z. Teodor Draizer i ego pervyi roman. ("Sestra Kerri") [Theodore Dreiser and his first novel. ("Sister Carrie")]. Internatsional'naia literatura, 1941, no. 11-12, p. 298-299.

Elistratova, A. Predislovie [Foreword]. *In:* Dreiser, T. Sestra Kerri [Sister Carrie]. Moscow, 1941. p. iii-vii.

1945 Anisimov, I. Teodor Draizer. Nekrolog. [Theodore Dreiser. An obituary]. Pravda, December 31, 1945.

1946 Elistratova, A. Posmertnyi roman Draizera [The posthumous novel by Dreiser]. (*The Bulwark*. New York, 1946). Literaturnaia gazeta, July 13, 1946.

Isbakh, A. Teodor Draizer i Rossiia [Theodore Dreiser and Russia]. Literaturnaia gazeta, January 5, 1946.

Nemerovskaia, O. Teodor Draizer [Theodore Dreiser]. Zvezda, 1946, no. 4, p. 147-151.

Tikhonov, N. Pamiati bol'shogo khudozhnika [To the memory of a great artist]. Literaturnaia gazeta, January 5, 1946.

1948 Bobrova, M. Predislovie [Foreword]. *In:* Dreiser, T. Amerikanskaia tragediia [An American tragedy]. Moscow, 1948. p. 3-16.

1949 Anisimov, I. Vot ona, kapitalisticheskaia Amerika! Zametki o tvorchestve T. Draizera [There she is, capitalist America! Notes about the work of T. Dreiser]. Izvestiia, August 24, 1949.

1950 Anisimov, I. Amerika, kak ona est' [America as it is]. *In:* Dreiser, T. Ocherki i rasskazy [Essays and tales]. Moscow, 1950. p. 3-15.

Dynnik, V. Ocherki i rasskazy T. Draizera—kniga oblichitel'nykh dokumentov. (Ocherki i rasskazy. Moscow, 1950). [The essays and tales of T. Dreiser—a book of accusing documents. (Essays and tales. Moscow, 1950)]. Literatura v shkole, 1950, no. 6, p. 71-73.

Panova, V. V zashchitu pamiati Draizera. Pis'mo v redaktsiiu "Literaturnoi gazety" [In defense of Dreiser's memory. A letter to the editorial board of "Literaturnaia gazeta"]. Literaturnaia gazeta, February 25, 1950.

Razgovorov, N. Teodor Draizer obviniaet. (Ocherki i rasskazy. Moscow, 1950) [Theodore Dreiser accuses. (Essays and tales. Moscow, 1950)]. Literaturnaia gazeta, May 24, 1950.

Samokhvalov, N. I. Razoblachenie "amerikanskogo obraza zhizni" v tvorchestve Teodora Draizera. (Romany i publitsistika) [The unmasking of the "American way of life" in the works of Theodore Dreiser. (Novels and journalistic writings)]. Abstract of dissertation presented for the degree of Candidate of Philological Sciences. Moscow, 1950. 15 p.

Draizer [Dreiser], T. Sobranie sochinenii v 12 tt. [Collected works in 12 volumes]. Moscow, Goslitizdat, 1950-1955.

    Contents: v. 1: Sestra Kerri [Sister Carrie]. I. Anisimov, Teodor Draizer [Theodore Dreiser]. p. v-lxvii.

    v. 2: Dzhenni Gerkhardt [Jennie Gerhardt]. Istoriko-literaturnaia spravka [Historico-literary note]. p. 346-347.

    v. 3: Finansist [The financier]. Istoriko-literaturnaia spravka [Historico-literary note]. p. 550-551.

    v. 4: Titan [The titan]. Istoriko-literaturnaia spravka [Historico-literary note]. p. 593-594.

    v. 5: Stoik [The stoic]. I Anisimov, Zavershenie "Trilogii zhelaniia" [The completion of the "Trilogy of longing"]. p. 383-394.

    v. 6, pt. 2: Genii [The "genius"]. I. Anisimov, Posleslovie [Afterword]. p. 419-426.

    v. 8: Amerikanskaia tragediia [An American tragedy]. Istorikoliteraturnaia spravka [Historico-literary note]. p. 463.

    v. 9: Oplot [The bulwark]. Istoriko-literaturnaia spravka [Historico-literary note]. p. 326-327.

    v. 10: Rasskazy [Tales]. Istoriko-literaturnaia spravka [Historico-literary note]. p. 743-744.

    v. 11: Publitsistika [Journalistic writings]. I. Anisimov, Publitsistika Draizera. (1917-1935) Bibliograficheskaia spravka [Dreiser's journalism 1917-1935. Bibliographic note]. p. 596-620.

    v. 12: Publitsistika poslednikh let [Journalism of the later years]. I. Anisimov, Draizer i ego publitsistika poslednikh let [Dreiser and his journalism of the later years]. p. 373-392. D. Kraminov, Kniga Draizera "Amerika stoit spasat'" [Dreiser's book "America is worth saving"]. p. 393-398. Bibliograficheskaia spravka [Bibliographic note]. p. 399-401.

1951 Anisimov, I. Oblichitel' amerikanskogo imperializma [An accuser of American imperialism]. Pravda, August 30, 1951.

Dubashinskii, M. Teodor Draizer—vydaiushchii amerikanskii pisatel' i vernyi drug Sovetskogo Soiuza [Theodore Dreiser—an outstanding

71

American writer and a true friend of the Soviet Union]. Inostrannye iazyki v shkole, 1951, no. 2, p. 41-49.

Zasurskii, Ia. N. Draizer v bor'be s imperialisticheskoi Amerikoi [Dreiser in the struggle with imperialist America]. *In:* Dreiser, Th. *Essays and Articles*[1]. Moscow, 1951. p. 5-16.

Zasurskii, Ia. Put' Teodora Draizera k kommunismu [Theodore Dreiser's road to Communism]. Abstract of dissertation presented for the degree of Candidate of Philological Sciences. Moscow, 1951. 19 p.

Krugleevskaia, V. V. Put' Teodora Draizera, obshchestvennogo deiatelia i pisatelia, k kommunisticheskoi partii. (Na materiale zhizni i tvorchestva Draizera 30-40-kh godov) [The road of Theodore Dreiser, a public figure and writer, to the Communist Party. (Based on material from Dreiser's life and work in the 1930's and 1940's)]. Abstract of dissertation presented for the degree of Candidate of Philological Sciences. Leningrad, 1951. 18 p.

1952 Anisimov, I. Oblichitel' amerikanskogo imperializma [An accuser of American imperialism]. *In:* Dreiser, T. Tragicheskaia America [Tragic America]. Moscow, 1952. p. 3-11.

Zasurskii, Ia. N. and R. M. Samarin. Teodor Draizer v bor'be protiv amerikanskogo imperializma [Theodore Dreiser in the struggle against American imperialism]. Moscow, Izdatel'stvo Moskovskogo gosudarstvennogo universiteta, 1952. 110 p.

Nikolaev, V. Draizer obvinaiet amerikanskii imperializm. ("Tragicheskaia Amerika") [Dreiser attacks American imperialism. ("Tragic America")]. Bol'shevik, 1952, no. 13, p. 71-80.

Samokhvalov, N. I. Teodor Draizer — oblichitel' amerikanskogo imperializma [Theodore Dreiser — an accuser of American imperialism]. Moscow, "Znanie," 1952. 32 p.

Toper, P. Gnevnoe slovo pravdy. ("Tragicheskaia Amerika." Moscow, 1952) [The angry word of truth. ("Tragic America." Moscow, 1952)]. Znamia, 1952, no. 11, p. 188-192.

Fedunov, P. Golos chestnogo pisatelia. ("Tragicheskaia Amerika." Moscow, 1952) [The voice of an honest writer. ("Tragic America." Moscow, 1952)]. Pravda, September 14, 1952.

1953 Bukhtiiarova, N. S. Sintaksis nesobstvennopriamoi rechi v proizvedeniiakh T. Draizera [The syntax of indirect discourse in the works of T. Dreiser]. Abstract of dissertation presented for the degree of Candidate of Philological Sciences. Leningrad, 1953. 20 p.

Gorbunov, A. M. Teodor Draizer i amerikanskii narod. (K probleme polozhitel'nogo geroia v tvorchestve Draizera posleoktiabr'skogo perioda) [Theodore Dreiser and the American people. (Concerning the problem of the positive hero in Dreiser's work of the post-

---

[1] A book in the English language published in the Soviet Union.

October period)]. Abstract of dissertation presented for the degree of Candidate of Philological Sciences]. Moscow, 1953. 16 p.

Draizer [Dreiser], E. [H.]. Moia zhizn' s Draizerom [My life with Dreiser]. *Abridged translation.* Moscow, Inostrannaia literatura, 1953. 167 p. *Also in:* Dreiser, T. Sobranie sochinenii v 12 tt [Collected works in 12 volumes]. v. 12. Moscow, "Pravda," 1955. p. 259-390. *Review:* Elistratova, A. Vospominaniia o Draizere [Reminiscences of Dreiser]. Literaturnaia gazeta, April 23, 1953.

Krugleevskaia, V. V. Teodor Draizer v bor'be za mir [Theodore Dreiser in the struggle for peace]. Uchenye zapiski Severo-Osetinskogo pedagogicheskogo instituta, 1953, v. 19, p. 97-106.

1954 Anikst, A. Teodor Draizer i ego roman "Dzhenni Gerkhardt" [Theodore Dreiser and his novel "Jennie Gerhardt"]. *In:* Dreiser, T. Dzhenni Gerkhardt [Jenny Gerhardt]. Moscow, 1952. p. 3-14.

Zasurskii, Ia. Predislovie [Foreword]. *In:* Dreiser, Th. *The Financier*[1]. Moscow, 1954. p. iii-xv.

1955 Mazetskii, G. P. Kriticheskii realizm Teodora Draizera [The critical realism of Theodore Dreiser]. Abstract of dissertation presented for the degree of Candidate of Philological Sciences. L'vov, 1955. 16 p.

1956 Krugleevskaia, V. V. "Oplot" T. Draizera kak vydaiushcheesia proizvedenie realisticheskoi literatury SShA ["The bulwark" of T. Dreiser as an outstanding work of the realist literature of the US]. Uchenye zapiski Severo-Osetinskogo pedagogicheskogo instituta, 1956, v. 21, vyp. 2. Seriia obshchestvennykh nauk. p. 171-184.

Lozovskii, A. I. Tvorchestvo Teodora Draizera, 1900-1929 [Theodore Dreiser's work, 1900-1929]. Abstract of dissertation presented for the degree of Candidate of Philological Sciences. Moscow, 1956. 11 p.

Postnov, G. S. Realisticheskie romany Teodora Draizera, 1900-1915 [Theodore Dreiser's realistic novels, 1900-1915]. Abstract of dissertation presented for the degree of Candidate of Philological Sciences. Moscow, 1956. 16 p.

Topuridze, E. E. K probleme iskusstva v tvorchestve Teodora Draizera [On the problem of art in the work of Theodore Dreiser]. Abstract of dissertation presented for the degree of Candidate of Philological Sciences. Tbilisi, 1956. 20 p.

1957 Zasurskii. Ia. N. Teodor Draizer—pisatel' i publitsist [Theodore Dreiser—writer and journalist]. Moscow, Izdatel'stvo Moskovskogo gosudarstvennogo universiteta, 1957. 223 p. *Review:* Rumiantseva, I. Voprosy literatury, 1959, no. 1, p. 244-247.

Postnov, Iu. Predislovie [Foreword]. *In:* Dreiser, Th. *The Titan*[1]. Moscow, 1957. p. iii-xv.

1958 Anisimov, I. Put', prolozhennyi Draizerom [The path broken by Drei-

---

[1] A book in the English language published in the Soviet Union.

ser]. (*The Stature of Theodore Dreiser*). Inostrannaia literatura, 1958, no. 11, p. 219-232.

Dubashinskii, I. Predislovie [Foreword]. *In:* Dreiser, Th. *Sister Carrie*[1]. Moscow, 1958. p. 3-14.

Kornilova, E. Sbornik statei o Draizere [A collection of articles about Dreiser]. Voprosy literatury, 1958, no. 6, p. 233-239.

Krugleevskaia, V. V. Teodor Draizer v bor'be protiv rasovoi diskriminatsii v SShA [Theodore Dreiser in the struggle against race discrimination in the US]. Uchenye zapiski Severo-Osetinskogo pedagogicheskogo instituta, 1958, v. 23, vyp. 3. Seriia filologicheskikh nauk. p. 67-79.

Savurenok, A. K. Publitsistika T. Draizera 1920-kh godov [T. Dreiser's journalism of the 1920's]. Vestnik Leningradskogo gosudarstvennogo universiteta, 1958, no. 2. Seriia istorii, iazyka i literatury, vyp. 1. p. 83-92.

Teodor Draizer ob instsenirovke "Sestry Kerri" [Theodore Dreiser on the dramatization of "Sister Carrie"]. Inostrannaia literatura, 1958, no. 7, p. 249-251.

Chistikov, E. I. Teodor Draizer, 1871-1945 [Theodore Dreiser, 1871-1945]. Frunze, 1958. 48 p.

Shpakova, A. P. K voprosu ob ideino-khudozhestvennom svoeobrazii "Trilogii zhelaniia" T. Draizera [On the problem of the ideological and artistic traits of the "Trilogy of longing" of T. Dreiser]. Uchenye zapiski Akademii obshchestvennykh nauk, 1958, vyp. 35. Idei i obrazy khudozhestvennoi literatury, p. 206-241.

1959 Anisimov, I. "Amerikanskaia tragediia" i "Tragicheskaia America" ["An American tragedy" and "Tragic America"]. *In:* Dreiser, T. Amerikanskaia tragediia [An American tragedy]. pt. 1. Moscow, 1959. p. 5-25.

Mazets'kii, G. P. K kharakteristike romana T. Draizera "Amerikanskaia tragediia" [A characterization of T. Dreiser's novel "An American tragedy"]. Naukovy zapysky Stanislavs'koho pedahogychnoho instytuta, Filologichna seriia. 1959, t. 3, p. 55-61.

Mazets'kii, G. P. O stile romanov Draizera (na materiale "Trilogii zhelaniia") [Concerning the style of Dreiser's novels (on the basis of the materials of the "Trilogy of longing")]. Naukovy zapysky Stanislavs'koho pedahogychnoho instytuta, Filologichna seriia. 1959, t. 2, p. 53-65.

Shpakova, A. P. Amerikanskaia deistvitel'nost' v izobrazhenii Teodora Draizera. (Roman "Amerikanskaia tragediia") [American reality as depicted by Theodore Dreiser. (The novel "An American tragedy")]. Moscow, 1959. 52 p.

---

[1] A book in the English language published in the Soviet Union.

Shpakova, A. P. Amerikanskaia deistvitel'nost' v izobrazhenii Teodora Draizera. [American reality as depicted by Theodore Dreiser]. Abstract of dissertation presented for the degree of Candidate of Philological Sciences. Moscow, 1959. 21 p.

1960 Gilenson, B. "...Ia voskhishchaius' Rossiei..." (S publikatsiei pisem) ["...I am enchanted by Russia..." (On the publication of letters)]. Literaturnaia gazeta, December 27, 1960.

Ivashchenko, A. F. Roman Teodora Draizera "Dzhenni Gerkhardt." [Theodore Dreiser's novel "Jennie Gerhardt"]. *In:* Dreiser, T. Dzhenni Gerkhardt [Jennie Gerhardt]. Moscow, 1960. p. 5-16.

Mazetskii, G. P. Obraz Kaupervuda v "Trilogii zhelanii" T. Draizera. (K voprosu o sviazi mirovozzreniia i khudozhestvennogo masterstva pisatelia) [The character of Cowperwood in the "Trilogy of longing" of T. Dreiser. (On the problem of the relationship of the Weltanschauung and artistic mastery of the writer]. Naukovy zapysky Stanislavs'koho pedahogichnoho instytuta. Filologichna seriia, 1960, t. 4, p. 93-103.

Sergeeva, I. N'iu-Iork—Blizhne Borisovskoe [New York to Blizhne-Borisovskoe]. Literaturnaia gazeta, July 19, 1960.

Teodor Draizer (1871-1945). Metodicheskie materialy k vecheru, posviashchennomu 15-letiiu so dnia smerti [Theodore Dreiser (1871-1945). Materials for planning of evenings devoted to the fifteenth anniversary of his death]. Moscow, 1960. 18 p. (Issued by All-Union State Library of Foreign Literature).

Fedorov, G. Imeni Draizera [In Dreiser's name]. Literatura i zhizn', May 25, 1960.

Shelepenkov, B. Draizer i russkie krest'iane [Dreiser and Russian peasants]. Izvestiia, September 5, 1960.

1961 Mazetskii, G. P. K kharakteristike romana T. Draizera "Oplot" [A characterization of T. Dreiser's novel "The bulwark"]. Naukovi zapysky Stanislavs'koho pedahohichnoho instytuta, 1961, t. 5. Pratsi kafedr ukrains'koi movy ta literatury, rossis'koi movy ta literatury. p. 78-86.

Sergeeva, I. Draizer v Blizhne-Borisovskom [Dreiser in Blizhne-Borisovskoe]. Literaturnaia gazeta, September 23, 1961.

1962 Lozovskii, A. I. Draizer v SSSR [Dreiser in the USSR]. Uchenye zapiski Moskovskogo oblastnogo pedagogicheskogo instituta, 1962. t. 111. K problemam kriticheskogo realizma v zarubezhnoi literature 20 veka [On the problems of critical realism in foreign literature of the 20th century]. Sb. 2, p. 167-177.

Lozovskii, A. I. Draizer—novellist. (Sbornik "Osvobozhdenie i drugie rasskazy") [Dreiser as short story writer. (The collection "Liberation and other stories"—i.e. *Free and Other Stories*)]. Uchenye zapiski Permskogo universiteta, 1962, t. 23, vyp. 2, p. 40-53.

Shpakova, A. Predislovie [Foreword]. *In:* Dreiser, Th. *The Stoic.*[1] Moscow, 1962. p. 3-17.

1963 Draizer [Dreiser], T. "...Izobrazhat' kharakter i dukh deistvitel'nosti..." (Iz perepiski) ["...To show the character and spirit of reality..." (From correspondence)]. Introductory article and notes by B. Gilenson. Voprosy literatury, 1963, no. 5, p. 183-200.

Zasurskii, Ia. Review of: Shapiro, Ch. *Theodore Dreiser: Our Bitter Patriot.* 1962. Sovremennaia khudozhestvennaia literatura za rubezhom, 1963, no. 12, p. 107-109.

Kharris [Harris], M. T. Naperekor temnym silam [In opposition to the dark forces]. Literaturnaia gazeta, June 25, 1963.

DIUBUA Vil'iam Edvard   DU BOIS William Edward

1934 Kh'iuz [Hughes], L. D-r Diubua—chelovek s borodkoi [Dr. Du Bois—a man with a small beard]. Internatsional'naia literatura, 1934, no. 3-4, p. 205-206.

1958 Belfreidzh, S. [Belfrage, C.]. Slavnyi iubilei. (K 90-letiiu Uil'iama Diubua) [A glorious jubilee. (On the 90th birthday of William Du Bois)]. Inostrannaia literatura, 1958, no. 2, p. 221-226.

90—i.e. Devianosto—letie Uil'iama Diubua [The 90th birthday of William Du Bois]. Vestnik Akademii nauk SSSR, 1958, no. 5, p. 134-135.

Zlobin, G. Chernoe plamia [The black flame]. (*The Ordeal of Mansart.* New York, 1957). Inostrannaia literatura, 1958, no. 2, p. 259-261.

Litoshko, E. Bol'shaia iarkaia zhizn' [A great, brilliant life]. Pravda, February 28, 1958.

Uil'iamu Diubua—90 let [William Du Bois is 90 years old]. Literaturnaia gazeta, February 22, 1958.

1960 Gorokhov, V. Doroga dlinoi v 92 goda [A road 92 years long]. Literatura i zhizn', July 3, 1960.

1961 Zhukov, V. Tovarishch Uil'iam Diubua [Comrade William Du Bois]. Pravda, November 24, 1961.

Zlobin, G. Chernoe plamia razgoraetsia iarche [The black flame burns more brightly]. (*Mansart Builds a School.* New York, 1959). Inostrannaia literatura, 1961, no. 3, p. 262-263.

1962 Diubua, U. E. B. [Du Bois, W. E. B.]. Vospominaniia [Memoirs]. Moscow, 1962. *Reviews:* Sheinis, Z. Put' bortsa [The path of a fighter]. Novoe vremia, 1962, no. 39, p. 30-31; G. Z. (Review of: *Worlds of Color.* New York, 1961). Sovremennaia khudozhestvennaia literatura za rubezhom, 1962, no. 1, p. 67-70; Zlobin, G. Dva tsveta mira [Two colors of the world]. (*Worlds of Color.* New York, 1961). Inostrannaia literatura, 1962, no. 6, p. 281-283.

[1] A book in the English language published in the Soviet Union.

Pittman, D. Logika odnoi zhizni [The logic of one life]. Inostrannaia literatura, 1962, no. 8, p. 232-287.

1963 Bekker, M. Predislovie [Foreword]. *In:* Mansart stroit shkolu [Mansart builds a school]. Moscow, 1963. p. 5-14.

Dolmatovskii, E. Pamiati Uil'iama Diubua [To the memory of William Du Bois]. Inostrannaia literatura, 1963, no. 10, p. 253-255.

Kolesnichenko, T. Myslitel', poet, borets [Thinker, poet, fighter]. Pravda, February 23, 1963.

Kotov, M. Bol'shaia zhizn' [A great life]. Izvestiia, August 29, 1963. (Moscow evening edition).

Kuznetsov, V. Rytsar' pravda [A knight of the truth]. Neva, 1963, no. 12, p. 207-209.

Levchenko, I. Poet ne umiraet [A poet does not die]. Literaturnaia gazeta, August 31, 1963.

Romanova, E. Svet "chernogo plameni" [The light of the "black flame"]. Literaturnaia gazeta, February 23, 1963.

Uinston, G. [Winston, H.]. Svetlaia zhizn' bortsa [The luminous life of a fighter]. Izvestiia, February 22, 1963. (Moscow evening edition).

D'IUSSO Arno   D'USSEAU Arnaud

1956 Romanova, E. V. V odnom iz otelei N'iu-Iorka. ("Dama iz togo zhe koridora") [In one of the hotels in New York. ("A lady from the same corridor"[1])]. Sovetskaia kul'tura, April 5, 1956.

EMERSON Ral'f Uoldo   EMERSON Ralph Waldo

1847 Ral'f Val'do Emerson amerikanskii poet i filosof [Ralph Waldo Emerson, an American poet and philosopher]. Biblioteka dlia chteniia, 1847, t. 85, otd. VII, p. 36-69.

1864 Angliia s tochki zreniia amerikantsa. ("Cherty angliiskoi zhizni") [England from the point of view of an American. ("Traits of English life"—i.e. *English Traits*)]. Otechestvennye zapiski, 1864, no. 5, p. 203-223.

1882 Novikova, O. A. (Kireeva). Ral'f V. Emerson [Ralph W. Emerson]. Rus' (Moscow), May 8, 1882. (Signed: O. K.)

Ral'f-Val'do Emerson. (Nekrolog) [Ralph Waldo Emerson. (Obituary)]. Zagranichnyi vestnik, 1882, no. 5, otd. II, p. 118.

1885 Urusova, V. D. Ralf-Ualdo Emerson [Ralph Waldo Emerson]. Literaturnoe prilozhenie k gazete "Grazhdanin," 1885, no. 9, (otd. II), p. 1-12.

[1] *Ladies of the Corridor* (Dorothy Parker, co-author).

1900 Emerson. (Kritikobiograficheskii etiud) [Emerson. (Critico-biographic study)]. Novyi zhurnal inostrannoi literatury, 1900, no. 10, p. 362-371.

1901 Emerson—pisatel', filosof i moralist. (Kriticheskii ocherk) [Emerson, writer, philosopher and moralist. (Critical sketch)]. *In:* Emerson, R. W. Sochineniia [Works]. St. Petersburg, 1901. p. 1-21. *Also in:* Novyi zhurnal inostrannoi literatury, 1901, no. 2, p. 1-19.

1902 Ral'f Emerson [Ralph Emerson]. Novyi zhurnal inostrannoi literatury, iskusstva i nauki, 1902, no. 12 (2nd pagination), p. 161-162. *Also, in:* Plutarkh XIX veka [Plutarch of the 19th century]. v. 2. St. Petersburg, 1903, p. 161-162.

1903 Amerikanskii filosof i poet Ral'f Emerson (1803-1882). Po sluchaiu stoletiia so dnia ego rozhdeniia [The American philosopher and poet Ralph Emerson, 1803-1882. On the centennial of his birth]. Novyi mir, 1903, no. 108, p. 23.

Ral'f Val'do Emerson [Ralph Waldo Emerson]. Vestnik inostrannoi literatury, 1903, no. 6, p. 326-330.

1904 Bitner, V. Predislovie [Foreword]. *In:* Emerson, R. W. Velikie liudi [Great people—i.e. *Representative Men*]. St. Petersburg, 1904, p. iii-iv.

1909 Abramovich, N. T. Karleil' i R. Emerson. (Mir v otkrovenii misticheskogo individualizma) [Carlyle and R. Emerson. (The world in the revelation of mystic individualism)]. Russkaia mysl', 1909, no. 10, p. 69-97; no. 11, p. 54-75. *Also in:* Abramovich, N. Khudozhniki i mysliteli [Artists and thinkers]. St Petersburg, Moscow, 1911. p. 10-70.

1912 Aikhenval'd, Iu. Predislovie k russkomu perevodu [Foreword to the Russian translation]. Morley, J. Vvedenie [Introduction]. *In:* Emerson, R. Izbranniki chelovechestva [The chosen ones of humanity—i.e. *Representative Men*]. Moscow, 1912. p. v-xiii; p. 1-43.

1944 Chukovskii, K. Uitman i Emerson [Whitman and Emerson]. *In:* Whitman, W. Izbrannye stikhotvoreniia i proza [Selected poetry and prose]. Moscow, 1944, p. 194-195.

1954 Whitman, W. Knigi Emersona (ikh temnye storony) [Emerson's books (their darker side)]. *In:* Whitman, W. Izbrannoe [Selections]. Moscow, 1954. p. 264-266.

1955 Sillen, S. Zhivoi Emerson [The living Emerson]. *In:* Progressivnye deiateli SShA v bor'be za peredovuiu ideologiiu [Progressive figures of the US in the struggle for a progressive ideology]. Moscow, 1955. p. 379-388.

1947 Mendel'son, M. Gideon Dzhekson i drugie. (Rasovaia diskriminatsiia i amerikanskaia literatura poslednikh let) [Gideon Jackson and others. (Race discrimination and American literature in recent years)]. Novyi mir, 1947, no.5, p. 150-167.

1948 Anikst, A. Progressivnyi amerikanskii pisatel' Govard Fast. [The progressive American writer, Howard Fast]. Report of a public lecture. Moscow, "Pravda," 1958. 32 p.

Elistratova, A. Govard Fast [Howard Fast]. *In:* Fast, H. Posledniaia granitsa [The last frontier]. Moscow, 1948. p. 5-18.

Mendel'son, M. Govard Fast i ego kniga [Howard Fast and his book]. Znamia, 1948, no. 9, p. 183-189.

Mendel'son, M. Chetyre dnia v Klarktone [Four days in Clarkton]. Literaturnaia gazeta, April 21, 1948.

1949 Galanov, B. Doroga svobody Gideona Dzheksona [Gideon Jackson's road to freedom]. (Doroga svobody [Freedom road]. Moscow, 1949). Znamia, 1949, no. 11, p. 189-192.

1951 Miller-Budnitskaia, R. Kniga o prestupleniiakh amerikanskogo fashizma [A book about the crimes of American fascism]. (Pikskill, SShA [Peekskill, U.S.A.]). Oktiabr', 1951, no. 10, p. 180-182.

Smirnov, S. Kniga o bor'be prostykh liudei Ameriki [A book about the struggle of the common people of America]. (Klarkton [Clarkton]. Moscow, 1950). Novyi mir, 1951, no. 1, p. 255-258.

1952 Romanova, E. S. Govard Fast [Howard Fast]. *In:* Progressivnaia literatura stran kapitalizma [Progressive literature of the capitalist countries]. Moscow, 1952. p. 308-326.

1953 Levidova, I. M. Govard Fast. Bibliografiia s predisloviem [Howard Fast. A bibliography with a foreword]. Moscow, All-Union State Library of Foreign Literature, 1953. 26 p.

1954 Dubashinskii, I. Govard Fast [Howard Fast]. *In:* Sovremennaia progressivnaia literatura zarubezhnykh stran v bor'be za mir [Contemporary progressive literature of foreign countries in the struggle for peace]. Moscow, 1954. p. 181-223.

Orlova, R. Tvorchestvo Govarda Fasta i ego kniga "Podvig Sakko i Vantsetti" [The works of Howard Fast and his book "The great deed of Sacco and Vanzetti"—i.e. *The Passion of Sacco and Vanzetti*]. Molodoi kommunist, 1954, no. 4, p. 116-120.

Romanova, E. Novyi roman Govarda Fasta. ("Sailas Timbermen") [Howard Fast's new novel. ("Silas Timberman")]. Literaturnaia gazeta, October 2, 1954.

Romm, A. S. "Doroga svobody." Roman G. Fasta ["Freedom road."

[1] [Footnote in original text]. As is well known, in 1957 H. Fast repudiated his socialist convictions and left the progressive forces of the US.

The novel by H. Fast]. Uchenye zapiski Leningradskogo pedago-gicheskogo instituta, t. 9. Fakul'tet iazyka i literatury, vyp. 3, 1954, p. 254-270.

Toper, P. Pravda vostorzhestvuet! (Podvig Sakko i Vantsetti) [Truth will triumph. (The great deed of Sacco and Vanzetti—i.e. *The Passion of Sacco and Vanzetti*)]. Znamia, 1954, no. 7, p. 183-190.

Shmeleva, S. K. Poslevoennaia publitsistika Govarda Fasta [Howard Fast's postwar journalism]. Uchenye zapiski Saratovskogo gosu-darstvennogo universiteta, 1954, t. 41. vyp. filol., p. 249-262.

1955 Anikst, A. Roman o chestnykh liudiakh Ameriki [A novel about the honest people of America]. ("Silas Timberman"). Znamia, 1955, no. 5, p. 181-183.

Berezark, I. Tragediia prostogo amerikantsa [The tragedy of an ordinary American]. ("Sailas Timbermen" ["Silas Timberman"]). Neva, 1955, no. 2, 175-176.

Golysheva, A. I. Roman Govarda Fasta "Doroga svobody" [Howard Fast's novel "Freedom road"]. Uchenye zapiski Pskovskogo peda-gogicheskogo instituta, 1955, vyp. 3, p. 3-58.

Golysheva, A. I. Roman Govarda Fasta "Posledniaia granitsa" [Howard Fast's novel "The last frontier"]. Uchenye zapiski Pskovskogo pedagogicheskogo instituta, 1955, vyp. 3, p. 59-109.

Elistratova, A. Novatorstvo Govarda Fasta [Howard Fast's innovations]. Inostrannaia literatura, 1955, no. 3, p. 202-210.

Tikhomirova, I. Oruzhie bor'by za mir. ("Sailas Timbermen") [A weapon in the struggle for peace. ("Silas Timberman")]. Zvezda, 1955, no. 7, p. 178-181.

Troitskii, Iu. N. "Podvig Sakko i Vantsetti" Govarda Fasta [Howard Fast's "The great deed of Sacco and Vanzetti"—i.e. *The Passion of Sacco and Vanzetti*]. Uchenye zapiski Tul'skogo pedagogicheskogo instituta, 1955, vyp. 6, p. 214-244.

1956 Zil'berbord, B. A. Govard Fast—borets za mir i demokratiiu [Howard Fast—a fighter for peace and democracy]. Abstract of dissertation presented for the degree of Candidate of Philological Sciences. Chernovtsy, 1956. 19 p.

1957 Golysheva, A. Roman Govarda Fasta "Klarkton" [Howard Fast's novel "Clarkton"]. Uchenye zapiski Pskovskogo pedagogicheskogo insti-tuta, 1957, vyp. 4, p. 139-174.

Dezertirstvo pod ognem. Po stranitsam progressivnoi pechati SShA [Desertion under fire. Through the pages of the progressive press of the US]. Literaturnaia gazeta, August 24, 1957.

1958 Gribachev, N. Govard Fast—psalomshchik revizionizma [Howard Fast—a psalm-singer of revisionism]. Literaturnaia gazeta, January 30, 1958.

Izakov, B. Dve ispovedi Govarda Fasta [Two confessions of faith by Howard Fast]. Inostrannaia literatura, 1958, no. 2, p. 214-220.

1933 Ivasheva, V. Review of: *The Sound and the Fury*. Literaturnaia gazeta, September 11, 1933.
1935 Abramov, A. Review of: *Dr Martino and Other Stories*. New York, 1935. Inostrannaia kniga, 1935, no. 3, p. 17-18.
1955 Romanova, E. Antivoennye motivy v tvorchestve Uil'iama Folknera [Antiwar motifs in the writing of William Faulkner]. Inostrannaia literatura, 1955, no. 6, p. 170-176.
1956 Robson, E. "Srednii put'" i novoe v negritianskom dvizhenii ["The middle of the road" and the new features in the Negro movement]. Mezhdunarodnaia zhizn', 1956, no. 5, p. 100-107.
1957 Novyi roman Folknera [Faulkner's new novel]. (*The Town*). Literaturnaia gazeta, June 15, 1957.
1958 Kashkin, I. Folkner—rasskazchik [Faulkner—the story writer]. *In:* Faulkner, W. Sem' rasskazov [Seven stories]. Moscow, 1958. p. 162-178.
Orlova, R. and L. Kopelev. Mify i pravda amerikanskogo Iuga. (Zametki o tvorchestve Folknera) [The myths and truth of the American South. (Remarks on Faulkner's writings)]. Inostrannaia literatura, 1958, no. 3, p. 206-220.
1959 Kashkin, I. Ob avtore [Concerning the author]. *In:* Faulkner, W. Podzhigatel' [Barn burning—i.e. *Light in August?*]. Moscow, 1959. p. 3-6.
Proshchanie so Snoupsami [A farewell to the Snopes]. (*The Hamlet. The Town. The Mansion.*) Literaturnaia gazeta, December 17, 1959.
1960 Izakov, B. Miatushchaiasia dusha [A restless spirit]. Moskva, 1960, no. 2, p. 97-98.
1961 Louson, D. G. [Lawson, J. H.?]. Uil'iam Folkner [William Faulkner]. Inostrannaia literatura, 1961, no. 9, p. 178-186.
1962 Nedelin, V. Review of: *The Reivers*. New York, 1962. Sovremennaia khudozhestvennaia literatura za rubezhom, 1962, no. 9-10, p. 61-64.
Levidova, I. Saga o sumrachnoi dinastii [A saga about a gloomy dynasty]. ("Osobniak" ["The mansion"]). Novyi mir, 1962, no. 7, p. 265-269.
Palievskii, P. Chelovek pobedit [Man is victorious]. Literaturnaia gazeta, July 10, 1962.
Startsev, A. Znakomstvo s Folknerom [An acquaintance with Faulkner]. ("Osobniak" ["The mansion"]). Literaturnaia gazeta, March 13, 1962.
Shoshitaishvili, Z. Pamiati Uil'iama Folknera [In memory of William Faulkner]. Literaturnaia Gruziia (Tbilisi), 1962, no. 8, p. 73-74.
1963 V. N. Review of: Hoffman, F. and O. Vickery, eds. *William Faulkner: Three Decades of Criticism*. 1960; Hoffman, F. *William Faulkner*.

New York, 1961. Sovremennaia khudozhestvennaia literatura za rubezhom, 1963, no. 2, p. 64-67.

Mendel'son, M. Ad na zemle i Uil'iam Folkner. [Hell on earth and William Faulkner]. Voprosy literatury, 1963, no. 9, p. 129-155.

FITSDZHERALD Frensis Skott   FITZGERALD Francis Scott

1957 Oldridzh, Dzh. [Aldridge, J.]. Razdum'ia o sud'bakh molodezhi na Zapade [Thoughts about the fate of youth in the West]. Literaturnaia gazeta, May 16, 1957.

1960 Landor, M. Tragediia amerikanskogo pisatelia [The tragedy of an American writer]. (Mizener, A. *The Far Side of Paradise. A Biography of F. Scott Fitzgerald.* New York, 1959.) Voprosy literatury, 1960, no. 10, p. 224-230.

FORSAIT Robert   FORSYTHE Robert (CRICHTON Kyle S.)

1936 Karmon, U. [Carmon, W.?]. Robert Forsait—amerikanskii satirik [Robert Forsythe—an American satirist]. Internatsional'naia literatura, 1936, no. 9, p. 160-162.

FRENK Uoldo   FRANK Waldo David

1928 Lann, E. Literatura sovremennoi Ameriki. Val'do Frenk [The literature of contemporary America. Waldo Frank]. Novyi mir, 1928, no. 2, p. 237-249.

1932 Abramov, A. Novaia kniga amerikanskogo pisatelia Uoldo Frenka [A new book by the American writer Waldo Frank]. (*Dawn in Russia.* New York, 1932). Literaturnaia gazeta, October 17, 1932.

Izakov. "Voskhod v Rossii." Novaia kniga Val'do Franka ["Dawn in Russia." The new book by Waldo Frank]. Pravda, December 28, 1932.

1935 Dmitrievskii, Vl. Rozhdenie revoliutsionnogo pisatelia [The birth of a revolutionary writer]. Internatsional'naia literatura, 1935, no. 10, p. 137-141.

Lann, E. Uoldo Frenk [Waldo Frank]. 30—i.e. Tridtsat'—dnei, 1935, no. 8, p. 49. (Signed: E. L.)

Lann, E. Uoldo Frenk [Waldo Frank]. Literaturnaia gazeta, October 20, 1935.

Lann, E. Essei ob Uoldo Frenke [An essay about Waldo Frank]. Internatsional'naia literatura, 1935, no. 12, p. 69-85.

Polemika Uoldo Frenka s Mal'kolmom Kauli. ("Smert' i rozhdenie Davida Markenda." Moscow, 1936 [*sic*]) [The polemics between Waldo Frank and Malcolm Cowley. ("The death and birth of David

Markand." Moscow, 1936)]. Internatsional'naia literatura, 1935, no. 3, p. 140-142.

Startsev, A. Uoldo Frenk [Waldo Frank]. Izvestiia, August 15, 1935.

1936 Abramov, A. Review of: Smert' i rozhdenie Devida Markenda [The death and birth of David Markand]. Moscow, 1936. Internatsional'naia literatura, 1936, no. 12, p. 205-207.

Dinamov, S. Poslednii roman Uoldo Frenka [Waldo Frank's latest novel]. *In:* Frank, W. Smert' i rozhdenie Devida Markenda [The death and birth of David Markand]. Moscow, 1936. p. 543-558. *Also, abridged, in:* Frank, W. Smert' i rozhdenie Devida Markenda [The death and birth of David Markand]. Moscow, Zhurgiz, 1936. p. 3-5.

Dinamov, S. Roman o krizise burzhuaznogo soznaniia. ("Smert' i rozhdenie Devida Markenda") [A novel about the crisis in the bourgeois soul. ("The death and birth of David Markand")]. Oktiabr', 1936, no. 3, p. 207-215.

Nemerovskaia, O. Navstrechu realizmu. ("Smert' i rozhdenie Devida Markenda") [Toward realism. ("The death and birth of David Markand")]. Literaturnyi Leningrad, June 6, 1936.

Startsev, A. Review of: Smert' i rozhdenie Devida Markenda [The death and birth of David Markand.]. Literaturnoe obozrenie, 1936, no. 10, p. 29-31.

Eishiskina, N. Smert' i rozhdenie Devida Markenda [The death and birth of David Markand]. Literaturnaia gazeta, February 29, 1936.

1937 Chakovskii, A. Review of: Smert' i rozhdenie Devida Markenda [The death and birth of David Markand]. Kniga i proletarskaia revoliutsiia, 1937, no. 5, p. 152-153.

FRANKLIN Bendzhamin   FRANKLIN Benjamin

1790 Nekrolog [Obituary]. Sanktpeterburgskie vedomosti, 1790, no. 50, June 21, p. 817.

1799 Turgenev, A. Zhizn' Franklinova [Franklin's life]. *In:* Franklin, B. Otryvok iz zapisok Franklinovykh... [Selection from the writings of Franklin...]. Translated from the French by A. N. Turgenev. Moscow, 1799. p. 3-15. (Signed: A. T.)

1830 Zhizn' Franklina [The life of Franklin]. *In:* Franklin, B. Uchenie Risharda Dobrodushnogo, ili, Sposob platit' nalogi [The teaching of Richard the Good-natured, or, A way to pay taxes]. Moscow, 1830. p. iii-iv. (Signed: Perevodchik [Translator].)

Glinka, S. Preduvedomlenie (k publikatsii perevoda "Nauka dobrogo Rikharda") [A word of introduction (to the publication of a translation of "The science of Goodman Richard")]. *In:* Moskovskii al'manakh dlia iunykh russkikh grazhdan... [Moscow almanac for young Russian citizens...]. Moscow, 1830. p. iii-viii.

1862 Rostovskaia M. Ven'iamin Franklin. Rasskaz dlia iunoshestva [Benjamin Franklin. A story for youth]. St. Petersburg, Vol'f, 1862. 116 p. 2nd ed., 1906.

1863 Min'e, F. O. Zhizn' Franklina [The life of Franklin]. St. Petersburg, 1863. 114 p. *Also:* Moscow, 1870. 169 p.

1888 Benzhamen Franklin (1706-1790) [Benjamin Franklin, 1706-1790]. Moscow,Obshchestvo dlia rasprostraneniia poleznykh knig,1888.35 p.
Demulen, G. Franklin [Franklin]. Kursk, 1888. 33 p.

1891 Abramov, Ia. V. Franklin, ego zhizn', obshchestvennaia i nauchnaia deiatel'nost' [Franklin, his life, social, public and scientific activity]. St. Petersburg, 1891, 79 p.

1892 Munt-Valueva, A. P. Ven'iamin Franklin [Benjamin Franklin]. 2nd ed. St. Petersburg, 1892. 50 p. *Review:* Iv. F. Vospitanie i obuchenie, 1892, no. 11, p. 418. 3rd ed. 1895.

1898 Sleptsov, A. A. Veniamin Franklin [Benjamin Franklin]. 2nd ed. St. Petersburg, 1898. 92 p. (Author's pseudonym: P. Korsunskii.) *Other editions:* 1905, 1913.

1904 Annenskaia, A. N. Detstvo i iunost' Ven'iamina Franklina [Childhood and youth of Benjamin Franklin]. 2nd ed. St. Petersburg, 1904. 258 p.
Voronova, Z. L. Franklin—tipograf [Franklin the printer]. St. Petersburg, 1904. 52 p.

1934 Vladimirov, V. N. Franklin [Franklin]. Moscow, Zhurnal'no-gazetnoe ob"edinenie, 1934. 224 p.

1940 Startsev, A. Veniamin Franklin i russkoe obshchestvo XVIII veka [Benjamin Franklin and Russian society of the 18th century]. Internatsional'naia literatura, 1940, no. 3-4, p. 208-221.

1941 Radovskii, M. I. Veniamin Franklin. Kratkii biograficheskii ocherk [Benjamin Franklin. A short biographical sketch]. Moscow, Leningrad, Gosenergoizdat, 1941. 80 p.

1955 Baskin, M. P. Vydaiushchiisia amerikanskii myslitel' [An outstanding American thinker]. Voprosy filosofii, 1955, no. 6, p. 70-80.

1956 Baskin, M. P. Veniamin Franklin [Benjamin Franklin]. *In:* Franklin, B. Izbrannye proizvedeniia [Selected works]. Moscow, 1956. p. 5-50.
Beliavskaia, I. A. B. Franklin—deiatel' natsional'no-osvoboditel'nogo dvizheniia amerikanskogo naroda [B. Franklin, a leader in the national liberation struggle of the American people]. Voprosy literatury, 1956, no. 10, p. 32-45.
Efimov, A. V. Obshchestvennaia deiatel'nost' Veniamina Franklina [The public activity of Benjamin Franklin]. Vestnik Akademii nauk SSSR, 1956, no. 3, p. 86-96.
Kapitsa, P. L. 250—i.e. Dvesti piat'desiat'—let so dnia rozhdeniia Veniamina Franklina [250 years since the birth of Benjamin Franklin]. Pravda, January 17,1956.
Kuznetsov, I. Veniamin Franklin—vydaiushchiisia amerikanskii uche-

nyi i obshchestvennyi deiatel' [Benjamin Franklin—an outstanding American scholar and public figure]. Kommunist, 1956, no. 1, p. 109-118.

Naidenov, N. Veniamin Franklin [Benjamin Franklin]. Sovetskaia kul'tura, January 17, 1956.

Radovskii, M. I. Avtograf Veniamina Franklina [An autograph by Benjamin Franklin]. Istoricheskii arkhiv, 1956, no. 4, p. 259-260.

Radovskii, M. Novye materialy o Veniamine Frankline [New materials about Benjamin Franklin]. Novoe vremia, 1956, no. 10, p. 31.

Sotin, B. S. Bendzhamin Franklin [Benjamin Franklin]. Nauka i zhizn', 1956, no. 1, p. 59-60.

Startsev, A. Franklin [Franklin]. Inostrannaia literatura, 1956, no. 1, p. 172-176.

Stekol'nikov, I. Veniamin Franklin [Benjamin Franklin]. Izvestiia, January 17, 1956.

Franklin, B. Avtobiografiia [Autobiography]. In: Franklin, B. Izbrannye proizvedeniia [Selected works]. Moscow, 1956. p. 418-554.

1957 Radovskii, M. I. Russko-amerikanskie nauchnye sviazi v 18-19 vv. (Franklin i sovremennye emu russkie uchenye) [Russo-American scholarly ties in the 18th and 19th centuries. (Franklin and his contemporary Russian scholars)]. Vestnik istorii mirovoi kul'tury, 1957, no. 2, p. 100-106.

1958 Radovskii, M. I. Veniamin Franklin i ego sviazi s Rossiei [Benjamin Franklin and his ties with Russia]. Moscow, Leningrad, Izdatel'stvo Akademii nauk SSSR, 1958. 76 p.

FROST ROBERT   FROST ROBERT

1960 Stikhi Roberta Frosta. (Predislovie k perevodam) [The poems of Robert Frost. (Foreword to translations)]. Literaturnaia gazeta, March 3, 1960.

1962 Kashkin, I. Dva stikhotvoreniia Roberta Frosta. (K publikatsii) [Two poems by Robert Frost. (On their publication)]. Ogonek, 1962, no. 38, p. 28.

Kashkin, I. Robert Frost [Robert Frost]. Inostrannaia literatura, 1962, no. 10, p. 195-201.

Levonevskii, D. Robert Frost v Pushkinskom Dome [Robert Frost in the Pushkinskii Dom (of the Academy of Sciences)]. Literatura i zhizn', September 7, 1962.

Surkov, A. Molodoe serdtse poeta [The young heart of a poet]. Pravda, September 10, 1962.

Surkov, A. Otkrytoe pis'mo amerikanskomu poetu Robertu Frostu [An open letter to the American poet Robert Frost]. Inostrannaia literatura, 1962, no. 11, p. 7-9.

Zenkevich, M. Robert Frost i ego poeziia [Robert Frost and his poetry]. *In:* Frost, R. Iz deviati knig [From nine books]. Moscow, 1962. p. 5-10.

1963 Kashkin, I. Review of: *You Come Too.* New York, 1962. Sovremennaia khudozhestvennaia literatura za rubezhom, 1963, no. 1, p. 78-80.

Robert Frost. Sobstvennyi golos [Robert Frost. His own voice]. Za rubezhom, 1963, no. 5, p. 24.

Sergeev, A. Pamiati Roberta Frosta [In memory of Robert Frost]. Literaturnaia Rossiia, February 1, 1963.

Simonov, K. Pamiati Roberta Frosta [In memory of Robert Frost]. Literaturnaia gazeta, January 31, 1963.

Surkov, A. Velikii poet [A great poet]. Izvestiia, January 31, 1963.

Khrushchev, N. S. Vydaiushchiisia poet i grazhdanin SShA. Sem'e Roberta L. Frosta. 29 ianvaria 1963 goda [An outstanding poet and citizen of the US. To the family of Robert L. Frost. January 29, 1963]. *In:* Khrushchev, N. S. Vysokoe prizvanie literatury i iskusstva [The high calling of literature and art]. Moscow, 1963. p. 245.

FULLER Genri Bleik   FULLER Henry Blake

1957 Samokhvalov, N. I. Genri Fuller—znamenosets amerikanskogo kriticheskogo realizma kontsa XIX veka [Henry Fuller—standard-bearer of American critical realism of the end of the 19th century]. Uchenye zapiski Krasnodarskogo pedagogicheskogo instituta, 1957, vyp. 21. Kafedra russkoi i zarubezhnoi literatury, p. 216-245.

1959 Samokhvalov, N. Predislovie [Foreword]. *In:* Fuller, G. Padenie Ebnera Dzhoisa [The downfall of Abner Joyce]. Moscow, 1959. p. 3-18.

Nedelin, V. Review of: Padenie Ebnera Dzhoisa [The downfall of Abner Joyce]. Moscow, 1959. Inostrannaia literatura, 1960, no. 5, p. 259.

FULLER Sara Margaret   FULLER Sarah Margaret

1852 Zapiski Margarity Fuller Ossoli [The notebooks of Margaret Fuller Ossoli]. Biblioteka dlia chteniia, 1852, t. 115, otd. VII, p. 192-199.

Zapiski Margarity Foller Ossoli [The notebooks of Margaret Fuller Ossoli]. Otechestvennye zapiski, 1852, no. 3 (otd. VIII), p. 103-105.

Margarita Foller [Margaret Fuller]. Panteon, 1852, t. VI, no. 12, otd. IV, p. 1-14.

1925 Dinamov, S. Review of: Prokliatyi agitator [Damned agitator[1]]. Moscow, 1925. Knigonosha, 1925, no. 18, p. 13.

Zonin, A. Review of: Prokliatyi agitator [Damned agitator[1]]. Moscow, 1925. Oktiabr', 1925, no. 3-4, p. 241-242.

Kheivud, V. [Haywood, W.]. Predislovie [Foreword]. *In:* Gold, M. Prokliatyi agitator [Damned agitator[1]]. Moscow, 1925. p. 5-8.

1928 Dinamov, S. Pisatel' revoliutsionnoi Ameriki, Maikl Gold [A writer of revolutionary America, Michael Gold]. Vestnik inostrannoi literatury, 1928, no. 6, p. 139-141. (Signed: D.)

1930 Aleksandrov, G. Review of: 120—i.e. Stodvadtsat'—millionov [120 million]. Moscow, Leningrad, 1930. Molodaia gvardiia, 1930, no. 22, 108-109.

Ippolit, N. Review of: 120—i.e. Stodvadtsat'—millionov [120 million]. Moscow, Leningrad, 1930. Kniga i revoliutsiia, 1930, no. 23-24, p. 70-71.

Levit, T. Novyi zhanr? (Evrei bez deneg) [A new genre? (Jews without money)]. Vestnik inostrannoi literatury, 1930, no. 2, p. 201-203. (Signed: T. L.)

Maikl Gold [Michael Gold]. Literatura i iskusstvo, 1930, no. 2, p. 118-119.

1931 Aleksandrov, G. Predislovie [Foreword]. *In:* Gold, M. Evreiskaia bednota [The Jewish poor—i.e. *Jews Without Money*]. Moscow, Leningrad, 1931. p. 3-7.

Aleksandrov, G. Review of: Evreiskaia bednota [The Jewish poor—i.e. *Jews Without Money*]. Moscow, 1931. Molodaia gvardiia, 1931, no. 11-12, p. 111.

Barsukov, N. and E. Riabchikov. Proletarskii shturm. O Maikle Golde [The proletarian attack. Concerning Michael Gold]. Natisk, 1931, no. 5-7, p. 86-89.

Vetrov, I.—Knizhnik-Vetrov. Review of: 120—i.e. Stodvadtsat'—millionov [120 million]. Moscow, Leningrad, 1931. Zvezda, 1931, no. 1, p. 235-236. (Signed: I. N.)

Kal'verton [Calverton], V. F. Tvorchestvo Maikl Golda [The work of Michael Gold]. Literaturnaia gazeta, June 30, 1931.

Levit, T. Review of: Evreiskaia bednota [The Jewish poor—i.e. *Jews Without Money*]. Krasnaia nov', 1931, no. 5-6, p. 244-245.

Levit, T. Review of: 120—i.e. Stodvadtsat'—millionov [120 million]. Moscow, Leningrad, 1931. Literatura i iskusstvo, 1931, no. 2-3, p. 201-202. (Signed: T. L.)

Startsev, A. Maikl Gold [Michael Gold]. Na literaturnom postu, 1931, no. 12, p. 22-26.

---

[1] Original English title not known.

1932 Ridnik, V. Review of: Evreiskaia bednota [The Jewish poor—i.e. *Jews Without Money*]. Moscow, 1931. Na pod"eme, 1932, no. 3, p. 154-156.

Eishiskina, N. "Evrei bez deneg" M. Golda ["Jews without money" of M. Gold]. Marksistsko-leninskoe iskusstvoznanie, 1932, no. 5-6, p. 173-176.

1933 Karmon, U. [Carmon, W.]. Rabota s Maikl Goldom [Working with Michael Gold]. Internatsional'naia literatura, 1933, no. 5, p. 131-133.

Eishiskina, N. Novyi etap tvorchestva Maikla Golda [A new stage in the work of Michael Gold]. Internatsional'naia literatura, 1933, no. 5, p. 119-123.

1934 Maikl Gold [Michael Gold]. Za rubezhom, 1934, no. 18, p. 9.

1936 Balashov, P. Review of: Gold, M. and M. Blenkfort [Blankfort]. Dzhon Braun [John Brown—i.e. *Battle Hymn*]. 1936. Za rubezhom, 1936, no. 17, p. 386.

1937 Balashov, P. Review of: Gold, M. and M. Blenkfort [Blankfort]. Dzhon Brown [John Brown—i.e. *Battle Hymn*]. Moscow, 1937. Literaturnoe obozrenie, 1937, no. 16, p. 45-48.

Del'man. Review of: Gold, M. and M. Blenkfort [Blankfort]. Dzhon Brown [John Brown—i.e. *Battle Hymn*]. Moscow, 1937. Literaturnaia gazeta, August 5, 1937.

Elistratova, A. Review of: *Change the World*. New York, 1936. Internatsional'naia literatura, 1937, no. 5, p. 224. (Signed: A. E.)

K'iunits, D. [Kunitz, J.]. Posleslovie [Afterword]. *In:* Gold, M. and M. Blenkroft [Blancroft[1]]. Dzhon Brown [John Brown—i.e. *Battle Hymn*]. Moscow, 1937. p. 129-133.

1941 Karmon, U. [Carmon, W.]. Maikl Gold i "N'iu messes" 1911-1916-1941 [Michael Gold and the *New Masses*, 1911-1916-1941]. Internatsional'naia literatura, 1941, no. 5, p. 216-218.

Iubilei Maikla Golda [The jubilee of Michael Gold]. Internatsional'naia literatura, 1941, no. 3, p. 180-181.

1955 Levidova, I. Iubileinyi sbornik Maikla Golda [A jubilee collection of the work of Michael Gold]. (*The Mike Gold Reader*. New York, 1954). Inostrannaia literatura, 1955, no. 1, p. 269.

GOU Dzheims   GOW James

1946 Anisimov, I. Amerikanskaia p'esa o rasovoi diskriminatsii (Glubokie korni) [An American play about racial discrimination (Deep roots—i.e. *Deep Are the Roots*)]. Pravda, August 9, 1946.

1947 Al'tman, I. Brett Charlz i "drugie" ("Glubokie korni") [Brett Charles and the "others" ("Deep roots"—i.e. *Deep Are the Roots*)]. Literaturnaia Gazeta, May 1, 1947.

Zhukov, Iu. Gluboki korni! ("Glubokie korni") [The roots *are* deep! ("Deep roots"—i.e. *Deep Are the Roots*)]. Pravda, April 27, 1947.

Maliugin, L. Globokie korni ("Glubokie korni") [Deep roots ("Deep are the roots")]. Sovetskoe iskusstvo, May 1, 1947.

Riurikov, B. Razoblachennaia idilliia ("Glubokie korni") [The unmasked idyll ("Deep are the roots")]. Teatr, 1947, no. 6, p. 7-17.

Surkov, E. Sorvannye maski. P'esa amerikanskikh dramaturgov D. Gou i A. d'Iusso "Glubokie korni" na sovetskoi stsene [The masks ripped off. The play of the American playwrights J. Gow and A. D'Usseau "Deep Are the Roots" on the Soviet stage]. Izvestiia, July 17, 1947.

Suchkov, B. Razoblachennaia legenda ("Glubokie korni") [An unveiled legend ("Deep are the roots")]. Kul'tura i zhizn', April 30, 1947.

1951 Kornilova, E. Predislovie [Foreword]. *In:* Gou, Dzh. and A. d'Iusso [Gow, J. and A. d'Usseau]. Glubokie korni [Deep are the roots]. Moscow, 1951. p. 3-6.

GREKHEM Shirli   GRAHAM Shirley

1960 Filatova, L. "Chelovek s diplomom na spine." ("Frederik Duglas." Moscow, 1959) ["A man with a diploma on his back" ["Frederick Douglass"—i.e. *There Was Once a Slave*. Moscow, 1959)]. Molodaia gvardiia, 1960, no. 3, p. 235-236.

1962 Bekker, M. Predislovie [Foreword]. *In:* Graham, Sh. Vash pokornyi sluga [Your humble servant—i.e. *Your Most Humble Servant*]. Moscow, 1962. p. 5-12.

KHALPER Al'bert   HALPER Albert

1935 Kholper, A. [Halper, A.]. Avtobiografiia [Autobiography]. Internatsional'naia literatura, 1935, no. 7, p. 133.

1937 Balashov, P. Review of: Slovolitnia [The type-foundry—i.e. *The Foundry*]. Moscow, 1937. Literaturnoe obozrenie, 1937, no. 13, p. 20-23.

Balashov, P. Al'bert Khalper.—"Slovolitnia" [Albert Halper.—"The type-foundry"—i.e. *The Foundry*]. Internatsional'naia literatura, 1937, no. 5, p. 229.

GART Frensis Bret   HARTE Francis Bret

1873 (Bret-Gart) [Bret Harte]. Vestnik evropy, 1873, no. 10, p. 599-601.

Predislovie k "Kalifornskim argonavtam" [Foreword to "The California argonauts"]. Delo, 1873, no. 10, p. 76-79.

Sreznevskaia, O. I. Bret-Gart [Bret Harte]. Russkii vestnik, 1873, no. 9, p. 352-368. (Signed: O. S.)

1874 Bret Gart [Bret Harte]. Niva, 1874, no. 15, p. 238-239.

N. V. Obrazchik sovremennoi khudozhestvennosti [A model of contemporary literature]. (Review of: Rasskazy, ocherki, legendy [Tales, essays, legends]. St. Petersburg, 1874). Delo, 1874, no. 3, otd. II, p. 21-27.

1880 Bret-Gart. (Biograficheskii ocherk) [Bret Harte. (Biographical sketch)]. Ogonek, 1880, no. 31, p. 584-585.

Review of: *The Twins of Table Mountain and Other Stories*. Ezhenedel'noe novoe vremia, 1880, t. 5, no. 61, p. 575-576.

1887 Razmadze, A. S. Bret-Gart. (Biograficheskii ocherk) [Bret Harte. (Biographical sketch)]. *In:* Harte, B. Kaliforniiskie rasskazy [California tales]. Moscow, 1887, p. iii-xiv. (Signed: A. R.)

1891 Frensis Bret-Gart [Francis Bret Harte]. Novosti inostrannoi literatury, 1891, no. 10, p. 10-11.

1894 Literaturnyi debiut Bret-Garta [Bret Harte's literary debut]. Knizhki nedeli, 1894, no. 7, p. 247-248.

1895 Iz literaturnykh priznanii 22 avtorov. Frensis Bret-Gart [From the literary confessions of 22 authors. Francis Bret Harte]. Vestnik inostrannoi literatury, 1895, no. 1, p. 19-23.

Koialovich, M. Poet Kalifornii. Literaturnyi eskiz [A poet of California. A literary sketch]. Vestnik inostrannoi literatury, 1895, no. 8, p. 99-106.

Review of: Sobranie sochinenii [Collected works]. St. Petersburg, 1895. Russkaia mysl', 1895, no. 8 (2nd pagination), p. 376-379.

Chuiko, V. Frensis Bret-Gart [Francis Bret Harte]. *In:* Harte, Bret. Sobranie sochinenii [Collected works]. v. 1. St. Petersburg, 1895. p. vii-xxiv.

1899 Bret-Gart [Bret Harte]. Literaturnye vechera "Novogo mira," 1899, no. 11, p. 173-174.

1901 Press, A. Frensis Bret-Gart. Kharakteristika [Francis Bret Harte. A character sketch]. *In:* Press, A. Pisateli XIX veka [Writers of the 19th century]. v. 1. St. Petersburg, 1901. p. 120-153. 2nd ed.: V tsarstve knig [In the world of books]. St. Petersburg, 1908. p. 155-178.

1902 Baturinskii, V. Poet vseproshcheniia [A poet of universal forgiveness]. Novoe delo, 1902, no. 6, p. 123-138.

Bret-Gart [Bret Harte]. (Obituary). Vestnik inostrannoi literatury, 1902, no. 6, p. 349-351.

Bykov, P. V. Poet Kalifornii (Bret-Gart). Ocherk. [The poet of California (Bret Harte). Essay]. Sever, 1902, no. 45, col. 1429-1436.

Lovtsova, M. Frensis Bret-Gart [Francis Bret Harte]. Iunyi chitatel', 1902, no. 12, p. 104-106. (Signed: M. L.)

(Obituary). Istoricheskii vestnik, 1902, p. 1136-1137.

Frensis Bret-Gart [Francis Bret Harte]. Novyi zhurnal inostrannoi literatury, 1902, no. 6 (2nd pagination), p. 329-332. *See also:* Plutarkh xix veka [Plutarch of the 19th century]. v. 1. St. Petersburg, 1902. p. 139-140.

1905 G. K. Review of: Kaliforniiskie rasskazy [California tales]. St. Petersburg, 1905. Pravda, 1905, no. 2, p. 162-164.

S. Foreword to: Harte, Bret. Kaliforniiskie rasskazy [California tales]. St. Petersburg, 1905. p. 3-4.

1909 Poet amerikanskoi demokratii [A poet of American democracy]. Novyi zhurnal literatury, iskusstva i nauki, 1909, no. 1, p. 76-80.

1915 E. K. Frensis Bret-Gart. Biograficheskii ocherk [Francis Bret Harte. Biographical sketch]. *In:* Harte, Bret. Sobranie sochinenii [Collected works]. Moscow, 1915. p. 3-8.

1925 Dinamov, S. Review of: Iskateli zolota [The goldseekers]. Moscow, 1925. Knigonosha, 1925, no. 11, p. 16. (Signed: S. D.)

1927 Kulle, R. Bret-Gart (1837-1902) [Bret Harte (1837-1902)]. Krasnaia panorama, 1927, no. 42, p. 13-14. *See also:* Literaturnye sredy (prilozhenie k "Krasnoi gazete"), 1927, no. 25, p. 6.

1928 Grossman, L. P. Frensis Bret-Gart [Francis Bret Harte]. *In:* Harte, Bret. Polnoe sobranie sochinenii [Complete collected works]. Leningrad, 1928. v. 1, p. i-xii.

Uzin, V. S. F. Bret-Gart [F. Bret Harte]. *In:* Harte, Bret. Schast'e Revushchego Stana [The Luck of Roaring Camp]. Moscow, 1928. p. 3-9.

Shchegolev, P. E. N. G. Chernyshevskii o Bret Garte (s publikatsiei pis'ma Chernyshevskogo) [N. G. Chernyshevskii on Bret Harte (with the publication of a letter from Chernyshevskii)]. *In:* Literaturno-khudozhestvennyi sbornik "Krasnoi Panoramy," 1928, December, p. 53-55. *See also:* Chernyshevskii, N. G. Polnoe sobranie sochinenii [Complete collected works]. v. 15. Moscow, 1950, p. 228-242. (Including publication of a translation of "Miggles").

1939 Startsev, A. Bret-Gart i kaliforniiskie zolotoiskateli [Bret Harte and the California goldseekers]. *In:* Harte, Bret. Kaliforniiskie povesti [California tales]. Moscow, 1939. p. 3-59.

1941 Tven, M. [Mark Twain]. Bret-Gart [Bret Harte]. Internatsional'naia literatura, 1941, no. 11-12, p. 265-277. *See also:* Mark Twain. Sobranie sochinenii [Collected works]. v. 12. Moscow, 1961. p. 290-301.

1945 Startsev, A. Predislovie. Chernyshevskii o Bret Garte [Foreword. Chernyshevskii on Bret Harte]. *In:* Harte, Bret. Schast'e Revushchego Stana i drugie rasskazy [The Luck of Roaring Camp and other tales]. Moscow, 1945. p. 1-7, 296-302.

1956 Glikman, I. Frensis Bret-Gart [Francis Bret Harte]. *In:* Harte, Bret. Izbrannye proizvedeniia [Selected works]. Moscow, 1956. p. iii-xxiv. *Another edition:* Moscow, Leningrad, 1960. p. 3-24.

1958 Lidskii, Iu. Ia. Realisticheskaia novella Bret Garta [The realistic short story of Bret Harte]. Trudy molodykh uchenykh, Kievskii meditsinskii (*sic*) institut, 1958, p. 394-399.

1961 Lidskii, Iu. Pisatel'-realist Bret Gart [Bret Harte, a realistic writer]. Kiev, Akademiia nauk Ukrainskoi SSR, 1961. 72 p.

Lidskii, Iu. Ia. Realisticheskii rasskaz Bret Garta [The realistic tale of Bret Harte]. Abstract of dissertation presented for the degree of Candidate of Philological Sciences. Kiev, 1961. 15 p.

Tven, M. [Mark Twain]. (Bret-Gart) [Bret Harte]. *In:* Tven, M. Sobranie sochinenii [Collected works]. v. 12. Moscow, 1961. p. 355-377.

GOTORN Nataniel'[1]   HAWTHORNE Nathaniel

1852 Vmesto predisloviia [In place of a foreword]. *In:* Gotorn [Hawthorne], N. Dom o semi shpiliakh [The house of the seven spires — i.e. *The House of the Seven Gables*]. St. Petersburg, 1852. p. 3-8. (*Supplement to:* Sovremennik, 1852, no. 9, 10).

1854 Review of: *Twice-Told Tales. The Scarlet Letter.* Otechestvennye zapiski, 1854, no. 4, otd. VII, p. 101-102.

1860 Mikhailov, M. I. Amerikanskie poety i romanisty. (Gotorn) [American poets and novelists. (Hawthorne)]. Sovremennik, 1860, no. 10, otd. III, p. 217-232. (Signed: —X—.)

Chernyshevskii, N. G. Sobranie chudes, povesti, zaimstvovannye iz mifologii. Sochinenie amerikanskogo pisatelia Natanielia Gotorna. (A collection of wonders. Tales borrowed from mythology. The work of the American writer Nathaniel Hawthorne — i.e. A *Wonder Book*]. St. Petersburg, 1860. Sovremennik, 1860, no. 6, otd. III, p. 230-245. *See also:* Chernyshevskii, N. G. Polnoe sobranie sochinenii [Complete collected works]. v. 7. Moscow, 1950. p. 440-453.

1864 Angliia s tochki zreniia amerikantsa [England from the point of view of an American]. (*Our Old Home*). London, 1863. Otechestvennye zapiski, 1864, no. 5, p. 203-223.

Smert' Gotorna. Kratkii ocherk ego zhizni. [The death of Hawthorne. A short sketch of his life]. Zagranichnyi vestnik, 1864, t. 2, no. 6, p. 568-570.

1872 Nataniel' Gotorn, izvestnyi amerikanskii romanist [Nathaniel Hawthorne, the noted American novelist]. Syn otechestva (Literaturnoe prilozhenie), 1872, no. 7, p. 92-98, no. 8, p. 108-112.

1879 Kenel', L. Amerikanskie romanisty. Nataniel' Gotorn. [American novelists. Nathaniel Hawthorne]. Ezhenedel'noe novoe vremia, 1879, t. IV, no. 40, p. 51-59. *See also:* Chitatel', 1898, no. 4, p. 149-160.

---

[1] Also transliterated as "Khotorn" in Soviet works of reference.

1897 Review of: Kniga chudes [A book of wonders—i.e. *A Wonder Book*]. St. Petersburg, 1897. Revel'skie izvestiia, February 23, 1897.

1900 Nataniel' Gotorn [Nathaniel Hawthorne]. *In:* Hawthorne, N. Fantasticheskie rasskazy [Fantastic tales]. Moscow, 1900. p. i-viii.

1912 Maevskii, I. Nataniel' Khautorn. 1804-1864 [Nathaniel Hawthorne, 1804-1864]. *In:* Hawthorne, N. Sobranie sochinenii [Collected works]. v. 1. Moscow, 1912. p. ix-xiii. (Signed: I. M.)

1913 Maevskii, I. A. (Predislovie [Foreword]). *In:* Hawthorne, N. Sobranie sochinenii [Collected works]. v. 2. Moscow, 1913. p. 5-6.

1957 Levinton, A. Nataniel' Gotorn i ego roman "Alaia bukva" [Nathaniel Hawthorne and his novel "The Scarlet Letter"]. *In:* Hawthorne, N. Alaia bukva [The scarlet letter]. Moscow, 1957. p. iii-xxiv.

1958 Egorov, B. F. Kogo parodiroval N. G. Chernyshevskii v retsenzii na knigu N. Gotorna? [Whom did N. G. Chernyshevskii parody in the review of N. Hawthorne's book?]. *In:* Voprosy izucheniia russkoi literatury XI-XX vekov [Problems of the study of Russian literature of the 11th to 20th centuries]. Moscow, Leningrad, 1958. p. 321-322.

1959 Bel'skii, A. Predislovie [Foreword]. *In:* Hawthorne, N. *The Scarlet Letter*. Moscow, 1959. p. 3-17.

1963 Nikoliukin, A. Review of: Wagenknecht, E. *Nathaniel Hawthorne: Man and Writer*. New York, 1961. Sovremennaia khudozhestvennaia literatura za rubezhom, 1963, no. 4, p. 101-103.

KHEIVUD Vil'iam   HAYWOOD William D.

1932 Kheivud, B. [Haywood, W.]. Kniga Billia Kheivuda. Avtobiografiia Vil'iama D. Kheivuda [Bill Haywood's book. The autobiography of William D. Haywood]. Translated by D. Gorbov, with introductory article by N. Andreichik. Moscow, Leningrad, Gos. izd-vo khudozhestvennoi literatury, 1932. 358 p. *Reviews:* Zelinskii, K. Kniga "Bol'shogo Billia" ["'Big Bill's' book"]. Na literaturnom postu, 1932, no. 8, p. 20-23. *Also in:* Zelinskii, K. Kriticheskie pis'ma [Critical letters]. v. 2. Moscow, 1934. p. 79-87; Mazurin, B. Krasnaia nov', 1932, no. 6, p. 198-199.

KHERN Lafkadio   HEARN Lafcadio

1895 De Vorin'i [De Worigny?]. Neizvestnaia Iaponiia.—Lafkadio Girn [Unknown Japan—Lafcadio Hearn]. Mir bozhii, 1895, no. 10, p. 157-173.

1900 Buddiiskii pisatel' [A Buddhist writer]. Knizhki nedeli, 1900, no. 11, p. 269-270.

---

¹ A work in the English language published in the Soviet Union.

1905 V. K. Levkadio Khern o iapontsakh [Lafcadio Hearn on the Japanese]. Sem'ia, 1905, no. 13, p. 13.

1907 Gofmanstal', G. fon [Hofmannsthal, H. von]. O Lafkadio Kherne pod vpechatleniem izvestiia o ego smerti osen'iu 1904 goda [Concerning Lafcadio Hearn, under the impress of the news of his death in the autumn of 1904]. Russkaia mysl', 1907, no. 12, p. 150-151. *Also in:* Hearn, L. Dusha Iaponii [The soul of Japan]. Moscow, 1910. p. xv-xviii.

Lorie, S. Dusha Vostoka. Rasskazy iz iaponskoi zhizni Lafkadio Kherna [The soul of the East. Stories from Japanese life by Lafcadio Hearn]. Russkaia mysl', 1907, no. 12, p. 146-149. *Also, under title:* "Biograficheskie zametki" ["Biographical notes"] *in:* Hearn, L. Dusha Iaponii [The soul of Japan]. Moscow, 1910. p. v-xiv.

1910 Kostylev, N. Lafkadio Khern [Lafcadio Hearn]. Apollon, 1910, no. 11, p. 20-21.

1911 Lorie, S. Lafkadio Khern [Lafcadio Hearn]. *In:* Hearn, L. Iaponskie skazki [Japanese tales]. Moscow, 1911. p. 3-8.

1944 Chukovskii, K. Lafkadio Gern [Lafcadio Hearn]. *In:* Whitman, W. Izbrannye stikhotvoreniia i proza [Selected poetry and prose]. Moscow, 1944. p. 198-199.

KHEKT BEN   HECHT BEN

1927 Adonts, G. Review of: Genii naiznanku [A genius wrong-side out— i.e. *Count Bruga*]. Leningrad, 1927. Zhizn' iskusstva, 1927, no. 19, p. 12.

Dinamov, S. Amerikanskaia literatura i Ben Khekt. (Vmesto predisloviia k russkomu izdaniiu) [American literature and Ben Hecht. (In place of a preface to the Russian edition)]. *In:* Hecht, B. Igra v zhizn' [A game for life—original English title not determined]. Leningrad, 1927. p. 3-10.

Dinamov, S. Review of: Genii naiznanku [A genius wrong-side out— i.e. *Count Bruga*]. Leningrad, 1927. Pechat' i revoliutsiia, 1927, no. 6, p. 235-236.

Nikolaev, Ia. Review of: Igra v zhizn' [A game for life—original English title not determined]. Leningrad, 1927. Na literaturnom postu, 1927, no. 19, p. 81.

1928 Zhurbina, E. Pomes' zhurnalistiki i literatury. (1001—i.e. Tysiacha odin —den' v Chikago) [A mixture of journalism and literature. (1001 days in Chicago—i.e. *1001 Afternoons in Chicago*)]. Moscow, 1928. Zhurnalist, 1928, no. 5-6, p. 49.

Urban. Review of: 1001—i.e. Tysiacha odin—den' v Chikago [1001 days in Chicago—i.e. *1001 Afternoons in Chicago*]. Chitatel' i pisatel', April 7, 1928.

94

1940 Emel'ianov, B. S. Review of: Viva Vil'ia! [Viva Villa!]. Moscow, 1940. Literaturnaia gazeta, August 25, 1940.
1943 Trauberg, L. Kak sdelan stsenarii "Viva Vil'ia!" [How the scenario "Viva Villa!" was written]. Eisenshtein, S. Posleslovie [Afterword]. *In:* Hecht, B. Viva Vil'ia! [Viva Villa!]. Moscow, 1943. p. 3-30, 189-195.

KHELLMAN Lilian   HELLMAN Lillian

1945 Kruti, I. Sem'ia Ferelli obretaet muzhestvo. ("Sem'ia Ferelli teriaet pokoi.") [The Farrelly family gains courage. ("The Farrelly family loses its quiet"—i.e. *Watch on the Rhine*)]. Sovetskoe iskusstvo, March 8, 1945.
Kulakovskaia, T. Review of: Sem'ia Ferelli teriaet pokoi [The Farrelly family loses its quiet—i.e. *Watch on the Rhine*]. Ogonek, 1945, no. 12-13, p. 12.
Mendel'son, M. Khelman i Pristli na moskovskoi stsene [Hellman and Priestley on the Moscow stage]. Teatr, 1945, no. 2, p. 14-19.
1949 Afanas'ev, O. O "dobrykh" i "zlykh" plantatorakh. ("Ledi i dzhentl'-meny") [About "good" and "evil" planters. ("Ladies and gentle-men")]. Teatr, 1949, no. 12, p. 95-98.
Emel'ianov, B. Mnimoe razoblachenie. ("Ledi i dzhentl'meny") [A pretended unmasking. ("Ladies and gentlemen")]. Sovetskoe iskusstvo, November 12, 1949.
1955 Kulakovskaia, I. Lilian Khellman [Lillian Hellman]. Sovetskaia kul'tura, July 19, 1955.
1958 Obraztsova, A. Dramaturgiia Lilian Khellman [Lillian Hellman's dramas]. *In:* Hellman, L. P'esy [Plays]. Moscow, 1958. p. 3-25.
1960 Smirnov, B. A. Traditsii russkoi klassicheskoi dramy i dramaturgiia Lilian Hellman [The tradition of Russian classical drama and the plays of Lillian Hellman]. *In:* Zapiski o teatre [Notes about the theater]. Leningrad, Moscow, 1960. p. 284-305.
1961 Obraztsova, A. Slomannye igrushki. ("Igrushki na cherdake") [Broken toys. ("Toys in the attic")]. Teatr, 1961, no. 3, p. 186-188.

KHEMINGUEI Ernest   HEMINGWAY Ernest

1929 Gold, M. Poet belykh vorotnichkov. (Ernest Kheminguei)[A poet of the white-collar class. (Ernest Hemingway)]. Na literaturnom postu, 1929, no. 11-12, p. 101-103.
1934 Dos Passos, J. O masterstve ("Proshchai, oruzhie!") [Concerning mastery. ("A farewell to arms")]. Znamia, 1934, no. 4, p. 105-107.
Kashkin, I. Dve novelly Khemingueia [Two short stories by Hemingway]. Internatsional'naia literatura, 1934, no. 1, p. 92-93.

Kashkin, I. Pomni o... [Remember...]. Literaturnaia gazeta, October 18, 1934.

Kashkin, I. "Smert' posle poludnia." (Ernest Kheminguei) ["Death in the afternoon." (Ernest Hemingway)]. Literaturnyi kritik, 1934, no. 9, p. 121-148.

Kashkin, I. Ernest Kheminguei [Ernest Hemingway]. *In:* Hemingway, E. Smert' posle poludnia [Death in the afternoon]. Moscow, 1934. p. 3-29.

Trupnyi zapakh [An odor of corpses]. (*Winner Take Nothing.* New York, 1933). Literaturnaia gazeta, March 14, 1934.

Eishiskina, N. V poiskakh prostoty [In search of simplicity]. Literaturnaia gazeta, November 4, 1934.

1935 Garin, N. Posleslovie [Afterword]. *In:* Hemingway, E. Fiesta [Fiesta — i.e. *The Sun Also Rises*]. Moscow, 1935. p. 222-224.

Zundelovich, Ia. Zametki chitatelia na poliakh knigi rasskazov E. Khemingueia [A reader's notes on the margins of a book of stories by E. Hemingway]. Krasnaia nov', 1935, no. 5, 232-234.

Loks, K. Pogibshee pokolenie. ("Fiesta") [A lost generation. ("Fiesta" — i.e. *The Sun Also Rises*)]. Literaturnaia gazeta, December 15, 1935.

Rostov, P. Zamknutyi mir. ("Smert' posle poludnia") [A closed world. ("Death in the afternoon")]. Literaturnyi Donbass, 1935, no. 7, p. 94-97.

Startsev, A. Review of: Fiesta [Fiesta — i.e. *The Sun Also Rises*]. Moscow, 1935. Izvestiia, December 23, 1935.

Stoletov, A. Review of: Smert' posle poludnia [Death in the afternoon]. Moscow, 1934. Pod"em (Voronezh), 1935, no. 2, p. 134-135.

Eishiskina, N. Khudozhnik "poteriannogo pokoleniia" [An artist of the "lost generation"]. Khudozhestvennaia literatura, 1935, no. 4, p. 38-40.

1936 Admoni, V. Review of: Proshchai, oruzhie! [A farewell to arms]. Literaturnyi sovremennik, 1936, no. 12, p. 197-200.

Angarov, A. Tragediia patsifizma. ("Proshchai, oruzhie!") [The tragedy of pacifism. ("A farewell to arms")]. Izvestiia, October 8, 1936.

Dinamov, S. Roman Khemingueia o voine. ("Proshchai, oruzhie!") [Hemingway's book about the war. ("A farewell to arms")]. Internatsional'naia literatura, no. 7, p. 165-170. *Also, with additions and with title:* "Predislovie" [Foreword], *in:* Hemingway, E. Proshchai, oruzhie! [A farewell to arms]. Moscow, 1936. p. 5-19.

Novoselov, N. Review of: Proshchai, oruzhie! [A farewell to arms]. Literaturnoe obozrenie, 1936, no. 20, p. 8-12.

Olesha, Iu. Review of: Fiesta [Fiesta — i.e. *The Sun Also Rises*]. Moscow, 1935. Literaturnoe obozrenie, 1936, no. 1, p. 29-31.

Sil'man, T. "Proshchai, oruzhie!" Khemingueia [Hemingway's "A farewell to arms"]. Zvezda, 1936, no. 11, p. 171-178.

Sil'man, T. Review of: Fiesta [Fiesta—i.e. *The Sun Also Rises*]. Literaturnyi Leningrad, February 26, 1936.

Sil'man, T. Ernest Kheminguei. Obzor tvorchestva amerikanskogo pisatelia [Ernest Hemingway. A survey of the works of an American writer]. Literaturnyi sovremennik, 1936, no. 3, p. 172-182.

Uilson, E. [Wilson, Edmund?]. Pis'mo sovetskim chitateliam o Kheminguee [A letter to Soviet readers about Hemingway]. Internatsional'naia literatura, 1936, no. 2, p. 151-154.

1937 Grinberg, I. Chto zhe dal'she? ("Proshchai, oruzhie!") [What further? ("A farewell to arms")]. Zvezda, 1937, no. 3, p. 180-190.

Mendel'son, M. Review of: *To Have and Have Not*. New York, 1937. Za rubezhom, 1937, no. 35, p. 794.

Miller-Budnitskaia, R. Ernest Kheminguei [Ernest Hemingway]. Internatsional'naia literatura, 1937, no. 6, p. 209-219.

Mingulina, A. Ernest Kheminguei [Ernest Hemingway]. Kniga i proletarskaia revoliutsiia, 1937, no. 8, p. 122-125.

Nemerovskaia, O. Ernest Kheminguei [Ernest Hemingway]. Rezets, 1937, no. 2, p. 14-16.

1938 Anisimov, I. V Amerike. (E. Sinkler i E. Kheminguei) [In America. (U. Sinclair and E. Hemingway)]. Oktiabr', 1938, no. 11, p. 186-196.

Anisimov, I. Novaia kniga Khemingueia. ("Imet' i ne imet'") [Hemingway's new book. ("To have and have not")]. Literaturnaia gazeta, May 15, 1938.

Anisimov, I. Predislovie [Foreword]. *In:* Hemingway, E. Imet' i ne imet' [To have and have not]. Moscow, 1938. p. 3-12.

Grigor'ev, V. Tvorcheskii put' Khemingueia. ("Imet' i ne imet'") [Hemingway's creative path. ("To have and have not")]. Knigi i proletarskaia revoliutsiia, 1938, no. 10-11, p. 201-204.

Druzin, V. V poiskakh nastoiashchego cheloveka. ("Imet' i ne imet'") [In search of a real man. ("To have and have not")]. Rezets, 1938, no. 18, p. 22-23.

Elistratova, A. "Imet' i ne imet'." Novyi roman Ernesta Khemingueia ["To have and have not." The new novel by Ernest Hemingway]. Pravda, July 16, 1938.

Kauli [Cowley], M. Tvorcheskii rost Khemingueia [Hemingway's creative growth]. Internatsional'naia literatura, 1938, no. 4, p. 146-148.

Nemerovskaia, O. Novyi roman Khemingueia. ("Imet' i ne imet'") [Hemingway's new novel. ("To have and have not")]. Literaturnyi sovremennik, 1938, no. 9, p. 214-216.

Nemerovskaia, O. O poiskakh geroizma [Concerning searches for heroism]. Znamia, 1938, no. 6, p. 272-287.

Ot redaktsii. (Predislovie k romanu "Imet' i ne imet'") [From the editors. (Foreword to the novel "To have and have not")]. Internatsional'naia literatura, 1938, no. 4, p. 22-23.

Pesis, B. Review of: Imet' i ne imet' [To have and have not]. Literaturnoe obozrenie, 1938, no. 19, p. 37-43.

Platonov, A. Gore bezoruzhnym! ("Proshchai, oruzhie!") [Woe to those without arms. ("A farewell to arms")]. Literaturnaia gazeta, June 30, 1938.

Platonov, A. Navstrechu liudiam. (Po povodu romanov Ernesta Khemingueia "Proshchai, oruzhie!" i "Imet' i ne imet'") [Toward a meeting with people. (On the basis of the novels of Ernest Hemingway "A farewell to arms" and "To have and have not"]. Literaturnyi kritik, 1938, no. 11, p. 158-171.

Stat'ia Khemingueia [An article by Hemingway]. Pravda, September 5, 1938.

Taggard, Zh. [Taggard, Genevieve]. Ernest Kheminguei [Ernest Hemingway]. Literaturnaia gazeta, February 15, March 1, 1938. *Second article under title:* Tvorcheskii put' E. Khemingueia [E. Hemingway's path of creativity].

Teggard, Zh. [Taggard, Genevieve]. "Piataia kolonna" Khemingueia. Pis'mo iz SShA ["The fifth column" of Hemingway. A letter from the US]. Literaturnaia gazeta, December 20, 1938.

1939 Berestov, O. Vecher E. Khemingueia [A Hemingway evening]. Rezets, 1939, no. 7, p. 23-24.

Bleiman, M. Poeziia bor'by i gumanizma. ("Piataia kolonna") [The poetry of struggle and humanism. ("The fifth column")]. Iskusstvo i zhizn', 1939, no. 5, p. 15-16.

Gerasimova, V. Blagorodnyi istochnik [A noble spring]. Internatsional'-naia literatura, 1939, no. 7-8 (first printing), p. 343.

Grinberg, I. Geroi beretsia za oruzhie. ("Piataia kolonna") [A hero takes up arms. ("The fifth column")]. Rezets, 1939, no. 9-10, p. 28-30.

Grits, T. P'esa o grazhdanskoi voine v Ispanii. ("Piataia kolonna") [A play about the civil war in Spain. ("The fifth column")]. Kniga i proletarskaia revoliutsiia, 1939, no. 5-6, p. 147-148.

Kashkin, I. Pereklichka cherez okean [An exchange of shouts across the ocean]. Krasnaia nov', 1939, no. 7, p. 196-201.

Kashkin, I. Slovo o neizvestnom kritike [A word about an unknown critic]. Literaturnaia gazeta, May 1, 1939.

Kashkin, I. Ernest Kheminguei [Ernest Hemingway]. Internatsional'naia literatura, 1939, no. 7-8 (first printing), p. 315-339.

Kashkin, I. Ernest Kheminguei [Ernest Hemingway]. Literaturnaia gazeta, February 26, 1939.

Pesis, B. Review of: Piataia kolonna [The fifth column]. Moscow, 1939. Literaturnoe obozrenie, 1939, no. 11, p. 33-36.

Solov'ev, B. Geroi Khemingueia. ("Piataia kolonna") [A Hemingway hero. ("The fifth column")]. Literaturnyi sovremennik, 1939, no. 10-11, p. 257-260.

Trenev, K. Zamechatel'nyi roman. ("Proshchai, oruzhie!") [A remarkable novel. ("A farewell to arms")]. Internatsional'naia literatura, 1939, no. 7-8 (first printing), p. 341.

Fedin, K. O knigakh Khemingueia [Concerning Hemingway's books]. Internatsional'naia literatura, 1939, no. 7-8 (first printing), p. 217.

Frid, Ia. Rasskazy Khemingueia [Hemingway's stories]. Literaturnoe obozrenie, 1939, no. 18, p. 48-53.

Kheminguei [Hemingway], E. Predislovie [Foreword]. Kashkin, I. K oglavleniiu [On the table of contents]. *In:* Hemingway, E. Piataia kolonna i pervye tridtsat' vosem' rasskazov [The fifth column and the first thirty-eight stories]. Moscow, 1939. p. 3-6, 647-654.

1955 Gorokhov, V. Kheminguei i ego novaia kniga ("Starik i more") [Hemingway and his new book. ("The old man and the sea")]. Novoe vremia, 1955, no. 37, p. 27-28.

1956 Agrikolianskii, V., A. Krasnovskii and D. Rachkov. Pis'mo studentov Ernestu Khemingueiu. ("Starik i more") [Students' letter to Ernest Hemingway. ("The old man and the sea")]. Inostrannaia literatura, 1956, no. 1, p. 233.

Drobyshevskii, V. Nepobedimyi. O povesti E. Khemingueia "Starik i more" [The unconquerable. Concerning E. Hemingway's story "The old man and the sea"]. Zvezda, 1956, no. 5, p. 166-170. *Review:* L'vov, S. Replika Vladislavu Drobyshevskomu [A reply to Vladislav Drobyshevskii]. Zvezda, 1958, no. 8, p. 188-189.

Illichevskii, A. Ernest Kheminguei i ego povest' "Starik i more" [Ernest Hemingway and his story "The old man and the sea"]. *In:* Hemingway, E. Starik i more [The old man and the sea]. Kiev, 1956. p. 3-5.

Kashkin, I. Perechityvaia Khemingueia [On re-reading Hemingway]. Inostrannaia literatura, 1956, no. 4, p. 194-206.

Loziuk, N. Chelovek ne mozhet borot'sia v odinochku. ("Starik i more") [A man cannot fight alone. ("The old man end the sea")]. Sovetskaia Ukraina (Kiev), 1956, no. 7, p. 171-173.

Etvud, U. [Atwood, W.?]. U Ernesta Khemingueia. Pis'mo iz N'iu-Iorka [With Ernest Hemingway. A letter from New York]. Ogonek, 1956. no. 51, p. 10-11.

1957 Kashkin, I. Kheminguei na puti k masterstvu [Hemingway on his path to mastery]. Voprosy literatury, 1957, no. 6, p. 184-204.

1959 Boiarskii, O. O pozdnem tvorchestve Khemingueia [Concerning Hemingway's later work]. Krym; al'manakh (Simferopol'), 1959, no. 20, p. 104-107.

Geptner, V. G. O "Zelenykh kholmakh Afriki" Ernesta Khemingueia [Concerning Ernest Hemingway's "Green hills of Africa"]. *In:* Hemingway, E. Zelenye kholmy Afriki [The green hills of Africa]. Moscow, 1959. p. 156-159.

Kashkin, I. Predislovie k glavam iz knigi "Zelenye kholmy Afriki" [Intro-

99

duction to chapters from the book "The green hills of Africa"]. In-ostrannaia literatura, 1959, no. 7, p. 164-165.

Kashkin, I. Ernest Kheminguei [Ernest Hemingway]. Kashkin, I. Kommentarii [Commentary]. *In:* Hemingway, E. Izbrannye proiz-vedeniia v dvukh tomakh [Selected works in two volumes]. Moscow, 1959. v. 1, p. 3-38; v. 2, p. 639-653.

Nekrasov, V. Predislovie k rasskazu "Posviashchaetsia Khemingueiu" [Foreword to the story "Dedicated to Hemingway"]. Literaturnaia gazeta, July 23, 1959.

Shklovskii, V. Kheminguei v ego poiskakh ot iunosti do starosti [Heming-way in his searching from youth to age]. *In:* Shklovskii, V. Khudo-zhestvennaia proza. Razmyshleniia i razbory [Literary prose. Thoughts and criticisms]. Moscow, 1959. p. 597-605. *Also:* 1961. p. 635-643.

1960 Alekseev, A. Don Ernesto zhivet pod Gavanoi. A. I. Mikoian v gostiakh u E. Khemingueia [Don Ernesto lives near Havana. A. I. Mikoian visits E. Hemingway]. Izvestiia, February 14, 1960.

Borovik, G. U Ernesta Khemingueia [At Ernest Hemingway's]. Ogonek, 1960, no. 14, p. 26-29.

Dva interv'iu Khemingueia [Two interviews with Hemingway]. Inostran-naia literatura, 1960, no. 1, p. 267-269.

Kashkin, I. O samom glavnom. Proza Ernesta Khemingueia [Concerning the most important. Ernest Hemingway's prose]. Oktiabr', 1960, no. 3, p. 215-223.

Kashkin, I. Ob osnovnom i glavnom [Concerning that which is basic and important]. *In:* Hemingway, E. Izbrannye proizvedeniia [Selected works]. Sverdlovsk, 1960, p. 724-733.

Kopelev, L. Naperekor otchaianiiu i smerti (Ernest Kheminguei) [In opposition to disillusionment and death (Ernest Hemingway)]. *In:* Kopelev, L. Serdtse vsegda sleva [The heart is always on the left]. Moscow, 1960, p. 200-238.

Litoshko, E. Sud'ba polkovnika Kantuella. O romane Ernesta Kheming-ueia "Za rekoi, v teni derev'ev" [The fate of Colonel Cantwell. Concerning Ernest Hemingway's novel "Across the river, into the sha-de of the trees"[1]]. Moskva, 1960, no. 7, p. 98-100. *Also, with title:* Predislovie [Preface], *in:* Hemingway, E. Za rekoi v teni derev'ev [Across the river, into the shade of the trees]. Moscow, 1961. p. 5-10.

Mikoian, S. Vstrecha s Khemingueem [A meeting with Hemingway]. Literaturnaia gazeta, May 7, 1960.

Moknachev, M. Kheminguei govorit: "Liudi dolzhny zhit' bez voiny" [Hemingway says, "People ought to live without war"]. Izvestiia, March 19, 1960.

[1] *Across the River and Into the Trees.*

Olesha, Iu. Chitaia Khemingueia [On reading Hemingway]. Literatura i zhizn', May 13, 1960.

Ernest Kheminguei o svoei rabote [Ernest Hemingway about his work]. Voprosy literatury, 1960, no. 1, p. 153-156.

1961 Bol'shoi pisatel'. Pamiati Khemingueia [A great writer. In memory of Hemingway]. Izvestiia, July 3, 1961 (Moscow evening edition).

Borovik, G. Serdtse Khemingueia [Hemingway's heart]. Ogonek, 1961, no. 28, p. 29.

Leonov, L. Pisatel' s mirovym golosom. [A writer with a world-wide voice]. Pravda, July 4, 1961.

Machavariani, V. Pamiati Ernesta Khemingueia [In memory of Ernest Hemingway]. Literaturnaia Gruziia, 1961, no. 8, p. 72.

Mikoian, S. Nashedshii dorogu k serdtsam [Having found the way to men's hearts]. Moskva, 1961, no. 8, p. 200-201.

Nort, D. [North, J.]. Ernest Kheminguei. (Iz vospominanii) [Ernest Hemingway. (From my memories)]. Inostrannaia literatura, 1961, no. 8, p. 224-227.

Orlova, R. Posle smerti Khemingueia. Po stranitsam zarubezhnoi pressy [After Hemingway's death. On the pages of the foreign press]. Novyi mir, 1961, no. 9, p. 173-178.

Urnov, M. Predislovie [Foreword]. In: Hemingway, E. Proshchai, oruzhie! [A farewell to arms]. Moscow, 1961. p. 5-15.

Finkel'shtein, I. Kheminguei, ego zhizn' i knigi [Hemingway, his life and books]. Voprosy literatury, 1961, no. 12, p. 219-221.

E. Kheminguei—"persona non grata." ("Op as noe leto") [E. Hemingway —persona non grata. ("A dangerous summer")]. Literaturnaia gazeta, January 26, 1961.

Chakovskii, A. Muzhestvennyi talant. Pamiati Ernesta Khemingueia [A courageous talent. In memory of Ernest Hemingway]. Literaturnaia gazeta, July 4, 1961.

Eisner, A. On byl s nami v Ispanii [He was with us in Spain]. Novyi mir, 1961, no. 9, p. 169-173.

1962 Belousov, S. Tam, gde zhil Kheminguei [There, where Hemingway lived]. Sovetskaia kul'tura, September 27, 1962.

Golikov, A. Tam, gde zhil Kheminguei [There, where Hemingway lived]. Ogonek, 1962, no. 43, p. 18-19.

Demidova, I. M. Antivoennaia tema v tvorchestve Khemingueia [The anti-war theme in Hemingway's works]. Uchenye zapiski Tashkent-skogo pedagogicheskogo instituta inostrannykh iazykov, 1962, vyp. 6, ch. 2, p. 443-459.

Kashkin, I. O pis'makh Khemingueia. (Posleslovie k publikatsii) [Concerning Hemingway's letters. (Afterword to their publication)]. Voprosy literatury, 1962, no. 10, p. 181-183.

Kashkin, I. Review of: Killinger, J. *Hemingway and Dead Gods.* New

York, 1960. Sovremennaia khudozhestvennaia literatura za rubezhom, 1962, no. 2, p. 96-97.

Kubil'ias [Cubillas?], V. On liubil Kubu i Kuba liubila ego. Poslednie
dni zhizni E. Khemingueia [He loved Cuba and Cuba loved him.
The last days of the life of E. Hemingway]. Izvestiia, July 21, 1962.

Mashchenko, R. V. O nekotorykh osobennostiakh tvorcheskogo metoda
Ernesta Khemingueia [Concerning some features of Ernest Heming-
way's creative method]. Pratsy Odesskogo universyteta, 1961, t. 151.
Zbirnyk stud. robit, vyp. 7, p. 50-56.

Mendel'son, M. Tragediia Khemingueia [Hemingway's tragedy]. In:
Sovremennaia literatura SShA [The contemporary literature of the
US]. Moscow, 1962. p. 111-156.

Simonov, K. "Ne uspeesh' oglianut'sia..." (Predislovie k publikatsii
pis'ma E. Khemingueia K. Simonovu ot 20 iiunia 1946 g.) ["You
can't even look around..." (Foreword to the publication of a letter
from E. Hemingway to K. Simonov, June 26, 1946)]. Izvestiia, July
2, 1962 (Moscow evening edition).

Ernest Kheminguei o literaturnom masterstve [Ernest Hemingway concerning literary mastery]. Inostrannaia literatura, 1962, no. 1,
p. 212-218.

1963 Dodd, M. V dome Khemingueia [In Hemingway's house]. Literaturnaia
gazeta, January 22, 1963.

Kashkin, I. Pod kupolom "Rotondy" [Under the cupola of "La Roton-
de"]. Literaturnaia gazeta, July 2, 1963.

Kashkin, I. Review of: The Wild Years. New York, 1962. Sovremennaia
khudozhestvennaia literatura za rubezhom, 1963, no. 12, p. 57-59.

Neizvestnaia fotografiia Khemingueia. (K publikatsii fotografii, vypol-
nennoi I. Ivensom v 1937 g. v Ispanii) [An unknown photograph of
Hemingway. (On the publication of the photograph taken by J. Ivens
in 1937 in Spain)]. Smena, 1963, no. 1, p. 14.

Orlova, R. Mifologiia—pravda—geroi [Mythology—the truth—the
hero]. Voprosy literatury, 1963, no. 11, p. 174-177.

Rukopisi izvlecheny iz seifov [Manuscripts taken from the safes]. Izvestiia, December 12, 1963 (Moscow evening edition).

Samarin, R. Ernest Kheminguei i ego "Starik i more" [Ernest Hemingway and his "The old man and the sea"]. In: Hemingway, E.
The Old Man and the Sea[1]. Moscow, 1963. p. 3-19.

El'iashevich, A. P. Ob ideino-eticheskoi pozitsii i stile Ernesta Khemingueia [Concerning the ideological-ethical position and style of Ernest
Hemingway]. Trudy Leningradskogo gosudarstvennogo bibliotech-
nogo instituta, 1963, t. 14. Problemy ideinosti i khudozhestvennosti
literatury, p. 289-312.

[1] A work in the English language published in the Soviet Union.

KHERBST Dzhozefina   HERBST Josephine

1936 Balashov, P. Poiski gumanizma. ("Zhalosti nedostatochno") [In search
     of humanism. ("Pity is not enough")]. Literaturnaia gazeta, October
     10, 1936.
     Sats, N. Review of: Zhalosti nedostatochno [Pity is not enough]. Mos-
     cow, 1936. Literaturnoe obozrenie, 1936, no. 23, p. 43-46.
     Startsev, A. Posleslovie [Afterword]. *In:* Herbst, J. Zhalosti nedosta-
     tochno [Pity is not enough]. Moscow, 1936. p. 369-374.
1938 Balashov, P. Predislovie [Foreword]. *In:* Herbst, J. Rasplata blizka [The
     reckoning is near at hand—i.e. The Executioner Waits]. Moscow,
     1938. p. 3-7.
     Kuz'min, B. Review of: Herbst, J. Rasplata blizka [The reckoning is
     near at hand—i.e. The Executioner Waits]. Moscow, 1938. Internat-
     sional'naia literatura, 1938, no. 5, p. 220-221.
     Naumov, V. Review of: Herbst, J. Rasplata blizka [The reckoning is
     near at hand—i.e. The Executioner Waits]. Moscow, 1938. Litera-
     turnoe obozrenie, 1938, no. 21, p. 44-47.
     Novyi roman Dzhozefiny Kherbst. ("Rasplata blizka") [A new novel by
     Josephine Herbst. ("The reckoning is near at hand"—i.e. The
     Executioner Waits]. Knizhnye novosti, 1938, no. 24, p. 23.
1939 Mingulina, A. Review of: *Rope of Gold.* New York, 1939. Internatsio-
     nal'naia literatura, 1939, no. 9-10, p. 247-250.
1941 Mendel'son, M. Review of: *Rope of Gold.* New York, 1939. Literatur-
     naia gazeta, April 27, 1941.

     GERSHSGEIMER Dzhozef   HERGESHEIMER Joseph

1925 Arefin, S. O tvorchestve Dzhozefa Gershsgeimer [Concerning the work
     of Joseph Hergesheimer]. *In:* Hergesheimer, J. Tri pokoleniia [Three
     generations—*The Three Black Pennys*]. Leningrad, Moscow, 1925.
     p. 3-6. *See also:* Hergesheimer, J. Kukla i zhenshchina [A doll and
     a woman—i.e. *Cytherea*]. 2nd ed. Leningrad, 1927. p. 207-208.
     Dinamov, S. Review of: Tri pokoleniia [Three generations—*The Three
     Black Pennys*]. Leningrad, Moscow, 1925; Kukla i zhenshchina [A
     doll and a woman—i.e. *Cytherea*]. Leningrad, Moscow, 1925.
     Knigonosha, 1925, no. 27, p. 15.
     Levidov, M. Kniga o "pozdnei strasti" [A book about "belated passion"].
     In: Hergesheimer, J. Kukla i zhenshchina [A doll and a woman—i.e.
     Cytherea]. Leningrad, Moscow, 1925. p. 5-8. 2nd ed., 1927. p. 3-6.

     GERRIK Robert   HERRICK Robert

1927 Dinamov, S. Review of: Eshche ne pozdno... [It's still not late...—i.e.

Homely Lilla]. Moscow, Leningrad, 1927. Pechat' i revoliutsiia, 1927, no. 8, p. 200-201.
1928 Blok, G. Review of: Lavka uchenosti [The bench of learning—i.e. *Chimes*]. Moscow, 1928. Kniga i profsoiuzy, 1928, no. 5-6, p. 32.
1930 Gerzon, S. Review of: Opustoshenie [Devastation—i.e. *Waste*]. Moscow, Leningrad, 1930. Kniga i revoliutsiia, 1930, no. 12, p. 44-45.
Review of: Opustoshenie [Devastation—i.e. *Waste*]. Vestnik inostrannoi literatury, 1930, no. 4, p. 166-167.

KHERSI Dzhon   HERSEY John

1945 Mendel'son, M. Dva amerikanskikh romana [Two American novels]. (*A Bell for Adano*. New York, 1944). Literaturnaia gazeta, February 10, 1945.
Obsuzhdenie romana Dzhona Khersi [A discussion of John Hersey's novel]. (*A Bell for Adano*. New York, 1944). Literaturnaia gazeta, January 27, 1945.
1960 Orlova, R. Chelovek, gotovyi nazhat' knopku [A man who is ready to push the button]. (*The War Lover*. New York, 1959). Literaturnaia gazeta, July 5, 1960.
1961 Orlova, R. Pravda neveroiatnogo [The truth of the unbelievable]. (*The Child Buyer*. New York, 1960). Inostrannaia literatura, 1961, no. 5, p. 259-262.

KHILDRET Richard   HILDRETH Richard

1950 Treskunov, M. S. Roman Richarda Khil'dreta "Belyi rab" [Richard Hildreth's novel "The white slave"]. *In:* Hildreth, R. Belyi rab [The white slave]. Leningrad, 1950. p. 359-370.
1951 Brandis, E. Zemlia tiranii i rabstva. ("Belyi rab") [A land of tyranny and slavery. ("The white slave")]. Zvezda, 1951, no. 1, p. 182-183.
Treskunov, M. Roman Richarda Khil'dreta "Belyi rab" [Richard Hildreth's novel "The white slave"]. *In:* Hildreth, R. Belyi rab [The white slave]. Moscow, Leningrad, 1951. p. iii-xx.
Chivilikhin, A. Iz rodoslovnoi amerikanskogo fashizma. ("Belyi rab") [From the family tree of American fascism. ("The white slave")]. Literaturnaia gazeta, June 30, 1951.
1952 Mikhailova, L. Amerikanskie rabovladel'tsy. ("Belyi rab") [American slave-owners. ("The white slave")]. Znamia, 1952, no. 1, p. 189-192.
1957 Fialkovskii, E. E. Richard Khildret i osobennosti ego khudozhestven-nogo masterstva [Richard Hildreth and the specific features of his artistic mastery]. Uchenye zapiski Adygeiskogo pedagogicheskogo instituta (Maykop), 1957, t. 1, p. 181-200.
Fialkovskii, E. E. Roman Richarda Khildreta "Belyi rab" [Richard

104

Hildreth's novel "The white slave"]. Uchenye zapiski Moskovskogo oblastnogo pedagogicheskogo instituta, 1957, t. 55. Trudy kafedry zarubezhnoi literatury, vyp. 5, p. 155-180.

1958 Fialkovskii, E. E. Abolitsionistskii roman Richarda Khildreta i problema stanovleniia kriticheskogo realizma v literature SShA [Richard Hildreth's abolitionist novel and the problem of the origin of critical realism in the literature of the US]. Abstract of dissertation presented for the degree of Candidate of Philological Sciences. Moscow, 1958. 18 p.

1960 Treskunov, M. Richard Khildret [Richard Hildreth]. *In:* Hildreth, R. Belyi rab [The white slave]. Moscow, Leningrad, 1960. p. 3-20.

KHILL Dzho   HILL Joe (HILLSTROM Joseph)

1940 Los'ev, V. Dzho Khill [Joe Hill]. Internatsional'naia literatura, 1940, no. 11-12, p. 327-329.

1954 Romanova, E. Chelovek, kotoryi nikogda ne umiral. P'esa o Dzho Khille [The man who never died. A play about Joe Hill]. Sovetskaia kul'tura, October 21, 1954.

1955 Dmitriev, Iu. and N. Osipov. Dzho Khill i ego stikhi [Joe Hill and his poems]. Smena, 1955, no. 23, p. 18-19.

1956 Sergeeva, N. Eto bylo 40 let nazad... [That was forty years ago...]. Novoe vremia, 1956, no. 10, p. 26-30.

1962 Dmitriev, Iu. Dzho Khill [Joe Hill]. Znanie—sila, 1962, no. 7, p. 44-47.
Steivis, B. Chelovek, kotoryi nikogda ne umiral [The man who never died]. Ogonek, 1962, no. 45, p. 24.
Edvards [Edwards], A. "Chelovek, kotoryi nikogda ne umiral" ["The man who never died"]. Trud, October 11, 1962.

KHOLMS Oliver Uendell   HOLMES Oliver Wendell

1861 Robin, G. Review of: *Elsie Venner.* London, 1861. Russkoe slovo, 1861, no. 3, otd. II, p. 23-30.

1887 Rantsov, V. L. O chem besedoval poet. Udachnyi priem populiarizatsii. ("Besedy poeta za zavtrakom s tovarishchami po trapeze i chitateliami") [What the poet chatted about. A successful form of popularization. ("Conversations of the poet at breakfast with his tablemates and readers"—i.e. *The Poet at the Breakfast Table*)]. Nov', 1887, t. XIX, no. 2, p. 104-112.

GOUARD Sidni   HOWARD Sidney

1939 Khenter [Hunter], E. Sidni Gouard [Sidney Howard]. Internatsional'naia literatura, 1939, no. 12, p. 250-252.

GOUELS Vil'iam Din[1]   HOWELLS William Dean

1890 Kriticheskie etiudy (Gauel's i Dzhems) [Critical studies (Howells and James)]. Kolos'ia, 1890, no. 4, p. 267-273.
1895 Maksimov, N. (Predislovie k ocherkam "Amerikanki") [(Foreword to the sketches "American women")]. Trud, 1895, no. 8, p. 358-366.
K perevodu romana "Gost' iz Al'trurii" [On the translation of the novel "A guest from Altruria"—i.e. A Traveler from Altruria]. Vestnik Evropy, 1895, no. 1, p. 212-213.
1961 Gilenson, B. Novye raboty o Gouellse [New works on Howells]. Voprosy literatury, 1961, no. 7, p. 223-229.
Samokhvalov, N. Uil'iam Din Khouells i amerikanskii kriticheskii realizm [William Dean Howells and American critical realism]. Uchenye zapiski Krasnodarskogo pedagogicheskogo instituta, 1961, vyp. 24. Russkaia i zarubezhnaia literatura, p. 146-194.
1963 Gilenson, B. A. U. D. Gouells i L. N. Tolstoi [W. D. Howells and L. N. Tolstoi]. Uchenye zapiski Gor'kovskogo universiteta, 1963, t. 60. L. N. Tolstoi. Stat'i i materialy, vyp. 5. p. 282-295.

KH'IUZ Lengston   HUGHES Langston

1931 Dinamov, S. Roman o "chernom poiase" Ameriki [A novel about "the black belt" of America]. (Not Without Laughter. New York, 1930). Na literaturnom postu, 1931, no. 20-21, p. 36-37. (Signed: S. D.) Also, enlarged, and with title: "Predislovie" [Foreword], in: Hughes, L. Smekh skvoz' slezy [Laughter through tears—i.e. Not Without Laughter]. Moscow, Leningrad, 1932. p. 3-8.
1932 Startsev, A. Realisticheskii roman o negrakh. ("Smekh skvoz' slezy") [A realistic novel about Negroes. ("Laughter through tears"—i.e. Not Without Laughter)]. Khudozhestvennaia literatura, 1932, no. 25-26, p. 15-16.
Filatova, L. Lengston Kh'iuz [Langston Hughes]. Literatura mirovoi revoliutsii, 1932, no. 9-10, p. 112-117.
Filatova, L. Pervyi roman Lengstona Kh'iuza. ("Smekh skvoz' slezy") [Langston Hughes' first novel. ("Laughter through tears"—i.e. Not Without Laughter)]. Kniga i proletarskaia revoliutsiia, 1932, no. 8-9, p. 146-147.
1933 Levontin, E. Stikhi chernogo proletariia. ("Zdravstvui, revoliutsiia") [Verses of a member of the black proletariat. ("Hello, revolution")]. Khudozhestvennaia literatura, 1933, no. 12, p. 10-11.
Chetunova, N. Review of: Hughes, L. Smekh skvoz' slezy [Laughter through tears—i.e. Not Without Laughter]. Moscow, Leningrad, 1932. Molodaia gvardiia, 1933, no. 2, p. 158-159.

[1] Also transliterated as „Khouel's" in Soviet works of reference.

1934 Lengston Kh'iuz [Langston Hughes]. Za rubezhom, 1934, no. 18, p. 18.
Novaia kniga Lengstona Kh'iuza [A new book by Langston Hughes].
Literaturnaia gazeta, July 24, 1934.
Trenin, V. Review of: Hughes, L. Zdravstvui, revoliutsiia [Hello, revo-
lution]. Moscow, Leningrad, 1933. Literaturnaia gazeta, March 26,
1934.
1935 Urnov, M. Review of: Hughes, L. *The Ways of White Folks.* New York,
1934. Inostrannaia kniga, 1935, no. 1, p. 22-23. *Also, abridged, in:*
Za rubezhom, 1935, no. 8, p. 170.
1936 Zenkevich, M. Review of: Hughes, L. Nravy belykh [The ways of white
folks]. Leningrad, n.d. Literaturnoe obozrenie, 1936, no. 13-14,
p. 62-63.
Mingulina, A. Review of: Hughes, L. Nravy belykh [The ways of white
folks]. Leningrad, 1936. Literaturnaia gazeta, May 20, 1936.
Khmel'nitskaia, T. Review of: Hughes, L. Nravy belykh [The ways of
white folks]. Literaturnyi sovremennik, 1936, no. 8, p. 218-220.
1939 Karavaeva, A. Ob Eptone Sinklere i Lengstone Kh'iuze [Concerning
Upton Sinclair and Langston Hughes]. Internatsional'naia literatura,
1939, no. 7-8 (first printing), p. 368.
Karmon, U. [Carmon, W.]. Lengston Kh'iuz—poet naroda [Langston
Hughes—a poet of the people]. Internatsional'naia literatura, 1939,
no. 1, p. 192-194.
1941 Avtobiografiia Lengstona Kh'iuza [The autobiography of Langston
Hughes]. Literaturnoe obozrenie, 1941, no. 2, p. 89.
Karmon, U. [Carmon, W.]. Novaia kniga Lengstona Kh'iuza [A new
book by Langston Hughes]. (*The Big Sea.* New York, 1940). Internatsional'naia literatura, 1941, no. 1, p. 184-185.
1955 Shinkar', T. Predislovie [Foreword]. *In:* Hughes, L. Nepriiatnoe proisshestvie s angelami i drugie rasskazy [The trouble with angels and
other stories]. Moscow, 1955. p. 3-6.
1956 Berezark, I. Simpl nachinaet prozrevat'... ("Nepriiatnoe proisshestvie s
angelami") [Simple begins to see things clearly... ("The trouble with
angels")]. Neva, 1956, no. 3, p. 177.
Bekker, M. Predislovie k publikatsii stikhotvorenii [Foreword to the
publication of poems]. Inostrannai literatura, 1956, no. 10, p. 88-90.
1960 Bekker, M. Predislovie [Foreword]. *In:* Hughes, L. Izbrannye stikhi
[Selected poems]. Moscow, 1960. p. 7-12.
1961 Gilenson, B. Stikhi Kh'iuza. ("Izbrannye stikhi") [Hughes' poems.
("Selected poems")]. Moskva, 1961, no. 7, p. 209-210.

KHERST Fanni   HURST Fannie

1925 Neustroev, I. Predislovie k russkomu izdaniiu [A foreword to the Russian
edition]. *In:* Hurst, F. Zolotye perezvony [Golden chimes—original

English title not determined]. Leningrad, 1925. p. 3-4. 2nd ed. Leningrad, 1927.

1926 Dinamov, S. Review of: Hurst, F. Maneken [Mannequin]. Leningrad, 1926. Knigonosha, 1926, no. 39, p. 28.

1938 A. V. Review of: Hurst, F. *Great Laughter*. London, 1937. Internatsional'naia literatura, 1938, no. 1, p. 206.

IRVING VASHINGTON   IRVING WASHINGTON

1825 *Foreword to the translation of a selection from* "Puteshestviia v Angliiu" ["A voyage to England"—i.e. "The Voyage" (?)]. Moskovskii telegraf, 1825, no. 4, p. 297.

1830 Review of: Khronika o pokorenii Grenady [A chronicle of the taking of Granada—i.e. *The Conquest of Granada*]. Moskovskii vestnik, 1830, ch. 1, p. 302-308.

1831 Review of: Povesti pokoinogo Ivana Petrovicha Belkina [Tales about the late Ivan Petrovich Belkin]. St. Petersburg, 1831. (Pushkin and Irving). Moskovskii telegraf, 1831, no. 21, p. 254-256.

1835 Vashington Irving [Washington Irving]. Biblioteka dlia chteniia, 1835, t. 9, otd. II, p. 107-119.

Poezdka v Lugovye Stepi. Poslednee sochinenie Vashingtona Irvinga [A trip to the Meadow Steppes. The most recent work of Washington Irving]. (*A Tour on the Prairies*. New York, London, 1835). Biblioteka dlia chteniia, 1835, t. 10, otd. II, p. 44-61.

1837 Review of: Istoriia zhizni i puteshestvii Khristofora Kolomba [A history of the life and voyages of Christopher Columbus]. Translated from the French. St. Petersburg, 1836. Biblioteka dlia chteniia, 1837, t. 20, otd. V, p. 49-86.

1849 Druzhinin, A. V. Review of: Dol'f Geiliger [Dolf Heyliger]. Sovremennik, 1849, no. 10, otd. V, p. 303-311. *See also:* Druzhinin, A. V. Sobranie sochinenii [Collected works]. v. 6. St. Petersburg, 1865, p. 154-160.

1854 Vashington Irving [Washington Irving]. Biblioteka dlia chteniia, 1854, t. 123, otd. III, p. 109-110.

Dobroliubov, N. A. Review of: Zhizn' Magometa [A life of Mohammed]. Moscow, 1857. Sovremennik, 1858, no. 2, otd. II, p. 168-175. *See also:* Dobroliubov, N. Polnoe sobranie sochinenii [Complete collected works]. v. 3. Moscow, 1936. p. 334-339.

1860 Vashington Irving. Nekrolog [Washington Irving. An obituary]. Illiustratsiia, February 4, 1860.

Nenerokomov, F. Vashington Irving [Washington Irving]. Russkoe slovo, 1860, no. 2, p. 58-64.

1864 Przheval'skii, V. *Foreword to the article* "Zavoevanie Ispanii mavrami." (Po Vashingtonu Irvingu) ["The conquest of Spain by the Moors."

(After Washington Irving)]. Zhurnal dlia roditelei i nastavnikov, 1864, no. 7-8, otd. II, p. 23-26.

1879 Glazunov, A. Ot perevodchika [From the translator]. *In:* Irving, W. Putevye ocherki i kartiny [Essays and pictures on the way — *Selections of stories and Essays*]. Moscow, 1879. p. v-ix. (Signed: A. G.)

Review of: Putevye ocherki i kartiny [Essays and pictures on the way — *Tales of a Traveller?*]. Otechestvennye zapiski, 1879, no. 4, p. 192-195.

1884 Bulgakov, F. Istoricheskii roman na Zapade. Kuper i Vashington Irving [The historical novel in the West. Cooper and Washington Irving]. Istoricheskii vestnik, 1884, no. 8, p. 392-398.

1906 Chudakov, G. Zapadnye paralleli k povesti Gogolia "Portret." (Gogol', Irving, i Gofman) [Western parallels to Gogol's tale "The portrait." (Gogol', Irving and Hoffmann)]. *In:* Eranos. Sbornik statei po literature i istorii v chest' N. P. Dashkevicha [Eranos. A collection of articles on literature and history in honor of N. P. Dashkevich]. Kiev, 1906. p. 267-276.

1926 Alekseev, M. P. K "Istorii sela Goriukhina." (Pushkin i "Istoriia N'iu-Iorka") [On the "History of the village of Goriukhin." (Pushkin and the "History of New York")]. *In:* Pushkin. Stat'i i materialy. [Pushkin. Articles and materials]. vyp. 2. Odessa, 1926, p. 70-87.

1933 Akhmatova, A. (Anna Andreevna). Posledniaia skazka Pushkina. ("Legenda ob arabskom zvezdochete" kak istochnik "Skazki o Zolotom petushke") [Pushkin's last tale. ("The Legend of the Arabian Astrologer" as a source of "The Tale of the Golden Cockerel")]. Zvezda, 1933, no. 1, p. 161-176.

1939 Gershenzon, M. Vashington Irving (1783-1859). (Biograficheskii ocherk) [Washington Irving (1783-1859). (Biographical sketch)]. *In:* Irving, W. Rasskazy i legendy [Tales and legends]. Moscow, Leningrad, 1939. p. 3-24.

1940 Mirskaia, Iu. Rasskazy Vashingtona Irvinga [The tales of Washington Irving]. Literaturnaia gazeta, May 10, 1940.

Chelovekov, F. Vashington Irving [Washington Irving]. Detskaia literatura, 1940, no. 1-2, p. 53-57.

1954 Lopyreva, E. Vashington Irving, 1783-1850 [Washington Irving, 1783-1859]. *In:* Irving, W. Novelly [Short stories]. Moscow, 1954. p. iii-viii.

1959 Prozorova, M. Otets amerikanskoi literatury [The father of American literature]. Literaturnaia gazeta, October 29, 1959.

1962 Nikoliukin, A. Review of: Wagenknecht, E. *Washington Irving: Moderation Displayed.* New York, 1962. Sovremennaia khudozhestvennaia literatura za rubezhom, 1962, no. 12, p. 139-141.

DZHEKSON Feliks   JACKSON Felix

1958 Urnov, M. Predislovie [Foreword]. *In:* Jackson, F. "...Da pomozhet
mne bog" ["So help me God!"]. Moscow, 1958. p. 5-11. *Also:*
2nd ed. Moscow, 1959. p. 5-11.
1959 Nodel', F. Donos ... na sebia ("...Da pomozhet mne bog") [Informing...
on oneself ("So help me God!")]. Molodaia gvardiia, 1959, no. 3,
p. 248-249.
1960 Gromakov, B. Prochtite etu knigu. ("...Da pomozhet mne bog") [Read
this book. ("So help me God!")]. Sovetskaia iustitsiia, 1960, no. 2,
p. 59-60.
Novikova, N. Review of: "...Da pomozhet mne bog" ["So help me
God!"]. Teatr, 1960, no. 5, p. 80-81.

DZHEIMS Genri   JAMES Henry

1881 Review of: *The Portrait of a Lady.* Zagranichnyi vestnik, 1881, October-
December, t. 1, otd. II, p. 244.
1890 Kriticheskie etiudy (Gauel's i Dzhems) [Critical studies (Howells and
James)]. Kolos'ia, 1890, no. 4, p. 267-273.
1905 Annibal, L. Review of: *The Golden Bowl.* 1905. Vesy, 1905, no. 6, p. 63-
64.
1941 Narkevich, A. Iu. Genri Dzhems (25 let so dnia smerti). (Bibliogra-
ficheskaia spravka) [Henry James (25th anniversary of his death).
(Bibliographic note)]. Literaturnoe obozrenie, 1941, no. 4, p. 79.
(Signed: A. N.)
1956 Samokhvalov, N. I. Genri Dzheims [Henry James]. Uchenye zapiski
Krasnodarskogo pedagogicheskogo instituta, 1956. vyp. 18. Filologiia. p. 106-129.
1963 Shou [Shaw], B. Dve novye p'esy ("Gai Domvill") [Two new plays
("Guy Domville")]. *In:* Shaw, B. O drame i teatre [On drama and
the theater]. Moscow, 1963. p. 126-130.

DZHEFFERSON Tomas   JEFFERSON Thomas

1948 Zakharova, M. N. O genezise idei T. Dzheffersona [On the genesis of
the ideas of T. Jefferson]. Voprosy istorii, 1948, no. 3, p. 40-59.
1963 Iz pisem Tomasa Dzheffersona. Po stranitsam istorii [From the letters of
Thomas Jefferson. Through the pages of history]. Literaturnaia
gazeta, June 13, 1953.
1955 Foner, F. [Ph.]. Ideolog amerikanskoi demokratii [The ideologist of
American democracy]. *In:* Progressivnye deiateli SShA v bor'be za
peredovuiu ideologiiu [Progressive leaders of the US in the struggle
for a progressive ideology]. Moscow, 1955. p. 356-378.

DZHONSON Dzhozefina   JOHNSON Josephine

1934 Review of: *Now in November*. Literaturnaia gazeta, October 26, 1934.
1938 Aleksandrov, R. Review of: "Teper' v noiabre" ["Now in November"].
      Moscow, 1938. Zvezda, 1938, no. 4, p. 242-243.
    Balashov, P. Review of: "Teper' v noiabre" ["Now in November"].
      Moscow, 1938. Literaturnoe obozrenie, 1938, no. 3, p. 33-36.
    Levenson, A. Review of: *Jordanstown*. New York, 1937. Za rubezhom,
      1938, no. 3, p. 50.
    Rubin, V. Review of: "Teper' v noiabre" ["Now in November"]. Mos-
      cow, 1938. Novyi mir, 1938, no. 5, p. 286-287.
    Rykova, N. Review of: "Teper' v noiabre" ["Now in November"].
      Moscow, 1938. Internatsional'naia literatura, 1938, no. 2-3, p. 370-
      371. (Signed: N. R.)

DZHONS Dzheims   JONES James

1951 Zhantieva, D. Po zakonu Pentagona. O "luchshem amerikanskom ro-
      mane 1951 goda" ("From Here to Eternity") [Following the Penta-
      gon's law. Concerning the "best American novel of 1951" ("From
      Here to Eternity")]. Literaturnaia gazeta, December 28, 1951.
1959 Orlova, R. Zhertvy i pobediteli odinochestva ("Pistolet") [Victims and
      conquerors of solitude ("The pistol")]. Literaturnaia gazeta, De-
      cember 3, 1959.
1963 Gribanov, B. Review of: *The Thin Red Line*. New York, 1962. Sovremen-
      naia khudozhestvennaia literatura za rubezhom, 1963, no. 2, p. 38-40.

KERUAK Dzhek   KEROUAC Jack

1959 Nedelin, V. Piligrimy nikuda [Pilgrims to nowhere]. (*The Dharma Bums*.
      New York, 1958). Inostrannaia literatura, 1959, no. 9, p. 262-263.
    "Verter" iz "podzemel'ia." ("Liudi podzemel'ia") ["Werther" from the
      "underground." ("People from the underground"—i.e. *The Subter-
      raneans*)]. Literaturnaia gazeta, September 5, 1959.
1962 Anastas'ev, N. Dva porazheniia [Two defeats]. (*Book of Dreams*).
      Molodaia gvardiia, 1962, no. 10, p. 304-310.
    Zhukov, D. Review of: *Book of Dreams*. Sovremennaia khudozhest-
      vennaia literatura za rubezhom, 1962, no. 1, p. 72-73.
1963 Orlova, R. Review of: *Big Sur*. New York, 1962. Sovremennaia khudo-
      zhestvennaia literatura za rubezhom, 1963, no. 4, p. 55-57.

KILLENS Dzhon   KILLENS John O.

1955 Limanovskaia, V. Review of: *Youngblood*. New York, 1954. Inostran-
      naia literatura, 1955, no. 3, p. 226-228.

111

1959 Landor, M. Schast'e nepokorstva [The happiness of insubordination]. (Molodaia krov' [Young blood]. Moscow, 1959). Druzhba narodova, 1959, no. 7, p. 252-253.

Robson [Robeson], E. Grekh molchaniia [The sin of silence]. (Molodaia krov' [Young blood]. Moscow, 1959). Ogonek, 1959, no. 25, p. 25.

1963 Zasurskii, Ia. Review of: *And Then We Heard the Thunder*. New York, 1963. Sovremennaia khudozhestvennaia literatura za rubezhom, 1963, no. 11, p. 53-56.

KINGSLI Sidni   KINGSLEY Sidney

1937 Volosov, M. Review of: *Dead End*. New York, 1936. Za rubezhom, 1937, no. 7, p. 146.

P. B. Review of: *Dead End*. New York, 1936. Internatsional'naia literatura, 1937, no. 9, p. 222.

LAN'ER Sidni   LANIER Sidney

1898 Amerikanskii poet-muzykant Sidnei Lan'er [The American poet-musician Sidney Lanier]. Vestnik inostrannoi literatury, 1898, no. 2, p. 309-312.

LARDNER Ring   LARDNER Ring W.

1934 Abramov, A. "Ironiia nenavisti" ["The irony of hate"]. Literaturnaia gazeta, February 28, 1934.

Abramov, A. Ring Lardner. Internatsional'naia literatura, 1934, no. 5, p. 121-123.

1935 Levidov, M. Predislovie [Foreword]. *In:* Lardner, R. Novelly [Short stories]. Moscow, 1935, p. 3-4. (Signed: M. L.)

1936 Nemerovskaia, O. Review of: Novelly [Short stories]. Moscow, 1935. Zvezda, 1936, no. 5, p. 259-261.

LORENS Lars   LAWRENCE Lars (STEVENSON Philip)

1956 Roman o rabochem klasse [A novel about the working class]. (*Out of the Dust*. New York, 1956). Literaturnaia gazeta, September 4, 1956.

1962 G. Z. Review of: *The Hoax*. London, 1961. Sovremennaia khudozhestvennaia literatura za rubezhom, 1962, no. 6, p. 43-46.

G. Z. Review of: *Old Father Antic*. London, 1961. Sovremennaia khudozhestvennaia literatura za rubezhom, 1962, no. 11, p. 52-57.

1963 Zlobin, G. Semena budushchego [Seeds of the future]. Inostrannaia literatura, 1963, no. 2, p. 189-196.

LI Kharper   LEE Harper

1961 Nedelin, V. Review of: Ubit' peresmeshnika... [To kill a mockingbird].
     Sovremennaia khudozhestvennaia literatura za rubezhom, 1961,
     no. 3, p. 56-58.
1963 Levidova, I. Attikus Finch i ego deti [Atticus Finch and his children].
     Novyi mir, 1963, no. 6, p. 264-268.
     Orlova, R. Khoroshie liudi shtata Alabama [The good people of the state
     of Alabama]. Literaturnaia gazeta, July 11, 1963.
     Sergeeva, N. Pravil'nye liudi [Just people]. Novoe vremia, 1963, no. 20,
     p. 29-31.

     LESUR MERIDEL   LE SUEUR Meridel

1941 Abramov, A. Review of: *Salute to Spring*. New York, 1940. Internatsio-
     nal'naia literatura, 1941, no. 6, p. 178-179.

     L'IUIS Sinkler   LEWIS Sinclair

1923 Adonts, G. G. Sinkler L'iuis [Sinclair Lewis]. Zhizn' iskusstva, 1923,
     no. 18, p. 13-14. (Signed: G. A.)
1924 Aigustov, G. Review of: Mister Bebbit [Mister Babbitt]. Moscow, 1924.
     Pechat' i revoliutsiia, 1924, no. 3, p. 255-256.
     Bobrov, S. Review of: Mister Bebbit [Mister Babbitt]. Moscow, 1924.
     Krasnaia nov', 1924, no. 5, p. 322-325.
     Gai, A. G. Normal'nye, zdorovye i krepkie [Normal, healthy and strong].
     (*Babbitt*). Krasnyi zhurnal dlia vsekh, 1924, no. 2, p. 121-123.
     Golub', L. Review of: Glavnaia ulitsa [Main street]. Leningrad, 1924.
     Russkii sovremennik, 1924, no. 4, p. 269.
     Dinamov, S. Review of: Glavnaia ulitsa [Main street]. Leningrad, 1924.
     Knigonosha, 1924, no. 38, p. 11.
     Dinamov, S. Review of: Mister Bebbit [Mister Babbitt]. Moscow, 1924.
     Knigonosha, 1924, no. 16, p. 10.
     Levidov, M. Predislovie [Foreword]. *In:* Lewis, S. Mister Bebbit
     [Mister Babbitt]. Moscow, Petrograd, 1924. p. 3-6; 2nd ed. 1926.
     Mandel'shtam, R. Review of: Glavnaia ulitsa [Main street]. Leningrad,
     1924. Vestnik knigi, 1924, no. 9-10, p. 65.
1925 Dinamov, S. Review of: Na vol'nom vozdukhe. Polet sokola [Free
     air. The flight of the falcon—i.e. *The Trail of the Hawk*]. Leningrad,
     1925. Knigonosha, 1925, no. 8, p. 18.
     Leont'ev, B. Review of: Glavnaia ulitsa [Main street]. Leningrad, 1924.
     Polet sokola [Flight of the falcon—i.e. *The Trail of the Hawk*].
     Leningrad, 1925. Novyi mir, 1925, no. 2, p. 153-155.
1926 Aseev, N. Knigi na stole. O Sinklere L'iuise [Books on the table. About
     Sinclair Lewis]. 30—i.e. Tridtsat'—dnei, 1926, no. 5, p. 87-88.

                                                                    113

Benni, Ia. Review of: Una Golden [Una Golden—i.e. *The Job*]. Leningrad, 1926. Pechat' i revoliutsiia, 1926, no. 7, p. 218-219.

Kulle, R. Review of: Mentrap [Mantrap]. Leningrad, 1926. Pechat' i revoliutsiia, 1926, no. 8, p. 212-213.

1927 Kulle, R. Sinkler L'iuis [Sinclair Lewis]. Novyi mir, 1927, no. 5, p. 173-182. *Also, with additions, in:* Kulle, R. Etiudy o sovremennoi zapadnoevropeiskoi i amerikanskoi literature [Studies in contemporary Western European and American literature]. Moscow, Leningrad, 1930. p. 24-46.

Moravskii, E. Review of: Mentrap [Mantrap]. Leningrad, 1927. Zvezda, 1927, no. 1, p. 182-184.

Tsingovatov, A. Review of: El'mer Gantri [Elmer Gantry]. Leningrad, 1927. Kniga i profsoiuzy, 1927, no. 11-12, p. 57-58. (Signed: A. Ts.)

1928 Danilin, Iu. Review of: El'mer Gantri [Elmer Gantry]. Leningrad, 1927. Na literaturnom postu, 1928, no. 1, p. 83-84. (Signed: Diar.)

Dinamov, S. Sinkler L'iuis [Sinclair Lewis]. Pechat' i revoliutsiia, 1928, no. 1, p. 118-122.

Ezh. S. Review of: El'mer Gantri [Elmer Gantry]. Leningrad, 1927. Chitatel' i pisatel', January 21, 1928.

Kulle, R. Stoprotsentnyi Bebbit. ("Chelovek, kotoryi znal Kulidzha" Sinklera L'iuisa) [A hundred-percent Babbitt. ("The man who knew Coolidge" of Sinclair Lewis)]. Vestnik inostrannoi literatury, 1928, no. 6, p. 151-153. (Signed: R. K.)

Lewis, S. Avtoportret. (Sinkler L'iuis o samom sebe) [Self-portrait. (Sinclair Lewis about himself)]. Chitatel' i pisatel', January 21, 1928.

1929 Blok, G. Review of: Prostaki [The simpletons—i.e. *The Innocents*]. Moscow, 1928; Chelovek, kotoryi znal Kulidzha [The man who knew Coolidge]. Moscow, 1928. Molodaia gvardiia, 1929, no. 2, p. 94-95.

Garris [Harris], Ch. Sinkler L'iuis stanovitsia Bebbitom [Sinclair Lewis is becoming Babbitt]. Vestnik inostrannoi literatury, 1929, no. 2, p. 232-233.

Kogan, P. S. Predislovie [Foreword]. *In:* Lewis, S. El'mer Gentri [Elmer Gantry]. Moscow, 1929. p. 3-8.

Eishiskina, N. Iz amerikanskoi literatury. O novom romane Sinklera L'iuisa "Dodsworth" [From American literature. On the new novel by Sinclair Lewis, "Dodsworth"]. Novyi mir, 1929, no. 8-9, p. 299-301.

1930 Popov, M. Novyi roman Sinklera L'iuisa [The new novel by Sinclair Lewis]. Vestnik inostrannoi literatury, 1930, no. 1, p. 203-204.

Eishiskina, N. Sinkler L'iuis i Teodor Draizer [Sinclair Lewis and Theodore Dreiser]. Russkii iazyk v sovetskoi shkole, 1930, no. 1, p. 177-180.

1931 Elistratova, A. Review of: *Cheap and Contented Labor. The Picture of a*

Southern Mill Town in 1929. Inostrannaia kniga, literaturno-khudozhestvennaia seriia, 1931, no. 1, p. 5. (Signed: A. E.)

Levit, T. Istoriia odnogo optimizma [The history of an optimism].
Literatura i iskusstvo, 1931, no. 2-3, p. 175-181.

1933 Levidov, M. Sinkler L'iuis i Dzhon Bebbit [Sinclair Lewis and John
Babbitt (*sic*)]. Literaturnaia gazeta, November 29, 1933.

1934 Gan, A. Novyi roman Sinklera L'iuisa [The new novel of Sinclair Lewis].
(*Work of Art.* New York, 1934). Literaturnaia gazeta, February 12,
1934. (Signed: A. G.)

Khiks [Hicks], G. Review of: *Work of Art.* New York, 1934. Inostrannaia literatura, 1934, no. 2, p. 119-120.

1935 Dinamov, S. Pisatel' i revoliutsiia [The writer and revolution]. Izvestiia,
June 8, 1935.

Osipov, G. Review of: Errousmit [Arrowsmith]. Moscow, 1936.
Literaturnoe obozrenie, 1936, no. 17, p. 17-20.

Romm, V. Roman Sinklera L'iuisa o fashizme v Amerike. ("Zdes' eto ne
mozhet sluchit'sia") [The novel of Sinclair Lewis about fascism in
America. ("It can't happen here")]. Izvestiia, November 26, 1935.

1936 Brusilovskii, A. Review of: Enn Vikers [Ann Vickers]. Moscow, 1936.
Sotsialisticheskaia zakonnost', 1936, no. 10, p. 84-90.

Dmitrevskii, V. Sinkler L'iuis i ego tvorchestvo [Sinclair Lewis and his
work]. Molodaia gvardiia, 1936, no. 5, p. 111.

Litauer, V. Review of: Enn Vikers [Ann Vickers]. Moscow, 1936.
Literaturnoe obozrenie, 1936, no. 7, p. 34-36.

Sats, I. Sinkler L'iuis o sud'bakh chelovechestva. ("U nas eto nevozmozhno") [Sinclair Lewis about the fate of mankind. ("With us that is
impossible"—i.e. *It Can't Happen Here*)]. Literaturnyi kritik, 1936,
no. 11, p. 158-169.

Spir [Spear?], L. Tvorchestvo Sinklera L'iuisa [The work of Sinclair
Lewis]. Translated by L. Savel'ev. Internatsional'naia literatura,
1936, no. 9, p. 118-133.

Eishiskina, N. Dve knigi Sinklera L'iuisa. ("Errousmit"—"Enn Vikers")
[Two books by Sinclair Lewis. ("Arrowsmith"—"Ann Vickers")].
Literaturnaia gazeta, July 10, 1936.

1937 Deich, A. Sinkler L'iuis i ego roman o fashizme. ("U nas eto nevozmozhno") [Sinclair Lewis and his novel about fascism. ("With us
that is impossible"—i.e. *It Can't Happen Here*)]. Molodaia gvardiia,
1937, no. 10-11, p. 346-350.

Dinamov, S. S. Predislovie [Foreword]. *In:* Lewis, S. U nas eto nevozmozhno [With us that is impossible—i.e. *It Can't Happen Here*].
Moscow, 1937. p. 3-29. *Abridged, in:* Internatsional'naia literatura,
1937, no. 2, p. 180-187; Dinamov, S. Zarubezhnaia literatura [For-
eign literature]. Moscow, 1960. p. 396-417.

Dinamov, S. Review of: U nas eto nevozmozhno [With us that is impos-

115

sible—i.e. *It Can't Happen Here*]. Literaturnoe obozrenie, 1937, no. 6, p. 26-29.

Elistratova, A. Antifashistskii roman L'iuisa Sinklera. ("U nas eto nevozmozhno") [The anti-fascist novel of Lewis Sinclair (*sic*). ("With us that is impossible"—i.e. *It Can't Happen Here*)]. Kniga i proletarskaia revoliutsiia, 1937, no. 6, p. 114-117.

Semenov, M. Obvinitel'noe slovo Sinklera L'iuisa. ("U nas eto nevozmozhno") [The accusatory word of Sinclair Lewis. ("With us that is impossible—i.e. *It Can't Happen Here*)]. Sovetskoe iskusstvo, August 5, 1937.

1938 Zhivov, M. Dva amerikanskikh romana. ("U nas eto nevozmozhno") [Two American novels. ("With us that is impossible"—i.e. *It Can't Happen Here*)]. Internatsional'nyi maiak, 1938, no. 1, p. 16.

Khiks [Hicks], G. Pis'mo iz Ameriki [A letter from America]. (*The Prodigal Parents*. New York, 1938). Internatsional'naia literatura, 1938, no. 4, p. 194-196.

1947 Motyleva, T. Predislovie [Foreword]. *In:* Lewis, S. Gideon Plenish [Gideon Planish]. Moscow, 1947. p. 5-16.

1948 Anisimov, I. Predislovie [Foreword]. *In:* Lewis, S. Kingsblad—potomok korolei [Kingsblood—descendant of kings—i.e. *Kingsblood Royal*]. Moscow, 1948. p. 5-14.

Kozel'skii, S. U nikh eto est'. ..."U nas eto nevozmozhno" [This is the case with them. ... "With us this is impossible"—i.e. *It Can't Happen Here*]. Novyi mir, 1948, no. 10, p. 277-280.

Koziura, N. Kingsblad—potomok korolei [Kingsblood—descendant of kings—i.e. *Kingsblood Royal*]. Znamia, 1948, no. 11, p. 142-145.

Motyleva, T. Knigi obviniaiut. ("Korolevskaia krov'") [Books accuse. ("Royal blood"—i.e. *Kingsblood Royal*)]. Izvestiia, May 13, 1948.

Motyleva, T. Predislovie k romanu "Korolevskaia krov'" [Foreword to the novel "Royal blood"—i.e. *Kingsblood Royal*]. Novyi mir, 1948, no. 4, p. 140-142.

Motyleva, T. Put' Sinklera L'iuisa [Sinclair Lewis's path]. Literaturnaia gazeta, December 1, 1948.

Nemerovskaia, O. Pamflet o politicheskikh gangsterakh. ("Gideon Plenish") [A pamphlet about political gangsters. ("Gideon Planish")]. Zvezda, 1948, no. 9, p. 205-207.

Orlova, R. Dikie nravy. (O romane Sinklera L'iuisa "Korolevskaia krov'") [Savage morals. (About Sinclair Lewis's novel "Royal blood"—i.e. *Kingsblood Royal*)]. Molodoi bol'shevik, 1948, no. 8, p. 57-61.

Startsev, A. Rasshifrovannaia biografiia. ("Gideon Plenish." Moscow, 1948) [A deciphered biography. ("Gideon Planish." Moscow, 1948)]. Znamia, 1948, no. 3, p. 184-188.

Startsev, A. Soedinennye linchuiushchie shtaty. ("Korolevskaia krov'")

116

[The United States of Lynchdom. ("Royal blood"—i.e. *Kingsblood Royal*)]. Literaturnaia gazeta, March 17, 1948.

1949 Elistratova, A. Sinkler L'iuis zashchishchaet podzhigatelei voiny [Sinclair Lewis defends the warmongers]. Literaturnaia gazeta, October 19, 1949.

Khmel'nitskaia T. Roman o belom negre. ("Kingsblad, potomok korolei." Moscow, 1948) [A novel about a white Negro. ("Kingsblood, descendant of kings"—i.e. *Kingsblood Royal*. Moscow, 1948)]. Zvezda, 1949, no. 1, p. 202-204.

1955 Motyleva, T. O tvorchestve Sinklera L'iuisa [Concerning the writings of Sinclair Lewis]. Inostrannaia literatura, 1955, no. 4, p. 209-219.

1956 Motyleva, T. Predislovie [Foreword]. *In:* Lewis, S. Errousmit [Arrowsmith]. Moscow, 1956. p. 3-18.

1957 Mendel'son, M. Vospominaniia o Sinklere L'iuise [Memoirs about Sinclair Lewis]. (Lewis, G. H. *With Love from Gracie: Sinclair Lewis, 1912-1925.* New York, 1955). Inostrannaia literatura, 1957, no. 12, p. 247-248.

Startsev, A. Predislovie [Foreword]. *In:* Lewis, S. Ivovaia alleia [Willow alley—i.e. *Willow Walk*]. Moscow, 1957. p. 3-5.

1958 Gilenson, B. Sinkler L'iuis o Turgeneve [Sinclair Lewis on Turgenev]. Voprosy literatury, 1958, no. 9, p. 89.

1959 Levidova, I. M. Sinkler L'iuis. Bio-bibliograficheskii ukazatel' k 75-letiiu so dnia rozhdeniia [Sinclair Lewis. A bio-bibliographical guide for the 75th anniversary of his birth]. With preface by B. A. Gilenson. Moscow, Vsesoiuznaia knizhnaia palata, 1959. 88 p.

Mendel'son, M. Sinkler L'iuis i ego roman "Bebbit" [Sinclair Lewis and his novel "Babbitt"]. *In:* Lewis, S. Bebbit [Babbitt]. Moscow, 1959. p. 3-18.

1960 Egunova, N. Sinkler L'iuis—romanist i rasskazchik. [Sinclair Lewis—novelist and short story writer]; Lewis, S. Ia probivaius' v pechat'. Ia byvalyi gazetchik. Neopublikovannoe predislovie k "Bebbitu." Zametka o romane "Kingsblad, potomok korolei" [I appear in print. I the former newspaperman. An unpublished preface to "Babbitt." A note about the novel "Kingsblood, descendant of kings"—i.e. *Kingsblood Royal*]. *In:* Lewis, S. Kingsblad, potomok korolei. Rasskazy. Stat'i. Ocherki [Kingsblood, descendant of kings—i.e. *Kingsblood Royal*. Stories. Articles. Sketches]. Leningrad, 1960. p. 3-32, 657-688, 715-730.

Romm, A. Sinkler L'iuis i ego roman "Glavnaia ulitsa" [Sinclair Lewis and his novel "Main street"]. *In:* Lewis, S. Glavnaia ulitsa [Main street]. Moscow, Leningrad, 1960. p. 5-22.

Savurenok, A. Predislovie [Foreword]. *In:* Lewis, S. *Elmer Gantry.*[1] Moscow, 1960. p. 5-18.

---

[1] A work in the English language published in the Soviet Union.

1961 Gilenson, B. Roman Sinklera L'iuisa "Errousmit" (k voprosu o polozhitel'nom geroe v tvorchestve pisatelia) [Sinclair Lewis's novel
"Arrowsmith" (on the problem of the positive hero in the writer's
works)]. Uchenye zapiski Gor'kovskogo pedagogicheskogo instituta,
1961, vyp. 36. O zarubezhnoi literature (stat'i), p. 42-76.

Gilenson, B. Sbornik proizvedenii Sinklera L'iuisa [A collection of the
writings of Sinclair Lewis]. Inostrannaia literatura, 1961, no. 8,
p. 258-259.

Landor, M. Proshlo li vremia buntarei? [Has the time for rebels passed?].
Literaturnaia gazeta, April 11, 1961.

1962 Gilenson, B. A. Literaturno-kriticheskie vzgliady Sinklera L'iuisa [The
literary and critical views of Sinclair Lewis]. Uchenye zapiski Moskovskogo oblastnogo pedagogicheskogo instituta, 1962, t. III.
K problemam kriticheskogo realizma v zarubezhnoi literature 20
veka, sb. 2, p. 179-203.

Krivitskii, A. Vozmozhno li eto? ("U nas eto nevozmozhno") [Is this
possible? ("With us this is impossible"—i.e. *It Can't Happen Here*)].
Literaturnaia gazeta, March 27, 1962.

Mendel'son, M. Review of: Schorer, M. *Sinclair Lewis: An American
Life*. New York, 1961. Sovremennaia khudozhestvennaia literatura
za rubezhom, 1962, no. 7, p. 108-110.

Mendel'son, M. Review of: Schorer, M. *Sinclair Lewis: An American
Life*. New York, 1961. Voprosy literatury, 1962, no. 12, p. 209-213.

1963 Gilenson, B. Satirik i ego kritiki [A satirist and his critics]. (*Sinclair Lewis:
A Collection of Critical Essays*. Edited by M. Schorer. New York,
1962). Inostrannaia literatura, 1963, no. 9, p. 266-268.

Gilenson, B. Tvorchestvo Sinklera L'iuisa 20-kh gg. XX v. [Sinclair
Lewis's writings in the 1920's]. Abstract of dissertation presented for
the degree of Candidate of Philological Sciences. Moscow, 1963. 19 p.

Rasiaev, V. V. Sinkler L'iuis—oblichitel' amerikanskogo obraza zhizni
(po novym materialam) [Sinclair Lewis—a critic of the American
way of life (from new materials)]. Uchenye zapiski Azerbaidzhanskogo pedagogicheskogo instituta iazykov, Baku, 1963, vyp. 17 (seriia
filologicheskikh nauk), p. 99-117.

LONDON Dzhek   LONDON Jack

1910 Maevskii, I. A. Dzhek London [Jack London]. *In:* London, J. Sobranie
sochinenii [Collected works]. v. 1. Moscow, 1910, p. i-ii. (Signed:
G. M.); 2nd ed. Moscow, 1913. v. 1, p. 1-4; 3rd ed. v. 3. Moscow,
1914. p. 3-6.

1911 Kuprin, A. Zametka o Dzheke Londone [A note about Jack London].
Sinii zhurnal, 1911, no. 22, p. 13. *Also in:* Kuprin, A. Sobranie
sochinenii [Collected works]. v. 6. Moscow, 1958. p. 628-630.

Mirov, V. Review of: Beloe bezmolvie [The white silence]. (Sochineniia [Works]. v. 1. Moscow, 1910). Sovremennyi mir, 1911, no. 9, p. 340-341.

1912 Abramovich, N. Problema voli v sovremennoi literature. ch. 3: Dzhek London [The problem of the will in contemporary literature. Pt. 3: Jack London]. Novyi zhurnal dlia vsekh, 1912, no. 11, p. 63-66.

Andreev, L. Dzhek London [Jack London]. *In:* London, J. Sobranie sochinenii [Collected works]. v. 1. St. Petersburg, 1912. p. 1-4. *Also in:* London, J. Sobranie sochinenii [Collected works]. v. 1. Moscow, 1922. p. 1-4.

Andruson, L. Dzhek London [Jack London]. Novyi zhurnal dlia vsekh, 1912, no. 7, p. 75-82.

Bogoraz, V. G. Novaia Amerika. (Dzhek London, neistovyi kaliforniets) [A new America. (Jack London, the violent Californian)]. Novaia zhizn', 1912, no. 11, p. 129-155; no. 12, p. 122-148. (Signed: Tan.)

Brusianin, V. Dzhek London [Jack London]. Zhizn' dlia vsekh, 1912, no. 8, cols. 1283-1285.

Voitolovskii, L. Literaturnye siluety. Dzhek London [Literary silhouettes. Jack London]. Kievskaia mysl', July 28, 1912.

Derman, A. Dzhek London [Jack London]. Zavety, 1912, no. 7, p. 125-130.

Koltonovskaia, E. Dzhek London [Jack London]. Vestnik Evropy, 1912, no. 9, p. 391-395.

Kranikhfel'd, V. Literaturnye otkliki. Ch. 2: Dzhek London [Literary echoes. Pt. 2: Jack London]. Sovremennyi mir, 1912, no. 4, p. 306-311.

M-skoi, S. V. Dzhek London [Jack London]. Sever, 1912, no. 23-26, p. 12-16; no. 27-31, p. 15-16. (Signed: S. V. M-skoi.)

Pevets podlinnoi zhizni (Dzhek London) [The singer of real life (Jack London)]. Biulleten' literatury i zhizni, 1912, no. 20-21, p. 775-777.

1913 Dzhek London o samom sebe [Jack London about himself]. Biulleten' literatury i zhizni, 1913, no. 13, p. 609-617.

Review of: Polnoe sobranie sochinenii [Complete collected works]. v. 1. Moscow, 1912-1913. Russkoe bogatstvo, 1913, no. 3, p. 369-371.

Rubinova, R. Dzhek London. (Biograficheskii ocherk) [Jack London. (Biographical sketch)]. Iunaia Rossiia, 1913, no. 11, p. 1315-1329; no. 12, p. 1453-1466. *Also, abridged, in:* Rubinova, R. Dzhek London [Jack London]. Moscow, 1917. 32 p.

1914 Chukovskii, K. Sovremennye ocherki. 1. Dzhek London [Contemporary essays. 1. Jack London]. *In:* Chukovskii, K. Litsa i maski [Faces and masks]. St. Petersburg, 1914. p. 137-150.

1916 Bukhov, A. Dzhek London [Jack London]. Zhurnal zhurnalov, 1916, no. 48, p. 5.

Vlagin, M. Dzhek London i my [We and Jack London]. Lukomor'e, 1916, no. 49, p. 16.

119

Dzhek London. (Nekrolog) [Jack London. (An obituary)]. Russkoe slovo, 1916, November 13/26, 1916.

Kugel', A. R. Poet atavizma [The poet of atavism]. Den', November 13, 1916. (Signed: Homo Novus.)

Kuz'min, E. U Dzheka Londona [With Jack London]. Argus, 1916, no. 10, p. 54-61.

Kuprin, A. Dzhek London. (Nekrolog) [Jack London. (An obituary)]. Russkoe slovo, November 17/30, 1916. *Also in:* Molodaia gvardiia, 1963, no. 8, p. 235-236. *See also:* Sredi knig i zhurnalov [Among the books and magazines]. Stolitsa i usad'ba, 1916, no. 72, p. 25-26.

Levidov, M. Review of: Zheleznaia piata. Zvezdnye skitaniia [The iron heel. Wanderings among the stars—i.e. *The Star Rover*]. Letopis', 1916, no. 12, p. 250-253.

Levidova, S. Dzhek London. Nekrolog [Jack London. An obituary]. Letopis', 1916, no. 12, p. 250-253.

P. T. Dzhek London. (Nekrolog) [Jack London. (An obituary)]. Iunaia Rossiia, 1916, no. 12, cols. 1188-1191.

1917 Bukhov, A. Dzhek London. Ocherk [Jack London. An essay]. Zhurnal zhurnalov, 1917, no. 48, p. 6.

Rosinskii, V. N. Pevets bor'by [A singer of the struggle]. Vestnik znaniia, 1917, no. 1, p. 21-29.

El'-ka. Dzhek London. Kritiko-biograficheskii ocherk [Jack London. A critico-biographic essay]. Vskhody, 1917, no. 3-4, p. 169-176.

1918 Bezsal'ko, P. Kak Dzhek London stal sotsialistom [How Jack London became a socialist]. Griadushchee, 1918, no. 3, p. 12.

1919 Al'medingen, N. A. Dzhek London. Biograficheskii ocherk [Jack London. A biographical sketch]. *In:* London, J. Liubov' k zhizni. [Love of life]. Petrograd, 1919. p. 5-16. *Also:* Moscow, Petrograd, 1924. p. 3-11.

Zamiatin, E. Predislovie [Foreword]. *In:* London, J. Syn volka i drugie rasskazy [The son of the wolf and other tales]. Peterburg, 1919. p. 5-9.

F. R. Review of: Zheleznaia piata [The iron heel]. Moscow, 1918. Gorn, 1919, no. 2-3, p. 110-112.

1920 Eventov, A. Review of: Zheleznaia piata [The iron heel]. Vestnik rabotnikov iskusstv, 1920, no. 1, p. 13-15.

1922 Vol'kenshtein, V. Dzhek London [Jack London]. *In:* Avangard. Al'manakh. t. 1, no. 1. Moscow, 1922. p. 9-11.

1923 Loks, K. Review of: Serdtsa trekh [Hearts of three]. Moscow, 1923. Pechat' i revoliutsiia, 1923, no. 6, p. 250-251.

Rozental', L. Review of: Zheleznaia piata [The iron heel], 1923. Pechat' i revoliutsiia, 1923, no. 5, p. 297-300.

Chernovskii, A. Review of: Kak ia stal sotsialistom [How I became a socialist]. Moscow, 1923. Kniga i revoliutsiia, 1923, no. 4, p. 61-62.

Churilin, T. Review of: Serdtsa trekh [Hearts of three]. Moscow, 1923. Knigonosha, 1923, no. 10, p. 8 (Signed: T. Ch.)

1924 Vasilevskii, L. Review of: Lunnaia dolina [Moon valley]. Leningrad, Moscow, 1924. Zvezda, 1924, no. 5, p. 279-280.

Gorlin, A. N. Dzhek London. (Vmesto predisloviia) [Jack London. (In place of a foreword)]. *In:* London, J. Sila sil'nykh [The strength of the strong]. Moscow, Petrograd, 1924. p. 3-8.

Dinamov, S. Review of: Lunnaia dolina [Moon valley]. Leningrad, 1924. Knigonosha, 1924, no. 30, p. 9.

Dinamov, S. Review of: Torzhestvo pravosudiia [The triumph of justice —i.e. *The Benefit of Doubt*]. Moscow, Leningrad, 1924. Iukonskie rasskazy [Yukon tales]. Moscow, 1924. Knigonosha. 1924, no. 34, p. 8. (Signed: S. Din.)

Zaslavskii, D. O. Predislovie redaktora [Editor's foreword]. *In:* London, J. Bor'ba klassov [The class struggle]. Leningrad, 1924. p. 5-6; 2nd ed. 1925.

Kogan, P. S. O Dzheke Londone. [On Jack London]. London, Ch. Zhizn' Dzheka Londona [The life of Jack London]. *In:* London, J. Polnoe sobranie sochinenii [Complete collected works]. v. 1. Moscow, Leningrad, 1924. p. 5-239. *Also:* Moscow, Leningrad, 1928. p. 5-144.

Kogan, P. S. Predislovie [Foreword]. *In:* London, J. Torzhestvo pravosudiia [The triumph of justice]. Moscow, Leningrad, 1924. p. 3-8.

London, Ch. Predislovie [Foreword]. *In:* London, J. Polnoe sobranie sochinenii [Complete collected works]. v. 11, bk. 1. Gollandskaia doblest' [Dutch courage]. Moscow, Leningrad, 1924. p. 5-9. *Also in:* London, J. Gollandskoe muzhestvo [Dutch courage]. Leningrad, 1926. p. 5-8.

Ch. Review of: Bor'ba klassov [The class struggle]. Leningrad, 1924. Zvezda, 1924, no. 5, p. 283.

1925 Anibal, B. Review of: Igra [The game—i.e. *Cherry*]. Leningrad, 1925. Novyi mir, 1925, no. 5, p. 156-157.

Dzhek London o sebe [Jack London about himself]. *In:* London, J. Polnoe sobranie sochinenii [Complete collected works]. v. 14, book 2. Moscow, Leningrad, 1925. p. 85-91; 2nd ed. v. 24. Moscow, Leningrad, 1929. p. 302-306.

London, J. Kak ia ponimaiu zhizn' [How I view life]. *In:* London, J. Glaza Azii [Eyes of Asia]. Leningrad, 1925. p. 18-33. *Abridged, and differing translation:* Chto mne dokazala zhizn' [What life showed me]. Krasnaia niva, 1925, no. 9, p. 207-208.

Obruchev, S. Review of: Za kulisami tsirka [Behind the scenes of the circus—i.e. *Michael, Brother of Jerry*]. Pechat' i revoliutsiia, 1925, no. 4, p. 287.

Sologub, F. Dzhek London. (K romanu "Glaza Azii") [Jack London.

(On the novel "Eyes of Asia")]. *In:* London, J. Glaza Azii [Eyes of Asia]. Leningrad, 1925, p. 7-17.

Iung [Young?], F. Dzhek London kak poet rabochego klassa [Jack London as a poet of the working class]. Translated by A. Arion. Leningrad, Moscow, "Kniga", 1925. 123 p. *Reviews:* Lelevich, G. Pechat' i revoliutsiia, 1925, no. 5-6, p. 511-513; Friche, V. Knigonosha, 1925, no. 9, p. 18; Munblit, G. Komsomoliia, 1926, no. 3, p. 7-8.

1926 Gitel', O. Tvorchestvo Dzheka Londona (1876-1916) [The works of Jack London, 1876-1916]. Narodnyi uchitel', 1926, no. 12, p. 116-120.

Loks, K. Review of: Glaza Azii [Eyes of Asia]. Leningrad, 1925. Pechat' i revoliutsiia, 1926, no. 2, p. 223-224.

London, Ch. O moem muzhe. Iz vospominanii [About my husband. From my memoirs]. With foreword by D. Gorbov: Poet bor'by i stroitel'stva [A poet of struggle and creation]. 30—i.e. Tridtsat'—dnei, 1926, no. 9, p. 20-29. *In full in:* London, Dzh. Polnoe sobranie sochinenii [Complete collected works]. v. 1. Moscow, Leningrad, 1927. p. 19-239.

1927 Baratov-Umanskii, B. Posleslovie k knige "Pod gnetom." Beseda po prochitannomu [Afterword to the book "Under the yoke." A talk about that which has been read]. *In:* London, J. Pod gnetom [Under the yoke—original title not determined]. Moscow, Leningrad, 1927, p. 129-141.

Golubkov, V. Dzhek London—v shkole [Jack London—in school]. *In:* Inostrannye pisateli v shkole [Foreign writers in school]. Moscow, Leningrad, 1927. p. 155-162.

Guber, P. Dzhek London. Biograficheskii ocherk [Jack London. Biographical sketch]. *In:* London, J. Sobranie sochinenii [Collected works]. v. 12. Moscow, Leningrad, 1926. p. 355-406; 2nd ed. Moscow, Leningrad, 1927.

Matsa, I. Romantika prirody i sily. ("Naturromantizm." Dzh. London i drugie) [The romance of nature and of strength. ("Nature romanticism." J. London and others)]. *In:* Matsa, I. Literatura i proletariat na Zapade [Literature and the proletariat in the West]. Moscow, 1927. p. 53-69.

Novskii, I. O Dzheke Londone [About Jack London]. *In:* Novskii, I. Neobychainye prikliucheniia Dzherri i ego brata Maikelia na sushe i na more [The unusual adventures of Jerry and his brother Michael on land and at sea]. (After J. London). Moscow, Leningrad, 1927. p. vii-xxxiv.

Perekati-Pole, G. K. Review of: Polnoe sobranie sochinenii [Complete collected works]. v. 1-12. Oktiabr', 1927, no. 2, p. 193-195.

Frimen, Dzh. [Freeman, J.?]. Dzhek London kak revoliutsioner [Jack

London as a revolutionary]. Na literaturnom postu, 1927, no. 2, p. 46-51.

Friche, V. M. Pisateli-sotsialisty. (Dzh. London i U. Sinkler) [Socialist writers (J. London and U. Sinclair)]. *In:* Friche, V. M. Ocherk razvitiia zapadnykh literatur [Outline of the development of Western literatures]. 3rd rev. ed. Khar'kov, 1927. p. 229-235.

Iung, F. Dzhek London (1876-1916) [Jack London, 1876-1916]. Golub-kov, V. Amerikanskii proletariat i Dzhek London [The American proletariat and Jack London]. (Signed: V. G.) *In:* London J. Rasskazy [Stories]. Moscow, Leningrad, 1927. p. 119-134.

1929 Beliaev, A. Predislovie [Foreword]. *In:* London, J. Polnoe sobranie sochinenii [Complete collected works]. v. 23, bks. 45-47: Zheleznaia piata [The iron heel]. Moscow, Leningrad, 1929. p. 5-6.

Beliaev, A. Predislovie [Foreword]. *In:* London, J. Polnoe sobranie sochinenii [Complete collected works]. v. 17-18, bks. 34-36: Lunnaia dolina [Moon valley — i.e. *The Valley of the Moon*]. Moscow, Leningrad, 1929, p. 3-5.

Beliaev, A. Predislovie [Foreword]. *In:* London, J. Polnoe sobranie sochinenii [Complete collected works]. v. 13, bks. 25-26: Martin Iden [Martin Eden]. Moscow, Leningrad, 1929. p. 3-4.

Gimel'farb, B. Dzhek London [Jack London]. *In:* London, J. Martin Iden [Martin Eden]. Moscow, Leningrad, 1929. p. 3-10.

Danilin, Iu. Dzhek London uchitsia pisatel'stvu [Jack London studies writing]. Na literaturnom postu, 1929, no. 23, p. 86-95.

Dzhek London. (Mastera siuzhetnoi prozy) [Jack London. (Masters of descriptive prose)]. *In:* Bor'ba mirov. Al'manakh. 1929, no. 1, p. 119-128. (Supplement to the journal *Vokrug sveta*). (Signed: Literaturoved.)

1930 Kulle, R. Genial'nyi brodiaga. (Dzhek London) [A tramp with genius. (Jack London)]. *In:* Kulle, R. Etiudy o sovremennoi zapadno-evropeiskoi i amerikanskoi literature [Studies in contemporary Western European and American literature]. Moscow, Leningrad, 1930. p. 47-83.

1931 Boroda, M. Kak rabotal Dzhek London. Ob organizatsii i kul'ture truda pisatelia [How Jack London worked. On the organization and method of the writer's craft]. Na pod"eme, 1931, no. 7, p. 153-158.

1932 Rykova, N. Predislovie [Foreword]. *In:* London, J. Rasskazy [Stories]. Moscow, Leningrad, 1932. p. 3-15.

1933 Dinamov, S. Zametki o Dzheke Londone [Notes on Jack London]. 30 — i.e. Tridtsat' — dnei, 1933, no. 9, p. 52-58.

Peluzo, E. Iz dnei znakomstva s Dzhekom Londonom [From the days of my acquaintance with Jack London]. Krasnaia nov', 1933, no. 1, p. 186-193.

1934 Kassil', L. London — malysham. ("Skazanie o Kishe." Moscow, 1933)

[London for children. ("The tale of Kisha." Moscow, 1933)].
Detskaia i iunosheskaia literatura, 1934, no. 3, p. 14-16.
1935 Peluzo, E. Moi vstrechi s Dzhekom Londonom [My meetings with Jack
London]. Literaturnyi Leningrad, January 8, 1935.
1936 Anikst, A. Dzhek London [Jack London]. Knizhnye novinki, 1936, no.
30, p. 22-24.
Sergeev, A. Review of: Belyi klyk [White fang]. Moscow, Leningrad,
1936. Detskaia literatura, 1936, no. 16, p. 11-15.
1937 Balashov, P. Review of: Khvat Belliu. Khvat i Malysh [Bellew the rake.
The Rake and Tiny—i.e. *Smoke Bellew. Smoke and Shorty*]. Moscow, 1937. Literaturnoe obozrenie, 1937, no. 21, p. 47-49.
1938 Sytin, V. Knigi Dzheka Londona. ("Serdtsa trekh." "Belyi klyk." Moscow, 1937) [Books by Jack London. ("Hearts of three." "White fang."
Moscow, 1937)]. Chto chitat', 1938, no. 2, p. 58-60.
1939 Paskhin, N. Tvorcheskii put' Dzheka Londona (1876-1916) [The creative
path of Jack London, 1876-1916]. Chto chitat', 1939, no. 7-8, p. 45-
48.
1940 Lundberg, E. Review of: Rasskazy [Stories]. Moscow, Leningrad, 1939.
Detskaia literatura, 1940, no. 5, p. 38-48.
1941 Vainshtein, G. Dzhek London [Jack London]. Literaturnoe obozrenie,
1941, no. 2, p. 83-85.
Levit, T. Dzhek London [Jack London]. Molodaia gvardiia, 1941, no. 1,
p. 159-160. (Signed: T. L.)
Nagel', V. Dzhek London [Jack London]. Literaturnaia gazeta, January
12, 1941.
Nemerovskaia, O. Dzhek London [Jack London]. Krasnoflotets, 1941,
no. 1, p. 51-53.
1945 Lenobl' [Lenoble?], G. Dzhek London [Jack London]. *In:* London, J.
Smok Bel'iu [Smoke Bellew]. Moscow, Leningrad, 1945. p. 3-8.
1946 Kucheriavenko, V. and E. Lepke. Na rodine Dzheka Londona [In
Jack London's native region]. Dal'nii Vostok, 1946, no. 5-6, p. 223-
230.
Startsev, A. Predislovie [Foreword]. *In:* London, J. Beloe bezmolvie i
drugie rasskazy [The white silence and other stories]. Moscow,
Leningrad, 1946. p. 3-6.
1947 Startsev, A. Grubaia oshibka. ("Prikliucheniia rybach'ego patrulia."
Moscow, Leningrad, 1947) [A glaring mistake. ("The adventures of
the fishery patrol"—i.e. *Tales of the Fish Patrol*)]. Literaturnaia
gazeta, May 24, 1947.
1948 Lorie, M. Dzhek London (1876-1916) [Jack London, 1876-1916]. *In:*
London, J. Rasskazy [Stories]. Moscow, Leningrad, 1948. p. 3-8.
Troitskii, Iu. Posleslovie [Afterword]. *In:* London, J. Martin Iden
[Martin Eden]. Moscow, 1948. p. 376-378.
1949 Kucheriavenko, V. V Oklende, na rodine Dzheka Londona. (Iz zapisok

124

sovetskogo moriaka) [In Oakland, Jack London's native region. (From the notes of a Soviet seaman)]. Zvezda, 1949, no. 7, p. 136-141.

Kheml'nitskaia, T. Avtobiograficheskii roman Dzheka Londona "Martin Iden" [Jack London's autobiographical novel, "Martin Eden"]. *In:* London, J. Martin Iden [Martin Eden]. Leningrad, 1949. p. 367-373.

1950 Merkel', Z. Predislovie [Foreword]. *In:* London, J. *Short Stories.*[1] Moscow, 1950. p. 3-13.

Mironova, A. Dzhek London [Jack London]. *In:* London, J. Rasskazy i ocherki [Stories and sketches]. Moscow, 1950. p. 3-8.

1951 Fedunov, P. Posleslovie [Afterword]. *In:* London, J. Izbrannoe [Selections]. Moscow, 1951. p. 714-733. *Abridged, in:* London, J. Martin Iden [Martin Eden]. Moscow, 1958. p. 348-358; London, J. *Martin Eden.*[1] Moscow, 1960. p. 3-12.

1952 Naer, V. Predislovie [Foreword]. *In:* London, J. Rasskazy [Stories]. Moscow, 1952. p. 3-10.

Khutsishvili, N. Dzhek London [Jack London]. *In:* London, J. Rasskazy [Stories]. Moscow. 1952, p. 3-7.

1953 Mironova, A. Dzhek London [Jack London]. *In:* London, J. Rasskazy [Stories]. Moscow, 1953. p. 197-199. *Also in:* London, J. Liubov' k zhizni [Love of life]. Gor'kii, 1955. p. 185-187.

Sukhoverov, S. Dzhek London i rabochee dvizhenie [Jack London and the labor movement]. Enisei. Al'manakh. Kn. 12 (Krasnoyarsk), 1953. p. 254-262.

Fedunov, P. Predislovie [Foreword]. *In:* London, J. *Martin Eden.*[1] Moscow, 1953, p. 3-14.

1954 Fedunov, P. Dzhek London [Jack London]. *In:* London, J. Sochineniia [Works]. v. 1. Moscow, 1954. p. 5-38.

1955 Romm, A. P'esa D. Londona "Krazha" [Jack London's play "Theft"]. *In:* London, J. Krazha [Theft]. Moscow, 1955, p. 98-104.

1956 Badanova, I. M. Kniga revoliutsionnogo gneva. ("Zheleznaia piata") [A book of revolutionary wrath. ("The iron heel")]. Uchenye zapiski Tashkentskogo pedagogicheskogo instituta inostrannykh iazykov, 1956, vyp. 1, p. 151-173.

Bannikov, N. Kak byli napisany "Liudi bezdny." [How "The people of the abyss" was written]. Ogonek, 1956, no. 5, p. 13.

Bogoslovskii, V. London. Ocherk tvorchestva [London. A sketch of his work]. Uchenye zapiski Moskovskogo oblastnogo pedagogicheskogo instituta, 1956, t. 37. Trudy kafedry zarubezhnoi literatury, vyp. 3, p. 3-76.

Bykov, V. Muzhestvennyi talant [A virile talent]. Smena, 1956, no. 23, p. 20.

[1] A work in the English language published in the Soviet Union.

Kush, O. Razmyshleniia nad tomom sochinenii Dzheka Londona [Thoughts on a volume of the works of Jack London]. (Sochineniia v 7 tomakh, t. 3. Moscow, 1956). Neva, 1956, no. 3, p. 176.

Okov, Iu. Pisatel' Dzhek London i senator Vil'iam Noulend [The writer Jack London and Senator William Knowland]. Sovetskaia kul'tura, November 15, 1956.

Omilianchuk, P. Posleslovie [Afterword]. *In:* London, J. Rasskazy [Stories]. Moscow, 1956. p. 524-525.

Pollit, G. [Pollitt, Harry]. "Zheleznaia piata." ["The iron heel"]. Smena, 1956, no. 23, p. 21.

Savchenko, Dzhek London [Jack London]. Sem'ia i shkola, 1956, no. 12, p. 21.

1957 Gruzinskaia, N. Severnye rasskazy D. Londona [The northern stories of J. London]. Sbornik studencheskikh nauchnykh rabot po gumanitarnomu tsiklu, Moskovskii oblastnoi pedagogicheskii institut, 1957, t. 2, p. 59-79.

Sukhoverov, S. I. M. Gor'kii za rubezhom. (D. London i M. Gor'kii) [M. Gor'kii abroad. (J. London and M. Gor'kii)]. *In:* Nauchnometodicheskii sbornik Shadrinskogo pedagogicheskogo instituta, 1957, vyp. 1, p. 141-170.

1958 Antonova, T. "Severnye rasskazy" Dzheka Londona [The "northern stories" of Jack London]. Uchenye zapiski Moskovskogo gosudarstvennogo pedagogicheskogo instituta, 1958, t. 130. Kafedra zarubezhnoi literatury, vyp 3, p. 231-242.

Kumkes, S. and Iu. Lipets. Dzhek London—puteshestvennik [Jack London—traveller]. *In:* London, J. Puteshestvie na "Snarke" [The cruise of the "Snark"]. Moscow, 1958, p. 203-206.

Sukhoverov, S. I. Dzhek London v SSSR [Jack London in the USSR]. Uchenye zapiski Shadrinskogo pedagogicheskogo instituta, 1958, vyp. 2, Russkii iazyk i literatura, p. 102-143.

1959 Bogoslovskii, V. N. Severnye rasskazy Dzheka Londona [The northern stories of Jack London]. Uchenye zapiski Moskovskogo oblastnogo pedagogicheskogo instituta, 1959. t. 78. Trudy kafedry zarubezhnoi literatury, vyp. 6. Progressivnaia zarubezhnaia literatura 19 i 20 vekov, p. 63-116.

Kan [Kahn], A. V Lunnoi doline Dzheka Londona [In the Moon Valley of Jack London]. Smena, 1959, no. 16, p. 20-21.

Konferentsiia chitatelei po knige Dzheka Londona "Martin Iden." Metodicheskie materialy [Readers' conference on the book by Jack London, "Martin Eden." Guidance materials]. Moscow, Lenin State Library, 1959. 12 p.

1960 Badanova, I. Gor'kii i Dzhek London [Gor'kii and Jack London]. Uchenye zapiski Tashkentskogo pedagogicheskogo instituta inostrannykh iazykov, 1960, vyp. 4, p. 129-148.

Badanova, I. M. Protiv uzakonennogo grabezha. (Analiz khudozhest-vennykh obrazov p'esy Dzheka Londona "Krazha") [Against legal-ized robbery. (Analysis of the literary forms of Jack London's play "Theft")]. Uchenye zapiski Tashkentskogo pedagogicheskogo insti-tuta inostrannykh iazykov, 1960, vyp. 4, p. 149-171.

Bykov, V. Znakomstvo s Dzhekom Londonom prodolzhaetsia [The acquaintance with Jack London continues]. Smena, 1960, no. 10, p. 20-21.

Sukhoverkhov, S. I. Dzhek London vstupaet v zhizn'. (Rannii period zhizni i tvorchestva pisatelia) [Jack London enters into life. (The early period of the life and work of the writer)]. *In:* Programma i tezisy dokladov piatoi nauchnoi konferentsii professorsko-prepoda-vatel'skogo kollektiva Michurinskogo pedagogicheskogo instituta [The program and summary of reports of the fifth scholarly confer-ence of the professorial and instructional staff of the Michurinsk Pedagogical Institute]. 1960. 31 p.

Frans [France], A. Predislovie k pervomu izdaniiu "Zheleznoi piaty" vo frantsuzskom perevode [Foreword to the first edition of "The iron heel" in French translation]. *In:* France, A. Sobranie sochinenii [Collected works]. v. 8. Moscow, 1960. p. 756-759.

1961 Bannikov, N. Kratkaia letopis' zhizni i tvorchestva Dzheka Londona [A short chronicle of the life and work of Jack London]. *In:* London, J. Polnoe sobranie sochinenii [Complete collected works]. v. 14. Moscow, 1961. p. 488-494.

Bykov, V. K biografii Dzheka Londona [On Jack London's biography]. Inostrannaia literatura, 1961, no. 2, p. 257-259.

Dzhek London (1876-1916). Metodicheskie materialy k vecheru, posvia-shchennomu 45-letiiu so dnia smerti [Jack London, 1876-1916. Program materials for an evening commemorating the 45th anniver-sary of his death]. Moscow, 1961. 19 p.

Samarin, R. Dzhek London (1876-1916) [Jack London, 1876-1916]. *In:* London, J. Sobranie sochinenii [Collected works]. v. 1. Moscow, 1961. p. 3-36.

Samuilov, V. Izdanie v SSSR proizvedenii D. Londona (Statistiko-bibliograficheskaia spravka) [The publication of the works of J. London in the Soviet Union. (Statistical-bibliographic note)]. Novye knigi, 1961, no. 2, p. 80.

1962 Bogoslovskii, V. N. Dzhek London i rabochee dvizhenie [Jack London and the labor movement]. Uchenye zapiski Moskovskogo oblast-nogo pedagogicheskogo instituta. 1962, t. 111. K problemam kriticheskogo realizma v zarubezhnoi literature 20 veka, sb. 2, p. 73-144.

Bogoslovskii, V. N. Roman Dzheka Londona "Zheleznaia piata" [Jack London's novel "The iron heel"]. Uchenye zapiski Moskovskogo oblastnogo pedagogicheskogo instituta, 1962, t. 111. K problemam kriticheskogo realizma v zarubezhnoi literature 20 veka, sb. 2, p. 145-165.

Bykov, V. O voennykh reportazhakh Dzheka Londona [Concerning the military reporting of Jack London]. (With excerpts). Dal'nii Vostok, 1962, no. 3, p. 161-168.

Zhuravlev, I. D. London v Rossii [J. London in Russia]. Uchenye zapiski Dagestanskogo universiteta (Makhachkala), 1962. t. 13, p. 92-110.

1963 London, J. Kak ia nachal pechatat'sia. (Publikatsiia s primechaniami redaktora) [How I began to appear in print. (Publication with editorial notes)]. Voprosy literatury, 1963, no. 1, p. 149-152.

Badanova, I. M. Dzhek London i ego geroi. Tvorchestvo Dzheka Londona 1900-1910 gg. [Jack London and his heroes. The work of Jack London, 1900-1910]. Abstract of dissertation presented for the degree of Candidate of Philological Sciences. Moscow, 1963. 23 p.

Badanova, I. M. Dzhek London i ego geroi [Jack London and his heroes]. Uchenye zapiski Tashkentskogo pedagogicheskogo instituta inostrannykh iazykov, 1963, vyp. 7, ch. 1. Seriia filologicheskikh nauk, p. 3-45.

Bogoslovskii, V. N. K istorii realizma v SShA. Tvorchestvo Dzheka Londona i Eptona Sinklera (1900-1917) [On the history of realism in the USA. The work of Jack London and Upton Sinclair, 1900-1917]. Abstract of dissertation presented for the degree of Doctor of Philological Sciences. Moscow, 1963, 39 p.

Temkin, Ia. Otmecheno rukoi Lenina... [Noted in Lenin's hand...]. (Concerning a marginal note in J. London's pamphlet "The Good Soldier" in *Appeal to Reason*, December 4, 1915). Literaturnaia gazeta, October 1, 1963.

LONGFELLO Genri   LONGFELLOW Henry Wadsworth

1849 Danilevskii, G. O sovremennom napravlenii poezii v Soedinennykh shtatakh Severnoi Ameriki. (Longfello) [Concerning the contemporary trend of poetry in the United States. (Longfellow)]. Sanktpeterburgskie vedomosti, November 17, 1849.

1854 Longfello [Longfellow]. Otechestvennye zapiski, 1854, no. 4, otd. VII, p. 97-98.

1855 Genrikh Longfellou i sovremennaia literatura v Severnoi Amerike [Henry Longfellow and contemporary literature in North America]. Panteon, 1855, no. 3, otd. IV, p. 5-9.

1856 Review of: Pesn' o Gaiavate [The song of Hiawatha]. Sovremennik, 1856, no. 1, otd. V, p. 56-58.

1860 Mikhailov, M. I. Amerikanskie poety i romanisty. (Longfello) [American poets and novelists. (Longfellow)]. Sovremennik, 1860, no. 12, otd. III, p. 305-324. (Signed: X.)

1870 Genri Uedsuord Longfello [Henry Wadsworth Longfellow]. Vsemirnaia illiustratsiia, 1870, no. 76, p. 426.

1873 Longfello [Longfellow]. Niva, 1873, no. 42, p. 657-658.

1875 Gerbel', N. V. Genri Longfello [Henry Longfellow]. *In:* Gerbel', N. Angliiskie poety v biografiiakh i obraztsakh [English poets in biographies and extracts]. St. Petersburg, 1875. p. 382-384.

1877 Genrikh V. Longfello [Henry W. Longfellow]. Illiustrirovannaia gazeta, May 8, 1877.

1882 Arsen'ev, Iu. Vospominanie o Longfello [A memory of Longfellow]. Moskovskie vedomosti, March 17, 1882.

Genri Uodsvort Longfello [Henry Wadsworth Longfellow]. (An obituary). Zagranichnyi vestnik, 1882, no. 4, otd. II, p. 58-59.

Genri Uedsuord Longfello [Henry Wadsworth Longfellow]. (An obituary). Vsemirnaia illiustratsiia, 1882, no. 13, p. 258.

Lavrov, P. Genri Uodsvorts Longfello [Henry Wadsworth Longfellow]. Otechestvennye zapiski, 1882, no. 7, p. 57-80. (Signed: P. Kriukov.) *See also:* Lavrov, P. Etiudy o zapadnoi literature [Studies in Western literature]. Petrograd, 1923. p. 153-180.

Longfello. Nekrolog [Longfellow. An obituary]. Istoricheskii viestnik, 1882, no. 5, p. 478-479.

Longfello [Longfellow]. (An obituary). Niva, 1882, no. 15, p. 354.

Sovremennye inostrannye pisateli. Genri Uedsuord Longfello [Contemporary foreign writers. Henry Wadsworth Longfellow]. (An obituary). Ogonek, 1882, no. 14, p. 284-285.

Iazykov, D. Genri Uodsvort Longfello [Henry Wadsworth Longfellow]. (Bibliography). Zagranichnyi vestnik, 1882, no. 5, otd. II, p. 93.

1883 Mechnikov, L. I. Novosti inostrannoi literatury. Obizhennyi poet [News of foreign literature. An insulted poet]. Delo, 1883, no. 3, otd. II, p. 37-40. (Signed: L. M.)

1888 Review of: Baumgartner, A. *Longfellow's Dichtungen.* Freiburg, 1888. Severnyi vestnik, 1888, no. 5, otd. II, p. 123-125.

1890 Review of: Gaiavata. Skazka iz zhizni Severo-amerikanskikh indeitsev [Hiawatha. A tale from the life of the North American Indians]. St. Petersburg, 1890. Russkaia mysl', 1890, no. 7, p. 329-331.

Mikhailovskii, D. L. Predislovie [Foreword]. *In:* Longfellow, H. W. Gaiavata [Hiawatha]. St. Petersburg, 1890. p. v-xiv. 2nd ed. St. Petersburg, Moscow, 1913. p. v-xvii.

1894 Predislovie [Foreword]. *In:* Longfellow, H. W. Stikhotvoreniia [Poems]. St. Petersburg, 1894. p. 3-4.

1895 Review of: Longfellow, H. W. Stikhotvoreniia [Poems]. Mir bozhii, 1895, no. 7, otd. III, p. 6-9.

1896 Bunin, I. Ot perevodchika [From the translator]. (On the translation of *The Song of Hiawatha*). Orlovskii vestnik, May 2, 1896.

1899 Bunin, I. Ot perevodchika [From the translator]. *In:* Longfellow, H. W. Pesn' o Gaiavate [The song of Hiawatha]. Moscow, 1899. p. i-vii. *Also, with changes and abridged, in:* Longfellow, H. W. Pesn' o Gaiavate [The song of Hiawatha]. Moscow, 1959. p. 5-8.

Longfello. Ocherk [Longfellow. An essay]. Iunyi chitatel', 1899, no. 12, cols. 356-360.

Review of: Pesn' o Gaiavate [The song of Hiawatha]. Moscow, 1899. Zhivopisnoe obozrenie, 1899, no. 30, p. 607-608.

Review of: Pesn' o Gaiavate [The song of Hiawatha]. Moscow, 1899. Mir bozhii, 1899, no. 5, otd. II, p. 62.

Solov'ev, E. A. Review of: Pesn' o Gaiavate [The song of Hiawatha]. Zhizn', 1899, no. 10, p. 360-361. (Signed: A—ch.)

1901 Longfello, Genri. Biograficheskii ocherk amerikanskogo poeta s prilozheniem ego stikhotvorenii [Longfellow, Henry. A biographical sketch of the American poet, with a supplement of his poems]. Moscow, Obshchestvo rasprostraneniia poleznykh knig, 1901. 48 p.

1902 Gorbunov-Posadov, I. Vil'iam Channing i poet Genri Longfello [William Channing and the poet Henry Longfellow]. *In:* Gorbunov-Posadov, I. Osvoboditeli chernykh rabov [The liberators of the black slaves]. *Supplement to:* Stowe, H. B. Khizhina diadi Toma [Uncle Tom's cabin]. Moscow, 1902. p. 395-398. *Other editions:* 1907, 1910.

1903 Degen, E. Review of: Pesn' o Gaiavate [The song of Hiawatha]. St. Petersburg, 1903. Mir bozhii, 1903, no. 5, p. 89.

1904 Bal'mont, K. Review of: Pesn' o Gaiavate [The song of Hiawatha]. St. Petersburg, 1903. Vesy, 1904, no. 2, p. 61-62. (Signed: Don.)

Golenishchev-Kutuzov, A. L. Review of: Pesn' o Gaiavate [The song of Hiawatha]. St. Petersburg, 1903. Sbornik Obshchestva russkogo iazyka i slovesnosti, 1904, t. 78, no. 1, p. 61-62.

1907 Zhurakovskii, E. Angliiskaia poeziia. (Genri Vinevarto—*sic*—Longfello) [English poetry. (Henry Wadsworth Longfellow)]. *In:* Zhurakovskii, E. Konspektnyi kurs istorii vseobshchei literatury [Summary course of the history of world literature]. v. 2. Moscow, 1907. p. 248-250.

100—i.e. Sto—letie so dnia rozhdeniia Longfello [The hundredth anniversary of the birth of Longfellow]. Istoricheskii vestnik, 1907, no. 4, p. 330-331.

1908 Kholodniak, I. Review of: Pesn' o Gaiavate [The song of Hiawatha]. St. Petersburg, 1903. Zhurnal Ministerstva narodnogo prosveshcheniia, 1908, novaia seriia, ch. XVII, no. 10, p. 223-228.

1911 Peterson, O. Genri Longfello (1807-1882) [Henry Longfellow, 1807-1882]. *In:* Peterson, O. G. V. Longfello i ego proizvedeniia [H. W. Longfellow and his works]. St. Petersburg, 1911, p. 3-5.

Sviatlovskii, V. Gaiavata, kak istoricheskaia lichnost' i kak geroi poemy

Longfello. (Istoriko-etnograficheskoe issledovanie legendy o Gaiavate) [Hiawatha as a historical personage and as hero of the poem
by Longfellow. (Historico-ethnographic study of the legend of
Hiawatha)]. Zapiski Neofilologicheskogo obshchestva pri Impera-
torskom Sanktpeterburgskom universitete, vyp. 5. St. Petersburg,
1911. p. 1-58. *Review in:* Novyi zhurnal dlia vsekh, 1911, no. 28,
cols. 134-135.

1915 Chukovskii, K. I. Amerikanskii poet o russkom Bosfore [An American
poet on the Russian Bosporus]. Niva, 1915, no. 14, p. 264.

1916 Iokhel'son, V. I. Gaiavata i istochniki vdokhnoveniia Longfello [Hia-
watha and the sources of Longfellow's inspiration]. *In:* Longfellow,
H. Pesn' o Gaiavate [The song of Hiawatha]. Moscow, 1916. p. v-xlvii.

1917 Popov, A. Review of: Pesn' o Gaiavate [The song of Hiawatha]. Moscow, 1916. Izvestiia Moskovskogo literaturno-khudozhestvennogo
kruzhka, 1917, no. 17-18, p. 72-73.

Review of: Pesn' o Gaiavate [The song of Hiawatha]. Moscow, 1916.
Russkie zapiski, 1917, no. 1, p. 310-312.

1919 Nonin, S. Genri Longfello (1807-1882) [Henry Longfellow, 1807-1882].
In: Longfellow, H. Pesni nevoli [Songs of slavery—i.e. *Poems on
Slavery*]. Petrograd, 1919. **p. 2. (Signed:** S. No—n.)

Stoliarov. Review of: Pesn' o Gaiavate [The song of Hiawatha]. Moscow, 1918. Vestnik zhizni, 1919, no. 3-4, p. 164-165. (Signed: M. T.)

1928 Derzhavin, K. Pesn' o Gaiavate [The song of Hiawatha]. *In:* Longfellow,
H. Pesn' o Gaiavate [The song of Hiawatha]. Moscow, Leningrad,
1928. p. 3-13; 2nd ed. 1931, p. 3-13; 3rd ed. 1933, p. 3-11; Moscow,
1941, p. 3-12. *Review:* Lomov, I. N. Gosizdat i Gaiavata. (O pre-
dislovii K. Derzhavina) [The State Publishing House and Hiawatha.
(Concerning K. Derzhavin's preface)]. Molodaia gvardiia, 1929,
no. 16, p. 79-80.

1934 Bobrova. Mir indeiskikh skazanii i legend [The world of Indian tales and
legends]. (Pesn' o Gaiavate [The song of Hiawatha]. Moscow,
Leningrad, 1933). Detskaia i iunosheskaia literatura, 1934, no. 6,
p. 11-13.

1940 Alekseev, M. P. Genri Uedsvort Longfello [Henry Wadsworth Long-
fellow]. Zvezda, 1940, no. 8-9, p. 229-233.

1941 Nesterovskaia, A. Review of: Pesn' o Gaiavate [The song of Hiawatha].
Moscow, Leningrad, 1941. Literaturnoe obozrenie, 1941, no. 10,
p. 72-73.

Fish, G. Review of: Pesn' o Gaiavate [The song of Hiawatha]. Moscow,
Leningrad, 1941. Detskaia literatura, 1941, no. 5, p. 38-39.

1946 Alekseev, M. P. Stikhotvornaia antologiia Longfello o Rossii [Long-
fellow's poetic anthology about Russia[1]]. Nauchnyi biulleten'

---

[1] *Poems of Places*, vol. 20 (Russia).

Leningradskogo gosudarstvennogo universiteta, 1946, no. 8, p. 27-28.
1947 Udartseva, M. Vliianie "Kalevaly" na "Pesniu o Gaiavate" [The influence of the "Kalevala" on "The song of Hiawatha"]. Na rubezhe (Petrozavodsk), 1947, no. 10, p. 67-73.
1949 Udartseva, M. G. K voprosu o vliianii narodnogo karelofinskogo eposa "Kalevala" na proizvedenie Longfello "Pesnia o Gaiavate" [On the problem of the Karelo-Finnish popular epic "Kalevala" on Longfellow's work "The song of Hiawatha"]. *In:* Prirodnye resursy, istoriia i kul'tura Karelo-Finskoi SSR. vyp. 1. Petrozavodsk, 1949. p. 79-90.
1954 Uspenskii, L. "Kalevala" i "Gaiavata" ["Kalevala" and "Hiawatha"]. *In:* Uspenskii, L. Slovo o slovakh [A word about words]. Leningrad, 1954. p. 217-219. Rev. and enlarged ed. Leningrad, 1962. p. 288-290.
1956 Kornilova, E. Posleslovie Longfello i ego pesn' o Gaiavate [Longfellow's afterword and his song of Kiawatha]. *In:* Longfellow, H. Pesn' o Gaiavate [The song of Hiawatha]. Moscow, 1956. p. 176-182.
1957 Elistratova, A. Genri Longfello. K 150-letiiu so dnia rozhdeniia [Henry Longfellow. On the 150th anniversary of his birth]. Pravda, February 27, 1957.
Zasurskii, Ia. N. Genri Uodsuort Longfello (1807-1882) [Henry Wadsworth Longfellow, 1807-1882]. Literatura v shkole, 1957, no. 2, p. 84-85.
Kornilova, E. Genri Longfello [Henry Longfellow]. Kul'tura i zhizn', 1957, no. 2, p. 53.
Kornilova, E. Poet-gumanist [A humanist-poet]. Izvestiia, February 27, 1957.
"Kto byl mister Longfello?" ["Who was Mr. Longfellow?"]. Literaturnaia gazeta, February 28, 1957.
Levin, Iu. D. Genri Longfello [Henry Longfellow]. *In:* Mikhailov, M. L. Stikhotvoreniia [Poems]. Leningrad, 1957. p. 449-451.
Mikhal'skaia, N. Longfello [Longfellow]. Narodnoe obrazovanie, 1957, no. 2, p. 100-102.
Nersesova, M. Genri Longfello [Henry Longfellow]. Sovetskaia kul'tura, February 26, 1957.
1958 Sedov, B. Pochtovaia marka v chest' Longfello [A postage stamp in honor of Longfellow]. Sovetskaia kul'tura, April 12, 1958.
Tomashevskii, B. Genri Longfello [Henry Longfellow]. *In:* Longfellow, H. Izbrannoe [Selections]. Moscow, 1958. p. iii-xxxix.
1959 Rongonen, L. I. Istoriia sozdaniia i analiz "Pesen o rabstve" Longfello [The history of the creation and an analysis of "Songs about slavery" —i.e. *Poems on Slavery*—by Longfellow]. Uchenye zapiski Karel'-skogo pedagogicheskogo instituta, 1959, t. 9, p. 172-183.
Rongonen, L. I. and M. G. Udartseva. K voprosu o iazyke i stile "Pesni o Gaiavate" Longfello [On the problem of the language and style of

132

"The song of Hiawatha" by Longfellow]. Uchenye zapiski Karel'-skogo pedagogicheskogo instituta, 1959, t. 6, p. 127-138.

1960 Lugovskoi, Vl. Slovo o Longfello [A word about Longfellow]. *In:* Lugovskoi, Vl. Razdum'e o poezii [Thoughts on poetry]. Moscow, 1960. p. 114-137.

1962 Genri Longfello (1807-1882). Metodicheskie materialy k vecheru, posvi-ashchennomu 80-letiiu so dnia smerti [Henry Longfellow, 1807-1882. Materials for a program marking the 80th anniversary of his death]. Moscow, 1962. 14 p.

Rongonen, L. I. O rannei poezii Longfello [Concerning the early poetry of Longfellow]. Uchenye zapiski Karel'skogo pedagogicheskogo instituta, 1962, t. 12, p. 185-197.

1963 Marti, Kh. [Jose]. Longfello [Longfellow]. *In:* Marti, Kh. [Jose]. Severo-amerikanskie stseny [North American scenes]. Moscow, 1963. p. 259-263.

Shalamov, V. Rabota Bunina nad perevodom "Pesni o Gaiavate" [Bunin's work on the translation of "The song of Hiawatha"]. Voprosy literatury, 1963, no. 1, p. 153-158.

MAKLISH Archibal'd   MACLEISH Archibald

1938 Startsev, A. Review of: *Land of the Free.* New York, 1938. Internatsio-nal'naia literatura, 1938, no. 12, p. 205-207.

MEILER Norman   MAILER Norman

1963 Levidova, I. Review of: *Deaths for the Ladies and Other Disasters.* New York, 1962. Sovremennaia khudozhestvennaia literatura za rubezhom, 1963, no. 1, p. 50-52.

MAL'TS Al'bert   MALTZ Albert

1934 Balashov, P. Mir, voina, revoliutsiia. (O p'ese "Mir na zemle" Al'berta Mal'tsa i Dzhordzha Skliara) [Peace, war, revolution. (About the play "Peace on earth" by Albert Maltz and George Sklar)]. Znamia, 1934, no. 8, p. 253-255.

1935 Balashov, P. Review of: *The Black Pit.* New York, 1935. Za rubezhom, 1935, no. 22, p. 482.

Iu. V. Tretii zlobstvuiushchii [The third malicious one]. (*The Black Pit.* New York, 1935). 30—i.e. Tridtsat'—dnei, 1935, no. 9, p. 84-86.

1939 Balashov, P. Review of: Chelovek na doroge [Man on a road]. Litera-turnaia gazeta, June 30, 1939.

Balashov, P. Uspekh molodogo novellista [The success of a young short story writer]. Internatsional'naia literatura, 1939, no. 1, p. 171-173.

1940 M. M. Novyi roman A. Mal'tsa. ("Podzemnyi potok") [The new novel by A. Maltz. ("The underground stream")]. Literaturnaia gazeta, August 18, 1940.

Khmel'nitskaia, T. Novelly Al'berta Mal'tsa [The short stories of Albert Maltz]. Leningrad, 1940, no. 3, p. 21-22.

1941 Abramov, A. Review of: *The Way Things Are*. New York, 1938. Literaturnoe obozrenie, 1941, no. 4, p. 64-66.

Balashov, P. Predislovie [Foreword]. *In:* Maltz, A. Chelovek na doroge [Man on a road]. Moscow, 1941. p. 3-6.

Bezrukikh, P. Review of: Chelovek na doroge [Man on a road]. 30—i.e. Tridtsat'—dnei, 1941, no. 4, p. 79-80.

Rubin, V. Review of: Glubinnyi potok [Deep current—i.e. *The Underground Stream*]. Internatsional'naia literatura, 1941, no. 1, p. 160-162.

1949 Limanovskaia, V. Ot perevodchika (posleslovie k povesti "Glubinnyi potok") [From the translator (afterword to the novel "Deep current" —i.e. *The Underground Stream*)]. Zvezda, 1949, no. 6, p. 110-111.

1950 Alipov, N. Predislovie [Foreword]. *In:* Maltz, A. Poriadok veshchei [The order of things—i.e. *The Way Things Are*]. Moscow, 1950, p. 3-5.

Nemerovskaia, O. Bor'ba prinimaet novye formy ("Glubinnyi istochnik." Moscow, 1949) [The struggle takes on new forms ("Deep spring"— i.e. *The Underground Stream*. Moscow, 1949)]. Zvezda, 1950, no. 5, p. 186-187.

1951 Mendel'son, M. Al'bert Mal'ts [Albert Maltz]. *In:* Maltz, A. Izbrannoe [Selected works]. Moscow, 1951. p. 3-24.

Mendel'son, M. Predislovie [Foreword]. *In:* Maltz, A. *Selected Stories*.[1] Moscow, 1951. p. 3-15.

1952 Anikst, A. Muzhestvennyi borets protiv voiny i fashizma [A courageous fighter against war and fascism]. Sovetskoe iskusstvo, March 26, 1952.

Bannikov, N. Predislovie [Foreword]. *In:* Maltz, A. Rasskazy [Stories]. Moscow, 1952. p. 3-6.

Gansovskii, S. Ot imeni amerikanskikh trudiashchikhsia. ("Izbrannoe." Moscow, 1951) [In the name of American workers. ("Selected works." Moscow, 1951)]. Zvezda, 1952, no. 3, p. 180-183.

Elistratova, A. Delo Pitera Morrisona, chestnogo amerikantsa. ("Delo Morrisona." 1952) [The case of Peter Morrison, an honest American. ("The Morrison case"—original English title not determined)]. Literaturnaia gazeta, August 19, 1952.

1954 Levidova, I. M. Al'bert Mal'ts. Bio-bibliograficheskii ukazatel' [Albert Maltz. Bio-bibliographic guide]. Moscow, Vsesoiuznaia gosudarstvennaia biblioteka inostrannoi literatury, 1954. 28 p.

[1] A book in the English language published in the Soviet Union.

1957 Novyi roman Al'berta Mal'tsa. ("Dolgii den' v korotkoi zhizni") [The new novel by Albert Maltz ("A long day in a short life")]. Literaturnaia gazeta, November 21, 1957.
1958 Al'bert Mal'ts. Materialy k vecheru, posviashchennomu 50-letiiu so dnia rozhdeniia [Albert Maltz. Materials for an evening in commemoration of the fiftieth anniversary of his birth]. Moscow, Vsesoiuznaia gosudarstvennaia biblioteka inostrannoi literatury, 1958. 7 p.
   Sheinin, L. Predislovie [Foreword]. *In:* Maltz, A. Dlinnyi den' v korotkoi zhizni [A long day in a short life]. Moscow, 1958. p. 5-20.
1959 Orlova, R. Vybor puti. ("Dlinnyi den' v korotkoi zhizni") [The choice of a road. ("A long day in a short life")]. Inostrannaia literatura, 1959, no. 3, p. 210-214.
1961 Orlova, R. U glubinnykh istochnikov gumanizma. Roman "Krest i strela" i ego mesto v tvorchestve Al'berta Mal'tsa [At the deep sources of humanism. The novel "The cross and the arrow" and its place in the work of Albert Maltz]. *In:* Maltz, A. Krest i strela [The cross and the arrow]. Moscow, 1961. p. 433-454.
1962 Baklanov, G. Obiazannost' byt' chelovekom. ("Krest i strela." Moscow, 1961) [The obligation to be a man. ("The cross and the arrow" Moscow, 1961)]. Inostrannaia literatura, 1962, no. 1, p. 251-254.
   Bannikov, N. Al'bert Mal'ts [Albert Maltz]. *In:* Maltz, A. Chelovek na doroge [Man on a road]. Moscow, 1962. p. 3-4.

MARKEND Dzhon Filipps   MARQUAND John Phillips

1942 Kramskoi, A. Review of: *H. M. Pulham, Esquire.* New York, 1941. Internatsional'naia literatura, 1942, no. 1-2, p. 214-215.
1945 Mendel'son, M. Dva amerikanskikh romana [Two American novels]. (*So Little Time.* New York, 1943). Literaturnaia gazeta, February 10, 1945.
1963 Samokhvalov, N. Markvend i ego roman [Marquand and his novel]. *In:* Marquand, J. P. G. M. Pulem, eskvair [H. M. Pulham, esquire]. Moscow, 1963. p. 441-443.

MASTERS Dekster   MASTERS Dexter

1957 Stal'skii, N. Zarevo vidno v kazhdom dome. ("Neschastnyi sluchai") [The dawn is visible in every house. ("The accident")]. Znamia 1957, no. 9, p. 214-218.
   Shvetsova, M. Tragediia Luisa Saksla. ("Neschastnyi sluchai") [The tragedy of Louis Saxl. ("The accident")]. Novoe vremia, 1957, no. 36, p. 28-30.
1958 Danin, D. Ispytanie optimizma. (O romane D. Mastersa "Neschastnyi sluchai") [A test of optimism. (Concerning D. Masters's novel "The accident")]. Novyi mir, 1958, no. 1, p. 240-249.

MASTERS Edgar Li   MASTERS Edgar Lee

1926 Kashkin, I. A. Edgar Li-Masters [Edgar Lee Masters]. *In:* Zapad i
      Vostok. Sbornik VOKSA [West and East. A collection for VOKS—
      Vsesoiuznoe obshchestvo dlia kul'turnykh sviazei s zagranitsei—All-
      Union Society for Cultural Relations with Foreign Countries].
      kn. 1 and 2. Moscow, 1926. p. 88-94.
1936 Kashkin, I. Edgar Li Masters [Edgar Lee Masters]. Internatsional'naia
      literatura, 1936, no. 3, p. 133-137.

MAKKEI Klod   MCKAY Claude

1923 V. V. Klod Mak-Kei [Claude McKay]. Krasnaia niva, 1923, no. 1, p. 15.
      Kozitsyn, M. Klod Mak-Kei [Claude McKay]. Literaturnyi ezhenedel'-
      nik, 1923, no. 8, p. 16.
      Okhrimenko, P. Ot perevodchika [From the translator]. *In:* McKay, C.
      Negry v Amerike [The Negroes in America]. Moscow, Petrograd,
      1923. p. 5-9.
1925 Vmesto predisloviia [In place of a foreword]. *In:* McKay, C. Sudom
      Lincha [Under lynch law—original English title not determined].
      Moscow, 1925. p. 3-5.
1929 Van Mais [Van Mise?] and V. Vil'son [W. Wilson?]. Predislovie [Fore-
      word]. *In:* McKay, C. Domoi v Garlem [Home to Harlem]. Mos-
      cow, Leningrad, 1929. p. 5-6.
      Vinogradskaia, S. Review of: Domoi v Garlem [Home to Harlem].
      Moscow, Leningrad, 1929. Kniga i revoliutsiia, 1929, no. 8, p. 59.
      Frid, Ia. Review of: Domoi v Garlem [Home to Harlem]. Moscow,
      Leningrad, 1929. Novyi mir, 1929, no. 6, p. 237-238.
1930 Vershinina, Z. Predislovie [Foreword]. *In:* McKay, C. Bandzho [Banjo].
      Moscow, Leningrad, 1930. p. 3-6.
      Pesis, B. Kurs na ar"ergard [Headed toward the rear guard]. (Bandzho
      [Banjo]. Moscow, Leningrad, 1930). Kniga i revoliutsiia, 1930, no.
      29-30, p. 16-18.

MELVILL German   MELVILLE Herman

1849 Deistvitel'nye i fantasticheskie puteshestviia Germana Mel'vilia. "Taipi."
      —"Omu."—"Vtornik." (S publikatsiei otryvkov) [The real and the
      fantastic journeys of Herman Melville. "Typee."—"Omoo."—"Mar-
      di." (With excerpts)]. Biblioteka dlia chteniia, 1849, t. 96, otd. VII,
      p. 77-90.
1853 German Mel'vil' [Herman Melville]. Moskvitianin, 1853, no. 15, otd.
      VIII, p. 125-126.
1854 German Mel'vil' (Severo-amerikanskii pisatel') [Herman Melville (a
      North American writer)]. Panteon, 1854, no. 3, otd. IV, p. 10-12.

1946 Mendel'son, M. Ot "Taipi" do Bikini [From "Typee" to Bikini]. Literaturnaia gazeta, July 27, 1946.
1960 Bakhta, V. Posleslovie [Afterword]. *In:* Melville, H. Omu [Omoo]. Moscow, 1960. p. 271-276.
1961 Startsev, A. German Melvili i ego "Mobi Dik" [Herman Melville and his "Moby-Dick"]. *And:* Zenkevich, B. A. Posleslovie [Afterword]. *In:* Melville, H. Mobi Dik ili Belyi Kit [Moby-Dick, or, The white whale]. Moscow, 1961. p. 9-20, 834-839. (2nd ed. Moscow, 1962).
   Andreev, K. Raziashchaia stal' Germana Melvilla—"Mobi Dik ili Belyi Kit" [The cutting edge of Herman Melville—"Moby-Dick, or, The white whale"]. Literaturnaia gazeta, December 9, 1961.
1963 Nikoliukin, A. Review of: Miller, J. E., Jr. *A Reader's Guide to Herman Melville.* Sovremennaia khudozhestvennaia literatura za rubezhom, 1963, no. 8, p. 86-88.

MENKEN Genri L'iuis   MENCKEN Henry Louis

1928 Sinkler, E. [Sinclair, U.]. Bezmiatezhnyi miatezhnik [The unrebellious rebel]. Na literaturnom postu, 1928, no. 13-14, p. 73-74.

MILBERN Dzhordzh   MILBURN George

1935 Dzhordzh Milbern. (Avtobiografiia) [George Milburn. (Autobiography)]. Internatsional'naia literatura, 1935, no. 11, p. 155.
1937 Balashov, P. Review of: *Catalogue.* New York, 1936. Za rubezhom. 1937, no. 2, p. 26.
   Borovoi, L. Review of: Deshevaia Amerika [Cheap America]; *Catalogue.* Literaturnoe obozrenie, 1937, no. 21, p. 41-42.
1938 Khmel'nitskaia, T. Tragicheskii grotesk. ("Deshevaia Amerika"—*Catalogue* Dzhordzha Milberna) [A tragic grotesque. ("Cheap America"—*Catalogue* of George Milburn)]. Literaturnyi sovremennik, 1938, no. 4, p. 220-229.
   Rubin, V. Review of: Preiskurant [Catalogue]. Moscow, 1937. Novyi mir, 1938, no. 8, p. 271-272.
1939 Tolkachev, E. Lozhka degtia. ("Preiskurant") [A spoonful of tar. ("Catalogue")]. Literaturnaia gazeta, June 30, 1939.

MILLER Artur   MILLER Arthur

1947 Berkutov, V. Goneniia na p'esu "Vse moi synov'ia" [The persecution of the play "All my sons"]. Izvestiia, September 12, 1947.
1948 Borshchagovskii, A. Review of the play: Vse moi synov'ia [All my sons]. Izvestiia, November 24, 1948.
   Golysheva, E. and Iu. Semenov. Artur Miller i ego p'esa. ("Vse moi

synov'ia") [Arthur Miller and his play. ("All my sons")]. Zvezda, 1948, no. 2, p. 114.

Dreiden, S. Dzho Keller i synov'ia. ("Vse moi synov'ia") [Joe Keller and sons. ("All my sons")]. Sovetskoe iskusstvo, September 18, 1948.

Matskin, A. Istoriia odnogo prestupleniia. ("Vse moi synov'ia") [The history of a crime. ("All my sons")]. Sovetskoe iskusstvo, November 27, 1948.

Munblit, G. Zapreshchennaia p'esa. ("Vse moi synov'ia") [A banned play. ("All my sons")]. Novyi mir, 1948, no. 9, p. 291-292.

1955 Adashevskii, K. Sila pravdy. ("Salemskii protsess") [The strength of truth. ("The Salem trial"—i.e. *The Crucible*)]. Sovetskaia kul'tura, December 24, 1955.

Balashova, N. Review of the play: Salemskii protsess [The Salem trial— i.e. *The Crucible*]. Teatr, 1955, no. 6, p. 137-139.

Turkov, A. Review of the play: Salemskii protsess [The Salem trial—i.e. *The Crucible*]. Sovetskaia kul'tura, July 14, 1955.

1956 Litinskii, G. Review of the play: Chelovek, kotoromu tak vezlo [The man to whom it happened that way—i.e. *Death of a Salesman*]. Teatr, 1956, no. 11, p. 127-128.

Shneiderman, I. Review of: Salemskie koldun'i [The Salem wizards—i.e. *The Crucible*]. Teatr, 1956, no. 2, p. 121-122.

1957 Artur Miller predan sudu [Arthur Miller is indicted]. Literaturnaia gazeta, February 28, 1957.

Zlobin, G. Surovoe ispytanie. (Zametki o dramaturgii A. Millera) [A harsh test—i.e. *The Crucible*. (Remarks on the dramaturgy of A. Miller)]. Inostrannaia literatura, 1957, no. 8, p. 184-190.

Keremetskii, Ia. Kakoi primer oni pokazyvaiut miru [The sort of example which they are showing to the world]. Sovetskaia kul'tura, June 25, 1957.

1959 Berkovskii, N. Zashchita zhizni. ("Smert' kommivoiazhera") [The defense of life. ("The death of a salesman")]. Teatr, 1959, no. 7, p. 50-60.

Kapralov, G. Tragediia Villi Lomena. ("Smert' kommivoiazhera") [The tragedy of Willy Loman. ("The death of a salesman")]. Pravda, July 28, 1959.

Neverov, N. P'esy Artura Millera [The plays of Arthur Miller]. Novoe vremia, 1959, no. 31, p. 23-30.

1960 Ben'iash, R. Liudi bez budushchego. ("Vospominanie o dvukh pone-del'nikakh") [People without a future. ("A memory of two Mon-days")]. Izvestiia, September 2, 1960.

Kapralov, G. Plata za zhizn'. ("Smert' kommivoiazhera") [A payment for life. ("The death of a salesman")]. Neva, 1960, no. 3, p. 193-195.

Mints, N. Idei, kotorye volnuiut mnogikh [Ideas which disturb many]. *In:* Miller, A. Vse moi synov'ia. Smert' kommivoiazhera. Surovoe ispytanie. Vid s mosta [All my sons. The death of a salesman. A harsh test—i.e. *The Crucible*. View from the bridge]. Moscow, 1960. p. 3-15.

Tsimbal, S. Review of: Vospominanie o dvukh ponedel'nikakh [A memory of two Mondays]. Teatr, 1960, no. 12, p. 64-67.

1961 Bereznitskii, Ia. Artur Miller pered sudom Erika Bentli [Arthur Miller before the judgment of Eric Bentley]. Teatr, 1961, no. 3, p. 180-183.

Koreneva, M. M. Amerikanskii dramaturg Artur Miller. (Zametki o masterstve) [The American playwright Arthur Miller. (Remarks about his mastery)]. Vestnik Moskovskogo universiteta. Filologiia, zhurnalistika, 1961, no. 6, p. 55-68.

Levidova, I. M. Artur Miller. Bio-bibliograficheskii ukazatel'. Vstupitel'naia stat'ia N. M. Eishiskinoi [Arthur Miller. Bio-bibliographic guide. Introductory guide by N. M. Eishiskina]. Moscow, Vsesoiuznaia knizhnaia palata, 1961. 55 p. Compiled with the cooperation of the Vsesoiuznaia gosudarstvennaia biblioteka inostrannoi literatury [All-Union State Library of Foreign Literature].

Orlova, R. S. S bol'iu—o cheloveke [Painfully—about mankind]. (P'esy [Plays]. Moscow, 1960). Novyi mir, no. 7, 1961, p. 267-271.

1962 Anastas'ev, N. Dva porazheniia [Two defeats]. (*The Misfits*. New York, 1961). Molodaia gvardiia, 1962, no. 10, p. 304-310.

Zlobin, G. Kto v otvete? [Who is responsible?]. (*The Misfits*. New York, 1961). Inostrannaia literatura, 1962, no. 1, p. 257-258.

Zlobin, G. Monografiia ob Arture Millere [A monograph about Arthur Miller]. (Welland, D. *Arthur Miller*. London, 1961). Voprosy literatury, 1962, no. 10, p. 238-239. *Also in:* Sovremennaia khudozhestvennaia literatura za rubezhom, 1962, no. 4-5, p. 116-119.

Miller, A. Chto podryvaet nash prestizh [What is undermining our prestige]. Literaturnaia gazeta, September 4, 1962.

Eishiskina, N. Artur Miller [Arthur Miller]. *In:* Sovremennaia zarubezhnaia drama [Contemporary foreign drama]. Moscow, 1962. p. 13-62.

1963 Anastas'ev, N. Poedinok ne sostoialsia [The duel did not take place]. ("Seilemskie ved'my" ["The Salem witches"—i.e. *The Crucible*]). Teatr, 1963, no. 4, p. 15-17.

Ul'ianov, G. Bunt Dzhona Proktora [The uprising of John Proctor]. ("Seilemskie ved'my" ["The Salem witches"—i.e. *The Crucible*]). Nauka i religiia, 1963, no. 5, p. 87-88.

MITCHEL Margaret   MITCHELL Margaret

1937 N. V. Review of: *Gone with the Wind*, 1936. Literaturnoe obozrenie, 1937, no. 8, p. 60.

1935 Karmon, U. [Carmon, W.]. Review of: *You Can't Sleep Here*. New York, 1934. Inostrannaia kniga, 1935, no. 1, p. 21-22.
1937 Ivasheva, V. Review of: *This Is Your Day*. New York, 1937. Internatsional'naia literatura, 1937, no. 8, p. 206-208.
1938 Vostokova, S. Review of: Spat' zdes' ne razreshaetsia [It is not permitted to sleep here—i.e. *You Can't Sleep Here*]. Moscow, 1938. Molodaia gvardiia, 1938, no. 11, p. 137-139.
     Levidov, M. Review of: Spat' zdes' ne razreshaetsia [It is not permitted to sleep here—i.e. *You Can't Sleep Here*]. Literaturnoe obozrenie, 1938, no. 11, p. 28-32.
     Firsov, A. Kniga o chelovecheskom dostoinstve [A book about human worth]. (Spat' zdes' ne razreshaetsia [It is not permitted to sleep here—i.e. *You Can't Sleep Here*]. Moscow, 1938). Literaturnyi kritik, 1938, no. 6, p. 235-237.

1925 Vikov, E. Review of: Sprut [The octopus]. Leningrad, 1925. Oktiabr', 1925, no. 8, p. 162.
     Zhits, F. Review of: Sprut [The octopus]. Leningrad, 1925. Novyi mir, 1925, no. 10, p. 153-154.
     Rozental', L. Review of: Sprut [The octopus]. Leningrad, 1925. Pechat' i revoliutsiia, 1925, no. 8, p. 254-255.
1926 Anisimov, I. Review of: Omut [The pool—i.e. *The Pit*]. Leningrad, 1925. Knigonosha, 1926, no. 1, p. 33.
     Rozental', L. Review of: Omut [The pool—i.e. *The Pit*]. Leningrad, 1925. Pechat' i revoliutsiia, 1926, no. 4, p. 218-219.
1927 Norris, K. Predislovie k amerikanskomu izdaniiu [Foreword to the American edition]. *In:* Norris, F. Bliks: Povest' iunoi liubvi [Blix: A tale of young love]. Leningrad, 1927. p. 5-6.
1929 Vl-ko. Review of: Sil'naia dukhom [Strong in spirit—i.e. *A Man's Woman*]. Leningrad, 1928. Krasnoe slovo (Khar'kov), 1929, no. 2, p. 107-108.
1937 A. S. Frenk Norris [Frank Norris]. Literaturnoe obozrenie, 1937, no. 21, p. 58.
1950 Bogoslovskii, V. Posleslovie [Afterword]. *In:* Norris, F. Sprut [The octopus]. Moscow, 1950. p. 448-454.
1953 Bogoslovskii, V. N. Literaturnye vzgliady Norrisa [Norris's literary views]. Uchenye zapiski Moskovskogo oblastnogo pedagogicheskogo instituta, 1953. t. 26. Trudy kafedry zarubezhnoi literatury, vyp. 1, p. 21-44.
1955 Bogoslovskii, V. N. Tvorchestvo Franka Norrisa, 1870-1902 [The work

of Frank Norris, 1870-1902]. Uchenye zapiski Moskovskogo oblastnogo pedagogicheskogo instituta, 1955, t. 34. Trudy kafedry zarubezhnoi literatury, vyp. 2, p. 67-117.
1956 Makarova, N. P. Roman Frenka Norrisa "Sprut." (Iz istorii amerikanskogo sotsial'nogo romana) [Frank Norris's novel "The octopus."
(From the history of the American social novel)]. Uchenye zapiski
Kemerovskogo pedagogicheskogo instituta, 1956, vyp. 1, p. 83-116.
Savurenok, A. K. "Epos pshenitsy" F. Norrisa [The "Epic of the Wheat"
of F. Norris]. Uchenye zapiski Leningradskogo gosudarstvennogo
universiteta, 1956, no. 212. Seriia filologicheskikh nauk, vyp. 28.
Zarubezhnaia literatura, p. 166-187.
1958 Babushkina, I. E. Kriticheskii realizm Frenka Norrisa. (Nekotorye
problemy tvorchestva pisatelei) [The critical realism of Frank Norris.
(Some problems of the creative work of writers)]. Uchenye zapiski
pervogo Moskovskogo pedagogicheskogo instituta inostrannykh
iazykov, 1958, t. 21. Kafedra literatury, p. 135-166.
Nol'man, M. Sotsial'naia epopeia Frenka Norrisa [The social epic of
Frank Norris]. In: Norris, F. Sprut [The octopus]. Moscow, 1958.
p. 227-237.
1959 Babushkina, I. E. Tvorcheskii put' Frenka Norrisa [The creative path of
Frank Norris]. Abstract of dissertation presented for the degree of
Candidate of Philological Sciences. Moscow, 1959. 16 p.
1962 Babushkina, I. Frenk Norris i ego roman "Sprut" [Frank Norris and his
novel "The octopus"]. In: Norris, F. The Octopus: A Story of
California.[1] Moscow, 1962. p. 3-14.

NORT Dzhozef   NORTH Joseph

1959 Nedelin, V. Pravdivaia, muzhestvennaia kniga [A true, courageous book].
(No Men Are Strangers. New York, 1958). Inostrannaia literatura,
1959, no. 6, p. 195-198.

ODETS Klifford   ODETS Clifford

1940 Miller-Budnitskaia, R. Mechta o chelovechnosti. Tri p'esy Klifforda
Odetsa [A dream of humaneness. Three plays of Clifford Odets].
Iskusstvo i zhizn', 1940, no. 10, p. 16-17.
Otten, N. Kratkaia spravka [A short note]. In: Odets, C. Zolotoi
mal'chik [Golden boy]. Moscow, Leningrad, 1940. p. 82-83.
Rait, R. P'esy Klifforda Odetsa [The plays of Clifford Odets]. Iskusstvo i
zhizn', 1940, no. 3, p. 46-47.
1941 Ketlinskaia, V. Review of: Zolotoi mal'chik [Golden boy]. Moscow,
Leningrad, 1940. Iskusstvo i zhizn', 1941, no. 2, p. 18-19.

[1] A work in the English language published in the Soviet Union.

Kostelianets, B. Gibel' Dzho Bonaparte [The downfall of Joe Bonaparte].
("Zolotoi mal'chik" ["Golden boy"]. Moscow, Leningrad, 1940).
Zvezda, 1941, no. 5, p. 182-183.

Levidov, M. Review of: Zolotoi mal'chik [Golden boy]. Moscow,
Leningrad, 1940. Literaturnoe obozrenie, 1941, no. 5, p. 63-66.

Miller-Budnitskaia, R. Review of: Zolotoi mal'chik [Golden boy].
Moscow, Leningrad, 1940. Zvezda, 1941, no. 5, p. 182-183.

Rykova, N. Dramy Klifforda Odetsa [The drama of Clifford Odets].
Literaturnyi sovremennik, 1941, no. 5, p. 144-148.

1942 M. Zh. Review of: Rokovoi chas [The fateful hour—i.e. *Clash by Night*].
Literatura i iskusstvo, March 8, 1942.

O'NIL Iudzhin   O'NEILL Eugene

1923 Klark [Clark], B. Evgenii O'Neil' i amerikanskaia drama [Eugene O'Neill
and American drama]. Beseda (Berlin], 1923, no. 1, p. 374-388.

1926 B. G. Review of: Kosmataia obez'iana [The hairy ape]. Pravda, January
19, 1926.

Blium, V. I. Review of: Kosmataia obez'iana [The hairy ape]. Izvestiia,
January 26, 1926. (Signed: Sadko.)

Blium, V. I. Review of: Liubov' pod viazami [Love under the elms[1]].
Zhizn' iskusstva, 1926, no. 49, p. 11.

Grossman, L. Review of: Liubov' pod viazami [Love under the elms].
Krasnaia niva, 1926, no. 48, p. 22.

Inber, V. Review of: Kosmataia obez'iana [The hairy ape]. Novyi
zritel', 1926, no. 5, p. 8.

Lunacharskii, A. O spektakle "Anna Kristi" [Concerning the play "Anna
Christie"]. *In:* Lunacharskii, A. O teatre [Concerning the theater].
Leningrad, 1926. p. 95-97.

Markov, P. Review of: Liubov' pod viazami [Love under the elms].
Pravda, November 19, 1926.

Pavlov, V. Druzheskaia zaokeanskaia dramaturgiia [Friendly trans-
Atlantic dramaturgy]. Novyi zritel', 1926, no. 43, p. 6.

Khersonskii, Kh. Review of: Liubov' pod viazami [Love under the elms].
Prozhektor, 1926, no. 23, p. 31.

Ia. A. Review of: Kosmataia obez'iana [The hairy ape]. Krasnaia niva,
1926, no. 7, p. 21.

Volkov, N. Review of: Liubov' pod viazami [Love under the elms].
Izvestiia, November 18, 1926.

1927 Derzhavin, K. Review of: Liubov' pod viazami [Love under the elms].
Zhizn' iskusstva, 1927, no. 19, p. 10.

Mazing, B. Review of: Kosmataia obez'iana [The hairy ape]. Krasnaia
gazeta, May 14, 1927.

[1] *Desire Under the Elms.*

142

Mazing, B. Review of: Liubov' pod viazami [Love under the elms]. Rabochii i teatr, 1927, no. 19, p. 6.

Mokul'skii, S. Review of: Kosmataia obez'iana [The hairy ape]. Zhizn' iskusstva, 1927, no. 21, p. 14-15.

1928 Kruti, I. Review of: Zoloto [Gold]. Sovremennyi teatr, 1928, no. 4, p. 66.

Eidel'man, Ia. Review of: Zoloto [Gold]. Zhizn' iskusstva, 1928, no. 4, p. 10.

1929 Volkov, N. Review of: Negr [The Negro—i.e. *All God's Chillun Got Wings*]. Izvestiia, February 27, 1929.

Litovskii, O. S. Review of: Negr [The Negro—i.e. *All God's Chillun Got Wings*]. Komsomol'skaia pravda, March 10, 1929. (Signed: Uriel'.)

Markov, P. Review of: Negr [The Negro—i.e. *All God's Chillun Got Wings*]. Krasnaia niva, 1929, no. 15, p. 21.

Mokul'skii, S. Review of: Negr [The Negro—i.e. *All God's Chillun Got Wings*]. Zhizn' iskusstva, 1929, no. 19, p. 24.

N. P. Review of: Negr [The Negro—i.e. *All God's Chillun Got Wings*]. Prozhektor, 1929, no. 19, p. 24.

Ravich, N. Review of: Negr [The Negro—i.e. *All God's Chillun Got Wings*]. Zhizn' iskusstva, 1929, no. 9, p. 8.

Tairov, A. "Negr" O'Neilia na stsene Kamernogo teatra ["The Negro"— i.e. *All God's Chillun Got Wings*—of O'Neill on the stage of the Kamernyi Theater]. Sovremennyi teatr, 1929, no. 8, p. 123.

Filippov, B. Vmesto predisloviia [In place of a foreword]. Movsheson, A. G. Iudzhen O'Neil' [Eugene O'Neill]. *In:* O'Neill, E. Koroleva Atlantiki ("Vorvan'") [The queen of the Atlantic ("Blubber"—i.e. *Ile*)]. Leningrad, Moscow, 1929. p. 3-8.

1930 Tairov, A. Ia. Rezhisserskie primechaniia [The remarks of a director]. *In:* O'Neill, E. Negr. (Chernoe getto) [The Negro—i.e. *All God's Chillun Got Wings*. (The black ghetto)]. Moscow, Leningrad, 1930, p. 5-14.

1933 Abramov, A. Obrechennye. Zhenshchina v burzhuaznoi dramaturgii. ("Strannaia intermediia") [The doomed. Woman in bourgeois drama. ("Strange interlude")]. Sovetskoe iskusstvo, March 8, 1933.

Tairov, A. Dramaturg i ego geroi. Tvorchestvo Iudzhina O'Neilia [The dramatist and his hero. The works of Eugene O'Neill]. Sovetskoe iskusstvo, November 26, 1933.

Tairov, A. Spor mezhdu "litsom" i "maskoi" [The quarrel between the "personage" and the "mask"]. Literaturnaia gazeta, January 17, 1933.

1934 Abramov, A. O'Neil' na koleniakh pered raspiatiem [O'Neill on his knees before the Crucifixion]. (*Days Without End*). Literaturnaia gazeta, December 12, 1934.

Zabludovskii, M. Ot realizma k mistitsizmu. (O'Neil') [From realism to mysticism. (O'Neill)]. Literaturnyi kritik, 1934, no. 7-8, p. 210-217.

Lunacharskii, A. "Kosmataia obez'iana" ["The hairy ape"]. *In:* Kamernyi teatr [The Kamernyi Theater]. Moscow, 1934. p. 37-40.

1935 Abramov, A. Review of: *Days Without End.* New York, 1934. Inostrannaia kniga, 1935, no. 1, p. 23-24. *Also, abridged, in:* Za rubezhom, 1935, no. 7, p. 146.
1936 Abramov, A. Konets buntarstva Iudzhina O'Neilia [The end of the seditious mood of Eugene O'Neill]. Internatsional'naia literatura, 1936, no. 2, p. 144-150.

O'Neil, Iudzhin Gladston [O'Neill, Eugene Gladstone]. Za rubezhom, 1936, no. 33, p. 770.
1937 Vigand, Ch. fon [Von Wiegand, Ch.]. Ot Karaibskogo moria k podnozhiiu kresta. (Put' Iudzhina O'Neilia) [From the Caribbean Sea to the foot of the cross. (The path of Eugene O'Neill)]. Internatsional'-naia literatura, 1937, no. 3, p. 175-186.

Nobelevskaia premiia 1936 g. [The Nobel Prize of 1936]. Literaturnaia gazeta, January 5, 1937.
1948 Kulikova, I. Besslavnyi put' [An inglorious path]. Teatr, 1948, no. 11, p. 47-54.
1956 Startsev, A. Neizvestnaia p'esa Iudzhina O'Nila [An unknown play by Eugene O'Neill]. (*Long Day's Journey Into Night*). [Publication not named], 1956, no. 11, p. 261-262.
1963 Zlobin, G. "On preobrazil nashu dramu." ["He transformed our drama"]. Literaturnaia gazeta, October 15, 1963.

PEIN Tomas   PAINE Thomas

1939 Startsev, A. Review of: Smith, F. *Thomas Paine—Liberator.* New York, 1938. Internatsional'naia literatura, 1939, no. 5-6, p. 214-216.
1959 Baskin, M. P. Tomas Pein [Thomas Paine]. *In:* Paine, T. Izbrannye sochineniia. [Selected works]. Moscow, 1959. p. 5-20.

Baskin, M. Tomas Pein—kritik religii [Thomas Paine, a critic of religion]. Nauka i religiia, 1959, no. 3, p. 92-93.
1960 Gromakov, B. S. Politicheskie pravovye vzgliady Tomasa Peina [The politico-juridical views of Thomas Paine]. Moscow, Gosiurizdat, 1960. 74 p.
1963 Tomas Pen v nemilosti [Thomas Paine in disfavor]. Literaturnaia gazeta, August 10, 1963.

PARKER Doroti   PARKER Dorothy

1940 Romanova, E. Review of: *Here Lies.* New York, 1939. Internatsional'-naia literatura, 1940, no. 9-10, p. 246-248.
1956 Romanova, E. V odnom iz otelei N'iu-Iorka. ("Damy iz togo zhe koridora") [In one of the hotels of New York. ("Ladies from the same corridor"—i.e. *Ladies of the Corridor*)]. Sovetskaia kul'tura, April 5, 1956.

1959 Kopelev, L. Predislovie [Foreword]. *In:* Parker, D. Novelly [Short stories]. Moscow, 1959. p. 3-14.

Lagunova, M. Predislovie [Foreword]. *In:* Parker, D. *Short Stories and Poems.*[1] Moscow, 1959. p. 3-8.

1960 Kopelev, L. Gorech' amerikanskikh budnei. (Novelly Doroti Parker) [The bitterness of everyday American life. (The short stories of Dorothy Parker)]. *In:* Kopelev, L. Serdtse vsegda sleva [The heart is always on the left]. Moscow, 1960. p. 352-363.

FILLIPS DEVID GREKHEM   PHILLIPS DAVID GRAHAM

1911 Fillips Devid Gregem, 1867-1911. (Nekrolog) [Phillips, David Graham, 1867-1911. (Obituary)]. Russkaia mysl', 1911, no. 3, otd. III, p. 51.

PO EDGAR ALLAN   POE EDGAR ALLAN

1852 Bodler, Sh. [Baudelaire, Ch.]. Edgar Ellen'-Poe. Severo-amerikanskii poet [Edgar Allan Poe. A North American poet]. Panteon, 1852, no. 9, otd. III, p. 1-34.

Grigor'ev, Ap. Obzor inostrannoi zhurnalistiki. (Edgar Po) [A survey of foreign journals. (Edgar Poe)]. Moskvitianin, 1852, no. 22, otd. VI, p. 13-15. (Signed: G.)

1856 Edgar Po [Edgar Poe]. Russkii invalid, November 1, 1856.

Edgar Poe, sovremennyi severo-amerikanskii pisatel'. Ego zhizn' i sochineniia [Edgar Poe, a contemporary North American writer. His life and works]. Syn otechestva, 1856, no. 14, p. 33-36.

1859 Govoriashchii mertvets. (O rasskaze "Fakty v dele m-ra Val'demara") [The speaking corpse. (Concerning the tale "The facts in the case of Mr. Valdemar")]. Saint Petersburg, 1859. 51 p.

1861 Dostoevskii, F. M. Tri rasskaza Edgara Poe [Three tales of Edgar Poe]. Vremia, 1861, t. 1, p. 230-231. (Signed: Red.) *Also in:* Dostoevskii, F. M. Polnoe sobranie sochinenii [Complete collected works]. v. 13. Moscow, Leningrad, 1930. p. 523-524.

Lopushinskii, E. Edgar Poe. (Amerikanskii poet) [Edgar Poe. (An American poet)]. Russkoe slovo, 1861, no. 11, otd. III, p. 1-30.

1864 Vern, Zh. [Verne, Jules?]. Edgar Poe i ego sochineniia [Edgar Poe and his works]. Modnyi magazin, 1864, no. 23, p. 353-356.

1866 Edgar Poe [Edgar Poe]. Zagranichnyi vestnik, 1866, no. 1, p. 67-78; no. 2, p. 348-367.

1874 Shelgunov, N. V. Edgar Po [Edgar Poe]. Delo, 1874, no. 4, p. 276-285. (Signed: N. Sh.)

Shelgunov, N. V. Edgar Po—kak psikholog [Edgar Poe as a psychologist]. Delo, 1874, no. 7-8, p. 350-366. (Signed: N. Sh.)

[1] A book in the English language published in the Soviet Union.

1880 Novaia biografiia i novoe izdanie sochinenii E. A. Poe [A new biography and a new edition of the works of E. A. Poe]. Ezhenedel'noe novoe vremia, 1880, t. 5, no. 63, p. 702-704.

Komarov, A. Edgar Allan Poe, ego zhizn' i tvoreniia [Edgar Allan Poe, his life and writings]. Ezhenedel'noe novoe vremia, 1880, t. 5, no. 61, p. 548-558; no. 62, p. 626-639.

1883 Vasilisk. Edgar Poe [Edgar Poe]. Rebus, 1883, no. 13, p. 118-120.

1885 Genneken, E. Zhizn' Edgara Allena Po [The life of Edgar Allan Poe]. *In:* Poe, E. Ocherki, rasskazy i mysli [Essays, stories and thoughts]. Moscow, 1885, p. i-lxiv.

1886 Aksakov, N. Psikhologiia Edgara Poe [The psychology of Edgar Poe]. Vsemirnaia illiustratsiia, 1886, no. 10, p. 191-194; no. 11, p. 210-211; no. 12, p. 234-238.

1895 Bal'mont, K. Predislovie [Foreword]. *In:* Poe, E. A. Ballady i fantasii [Ballads and fantasies]. Moscow, 1895. p. iii-xiv.

Klepatskii, G. Predislovie [Foreword]. *In:* Poe, E. Polnoe sobranie sochinenii [Complete collected works]. Kishinev, 1895. vyp. 1, p. 1-11.

Edgar Poe. (Biographicheskii ocherk) [Edgar Poe. (Biographical sketch)]. *In:* Poe, E. A. Izbrannye sochineniia [Selected works]. Saint Petersburg, 1895. p. iii-vii.

1896 Vengerova, Z. Review of: Neobyknovennye rasskazy [Unusual stories]. St. Petersburg, 1896. Obrazovanie, 1896, no. 10, p. 94-97.

1897 Lichnost' Edgara Poe [The personality of Edgar Poe]. Vestnik inostran-noi literatury, 1897, no. 9, p. 357-359.

Press, A. Edgar Allen Po. (Kharakteristika) [Edgar Allan Poe. (A character sketch)]. Kosmopolis, 1897, no. 2, p. 102-130. *Also in:* Press, A. Pisateli XIX veka [Writers of the 19th century]. v. 1. St. Petersburg, 1901. p. 177-216. 2nd ed.: Press, A. V tsarstve knig [In the world of books]. St. Petersburg, 1908. p. 195-222.

Rodonachal'nik simvolizma Edgar Poe [Edgar Poe, the originator of symbolism]. Russkii vestnik, 1897, no. 9, p. 316-323.

Edgar Po [Edgar Poe]. Istoricheskii vestnik, 1897, no. 10, p. 369-370.

Edgar Poe s patologicheskoi tochki zreniia [Edgar Poe from the patho-logical point of view]. Knizhki nedeli, 1897, no. 10, p. 262-265.

1898 Patologicheskaia literatura i bol'nye pisateli. Edgar Allan Poe [Patholo-gical literature and sick writers. Edgar Allan Poe]. Novyi zhurnal inostrannoi literatury, 1898, no. 2, p. 190-200.

1899 Mostovich, Ch. Amerikanskii Gofman [An American Hoffmann]. Knizhki nedeli, 1899, no. 11, p. 226-228.

Toporov, S. A. Mrachnyi genii [A gloomy genius]. Sem'ia, 1899, no. 42, p. 6. (Signed: S. T-v.)

1900 Gridinskii, Edgar Po (1809-1849) [Edgar Poe, 1809-1849]. Ezhemesiach-nye sochineniia, 1900, no. 10, p. 109-113.

Krasnosel'skii, A. V bor'be s prozoi zhizni. (K psikhologii neopredelen-nykh stremlenii). II. Edgar Po [In the struggle against the prose of life. (On the psychology of unfocussed strivings). II. Edgar Poe]. Russkoe bogatstvo, 1900, no. 11, otd. II, p. 46-55.

1901 A. B. Review of: Poe, E. A. Sobranie sochinenii [Collected works]. v. 1. Moscow, "Skorpion," 1901. Mir bozhii, 1901, no. 8, otd. II,p. 96-97.

A-i. Dekadentskaia poeziia. (Poe, E. A. Sobranie sochinenii. v. 1. Moscow, 1901) [Decadent poetry. (Poe, E. A. Collected works. v. 1. Moscow, 1901)]. Moskovskie vedomosti, June 4/17, 1901.

Bal'mont, K. Edgar Po, 1809-1849 [Edgar Poe, 1809-1849]. *In:* Poe, E. A. Sobranie sochinenii [Collected works]. v. 1. Moscow, 1901. p. vii-xii. *Also, with title:* "Genii otkrytii" ["The genius of discovery"], *in:* Bal'mont, K. Gornye vershiny [Mountain heights]. v. 1. Moscow, 1904. p. 49-53. *And in:* Poe, E. A. Sobranie sochinenii [Collected works]. 3rd ed. v. 1. Moscow, 1911. p. ix-xiv.

Sukhonin, S. Edgar Poe i odin iz ego "uchenykh" kritikov [Edgar Poe and one of his "scholarly" critics]. Vestnik vsemirnoi literatury, 1901, no. 5, p. 139-167.

1902 Edgar Poe [Edgar Poe]. *In:* Plutarkh XIX veka [Plutarch of the 19th century]. v. 1. St. Petersburg, 1902. p. 166.

1903 Gel'strem, V. A. Literaturnaia khronika. Kul't Edgara Po [Literary chronicle. The cult of Edgar Poe]. Novoe vremia, January 8/21, 1903. (Illustrated supplement). (Signed: V. G.)

1906 Blok, A. Review of: Poe, E. A. Sobranie sochinenii [Collected works]. v. 2. Moscow, 1906. Slovo, February 12, 1906. (Literary supplement, no. 2). (Signed: Al. Bl.) *Also in:* Blok, A. Sobranie sochinenii [Collected works]. v. 5. Moscow, Leningrad, 1962. p. 617-618.

Gorlenko, V. Novyi trud ob Edgare Poe [A new work about Edgar Poe]. *In:* Gorlenko, V. Otbleski [Reflections]. St. Petersburg, 1906. p. 86-97. *Also:* 2nd ed. St. Petersburg, 1908. p. 91-103.

Nalimov, A. Review of: Poe, E. A. Sobranie sochinenii [Collected works]. v. 2. Moscow, 1906. Rus', March 3, 1906. (Supplement).

Usov, A. Dekadentstvo. (Bodler i Po) [Decadence. (Baudelaire and Poe)]. *In:* Kratkii sistematicheskii slovar' vsemirnoi literatury [Short, systematic dictionary of world literature]. ch. 2. St. Petersburg, 1906. p. 135-143.

1907 Edgar Allen Po [Edgar Allan Poe]. Istoricheskii vestnik, 1907, no. 10, p. 325-328.

1908 Apostolov, N. Edgar Po [Edgar Poe]. *In:* Apostolov, N. Impressionizm i modernizm [Impressionism and modernism]. Kiev, 1908. p. 43-44.

1909 Anichkov, E. Bodler i Edgar Po [Baudelaire and Edgar Poe]. Sovre-mennyi mir, 1909, no. 2, p. 75-100. *Also, enlarged, in:* Anichkov, E. Predtechi i sovremenniki [Forerunners and contemporaries]. v. 1. St. Petersburg, 1910. p. 213-271.

Brazolenko, B. Edgar Po. (1809-1849-1909) [Edgar Poe, 1809-1849-1909]. Vestnik znaniia, 1909, no. 3, p. 348-352. *Also in:* Brazol', B. Kriticheskie grani [Facets of criticism]. St. Petersburg, 1910. p. 193-200.

Gosse, E. K stoletiiu so dnia rozhdeniia Edgara Po. Ocherk [On the centenary of the birth of Edgar Poe. Essay]. Novoe slovo, 1909, no. 4, p. 107-109.

Evropeiskie i amerikanskie iubilei. (100-letie so dnia rozhdeniia Edgara Po) [European and American jubilees. (100th anniversary of the birth of Edgar Poe)]. Istoricheskii vestnik, 1909, no. 5, p. 746-748.

Kuz'ko, P. Poet bezumiia i uzhasa—Edgar Poe. (1809-1849) [A poet of insanity and horror—Edgar Poe, 1809-1849]. Na Kavkaze (Ekaterinodar), 1909, no. 1, p. 86-89.

Edgar Poe. (Po povodu 100-letiia so dnia rozhdeniia) [Edgar Poe. (On the centenary of his birth)]. Priroda i liudi, 1909, no. 14, p. 213.

Engel'gardt, M. Edgar Po. Ego zhizn' i proizvedeniia [Edgar Poe. His life and works]. *In:* Poe, E. A. Sobranie sochinenii [Collected works]. 2nd ed. v. 1. St. Petersburg, 1909. p. vii-xxxi; *also in:* Poe, E. A. Polnoe sobranie sochinenii [Complete collected works]. v. 1, bk. 1. St. Petersburg, 1914. p. vii-xxxi.

1910 Aikhenval'd, Iu. Edgar Po. Pamiatka [Edgar Poe. A memorial]. *In:* Aikhenval'd, Iu. Otdel'nye stranitsy [Separate pages]. St. Petersburg, 1910. p. 75-81.

Bodler, Sh. [Baudelaire, Ch.]. Edgar Po. Zhizn' i tvorchestvo [Edgar Poe. Life and work]. Odessa, 1910. 71 p.

Drama Edgara Po [Edgar Poe's drama]. ("Politian"). Vestnik inostrannoi literatury, 1910, no. 6, p. 127-134.

Edgar Po i ego vliianie na sovremennuiu literaturu [Edgar Poe and his influence on contemporary literature]. Vestnik inostrannoi literatury, 1910, no. 12, p. 41-45.

1911 Edgar Po. (Biograficheskii ocherk); Primechaniia [Edgar Poe. (Biophical essay); notes]. *In:* Edgar Po v luchshikh russkikh perevodakh [Edgar Poe in the best Russian translations]. St. Petersburg, 1911. p. 3-8, 65-91.

1912 Bal'mont, K. Ocherk zhizni Edgara Po. Posleslovie perevodchika [A sketch of the life of Edgar Poe. An afterword from the translator]. *In:* Poe, E. A. Sobranie sochinenii [Collected works]. v. 5. Moscow, 1912, p. 1-107, 303-311.

Piast, V. Review of: Poe, E. A. Sobranie sochinenii [Collected works]. v. 5. Moscow, 1912. Apollon, 1912, no. 6, p. 49-50.

Friche, V. Strashnye rasskazy Edgara Po [The frightful tales of Edgar Poe]. *In:* Friche, V. Poeziia koshmara i uzhasa [The poetry of nightmare and horror]. Moscow, 1912. p. 182-194.

1913 Poe, E. Filosofiia tvorchestva. (Istoriia sozdaniia "Vorona") [The philosophy of creativity. (The history of the creation of "The Raven")].

In: Poe, E. A. Sobranie sochinenii [Collected works]. v. 2. Moscow, 1913. p. 167-182.

Po [Poe]. *In:* 34—i.e. Tridtsat' chetyre—biografii izvestneishikh russkikh i inostrannykh pisatelei [34 biographies of the best-known Russian and foreign writers]. St. Petersburg, 1913. p. 35-36.

Edgar Allan Po. (Biograficheskii ocherk) [Edgar Allan Poe. (Biographical sketch)]. *In:* Poe, E. A. Sobranie sochinenii [Collected works]. v. 1. St. Petersburg, 1913. p. iii-xiv.

1914 Briusov, V. Edgar Po [Edgar Poe]. *In:* Istoriia zapadnoi literatury [A history of Western literature]. v. 3. Moscow, 1914. p. 328-344.

L'vov-Rogachevskii, V. Edgar Po i Leonid Andreev [Edgar Poe and Leonid Andreev]. *In:* L'vov-Rogachevskii, V. Dve pravdy. Kniga o Leonide Andreeve [Two truths. A book about Leonid Andreev]. St. Petersburg, 1914. p. 169-186.

1921 Kotliarevskii, N. Edgar Poe i Sharl' Bodler [Edgar Poe and Charles Baudelaire]. *In:* Kotliarevskii, N. Deviatnadtsatyi vek [The nineteenth century]. Peterburg, 1921. p. 188-197.

1923 Grech, A. Review of: Zolotoi zhuk [The gold bug]. Peterburg, 1922. Pechat' i revoliutsiia, 1923, no. 2, p. 247-248.

1924 Briusov, V. Predislovie perevodchika.—Edgar Po. Biograficheskii ocherk; Kritiko-bibliograficheskii kommentarii [Translator's foreword.—Edgar Poe. Biographical sketch; Critico-bibliographic commentary]. *In:* Poe, E. A. Polnoe sobranie poem i stikhotvorenii [Complete collection of poems and verse]. Moscow, Leningrad, 1924. p. 5-16, 107-125.

Dinamov, S. Review of: Poe, E. A. Polnoe sobranie poem i stikhotvorenii [Complete collection of poems and verse]. Knigonosha, 1924, no. 34, p. 8.

1925 Aksenov, I. A. Review of: Poe, E. A. Polnoe sobranie poem i stikhotvorenii [Complete collection of poems and verse]. Pechat' i revoliutsiia, 1925, no. 1, p. 178-288.

1927 Kamegulov, A. Edgar Po. (Predislovie) [Edgar Poe. (Foreword)]. *In:* Poe, E. A. Ubiistvo v ulitse Morg [The murder in the rue Morgue]. Leningrad, 1927. p. 3-9.

1931 Dinamov,S. Nauchno-fantasticheskie novelly Edgara Po [The science fiction short stories of Edgar Poe]. Literatura i marksizm, 1931, no. 3, p. 51-64.

1933 Dinamov, S. Novelly Edgara Po [The short stories of Edgar Poe]. 30—i.e. Tridtsat'—dnei, 1933, no. 11-12, p. 60-64.

1934 Dinamov, S. Edgar Po—khudozhnik smerti i razlozheniia [Edgar Poe—an artist of death and decay]. Oktiabr', 1934, no. 4, p. 160-171. *Also, enlarged, and with title:* "Tvorchestvo Edgara Po" ["The work of Edgar Poe"], *in:* Poe, E. A. Izbrannye proizvedeniia [Selected works]. Moscow, 1935. p. 5-51. *And in:* Dinamov, S. Zarubezhnaia literatura [Foreign literature]. Moscow, 1960. p. 257-299.

1936 Startsev, A. Review of: Poe, E. A. Izbrannye rasskazy [Selected stories]. Moscow, 1935. Literaturnoe obozrenie, 1936, no. 4, p. 28-29.

1937 Bobrova, M. N. O proze Edgara Po [Concerning Edgar Poe's prose]. Izvestiia Irkutskogo pedagogicheskogo instituta, 1937, vyp. III, p. 23-63.

1939 Krzhizhanovskii, S. Edgar Allan Po [Edgar Allan Poe]. Literaturnaia gazeta, October 26, 1939.

1946 Paustovskii, K. Edgar Po [Edgar Poe]. *In:* Poe, E. A. Zolotoi zhuk [The gold bug]. Moscow, 1946. p. 3-8.

1954 Uitmen, U. [Whitman, W.]. Znachenie Edgara Po [The significance of Edgar Poe]. *In:* Whitman, W. Izbrannoe [Selections]. Moscow, 1954. p. 264-266.

1958 Bobrova, M. Predislovie [Foreword]. Bekker, M. Komentarii [Commentary]. *In:* Poe, E. A. Izbrannoe [Selections]. Moscow, 1958. p. 3-15, 334-341. 2nd ed. Moscow, 1959.

1959 Lashiz, S. Edgar Allan Po—"genial'nyi mistifikator" [Edgar Allan Poe— "a mystifier of genius"]. V zashchitu mira, 1959, no. 93, p. 72-78.

Eishiskina, N. Novoe izdanie Edgara Po [A new edition of Edgar Poe]. (Izbrannoe [Selections]. Moscow, 1958). Inostrannaia literatura, 1959, no. 9, p. 267-268.

1963 Nikoliukin, A. Review of: Moss, S. P. *Poe's Literary Battles.* 1963. Sovremennaia khudozhestvennaia literatura za rubezhom, 1963, no. 12, p. 104-106.

Eishiskina, N. Edgar Po, ego zhizn' i tvorchestvo [Edgar Poe, his life and work]. Voprosy literatury, 1963, no. 10, p. 206-211.

O. GENRI   O. HENRY (PORTER William Sidney)

1915 Predislovie [Foreword]. *In:* O. Henry. Serdtse Zapada [Heart of the West]. Petrograd, 1915. p. v-viii.

1916 Iv. K. Review of: Serdtse Zapada [Heart of the West]. Petrograd, 1915. Novyi zhurnal dlia vsekh, 1916, no. 4-6, p. 60.

Review of: Serdtse Zapada [Heart of the West]. Russkie zapiski, 1916, no. 2, p. 326-328.

Shaginian, M. Review of: Serdtse Zapada [Heart of the West]. Severnye zapiski, 1916, no. 6, p. 222.

1917 Emeri [Emery?]. O. Genry. Etiud o sovremennoi amerikanskoi literature [O. Henry. A study in contemporary American literature]. Niva, 1917, no. 45, p. 686-687.

1922 Dodonov, V. Bol'shoi gorod i chelovek v nem. (Ob amerikanskikh pisateliakh) [The big city and the man in it. (Concerning American writers)]. *In:* Zapad [The West]. vyp. 1. Moscow, 1922. p. 19-24.

Dodonov, V. N'iu-Iork i O. Genri [New York and O. Henry]. Ekran, 1922, no. 28, p. 3-9. *Also. abridged, in:* O. Henry. N'iu-Iorkskie

150

rasskazy [New York stories]. Moscow, Petrograd, 1923. p. 3-11.

Chukovskii, K. Predislovie k romanu "Koroli i Kapusta" [Foreword to the novel "Kings and cabbage"[1]]. Sovremennyi Zapad, 1922, no. 1, p. 17-18. (Signed: K. Ch.) *Also, enlarged, in:* O. Henry. Koroli i kapusta [Kings and cabbage]. Peterburg, Moscow, 1923, p. 7-8; 2nd ed. Moscow, Leningrad, 1924. p. 5-6. Moscow, Leningrad, 1926. p. 3-5.

1923 A. B. Review of: Koroli i kapusta [Kings and cabbage]. Moscow, 1923. Gorn, 1923, no. 9, p. 163-165.

A. G. Review of: Dusha Tekhasa [The spirit of Texas—i.e. *Heart of the West*]. Petrograd, 1923. Knigonosha, 1923, no. 11, p. 5.

Abashidze. Amerikanizatsiia literatury [The Americanization of literature]. Novyi mir (Petrograd), 1923, no. 1, p. 20-21.

Azov, Vl. O. Genri [O. Henry]. *In:* O. Henry. Amerikanskie rasskazy [American tales]. Moscow, Petrograd, 1923. p. iii-viii.

Aksenov, I. A. Review of: Dusha Tekhasa [The spirit of Texas—i.e. *Heart of the West*]. Petrograd, 1923. Pechat' i revoliutsiia, 1923, no. 5, p. 303-304.

Bobrov, S. Review of: Rasskazy [Stories]. Moscow, Petrograd, 1923. Pechat' i revoliutsiia, 1923, no. 4, p. 273-276.

Bol'shakov, K. Amerikanskii Mopassan (O. Genri) [An American Maupassant (O. Henry)]. Krasnaia niva, 1923, no. 5, p. 26-29.

Borisov, S. Review of: Koroli i kapusta [Kings and cabbage]. Moscow, 1923. Krasnaia niva, 1923, no. 29, p. 32.

Venetsianova, E. Komediia iz pestrykh loskut'ev [A comedy of motley scraps]. ("Koroli i kapusta" ["Kings and cabbage"]. Moscow, 1923). Literaturnyi ezhenedel'nik, 1923, no. 32, p. 15.

Gizetti, A. Golosa Zapada. 1. O. Genri [Voices of the West. 1. O. Henry]. Zapiski peredvizhnogo teatra, 1923, no. 63, p. 2.

Drei. O rasskazakh Genri [Concerning the stories by Henry]. Nash ponedel'nik (Gomel'), July 2, 1923.

Zhukov, P. Modnyi pisatel' [A fashionable writer]. Zori, 1923, no. 6, p. 14.

Zamiatin, E. Predislovie [Foreword]. *In:* O. Henry. Rasskazy [Stories]. Petersburg, Moscow, 1923. p. 7-12. *Also, abridged, and with title:* "Tvorchestvo O'Genri" ["The writing of O. Henry"], *in:* O. Henry. Blagorodnyi zhulik i drugie rasskazy [The noble swindler and other stories]. Moscow, Leningrad, 1924. p. 18-22.

Sobolev, Iu. Golosa iz-za rubezha [Voices from abroad]. ("Rasskazy" ["Stories"]. Moscow, Petrograd, 1923). Rossiia, 1923, no. 9, p. 30-31.

Chukovskii, K. O. Genri [O. Henry]. Sovremennyi Zapad, 1923, no. 3, p. 169-176.

---

[1] *Cabbages and Kings.*

1924 A. S. Review of: Puti, kotorye my izbiraem [The paths which we choose —i.e. *Roads of Destiny*]. Petrograd, 1923. Krasnyi zhurnal dlia vsekh, 1924, no. 3, p. 243.

"Amerikanskii Chekhov" ["The American Chekhov"]. Biulleten' literatury i zhizni, 1924, no. 3, p. 90-91.

Vmesto predisloviia [In place of a foreword]. *In:* O. Henry. Postskriptumy [Postscripts]. Moscow, Leningrad, 1924. p. 3-4.

Dinamov, S. Review of: Goriashchii svetil'nik [The burning lamp—i.e. *The Trimmed Lamp*]. Leningrad, 1924. Knigonosha, 1924, no. 35, p. 8.

Dinamov, S. Review of: Koroli i kapusta [Kings and cabbage]. Leningrad, 1924. Knigonosha, 1924, no. 41, p. 20. (Signed: D.)

Rashkovskaia, A. Review of: Puti, kotorye my izbiraem [The paths which we choose—i.e. *Roads of Destiny*]. Petrograd, 1923. Zapiski peredvizhnogo teatra, 1924, no. 68, p. 9.

Dinamov, S. Review of: Rasskazy zhulika. Shesterki—semerki. Postskriptumy. [The stories of a swindler—i.e. *The Gentle Grafter*. Sixes and sevens. Postscripts]. Moscow, Leningrad, 1924. Knigonosha, 1924, no. 26, p. 10.

Stepanov, A. Amerikanskii Chekhov [An American Chekhov]. ("Rasskazy" ["Stories"]. Moscow, 1923). Narodnyi uchitel', 1924, no. 1, p. 165-169.

Tarasov-Radionov, A. I. O. Genri [O. Henry]. Oktiabr', 1924, no. 2, p. 211. (Signed: Zh-ko, S.)

Chukovskii, K. Zhizn' O. Genri [O. Henry's life]. *In:* O. Henry. Blagorodnyi zhulik i drugie rasskazy [The noble swindler and other stories]. Moscow, Leningrad, 1924. p. 5-17.

Chukovskii, K. O. Genri, 1862-1910 [O. Henry, 1862-1910]. *In:* O. Henry. Rasskazy zhulika [The stories of a swindler—i.e. *The Gentle Grafter*]. Moscow, Leningrad, 1924. p. 7-8.

1925 Anibal, B. Review of: Novyi Bagdad. Chto govorit gorod [New Bagdad—i.e. *A Night in New Arabia*. What the city says—i.e. *The Voice of the City*]. Leningrad, 1925. Novyi mir, 1925, no. 6, p. 157-159.

Loks, K. Review of: Shumi—gorodok nad podzemkoi. Igrushechka-pastushechka. Chernyi Bill'. Sherstianaia koshechka [Make a noise—little city on the subway. The little toy shepherdess. Black Bill. The little woolen cat.—Original title not determined. *Madame Bo-Peep of the Ranches. The Hiding of Black Bill. The Discounters of Money*]. Petrograd, 1924. Pechat' i revoliutsiia, 1925, no. 1, p. 291-292.

L'vovskii, Z. Neskol'ko vstupitel'nykh slov [Some introductory words]. *In:* O. Henry. Tysiacha dollarov [One thousand dollars]. Leningrad, Moscow, 1925. p. 5-10.

Obruchev, S. Review of: Volchki [The tops—i.e. *Whirligigs*]. Leningrad, 1925. Pechat' i revoliutsiia, 1925, no. 7, p. 281-283.

Frid, Ia. Review of: Chetyre milliona [The four million]. Leningrad, 1925. Novyi mir, 1925, no. 7, p. 156.

Eikhenbaum, B. O. Genri i teoriia novelly [O. Henry and the theory of the short story]. Zvezda, 1925, no. 6, p. 291-308. *Also in:* Eikhenbaum, B. Literatura. Teoriia. Kritika. Polemika [Literature. Theory. Criticism. Polemics]. Leningrad, 1927. p. 166-209.

1926 Dzhennings [Jennings], E. O. Genri na dne [O. Henry in the lower depths]. Moscow, Leningrad, 1926. 197 p.; 2nd ed. 1927. 310 p. *Reviews:* Dinamov, S. Knigonosha, 1926, no. 9, p. 31-32; Tsingovatov, A. Molodaia gvardiia, 1926, no. 7, p. 169-171.

Eikhenbaum, B. M. Vil'iam-Sidnei Porter. (O. Genri) [William Sidney Porter. (O. Henry)]. *In:* O. Henry. Sobranie sochinenii [Collected works]. v. 4. Kovboi [Cowboy]. Moscow, Leningrad, 1926. p. 201-239.

1927 Azov, V. A. Predislovie k russkomu izdaniiu [Foreword to the Russian edition]. *In:* O. Henry. Lan' i ruchei [The deer and the brook—i.e. *The Poet and the Farmer*]. 2nd ed. Leningrad, 1927. p. 3-5.

Sol'skii, V. O. Genri [O. Henry]. Na literaturnom postu, 1927, no. 7, p. 42-48.

1928 Olenin, B. Amerikanskii "korotkii rasskaz" [The American "short story"]. Na pod"eme, 1928, no. 1-2, p. 58-60.

1932 Gorlin, A. N. Posleslovie [Afterword]. *In:* O. Henry. Izbrannye novelly [Selected short stories]. Leningrad, Moscow, 1932. p. 270-271. (Signed: G.)

Startsev, A. Master voskresnogo rasskaza [A master of the Sunday story]. Kniga stroiteliam sotsializma, 1932, no. 13-14, p. 23-24.

1935 Rukopis' O. Genri v knige retseptov [A manuscript by O. Henry in a book of prescriptions]. Pravda, May 12, 1935.

1936 B. N. O Genri v novom izdanii Goslitizdata [O. Henry in the new edition of the State Publishing House for Literature]. Knizhnye novinki, 1936, no. 30, p. 20-21.

1937 Balashov, P. O'Genri [O. Henry]. *In:* O. Henry. Rasskazy [Stories]. Moscow, 1937. p. 3-5.

Leites, A. Skovannyi smekh [Enchained laughter]. Izvestiia, September 10, 1937.

Chetunova, N. O'Genri [O. Henry]. Literaturnoe obozrenie, 1937, no. 16, p. 60. (Signed: N. Ch.)

Chetunova, N. Rasskazy O'Genri [O. Henry's stories]. Literaturnoe obozrenie, 1937, no. 6, p. 43-47.

1938 Nemerovskaia, O. O'Genri i ego novelly [O. Henry and his short stories]. *In:* O. Henry. Novelly [Short stories]. Moscow, 1938. p. 3-15.

Startsev, A. K. voprosu ob O'Genri [On the problem of O. Henry]. Internatsional'naia literatura, 1938, no. 2-3, p. 351-353.

1940 Abramov, A. Vstupitel'naia zametka k rannim novellam O. Genri [An introductory remark to the early short stories of O. Henry]. Internatsional'naia literatura, 1940, no. 5-6, p. 195.

Abramov, A. Eshche O. Genri [Once more O. Henry]. Literaturnoe obozrenie, 1940, no. 21, p. 61.

1944 Sil'man, T. O. Genri [O. Henry]. *In:* O. Henry. Rasskazy [Stories]. Moscow, 1944. p. 3-7.

1946 Sil'man, T. O. Genri [O. Henry]. *In:* O. Henry. Koroli i kapusta [Kings and cabbage]. Moscow, 1946. p. 3-14.

1949 Anikst, A. O. Genri, 1862-1910 [O. Henry, 1862-1910]. *In:* O. Henry *Short Stories.*[1] Moscow, 1949, p. iii-xi.

1951 Kandel', B. Predislovie [Foreword]. *In:* O. Henry. Rasskazy [Stories]. Moscow, Leningrad, 1951. p. 3-7.

1954 Anikst, A. O. Genry [O. Henry]. *In:* O. Henry. Izbrannye proizvedeniia v 2 tt. [Selected works in 2 volumes]. v. 2. Moscow, 1954. p. 558-579. Other editions: 1955, 1959, 1960.

1956 Zhan-Sharl' [Jean-Charles?]. O. Genri [O. Henry]. V zashchitu mira, 1956, no. 62-63, p. 115-120.

1958 Letina, A. Svoeobrazie kompozitsii novell O. Genri (Tsikl "Blagorodnyi zhulik") [The specific features of the composition of the short stories of O. Henry (The cycle "The noble swindler"—i.e. *The Gentle Grafter*)]. Sbornik nauchnykh rabot studentov. (Tezisy i sokrashchennye teksty) [Collection of the scholarly papers of students. (Abstracts and condensed texts)]. Sverdlovsk, 1958. p. 40-43.

1960 Levidova, I. M. O. Genri. Bio-bibliograficheskii ukazatel'. K 50-letiiu so dnia smerti [O. Henry. Bio-bibliographic guide. On the fiftieth anniversary of his death]. Moscow, 1960. 143 p. *Review:* Kush, O. P. Sovetskaia bibliografiia, 1961, no. 1, p. 73-75.

Nagibin, Iu. V radosti i v pechali [In joy and in sorrow]. Literaturnaia gazeta, June 11, 1960.

1962 Alekseeva, K. Natsional'noe dostoianie Ameriki [A national property of America]. Literaturnyi Azerbaidzhan, 1962, no. 9, p. 157.

Vladimirov, V. Garun al'-Rashid nad podzemkoi [Harun-al-Rashid on the subway]. Ogonek, 1962, no. 37, p. 30-31.

Gorelov, I. Oblichitel' i gumanist [An accuser and a humanist]. Trud, September 11, 1962.

Nagibin, Iu. Dobryi talant [A good talent]. Inostrannaia literatura, 1962, no. 9, p. 253-255.

Nikoliukin, N. Amerikanskii iumorist [An American humorist]. Literatura v shkole, 1962, no. 4, p. 94-96.

Samarin, R. Poistine zamechatel'nyi pisatel' [A truly remarkable writer]. Literatura i zhizn', September 12, 1962.

Khatchins, Dzh. [Hutchins, J.?]. Zdes' visit portret O. Genri [Here hangs

---

[1] A book in the English language published in the Soviet Union.

O. Henry's portrait]. Literaturnaia gazeta, September 11, 1962.
Khvalynskii, S. "My pisali krov'iu serdtsa..." ["We wrote with our heart's blood..."]. Pravda, September 12, 1962.

PAUND Ezra   POUND Ezra

1915 Vengerova, Z. Angliiskie futuristy [English futurists]. *In:* Strelets. Sb. 1. Petrograd, 1915. p. 91-104.
1949 Mendel'son, M. Amerikanskaia premiia fashistskomu poetu [An American prize for a fascist poet]. Kul'tura i zhizn', August 31, 1949.
1961 Surkov, A. Politicheskie prichiny i esteticheskie sledstviia [Political cause and esthetic results]. Inostrannaia literatura, 1961, no. 6, p. 230-233.

KUIN Maikl   QUIN Michael

1958 Amerikanskii poet Maikl Kuin [The American poet Michael Quin]. Literaturnoe obozrenie, 1938, no. 13-14, p. 124-125.

RID Dzhon   REED John

Lenin, V. I. Predislovie k amerikanskomu izdaniiu [Foreword to the American edition]. *In:* Reed, J. 10—i.e. Desiat'—dnei, kotorye potriasli mir [Ten days that shook the world]. Moscow, 1923. p. 7. (Signed: N. Lenin.) *Also in:* Lenin, V. I. Polnoe sobranie sochinenii [Complete collected works]. 4th ed. v. 36, p. 478.
1920 Reinshtein, B. Dzhon Rid [John Reed]. Kommunisticheskii internatsional, 1920, no. 14, cols. 2973-2980.
1923 Gladnev. Review of: 10—i.e. Desiat'—dnei, kotorye potriasli mir [Ten days that shook the world]. Moscow, 1923. Krasnyi zhurnal dlia vsekh, 1923, no. 7-8, p. 84-85.
Krupskaia, N. [i.e. Krupskaia, Nadezhda Konstantinovna, wife of V. I. Lenin]. Predislovie k russkomu izdaniiu [Foreword to the Russian edition]. *In:* Reed, J. 10—i.e. Desiat'—dnei, kotorye potriasli mir [Ten days that shook the world]. Moscow, 1923. p. 8-9. *Also:* Moscow, 1959. p. 6; *and,* Krupskaia, N. Ob iskusstve i literature [Concerning literature and art]. Leningrad, Moscow, 1963. p. 198-199.
F. S. Review of: 10—i.e. Desiat'—dnei, kotorye potriasli mir [Ten days that shook the world]. Moscow, 1923. Prizyv, 1923, no. 2, p. 193-195.
1924 Reinshtein, B. Kratkaia biografiia Dzhona Rida [A short biography of John Reed]. *In:* Reed, J. Desiat' dnei, kotorye potriasli mir [Ten days that shook the world]. Moscow, 1924. p. 3-10.

Sobolev, Iu. Desiat' dnei, kotorye potriasli mir [Ten days that shook the world]. Narodnyi uchitel', 1924, no. 2, p. 123-128.

Fleer, M. G. Review of: 10—i.e. Desiat'—dnei, kotorye potriasli mir [Ten days that shook the world]. Moscow, 1923. Krasnaia letopis', 1924, no. 1, p. 276-277. (Signed: M. F.)

Chernovskii, A. Review of: 10—i.e. Desiat'—dnei, kotorye potriasli mir [Ten days that shook the world]. Moscow, 1923. Zvezda, 1924, no. 1, p. 297.

Iarotskii, V. Posleslovie k vtoromu izdaniiu [Afterword to the second edition]. *In:* Reed, J. 10—i.e. Desiat'—dnei, kotorye potriasli mir [Ten days that shook the world]. 2nd, revised, ed. Moscow, 1924. p. 319-323.

Iarotskii, V. Review of: Reed, J. and I. Amter. Kapitalizm i rabochee dvizhenie v Amerike [Capitalism and the workers' movement in America]. Moscow, 1924. Pechat' i revoliutsiia, 1924, no. 6, p. 157-158.

1925 Williams, A. R. Foreword to the Russian translation. *In:* Reed, J. Revoliutsionnaia Meksika [Revolutionary Mexico]. Moscow, 1925. p. 4-10.

1928 Dos Passos, J. Dzhon Rid [John Reed]. Vestnik inostrannoi literatury, 1928, no. 11, p. 128-130.

Isbakh, A. Review of: Vdol' fronta [Along the front—i.e. *The War in Eastern Europe*]. Moscow, Leningrad, 1928. Oktiabr', 1928, no. 5, p. 242-243.

Krupskaia, N. Predislovie [Foreword]. *In:* Reed, J. Doch' revoliutsii [A daughter of the revolution]. Moscow, Leningrad, 1928. p. 5-9. *Also in:* Krupskaia, N. Ob iskusstve i literature [On art and literature]. Leningrad, Moscow, 1963. p. 199-202.

Starchakov, A. Predislovie [Foreword]. *In:* Reed, J. Vdol' fronta [Along the front—i.e. *The War in Eastern Europe*]. Moscow, Leningrad, 1928. p. 5-8.

F. A. Review of: Vdol' fronta [Along the front—i.e. *The War in Eastern Europe*]. Moscow, 1928. Kniga i profsoiuzy, 1928, no. 4, p. 41-42.

1930 Val'be, B. Dzhon Rid [John Reed]. Leningrad, "Krasnaia gazeta," 1930. 118 p. *Bibliography:* p. 116-117.

Val'be, B. Dzhon Rid. (Opyt literaturnoi kharakteristiki) [John Reed. (An essay in literary characterization)]. Leningrad, 1930, no. 5-6, p. 145-152.

Williams, A. R. Dzhon Rid [John Reed]. Prozhektor, 1930, no. 33, p. 26-27.

Dinamov, S. Tvorcheskii metod Dzhona Rida [The creative method of John Reed]. Na literaturnom postu, 1930, no. 15-16, p. 72-81.

1935 Dzhon Rid [John Reed]. Literaturnyi Leningrad, October 20, 1935.

Pamiati Dzhona Rida. Istoriia Dzhona Rida [In memory of John Reed.

The story of John Reed]. Internatsional'naia literatura, 1935, no. 11, p. 156-157.

1955 Polevoi, B. Legendarnyi Dzhon Rid [The legendary John Reed]. Inostrannaia literatura, 1955, no. 5, p. 239-243.

1957 Andreev, B. V te nezabyvaemye dni [In those unforgettable days]. (10 — i.e. Desiat'—dnei, kotorye potriasli mir [Ten days that shook the world]). Znanie—sila, 1957, no. 11, p. 42-43.

Anisimov, I. Zhizn', otdannaia budushchemu [A life devoted to the future]. Inostrannaia literatura, 1957, no. 11, p. 254-266.

Belfredzh, S. [Belfrage, C.]. Dzhon Rid, revoliutsioner [John Reed, revolutionary]. Literaturnaia gazeta, October 31, 1957.

Val'be, B. Dzhon Rid v krasnom Petrograde [John Reed in red Petrograd]. Zvezda, 1957, no. 8, p. 202-205.

Vladimirov, G. Tak sovershilas' revoliutsiia [Thus the revolution was made]. (10—i.e. Desiat'—dnei, kotorye potriasli mir [Ten days that shook the world]). Pod"em (Voronezh), 1957, no. 5, p. 214-215.

Inber, V. Dzhon Rid i ego kniga [John Reed and his book]. (10—i.e. Desiat'—dnei, kotorye potriasli mir [Ten days that shook the world]). Novoe vremia, 1957, no. 26, p. 29-31.

Lenin i Rid [Lenin and Reed]. Inostrannaia literatura, 1957, no. 11, p. 5-10.

Liorentsevich, I. Kniga o revoliutsii [A book about the Revolution]. (10—i.e. Desiat'—dnei, kotorye potriasli mir [Ten days that shook the world]). Neva, 1957, no. 11, p. 202-203.

Orlova, R. Pioner amerikano-sovetskoi druzhby [A pioneer of American-Soviet friendship]. Kul'tura i zhizn', 1957, no. 12, p. 43-44.

Stiuart, D. [Stewart, J.?]. Formirovanie vzgliadov Dzhona Rida [The formation of John Reed's outlook]. In: Reed, J. Izbrannye proizvedeniia [Selected works]. Moscow, 1957. p. 7-43.

1958 Williams, A. R. Dzhon Rid, soldat revoliutsii [John Reed, a soldier of the Revolution]. Ogonek, 1958, no. 43, p. 13.

Gilenson, B. Dzhon Rid o Turgeneve [John Reed concerning Turgenev]. Russkaia literatura, 1958, no. 3, p. 193-195.

Ivashchenko, A. F. Dzhon Rid [John Reed]. Moscow, "Znanie," 1958. 32 p.

Kramov, I. Dzhon Rid [John Reed]. Moskva, 1958, no. 2, p. 166-175.

Polianovskii, M. Odna iz "shesti devushek." Po sledam knigi "Desiat' dnei, kotorye potriasli mir" [One of "the six girls." On the traces of the book "Ten days that shook the world"]. Sovetskaia Rossiia, June 13, 1958.

1959 Anisimov, I. Literaturnoe tvorchestvo Dzhona Rida [The literary work of John Reed]. In: Reed, J. Vosstavshaia Meksika [Insurgent Mexico]. Moscow, 1959. p. 3-30.

Williams, A. Biografiia Dzhona Rida [A biography of John Reed]. In:

157

Reed, J. 10—i.e. Desiat'—dnei, kotorye potriasli mir [Ten days that shook the world]. Moscow, 1959. p. 343-351.

Sinel'nikov, A. Novoe o Dzhone Ride. Rasskazyvaet staryi bol'shevik Z. K. Karpinskaia [Something new about John Reed. Told by the Old Bolshevik Z. K. Karpinskaia]. Moskovskaia pravda, April 26, 1959.

1960 Drabkina, E. Posledniaia rech' Dzhona Rida [John Reed's last speech]. Novyi mir, 1960, no. 8, p. 279-282.

Kramov, I. Po dorogam mira i voiny [On roads of peace and of war]. (Vosstavshaia Meksika [Insurgent Mexico]. Novyi mir, 1960, no. 10, p. 258-262.

Raidmaa, E. Uznik No. 42. Dzhon Rid v finskoi tiur'me [Prisoner No. 42. John Reed in a Finnish prison]. Ogonek, 1960, no. 7, p. 25.

Simonov, K. "Vosstavshaia Meksika." Vmesto retsenzii ["Insurgent Mexico." In place of a review]. Ogonek, 1960, no. 40, p. 18.

Iarovoi, M. Dzhon Rid i ego geroi [John Reed and his heroes]. Izvestiia, October 29, 1960.

1961 Gilenson, B. "Ia videl rozhdenie novogo mira." (Publitsistika Dzhona Rida 1917-1920 godov) ["I saw the birth of a new world." (John Reed's reporting of 1917-1920)]. Voprosy literatury, 1961, no. 11, p. 158-171.

Dangulov, S. Dar potriasennogo mira [The gift of a shaken world]. Izvestiia, October 14, 1961.

Drabkina, E. Povest' o nenapisannoi knige [A tale about an unwritten book]. Novyi mir, 1961, no. 6, p. 135-170; no. 7, p. 191-230.

Nash drug, boets, kommunist. Neizvestnye pis'ma Dzhona Rida. (Publikatsiia Li Golda, predislovie Dzheimsa Oldridzha, posleslovie E. Drabkinoi) [Our friend, a fighter and a communist. Unknown letters of John Reed. (Publication by Lee Gold, foreword by James Aldridge, afterword by E. Drabkina)]. Inostrannaia literatura, 1961, no. 10, p. 208-220. *Review:* Kramov, I. Neizvestnye pis'ma Dzhona Rida [Unknown letters of John Reed]. Novyi mir, 1962, no. 1, p. 261-262.

1962 Afonin, M. I segodnia v nashem stroiu [And still in our ranks today]. Sovetskaia pechat', 1962, no. 11, p. 51-52.

Gilenson, B. A. On videl rozhdenie novogo mira [He saw the birth of a new world]. Moscow, Gospolitizdat, 1962. 80 p.

Gilenson, B. Pisatel', borets, kommunist [Writer, fighter, Communist]. Na rubezhe (Petrozavodsk), 1962, no. 5, p. 116-121.

Gilenson, B. Svet Dzhona Rida [The light of John Reed]. Literaturnaia gazeta, October 23, 1962.

Gladkov, T. Dzhon Rid [John Reed]. Moscow, "Molodaia gvardiia," 1962. 288 p.

Drabkina, E. Zveniashchaia struna [A sounding string]. Izvestiia, October 20, 1962.

Drabkina, E. Chelovek neobychainoi sud'by [A man of an uncommon fate]. Kul'tura i zhizn', 1962, no. 11, p. 27-29.

Karlail', G. [Carlyle, G.?]. Dzhon Rid—syn buri [John Reed—son of the storm]. Literatura i zhizn', October 21, 1962.

Karlail', G. [Carlyle, G.?]. "Ia videl budushchee, i ono zhivet" ["I saw the future, and it lives"]. Uchitel'skaia gazeta, November 6, 1962.

Kramov, I. Dzhon Rid [John Reed]. Moscow, Gospolitizdat, 1962. 131 p. *Abridged, in:* Kramov, I. Literaturnye portrety [Literary portraits]. Moscow, 1962. p. 46-160.

Kurochkina, O. and F. Firsov. Drug Oktiabr'skoi revoliutsii [A friend of the October Revolution]. Pravda, October 21, 1962.

Lerman, A. On videl rozhdenie novogo mira [He saw the birth of a new world]. Literaturnyi Azerbaidzhan, 1962, no. 10, p. 155-156.

Startsev, A. Poslednii god Dzhona Rida [John Reed's last year]. Znamia, 1962, no. 11, p. 219-223.

Uinston, G. [Winston, Harry]. "Mir sokhranit ego imia" ["The world will preserve his name"]. Literaturnaia gazeta, October 20, 1962.

Khovi [Hovey?], K. L'venok. (Dzhon Rid, kakim ia ego znal) [The lion cub. (John Reed as I knew him)]. Inostrannaia literatura, 1962, no. 9, p. 200-220; no. 10, p. 216-235.

Chelovek, vospevshii desiat' dnei, kotorye potriasli mir! [The man who sang of the ten days that shook the world!]. Nauka i zhizn', 1962, no. 11, p. 16-17.

Chumak, P. Dzhon Rid—sovetskii konsul [John Reed—Soviet consul]. Ogonek, 1962, no. 44, p. 7.

1963 Lerman, I. Dzhon Rid—poet i novellist [John Reed—poet and short story writer]. Dal'nii Vostok (Khabarovsk), 1963, no. 3, p. 167-170.

Pavlova, S. Dzhon Rid—pevets revoliutsii [John Reed, the singer of revolution]. Sovetskie profsoiuzy, 1963, no. 16, p. 40-41.

Pamiati bortsa [To the memory of a fighter]. Voprosy istorii KPSS, 1963, no. 8, p. 79-85.

ROBINSON Edvin Arlington   ROBINSON Edwin Arlington

1935 Kashkin, I. Ushel naslednik vekovykh traditsii [The inheritor of age-old traditions has passed away]. Literaturnaia gazeta, June 15, 1935.

1936 Kashkin, I. Edvin Arlington Robinson [Edwin Arlington Robinson]. Internatsional'naia literatura, 1936, no. 1, p. 104-114.

1944 Edvin Arlington Robinson [Edwin Arlington Robinson]. Literaturnaia gazeta, December 24, 1944.

ROLLINS Vil'iam   ROLLINS William

1934 Kniga o gastonskoi stachke [A book about the Gastonia strike]. (*The*

Shadow Before. New York, 1934). Literaturnaia gazeta, June 16, 1934.

Startsev, A. Review of: *The Shadow Before.* New York, 1934. Izvestiia, August 5, 1934.

1935 Garin, N. Predislovie [Foreword]. *In:* Rollins, V. Ten' vperedi [The shadow before]. Moscow, 1935. p. 5-10.

Startsev, A. "Ten' vperedi" Vil'iama Rollinsa ["The shadow before" of William Rollins]. Krasnaia nov', 1935, no. 5, p. 230-232.

Vostokova, S. Navstrechu bitvam [Toward the battles]. (Ten' vperedi [The shadow before]. Moscow, 1935). Iunyi kommunist, 1936, no. 7, p. 61-63.

1936 Elistratova, A. Review of: Ten' vperedi [The shadow before]. Moscow, 1935. Literaturnaia gazeta, April 24, 1936.

Eishiskina, N. Review of: Ten' vperedi [The shadow before]. Oktiabr', 1936, no. 5, p. 230-232.

Eishiskina, N. Review of: Ten' vperedi [The shadow before]. Moscow, 1935. Pravda, May 8, 1936.

SELINDZHER Dzherom devid   SALINGER Jerome David

1960 Orlova, R. Mal'chishka bezhit iz Ameriki. O romane Dzh. D. Selindzhera "Nad propast'iu vo rzhi." [A boy is running from America. About J. D. Salinger's novel "Above the abyss in the rye" —i.e. *The Catcher in the Rye*]. Literaturnaia gazeta, November 26, 1960.

Panova, V. O romane Dzh. D. Selindzhera. ("Nad propast'iu vo rzhi") [About J. D. Salinger's novel. ("Above the abyss in the rye" —i.e. *The Catcher in the Rye*)]. Inostrannaia literatura, 1960, no. 11, p. 138-141.

Dymshits, A. S etim nel'zia soglasit'sia... [It is impossible to agree with this...]. Literatura i zhizn', December 14, 1960.

1961 Vladimov, G. Tri dnia iz zhizni Kholdena. ("Nad propast'iu vo rzhi") [Three days from Holden's life. ("Above the abyss in the rye" —i.e. *The Catcher in the Rye*)]. Novyi mir, 1961, no. 2, p. 254-258.

Knipovich, E. Liudi nad propast'iu. ("Nad propast'iu vo rzhi") [People over the abyss. ("Above the abyss in the rye" —i.e. *The Catcher in the Rye*)]. Znamia, 1961, no. 6, p. 215-224.

Landor, M. Review of: Gwinn, F. and J. Blotner. *The Fiction of J. D. Salinger.* New York, 1960. Sovremennaia khudozhestvennaia literatura za rubezhom, 1961, no. 3, p. 102-104.

1963 Asarkan, I. A. Review of: Grustnyi motiv [A sad motif—i.e. Blue Melody]. Moscow, 1963. Novyi mir, 1963, no. 9, p. 284.

Orlova, R. Review of: *Raise High the Roof Beam, Carpenters* and *Seymour: An Introduction.* Boston, Toronto, 1963. Sovremennaia khudozhestvennaia literatura za rubezhom, 1963, no. 12, p. 59-62.

Orlova, R. Review of: *Salinger*. New York, 1962. Sovremennaia khudozhestvennaia literatura za rubezhom, 1963, no. 12, p. 144-147.

SENDBERG Karl   SANDBURG Carl

1928 Mendelevskii. Maiakovskii i Sendberg [Maiakovskii and Sandburg]. Vestnik inostrannoi literatury, 1928, no. 11, p. 141-144.
1935 Karl Sendborg. (Vstuplenie k publikatsii stikhov) [Carl Sandburg. (Introduction to the publication of his poems)]. Literaturnyi sovremennik, 1935, no. 5, p. 88.
1936 Kashkin, I. Karl Sendberg [Carl Sandburg]. Internatsional'naia literatura, 1936, no. 8, p. 109-119.
Novaia kniga Karla Sendberga [A new book by Carl Sandburg]. (*The People, Yes.* New York, 1936). Literaturnaia gazeta, October 10, 1936.
1942 Vinsent, S. Sendberg—syn strany Linkol'na [Sandburg—a son of Lincoln's country]. Internatsional'naia literatura, 1942, no. 12, p. 140-141.
1956 Kennedi, S. V traditsiiakh Uitmena. (Poeziia K. Sendberga) [In the traditions of Whitman. (The poetry of C. Sandburg)]. Inostrannaia literatura, 1956, no. 10, p. 197-200.
1959 Kashkin, I. Veteran amerikanskoi poezii [A veteran of American poetry]. Literaturnaia gazeta, July 25, 1959.
Kashkin, I. Veteran amerikanskoi poezii [A veteran of American poetry]. *In:* Sandburg, C. Stikhi raznykh let [Poems of various years]. Moscow, 1959. p. 5-15.
Narodnyi poet Ameriki [An American people's poet]. Literatura i zhizn', August 5, 1959.
Poet Karl Sendberg [Carl Sandburg sings]. Literaturnaia gazeta, August 4, 1959.
1960 Martynova, A. Narod—dusha ego poezii [The people—the soul of his poetry]. ("Stikhi raznykh let" ["Poems of various years"]. Moscow, 1959). Inostrannaia literatura, 1960, no. 6, p. 260-261.
Razgovorov, N. Eto moe litso [This is my face]. ("Stikhi raznykh let" ["Poems of various years"]. Moscow, 1959). Literaturnaia gazeta, October 8, 1960.
1961 Savich, O. Poet i ego perevodchik [A poet and his translator]. Literatura i zhizn', January 13, 1960.
Ivanov, R. F. Posleslovie [Afterword]. *In:* Sandburg, C. Linkol'n [Lincoln]. Moscow, 1961. p. 689-696.
Urnov, D. Review of: *Wind Song*. New York, 1960. Sovremennaia khudozhestvennaia literatura za rubezhom, 1961, no. 2, p. 101-102.
1963 Sergeev, A. Review of: *Honey and Salt*. New York, 1963. Sovremennaia khudozhestvennaia literatura za rubezhom, 1963, no. 12, p. 53-56.

1935 Saroyan, W. Avtobiografiia [Autobiography]. Internatsional'naia literatura, 1935, no. 10, p. 175-176.
1950 Prett [Pratt?], A. Kleveta na geroev Steinbeka [A slander of Steinbeck's heroes]. ("Love's old sweet song"). Literaturnaia gazeta, October 6, 1940.
1948 Morozov, M. Illiuzii i gor'kaia pravda [Illusion and bitter truth]. ("Jim Dandy"). Literaturnaia gazeta, February 25, 1948.
1949 Zaslavskii, D. Literaturnaia gnil' [Literary rot]. ("Jim Dandy"). Novoe vremia, 1949, no. 13, p. 24-27.
   Mendel'son, M. Dekadent-uteshitel' [A decadent consoler]. Literaturnaia gazeta, January 5, 1949.
1958 Vetoshkina, N. Predislovie [Foreword]. In: Saroyan, W. Chelovecheskaia komediia [The human comedy]. Moscow, 1958. p. 5-12.
   Orlova, R. and L. Kopelev. Grustnyi i bespechnyi, dobryi i nasmeshlivyi uteshitel' [A sad and light-hearted, kind and mocking consoler]. In: Saroyan, W. 60—i.e. Shest'desiat—mil' v chas [Sixty miles an hour]. Moscow, 1958. p. 3-16.
   Talanov, A. Ulybka do boli v shchekakh [A smile until the cheeks hurt]. (60—i.e. Shest'desiat—mil' v chas [Sixty miles an hour]. Moscow, 1958). Novyi mir, 1958, no. 4, p. 254-257.
1959 Gullakian, S. Liubov' k cheloveku. (K vykhodu v svet knig Vil'iama Saroiana na armianskom iazyke) [A love for man. (On the publication of the books of William Saroyan in the Armenian language)]. Literaturnaia Armeniia (Erevan), 1959, no. 3, p. 142-146.
   Zobina, M. "Estestvennyi" chelovek v sovremennom obshchestve [A "natural" man in contemporary society]. ("Prikliucheniia Vesli Dzheksona" ["The adventures of Wesley Jackson"]. Moscow, 1959). Novyi mir, 1959, no. 6, p. 255-258.
   Nedelin, V. "Smert', ne khodi v Itaku!" ["Death, do not go to Ithaca!"]. (Chelovecheskaia komediia [The human comedy]. Moscow, 1958). Inostrannaia literatura, 1959, no. 1, p. 253-254.
   Orlova, R. Chelovek s chuzhim ruzh'em [A man with another's gun]. In: Saroyan, W. Prikliucheniia Vesli Dzheksona [The adventures of Wesley Jackson]. Moscow, 1959. p. 305-312.
1960 Serebriakov, K. Vstrechi s Uil'iamom Saroianom [Meetings with William Saroyan]. Literaturnaia gazeta, September 29, 1960.
1961 Avakian, Kh. P'esa Vil'iama Saroiana v teatre imeni Sundukiana [A play by William Saroyan in the theater named for Sundukian]. (V gorakh moe serdtse [My heart's in the Highlands]). Literaturnaia Armeniia (Erevan), 1961, no. 8, p. 79-83.
   Akhverdian, L. Review of: V gorakh moe serdtse [My heart's in the Highlands]. Teatr, 1961, no. 11, p. 118-120.

162

1962 Orlova, R. Ironiia i gorech' [Irony and bitterness]. Inostrannaia literatura, 1962, no. 10, p. 257-259.
Saroyan, W. Pasport. (Glava iz avtobiograficheskoi knigi) [Passport. (A
chapter from an autobiographical book)]. Literaturnaia gazeta,
September 11, 1962.
1963 Levidova, I. Review of: *Boys and Girls Together*. New York, 1963.
Sovremennaia khudozhestvennaia literatura za rubezhom, 1963, no.
11, p. 56-59.

SAKSTON Aleksandr   SAXTON Alexander

1949 Abramov, A. Roman o chestnykh liudiakh Ameriki [A novel about the
honorable people of America]. (Bol'shaia Srednezapadnaia [The
great Middle-Western — i.e. *The Great Midland*]). Literaturnaia
gazeta, September 17, 1949.
Mendel'son, M. Roman ob amerikanskikh kommunistakh [A novel about
American communists]. (Bol'shaia Srednezapadnaia [The great
Middle-Western — i.e. *The Great Midland*]). Trud, September 17,
1949.
Pavlenko, P. Predislovie [Foreword]. *In:* Saxton, A. Bol'shaia Srednezapadnaia [The great Middle-Western — i.e. *The Great Midland*].
Moscow, 1949. p. 5-10.
1951 Dubashinskii, I. Predislovie [Foreword]. *In:* Saxton, A. *The Great Midland.*[1] Moscow, 1951. p. 3-8.

SIVER Edvin   SEAVER Edwin

1937 K'iunits, Dzh. [Kunitz, J.]. Drama amerikanskogo srednego klassa [The
drama of the American middle class]. (*Between the Hammer and the
Anvil*. New York, 1937). Internatsional'naia literatura, 1937, no. 7,
p. 208-210.

SHOU Irvin   SHAW Irwin

1936 Review of: *Bury the Dead*. Literaturnaia gazeta, May 30, 1936.
1941 Abramov, A. Novelly Irvina Shou [The short stories of Irwin Shaw].
Internatsional'naia literatura, 1941, no. 3-4, p. 68-69.
Borovoi, L. Zametki o spektakliakh [Notes on plays]. (Review of:
"Mirnye liudi" ["Peaceful people" — i.e. *The Gentle People*]). Teatr,
1941, no. 3, p. 126-127.
1962 Kalinenko, O. Ne napokaz. ("Ubiitsa") [Not just for show. ("The
murderer" — i.e. *The Assassin*)]. Teatral'naia zhizn', 1962, no. 11, p. 9.

[1] A book in the English language published in the Soviet Union.

Chuvikov, P. Predislovie [Foreword]. *In:* Shaw, I. Molodye l'vy [The young lions]. Moscow, 1962. p. 5-14.

SINKLER Epton   SINCLAIR Upton

Lenin, V. I. E. Sinkler [U. Sinclair]. Pravda, July 27, 1924. *Also in:* Lenin, V. I. Polnoe sobranie sochinenii [Complete collected works]. 5th ed. v. 26. p. 270-271.

1906 Chikagskaia epopeia i "Dzhungli," roman U. Sinklera [The Chicago epic and "The jungle," a novel by U. Sinclair]. Vestnik inostrannoi literatury, 1906, no. 10, p. 277-285.

Shklovskii, I. V. Review of: *The Jungle.* London, 1906. Russkoe bogatstvo, 1906, no. 7, otd. II, p. 19-39. (Signed: Sh.)

1907 Vasilevskii, L. M. Review of: Debri [The jungle]. Moscow, 1907. Sovremennyi mir, 1907, no. 2, otd. II, p. 76-77. (Signed: L. Vas-ii.)

Brusiakin, V. Romanist-sotsialist [A socialist novelist]. Novyi zhurnal dlia vsekh, 1912, no. 8, p. 97-110.

1912 Levinson, A. Review of: Sinclair, U. Sobranie sochinenii [Collected works]. v. 1-5. St. Petersburg, 1912. Sovremennyi mir, 1912, no. 6, p. 322-324.

1921 Friche, V. Ot voiny k revoliutsii [From war to revolution] (Dzhimmi Khiggins [Jimmy Higgins]). Krasnaia nov', 1921, no. 2, p. 204-214.

1922 Garri [Harry?]. Sto protsentov. Roman Uptona Sinklera [One hundred per cent. A novel by Upton Sinclair]. *In:* Zapad, vyp. 8, Moscow, 1922, p. 11-12.

Dodonov, V. Fakty i gnev. (Upton Sinkler) [Facts and anger. (Upton Sinclair)]. *In:* Zapad, vyp. 2, Moscow, 1922, p. 20-26.

Kogan, P. S. "Mashina." (Novaia p'esa Uiptona Sinklera) ["The Machine." (The new play by Upton Sinclair)]. Ekran, 1922, no. 30, p. 4.

Los'ev, V. Review of: Silviia [Silvia]. Moscow, 1922. Sibirskie ogni, 1922, no. 4, p. 193-196.

Sobolev, Iu. Review of: Sto protsentov [100%]. Petersburg, 1922. Pechat' i revoliutsiia, 1922, no. 8, p. 238-239.

Sredinskii, S. Svoboda pechati i kapitalizm. ("Mednaia marka") [Freedom of the press and capitalism. ("The copper label" — i.e. *The Brass Check*)]. Sovremennik, 1922, no. 1, p. 304-313.

Sredinskii, S. Upton Sinkler o "svobode pechati" [Upton Sinclair on the "freedom of the press"]. Molodaia gvardiia, 1922, no. 4-5, p. 283-294.

Friche, V. Amerikanskii bol'shevik ("Dzhimmi Khiggins") [An American bolshevik. ("Jimmy Higgins"). *In:* Friche, V. Korifei mirovoi literatury i Sovetskaia Rossiia [The leaders of world literature and Soviet Russia]. Moscow, 1922. p. 22-25.

Friche, V. Pis'ma o literature Zapada. Sovremennye Nibelungi. ("Tsa-

164

revich Gagen") [Letters about Western literature. Contemporary Nibelungen. ("Tsarevich Gagen" —i.e. *Prince Hagen*]). Moskovskii ponedel'nik, August 7, 1922.

Iurlov, A. Review of: Sto protsentov [100%]. Peterburg, 1922. Krasnaia nov', 1922, no. 6, p. 356.

Iasinskii, I. Review of: Sto protsentov [100%]. Peterburg, 1922. Kniga i revoliutsiia, 1922, no. 8, p. 44.

1923 Avdeev, V. K solntsu! ("Prints Gagen") [Toward the sun! ("Prince Hagen")]. Literaturnyi ezhenedel'nik, 1923, no. 29, p. 14-15.

V. I. Review of: *The Goose Step*. New York, 1923. Novyi mir (Petrograd), 1923, no. 1, p. 21.

Venetsianova, E. Agitator iz Nazareta. ("Menia zovut plotnikom") [An agitator from Nazareth. ("They call me carpenter")]. Moscow, 1923. Literaturnyi ezhenedel'nik, 1923, no. 24, p. 15.

Vol'kenshtein, V. Review of: Mashina [The machine]. Pechat' i revoliutsiia, 1923, no. 6, p. 251.

Dinamov, S. Review of: Okovy sbrosheny. (Konets "Dzhunglei") [The chains are cast off. (The end of "The jungle")]. Petrograd, 1923. Knigonosha, 1923, no. 28, p. 11.

Zhukov, P. Review of: Amerikanskaia krov' ("Sto protsentov") [American blood ("100%")]. Moscow, 1923. Kniga i revoliutsiia, 1923, no. 4 (28), p. 62.

Zvavich, I. Upton Sinkler i amerikanskie universitety. (Pis'mo iz Anglii) [Upton Sinclair and American universities. (A letter from England)]. Pechat' i revoliutsiia, 1923, no. 7, p. 25-39.

Kogan, P. S. O sotsial'noi drame "Ad." (Novaia p'esa Sinklera) [Concerning the social drama "Hell." (The new play by Sinclair)]. Krasnaia nov', 1923, no. 5, p. 340-346.

Kogan, P. S. Predislovie [Foreword]. *In:* Sinclair, U. Ad [Hell]. Moscow, 1923. p. 3-8.

S. K. Review of: Dzhimmi Khiggins [Jimmy Higgins]. Peterburg, 1921. Sto protsentov [100%]. Petersburg, 1922. Kazanskii bibliofil, 1923, no. 4, p. 140-141.

Slonimskii, A. Review of: Korol'-ugol' [King Coal]. Moscow, 1923. Kniga i revoliutsiia, 1923, no. 4, p. 57-58.

Upton Sinkler [Upton Sinclair]. Literaturnyi ezhenedel'nik, 1923, no. 16, p. 2.

Friche, V. U. Sinkler [U. Sinclair]. Krassnyi zhurnal dlia vsekh, 1923. no. 1-2, p. 55-57.

Churilin, T. Review of: Silviia [Sylvia]. Moscow, 1923. Knigonosha, 1923, no. 10, p. 8. (Signed: T. Ch.)

Iablonskaia, A. Epton Sinclair. ("Ispytaniia liubvi." Petrograd, Moscow, 1923) [Upton Sinclair. ("A test of love" —i.e. *Love's Pilgrimage*)]. Zori, 1923, no. 1, p. 12.

1924 Aksenov, I. A. Review of: Ad [Hell]. Petrograd, 1923. Pechat' i revoliutsiia, 1924, no. 1, p. 286-287.

Aksenov, I. A. Review of: Debri [The jungle]. Khar'kov, 1923. Pechat'
i revoliutsiia, 1924, no. 3, p. 256-257.

Birbraer, M. I. Epton Sinkler. Kharakteristika tvorchestva [Upton
Sinclair. A characterization of his work]. In: Epton Sinkler v klubakh
molodezhi [Upton Sinclair in youth clubs]. Moscow, 1924. p. 4-32.

Braudo, E. Review of: Zamuzhestvo Sil'vii [Sylvia's marriage]. Leningrad, Moscow, 1924. Pechat' i revoliutsiia, 1924, no. 4, p. 285.

Vygodskii, D. Vopl' o spravedlivosti [A cry for justice]. Leningrad, 1924,
no. 23, p. 13.

Gorbatov, G. Podlinnyi geroi nashego vremeni. ("Dzhimmi Khiggins")
[A true hero of our times. ("Jimmy Higgins")]. Moscow, 1923.
Narodnyi uchitel', 1924, no. 1, p. 161-165.

Dinamov, S. Review of: 2000-i god [The year 2000 — i.e. The Millennium].
Moscow, Leningrad, 1924. Knigonosha, 1924, no. 41, p. 20.

Dinamov, S. Review of: Korol' Midas [King Midas]. Leningrad, 1924.
Zamuzhestvo Sil'vii [Sylvia's marriage]. Leningrad, Moscow, 1924.
Mashina [The machine]. Moscow, 1924. Knigonosha, 1924, no. 21,
p. 10.

Dinamov, S. Review of: Samuel' iskatel' [Samuel the seeker]. Moscow,
1924. Knigonosha, 1924, no. 14, p. 10.

Dinamov, S. Review of: Chetyresta. (N'iu-Iork) [The four hundred.
(New York)]. Knigonosha, 1924, no. 13, p. 9-10. (Signed: S. Din.)

Dinamov, S. Review of: Iug i sever [The south and the north—i.e.
Manassas?]. Leningrad, 1924. Knigonosha, 1924, no. 43, p. 21-22.

Zhirmunskii, V. M. Review of: Manassas. New York, 1924. Sovremennyi zapad, 1924, no. 2, p. 184.

Iv. Iv. Review of: Mednaia marka [The copper label—i.e. The Brass
Check]. Khar'kov, 1924. Krasnyi zhurnal dlia vsekh, 1924, no. 2,
p. 163.

Leont'ev, B. O novykh knigakh Uptona Sinklera. ("Mednaia marka.
"Chetyresta") [Concerning the new books by Upton Sinclair. ("The
copper label"—i.e. The Brass Check. "The four hundred")]. Rabochii zhurnal, 1924, no. 2, p. 149-151.

M. B. Predislovie [Foreword]. In: Sinclair, U. Manassa. Povest' o voine
[Manassas. A tale of the war]. Leningrad, Moscow, 1924. p. 3-6.

Raivid, N. "Dzhungli." (Vmesto predisloviia) ["The jungle." (In place of
a foreword)]. In: Sinclair, U. Dzhungli [The jungle]. Ekaterinburg,
1924. p. 3-14.

Rozhdestvenskii, V. Review of: Artur Stirling [Arthur Stirling]. Leningrad, 1924. Russkii sovremennik, 1924, no. 3, p. 280-281.

Rozhitsyn, V. S. Predislovie [Foreword]. In: Sinclair, U. Vygody religii
[The profits of religion]. Moscow, 1924. p. 3-7.

166

1925 A. Ts. Predislovie [Foreword]. *In:* Sinclair, U. Samuel'-iskatel' [Samuel the seeker]. Moscow, 1925. p. 3-4.

Brandes, G. Vvedenie [Introduction]. *In:* Sinclair, U. Korol'-ugol' [King coal]. Leningrad, 1925. p. 5-6. *Also, in variant translation, with title:* Predislovie [Foreword]. *In:* Sinclair, U. Sobranie sochinenii [Collected works]. v. 6: Chernyi vlastelin [The black ruler]. Moscow, Leningrad, 1926. p. 5-7. *And in:* Sinclair, U. Chernyi vlastelin [The black ruler]. Moscow, Leningrad, 1927. p. 5-7.

Vol'kenshtein, V. Review of: Otets semeistva [Father of a family—i.e. *The Pot-Boiler*]. Moscow, 1925. Pechat' i revoliutsiia, 1925, no. 8, p. 250.

Danilov, A. Predislovie [Foreword]. *In:* Sinclair, U. Korol' Midas [King Midas]. 2nd ed. Leningrad, 1925. p. 5-8.

Dinamov, S. Review of: Krik o spravedlivosti [The cry for justice]. Leningrad, 1925. Knigonosha, 1925, no. 6, p. 17. (Signed: S. D.)

Dinamov, S. Predislovie k russkomu izdaniiu [Foreword to the Russian edition]. *In:* Sinclair, U. Krik o spravedlivosti [The cry for justice]. Leningrad, 1925. p. 5-10. (Signed: D.)

Dinamov, S. Review of: Porchenye [The spoiled ones—i.e. *Damaged Goods*]. Leningrad, 1925. Knigonosha, 1925, no. 11, p. 16.

Zaslavskii, D. Predislovie k russkomu izdaniiu [Foreword to the Russian edition]. *In:* Sinclair, U. Vopl' o spravedlivosti [The cry for justice]. Leningrad, Moscow, 1925. p. 5-14.

Zaslavskii, D. Predislovie k russkomu izdaniiu [A preface to the Russian edition]. *In:* Sinclair, U. Promyshlennaia respublika [The industrial republic]. Leningrad, 1925. p. 5-16.

Lunacharskaia, A. Review of: Prishestvie Khrista v leto 1921 [The coming of Christ in the summer of 1921]. Leningrad, 1924. Pechat' i revoliutsiia, 1925, no. 1, p. 289.

Mokul'skii, S. Obzhigatel' gorshkov [The kiln-tender—i.e. *The Pot-Boiler*]. Zhizn' iskusstva, 1925, no. 9, p. 10.

Nusinov, I. Review of: Kipiashchii gorshok [The boiling pot—i.e. *The Pot-Boiler*]. Moscow, 1925. Knigonosha, 1925, no. 10, p. 18-19.

Nusinov, I. Review of: Poiushchie uzniki [The singing prisoners—i.e. *Singing Jailbirds*]. Moscow, 1925. Knigonosha, 1925, no. 25, p. 15.

Plotnikov, I. Predislovie k russkomu izdaniiu [Foreword to the Russian edition]. *In:* Sinclair, U. Kniga ob obshchestve [A book about society—i.e. *Book of Life*]. Leningrad, 1925. p. 5-18.

Predislovie [Foreword]. *In:* Sinclair, U. Debri [The jungle]. Leningrad, 1925. p. 5-8.

Rashkovskaia, A. Review of: Kipiashchii gorshok [The boiling pot—i.e. *The Pot-Boiler*]. Moscow, 1925. Leningrad, 1925, no. 25, p. 17. (Signed: A. R-aia.)

Rozental', L. Review of: Iug i Sever [The South and the North—i.e.

Manassas?]. Leningrad, 1924. Pechat' i revoliutsiia, 1925, no. 4, p. 287-288.

Friche, V. Predislovie [Foreword]. *In:* Sinclair, U. Tiuremnye ptitsy poiut [Prison birds are singing—i.e. *Singing Jailbirds*]. Moscow, 1925. p. 3-7.

1926 Brudi. Review of: Neft' [Oil]. Moscow, 1926. Komsomoliia, 1926, no. 9, p. 77.

Duglas, Dzh. [Douglas, J.?]. Predislovie [Foreword]. *In:* Sinclair, U. Prikliucheniia malen'kogo sotsialista (Dzhimmi Khiggins) [The adventures of a small socialist (Jimmy Higgins)]. Moscow, 1926. p. 3-6.

Iakubovskii, G. Predislovie [Foreword]. *In:* Sinclair, U. Sto protsentov. Istoriia odnogo patriota [100%. The story of a patriot]. Moscow, 1926. p. 3-6.

1927 Vaisenberg, L. Epton Sinkler. Populiarnyi ocherk. [Upton Sinclair. A popular sketch]. Leningrad, Priboi, 1927. 72 p. *Also, abridged, in:* Sinclair, E. Sobranie sochinenii [Collected works]. v. 12. Moscow, Leningrad, 1927. p. 601-630.

Grigor'ev, Ia. Review of: Sekretar' Goveruna. (Pis'ma Mem k mame) [Secretary of the talkative one. (Mame's letters to her ma —i.e. *The Spokesman's Secretary*)]. Na literaturnom postu, 1927, no. 8, p. 61-62.

Loks. Review of: Neft' [Oil]. Pechat' i revoliutsiia, 1927, no. 1, p. 206.

Matsa, I. E. Sinkler i ego "Entwicklungsroman" [U. Sinclair and his "Entwicklungsroman"]. *In:* Matsa, I. Literatura i proletariat na Zapade [Literature and the proletariat in the West]. Moscow, 1927. p. 53-69.

Upton Sinkler [Upton Sinclair]. I. Efremian, A. Kritiko-biograficheskii ocherk [Critico-biographic sketch]; II. Bedov, A. U. Sinkler v shkole [U. Sinclair in the schools]. *In:* Inostrannye pisateli v shkole [Foreign writers in the schools]. Moscow, Leningrad, 1927. p. 163-178.

Friche, V. M. Pisateli-sotsialisty. (Dzh. London i U. Sinkler) [Socialist writers. (J. London and U. Sinclair)]. *In:* Friche, V. M. Ocherk razvitiia zapadnykh literatur [Outline of the development of Western literatures]. 3rd rev. ed. Khar'kov, 1927. p. 229-235.

1928 Ben, Dzh. Predislovie [Foreword]. *In:* Sinclair, U. Dzhungli [The jungle]. Moscow, 1928. p. 3-9.

Bogoslovskii, N. Review of: Neft' [Oil]. 2nd ed. Moscow, Leningrad, 1928. Kniga i profsoiuzy, 1928, no. 7, p. 25.

Danilin, Iu. Review of: Neft' [Oil]. Moscow, Leningrad, 1928. Novyi mir, 1928, no. 7, p. 254-255.

Dell, F. Epton Sinkler [Upton Sinclair]. Moscow, Leningrad, Gosizdat, 1928, 172 p. *Review:* A.B. Chitatel' i pisatel', February 18, 1928.

Dell, F. Epton Sinkler v Amerike [Upton Sinclair in America]. Vestnik inostrannoi literatury, 1928, no. 12, p. 88-89.

Dinamov, S. Pamflety Eptona Sinklera [The pamphlets of Upton Sinclair]. Vestnik inostrannoi literatury, 1928, no. 7, p. 152-153. (Signed: D.)

Dinamov, S. Epton Sinkler [Upton Sinclair]. Pechat' i revoliutsiia, 1928, no. 5, p. 125-136.

Sinclair, U. Kak ia pisal "Boston" [How I wrote "Boston"]. Vestnik inostrannoi literatury, 1928, no. 12, p. 117-118.

Predislovie [Foreword]. *In:* Sinclair, U. Dzhungli [The jungle]. Moscow, Leningrad, 1928. p. 3-6.

1929 Bessonov, N. Tiuremnye ptitsy [Prison birds—i.e. *Singing Jailbirds*]. Krasnaia panorama, 1929, no. 20, p. 13.

1930 Aleksandrov, G. Review of: Boston [Boston]. Moscow, Leningrad, 1930. Molodaia gvardiia, 1930, no. 11, p. 109-111.

Danilin, Iu. Kniga o Sakko i Vantsetti ("Boston." Moscow, Leningrad, 1930) [A book about Sacco and Vanzetti. ("Boston." Moscow, Leningrad, 1930)]. Novyi mir, 130, no. 6, p. 198-204.

Dzhermanetto, D. [Germanetto, D.?]. Predislovie [Foreword]. *In:* Sinclair, U. Boston [Boston]. v. 1. Moscow, Leningrad, 1930. p. 5-14.

Miroshnikov, N. Oblichitel'nyi dokument [An accusatory document]. ("Boston." Moscow, Leningrad, 1930). Sibirskie ogni, 1930, no. 9, p. 129-131.

Munblit, G. Predislovie [Foreword]. *In:* Sinclair, U. Dzhimmi Khiggins [Jimmy Higgins]. Moscow, Leningrad, 1930. p. 3-6.

Polonskaia, L. Review of: Boston [Boston]. Moscow, Leningrad, 1930. Izvestiia, May 9, 1930.

Popov, M. Novyi roman Eptona Sinklera. ("Mounten-Siti") [The new novel by Upton Sinclair. ("Mountain City")]. Vestnik inostrannoi literatury, 1930, no. 2, p. 200-201. (Signed: M. P.)

1931 Elistratova, A. Review of: *Mountain City.* New York, 1930. Inostrannaia kniga, literaturno-khudozhestvennaia seriia, 1931, no. 1, p. 3-4.

Put' Eptona Sinklera [The road of Upton Sinclair]. Literatura mirovoi revoliutsii, 1931, no. 4, p. 131-132.

Rykova, N. Review of: Boston [Boston]. Moscow, Leningrad, 1930. Zvezda, 1931, no. 1, p. 232-233.

Startsev, A. Epton Sinkler. Ocherk pervyi. "Dzhimmi Khiggins" i voina. [Upton Sinclair. First essay. "Jimmy Higgins" and the war]. Na literaturnom postu, 1931, no. 20-21, p. 25-29.

Startsev, A. Epton Sinkler i Amerika. 1. "Maunten-Siti"—roman "protsvetaniia" [Upton Sinclair and America. 1. "Mountain City"—a novel of "prosperity"]. 2. "Rimskii prazdnik"—roman krizisa ["Roman holiday"—a novel of crisis]. Na literaturnom postu, 1931, no. 33, p. 22-26, no. 34, p. 22-26.

1932 Vainshtein, Ts. Review of: Ispytaniia liubvi [A test of love—i.e. *Love's Pilgrimage*]. Moscow, Leningrad, 1932. Khudozhestvennaia literatura, 1932, no. 27, p. 13-14.

169

Elistratova, A. Review of: *The Wet Parade*. New York, 1931. Literatura mirovoi revoliutsii, 1932, no. 4, p. 106-108.

1933 Abramov, A. Epton Sinkler imeet chest' predstavit' Vill'iama Foksa [Upton Sinclair has the honor to introduce William Fox]. Sovetskoe kino, 1933, no. 10, p. 63-79.

Gol'denberg. Review of: Neft' [Oil]. Khudozhestvennaia literatura, 1933, no. 7, p. 41-43.

Elistratova, A. Amerikanskie zametki [American notes]. Literaturnaia gazeta, September 23, 1933.

Zaslavskii, D. Neudachnaia analogiia. ("Rimskie kanikuly." Leningrad, 1933) [An unsuccessful analogy. ("Roman holiday." Leningrad, 1933)]. Khudozhestvennaia literatura, 1933, no. 9, p. 38-40.

Miller-Budnitskaia, R. "Sotsialist chuvstva." (O tvorchestve Eptona Sinklera) ["A socialist in feeling." (Concerning the work of Upton Sinclair)]. Literaturnaia ucheba, 1933, no. 3-4, p. 92-109.

Rodzevich, S. Epton Sinkler. (Vmesto predisloviia) [Upton Sinclair. (In place of a preface)]. *In:* Sinclair, U. Rimskie kanikuly [Roman holiday]. Moscow, Leningrad, 1933. p. 263-291.

Khmel'nitskaia, T. Novaia kniga Eptona Sinklera. ("Rimskie kanikuly." Moscow, Leningrad, 1933) [The new book by Upton Sinclair. ("Roman holiday." Moscow, Leningrad, 1933)]. Literaturnyi kritik, 1933, no. 6, p. 136-139.

1934 Gardin, S. Epton Sinkler—reaktsionnyi utopist [Upton Sinclair—a reactionary utopianist]. Internatsional'naia literatura, 1934, no. 5, p. 132-135.

Levidov, M. Epicheskii Epton [Epic Upton]. Literaturnaia gazeta, January 24, 1934.

Rykova, N. Review of: Rimskie kanikuly [Roman holiday]. 1931; P'ianyi parad [The drunken parade—i.e. *The Wet Parade*]. Leningrad, Moscow, 1933. Literaturnyi sovremennik, 1934, no. 1, p. 154-156.

1937 A. Ia. "No pasaran!" Povest' Eptona Sinklera ob antifashistskoi voine v Ispanii ["No pasaran!" Upton Sinclair's story about the anti-fascist war in Spain]. Izvestiia, April 10, 1937.

Aleksinskaia, T. Torg chelovecheskim miasom [Trade in human meat]. *In:* Dooktiabr'skaia "Pravda" ob iskusstve i literature ["Pravda" of the pre-October period on literature and art]. Moscow, 1937. p. 220-222.

Balashov, P. Review of: *No pasaran!* Literaturnoe obozrenie, 1937, no. 14, p. 33-35.

Balashov, P. Epton Sinkler v zashchitu svobody [Upton Sinclair in defence of freedom]. Literaturnyi kritik, 1937, no. 9, p. 162-170.

Kniga Eptona Sinklera ob Ispanii. ("No pasaran!") [Upton Sinclair's book about Spain. ("No pasaran!")]. Pravda, March 26, 1937.

Mendel'son, M. Review of: *Co-op*. New York, 1936. Za rubezhom, 1937, no. 1, p. 2.

Mingulina, A. Novaia kniga Eptona Sinklera. ("No pasaran!") [The new book by Upton Sinclair. ("No pasaran!")]. Literaturnaia gazeta, April 20, 1937.

Mingulina, A. Posleslovie [Afterword]. *In:* Sinclair, U. "No pasaran!" —Oni ne proidut ["No pasaran!"—They will not pass]. Moscow, 1937, p. 203-207.

N. M. Review of: "No pasaran!" Internatsional'naia literatura, 1937, no. 12, p. 178.

Oborin, A. E. Sinkler v zashchitu revoliutsionnoi Ispanii. ("No pasaran!") [U. Sinclair in defence of revolutionary Spain. ("No pasaran!")]. Kniga i proletarskaia revoliutsiia, 1937, no. 10, p. 136-139.

Khovard, M. [Howard, M.?]. Novaia utopiia Eptona Sinklera [Upton Sinclair's new utopia]. ("Ko-op" ["Co-op"]). Internatsional'naia literatura, 1937, no. 1, p. 210-211.

Eidel'man, Ia. Litso fashizma [The face of fascism]. ("No pasaran!"). Literaturnaia gazeta, August 10, 1937.

1938   Aleksander [Alexander?], G. Review of: *Our Lady*. New York, 1938. Literaturnaia gazeta, December 26, 1938.

Anisimov, I. V Amerike. (E. Sinkler i. E Kheminguei) [In America. (U. Sinclair and E. Hemingway)]. Oktiabr', 1938, no. 11, p. 186-196.

Deich, A. Epton Sinkler [Upton Sinclair]. Izvestiia, September 21, 1938.

Elistratova, A. Roman-pamflet o kapitalisticheskoi Amerike [A pamphlet-novel about capitalist America]. (Avtomobil'nyi korol' [The automobile king—i.e. *The Flivver King*]. Moscow, 1938). Kniga i proletarskaia revoliutsiia, 1938, no. 12, p. 123-125.

Zhivov, M. Dva amerikanskikh romana [Two American novels]. (No pasaran! Moscow, 1937). Internatsional'nyi maiak, 1938, no. 1, p. 16.

Zalipskaia, N. Review of: Avtomobil'nyi korol' [The automobile king— i.e. *The Flivver King*]. Literaturnoe obozrenie, 1938, no. 17, p. 28-31.

K shestidesiatiletiiu Eptona Sinklera. (Privetstviia ot redaktsii zhurnala "Internatsional'naia literatura" i Soiuza sovetskikh pisatelei) [On Upton Sinclair's sixtieth anniversary. (Greetings from the editors of "Internatsional'naia literatura" and the Union of Soviet Writers)]. Internatsional'naia literatura, 1938, no. 9, p. 161-162.

Petrov, E. Epton Sinkler i Genri Ford [Upton Sinclair and Henry Ford]. Literaturnaia gazeta, September 20, 1938.

Segodnia Eptonu Sinkleru 60 let. Privetstvie Soiuza sovetskikh pisatelei [Today Upton Sinclair is sixty years old. Greetings of the Union of Soviet Writers]. Literaturnaia gazeta, September 20, 1938.

Sinclair, U. Kak sozdavalis' "Dzhungli" [How "The jungle" was written]. Internatsional'naia literatura, 1938, no. 9, p. 163-169.

Epton Sinkler—sovetskim pisateliam [Upton Sinclair to Soviet writers]. Literaturnaia gazeta, September 20, 1938.

1939 Karavaeva, A. Ob Eptone Sinklere i Lengstone Kh'iuze [Concerning Upton Sinclair and Langston Hughes]. Internatsional'naia literatura, 1939, no. 7-8 (first printing), p. 368.

Retsner, Ia. Mariia Antuanetta i frantsuzskaia revoliutsiia [Marie Antoinette and the French Revolution]. (*Marie Antoinette*. New York, 1939). Literaturnaia gazeta, July 20, 1939.

Rubin, V. Novyi roman Eptona Sinklera [A new novel by Upton Sinclair]. (*Little Steel*. New York, 1938). Internatsional'naia literatura, 1939, no. 2, p. 182-185.

1940 Mendel'son, M. Novyi roman Eptona Sinklera. ("Konets mira") [The new novel by Upton Sinclair. ("World's end")]. Literaturnaia gazeta, June 26, 1940.

Rokotov, T. Sumerki amerikanskogo liberalizma [The twilight of American liberalism]. (*Little Steel*. New York, 1938). Izvestiia, March 5, 1940.

Smirnov, Iu. Review of: *Little Steel*. New York, 1938. Molodaia gvardiia, 1940, no. 3, p. 156.

1942 Gal'perina, R. "Zuby drakona" ["The dragon's teeth"]. Pravda, December 29, 1942.

1943 Elistratova, A. Antifashistskaia trilogiia Sinklera [Sinclair's antifascist trilogy]. Internatsional'naia literatura, 1943, no. 1, p. 118-121.

Rokotov, T. Antifashistskii roman Eptona Sinklera. ("Zuby drakona") [Upton Sinclair's antifascist novel. ("The dragon's teeth")]. Ogonek, 1943, no. 2, p. 13.

1945 Elistratova, A. Antifashistskaia epopeiia Sinklera [Sinclair's antifascist epic]. Literaturnaia gazeta, March 24, 1945.

1947 Izakov, B. Predislovie [Foreword]. *In:* Sinclair, U. Krushenie mira [World's end]. Moscow, 1947. p. 5-14.

1948 Elistratova, A. Mezhdu dvukh mirov. Antifashistskaia epopeia Eptona Sinklera. [Between two worlds. The antifascist epic of Upton Sinclair]. ("Krushenie mira" ["World's end"]. Moscow, 1947). Literaturnaia gazeta, March 3, 1948.

Levinton, A. Krushenie starogo mira [The downfall of the old world]. ("Krushenie mira" ["World's end"]. Moscow, 1948). Zvezda, 1948, no. 10, p. 206-207.

Rubin, V. Predislovie [Foreword]. *In:* Sinclair, U. Mezhdu dvukh mirov [Between two worlds]. Moscow, 1948. p. v-xii.

1949 Pavlenko, P. Epton Sinkler—kar'erist i klevetnik [Upton Sinclair—careerist and slanderer]. Literaturnaia gazeta, April 20, 1949.

1950 Kislova, L. Epton Sinkler—podzhigatel' voiny [Upton Sinclair—war monger]. Literaturnaia gazeta, March 25, 1950.

Rozval, S. Epton Sinkler "kaetsia" [Upton Sinclair "repents"]. Literaturnaia gazeta, August 10, 1950.

1951 Kislova, L. Epton Sinkler vysluzhivaetsia [Upton Sinclair makes his way in the world]. Literaturnaia gazeta, April 3, 1951.
1958 Zasurskii, Ia. Posleslovie [Afterword]. *In:* Sinclair, U. Korol' Ugol' [King Coal]. Moscow, 1958. p. 373-382.
1959 Bogoslovskii, V. N. K istorii amerikanskogo realizma. Rannee tvorchestvo E. Sinklera [On the history of American realism. The early work of Upton Sinclair]. Uchenye zapiski Moskovskogo oblastnogo pedagogicheskogo instituta, 1959, t. 78. Trudy kafedry zarubezhnoi literatury, vyp. 6. Progressivnaia zarubezhnaia literatura 19 i 20 vekov, p. 27-61.
1962 Kulakovskaia, I. Review of: *Affectionately, Eve.* New York, 1961. Sovremennaia khudozhestvennaia literatura za rubezhom, 1962, no. 8, p. 55-56.
1963 Bogoslovskii, V. N. K istorii realizma v SShA. Tvorchestvo Dzheka Londona i Eptona Sinklera (1900-1917) [On the history of realism in the United States. The work of Jack London and Upton Sinclair (1900-1917)]. Abstract of dissertation presented for the degree of Doctor of Philological Sciences. Moscow, 1963. 39 p.
   Elistratova, A. Review of: *The Autobiography.* New York, 1962. Sovremennaia khudozhestvennaia literatura za rubezhom, 1963, no. 12, p. 100-103.
   London, J. Dzhungli [The jungle]. Nedelia, July 6, 1963, p. 6-7.

SMEDLI Agnes   SMEDLEY Agnes

1930 Frid, Ia. Review of: Doch' zemli [Daughter of earth]. Moscow, Leningrad, 1930. Novyi mir, 1930, no. 10, p. 205-206.
1934 Brodskii, R. Dve armii [Two armies]. ("Rasskazy o Kitae" ["Stories about China"]). Zalp, 1934, no. 12, p. 36-37.
   Vladimirskii, I. Predislovie [Foreword]; Startsev, A. Ob Agnese Smedli [About Agnes Smedley]. *In:* Smedley, A. Emi Siao. Rasskazy o Kitae [Emi Siao. Stories about China]. Khar'kov, 1934. p. 5-19, 279-285.
   Elistratova, A. Kontrasty kitaiskoi zhizni [The contrasts of Chinese life]. ("Kitaiskie sud'by" ["Chinese destinies"]. Moscow, 1934). Khudozhestvennaia literatura, 1934, no. 10, p. 31-34.
   Evg. L. Staryi i novyi Kitai [The old and new China]. Shturm (Sverdlovsk), 1934, no. 11, p. 114-116.
   Startsev, A. Kitaiskie sud'by [Chinese destinies]. Moscow, 1934. Krasnaia nov', 1934, no. 10, p. 206-207.
   Terent'ev, N. Review of: Kitaiskie sud'by [Chinese destinies]. Izvestiia, July 28, 1934
   Khamadan, A. Beloe i krasnoe [The white and the red]. ("Kitaiskie sud'by" ["Chinese destinies"]. Moscow, 1934). Pravda, September 11, 1934.

1935 Azorin. Review of: Rasskazy o kitaiskoi Krasnoi armii [Tales about the Chinese Red Army]. Moscow, 1935. Kommunisticheskaia molodezh', 1935, no. 11, p. 55-56.

Berezov, P. Review of: Kitaiskie sud'by [Chinese destinies]. Moscow, 1934. Novyi mir, 1935, no. 1, p. 297-299.

Glagolev, N. Kitaiskaia Krasnaia armiia pobezhdaet [The Chinese Red Army is winning]. (Rasskazy o kitaiskoi Krasnoi armii [Tales about the Chinese Red Army]. Moscow, 1935). Khudozhestvennaia literatura, 1935, no. 5, p. 41-44.

Zhdanov, N. Review of: Rasskazy o kitaiskoi Krasnoi armii [Tales about the Chinese Red Army]. Moscow, 1935. Literaturnyi sovremennik, 1935, no. 7, p. 218-229.

Karmon, V. (Carmon, W.). Agness Smedli [Agnes Smedley]. Raionnaia i politotdel'skaia pechat', 1935, no. 23, p. 30-31.

Ru-Sin. Armiia liubvi i nenavisti [An army of love and of hate]. (Rasskazy o kitaiskoi Krasnoi armii [Tales about the Chinese Red Army]. Moscow, 1935). Literaturnaia gazeta, May 10, 1935.

S. Review of: Rasskazy o kitaiskoi Krasnoi armii [Tales about the Chinese Red Army]. Moscow, 1935. Pod"em (Voronezh), 1935, no. 3, p. 97.

S-ov, V. Zhizn' Agnessy Smedli v opasnosti. Na zashchitu amerikanskoi revoliutsionnoi pisatel'nitsy [Agnes Smedley's life is in danger. In defense of the American revolutionary writer]. Literaturnaia gazeta, March 15, 1935. (Signed: V. S-ov.)

Khamadan, A. Kniga o doblesti i geroistve [A book about courage and heroism]. (Rasskazy o kitaiskoi Krasnoi armii [Tales about the Chinese Red Army]. Moscow, 1935). Pravda, May 8, 1935.

Khokhlov, G. Pravda o Kitae [The truth about China]. Znamia, 1935, no. 7, p. 201-209.

1936 Novoselov, N. Review of: Geroi Sovetskogo Kitaia [Heroes of Soviet China]. Moscow, 1936. Literaturnoe obozrenie, 1936, no. 22, p. 14-18.

Khamadan, A. Predislovie [Foreword]. In: Smedley, A. Geroi Sovetskogo Kitaia [Heroes of Soviet China]. Moscow, 1936. p. 5-10.

1957 Burchett, W. Liudi Kitaia [The people of China]. (The Great Road. The Life and Times of Chu Teh. New York, 1956). Novoe vremia, 1957, no. 52, p. 29-31.

SMIT LILIAN   SMITH LILLIAN

1947 Startsev, A. Review of: Strange Fruit. New York, 1944. Literaturnaia gazeta, August 2, 1947.

174

1933 Carmon, W. Predislovie [Foreword]. *In:* Spivak, J. Negr iz Dzhordzhii [A Negro from Georgia—i.e. *Georgia Nigger*]. Moscow, 1933. p. 3-6.

1934 Dinamov, S. Kniga strashnoi pravdy [A book of awesome truth]. (Negr iz Dzhordzhii [A Negro from Georgia—i.e. *Georgia Nigger*]. Moscow, 1933). Novyi mir, 1934, no. 12, p. 244.

Karmon, U. [Carmon, W.]. Spivak—reporter, kotoryi smeialsia [Spivak—a reporter who laughed]. Internatsional'naia literatura, 1935, no. 2, p. 123-128.

1935 S-ev, A. Mucheniki plantatsii i katorzhnykh komand [The martyrs of the plantations and the prison gangs]. (Negr iz Dzhordzhii [A Negro from Georgia—i.e. *Georgia Nigger*]. Moscow, Leningrad, 1933). Khudozhestvennaia literatura, 1935, no. 1, p. 45-47.

1948 Vronskii, B. Review of: Amerikanskii fashizm [American fascism—i.e. *A Pattern for American Fascism*]. Kul'tura i zhizn', October 21, 1948.

1949 Berezhkov, V. Vstupitel'naia stat'ia [Introductory article]. *In:* Spivak, J. "Spasiteli" Ameriki [The "saviors" of America]. Moscow, 1949. p. 5-16.

1950 Vygodskii, S. Fashizatsiia vnutripoliticheskoi zhizni SShA [The fascist trend in the domestic political life of the USA]. (Amerikanskii fashizm [American fascism — i.e. *A Pattern for American Fascism*]. Moscow, 1949). Propaganda i agitatsiia, 1950, no. 4, p. 59-62.

Minaev, V. "Amerikanskoe deistvie" v deistvii ["American action" in action]. ("Spasiteli" Ameriki [The "saviors" of America]. Moscow, 1949). Novyi mir, 1950, no. 5, p. 254-256.

Tarle, E. Zaokeanskie gitlerovtsy [Transoceanic Hitlerites]. (Amerikanskii fashizm [American fascism—i.e. *A Pattern for American Fascism*]. Moscow, 1949). Novyi mir, 1950, no. 2, p. 243-244.

1936 Rollins, V. Linkol'n Stefens [Lincoln Steffens]. Literaturnaia gazeta, August 15, 1936.

1937 Startsev, A. Krushenie odnogo liberalizma. (Linkol'n Steffens) [The destruction of one form of liberalism. (Lincoln Steffens)]. Internatsional'naia literatura, 1937, no. 12, p. 135-145.

Steffens, L. Iz avtobiografii [From his autobiography]. Internatsional'-naia literatura, 1937, no. 12, p. 146-166.

1940 Kozachinskii, A. Review of: Mal'chik na loshadi [A boy on a horse—i.e. *Boy on Horseback*]. Moscow, 1939. Literaturnaia gazeta, August 11, 1940.

Smirnov, Iu. Review of: Mal'chik na loshadi [A boy on a horse—i.e.

Boy on Horseback]. Moscow, 1939. Molodaia gvardiia, 1940, no. 3, p. 156-157.

Somov, A. Review of: Mal'chik na loshadi [A boy on a horse—i.e. *Boy on Horseback*]. Moscow, 1939. Detskaia literatura, 1940, no. 3, p. 51-52.

1941 Chechanovskii, M. Pis'ma Linkol'na Steffensa [The letters of Lincoln Steffens]. Literaturnaia gazeta, April 27, 1941.

1949 Chechanovskii, M. Predislovie [Foreword]. *In:* Steffens, L. Razgrebatel' griazi [The muckraker]. Moscow, 1949, p. 5-16.

1950 Brandis, E. Prestuplenie dvukhpartiinoi shaiki [The crime of the two-party gang]. (Razgrebatel' griazi [The muckraker]. Moscow, 1949). Oktiabr', 1950, no. 8, p. 188-191.

Nikiforov, L. "Chudovishche Korysti, Obmana i Lzhi" ["The Monster of Greed, Deceit and of Falsehood"]. (Razgrebatel' griazi [The muckraker]. Moscow, 1949. Izvestiia, March 11, 1950.

1961 Orlova, R. Iskatel' pravdy [A seeker after truth]. Inostrannaia literatura, 1961, no. 9, p. 243-248.

STEIN GERTRUDA   STEIN GERTRUDE

1936 Eishiskina, N. Primitivizm i prostota [Primitivism and simplicity]. Literaturnyi kritik, 1936, no. 1, p. 172-184.

STEINBEK DZHON   STEINBECK JOHN

1937 N. M. Review of: *In Dubious Battle*. New York, 1936. Internatsional'-naia literatura, 1937, no. 4, p. 221-222.

1939 Grou [Grow?], M. Strana, gde zreiut "Grozd'ia gneva" [A country where "The grapes of wrath" are ripening]. Literaturnaia gazeta, December 5, 1939.

N. V. Sud Lincha nad romanom Steinbeka [Lynch law for Steinbeck's novel]. Pravda, November 19, 1939.

Ol'gin, M. Review of: Grozd'ia gneva [The grapes of wrath]. Pravda, August 15, 1939.

Pressa SShA o romane Steinbeka "Grozd'ia gneva" [The press of the US about Steinbeck's novel "The grapes of wrath"]. Internatsional'naia literatura, 1939, no. 11, p. 240-241.

Rait [Wright?], R. "O myshakh i liudiakh." P'esa Dzhona Steinbeka ["Of mice and men." John Steinbeck's play]. Iskusstvo i zhizn', 1939, no. 9, p. 44-45.

1940 Abramov, A. Dzhon Steinbek [John Steinbeck]. Internatsional'naia literatura, 1940, no. 3-4, p. 222-232.

Amerikanskie reaktsionery protiv "Grozd'ev gneva" [American reactionaries against "The grapes of wrath"]. Literaturnoe obozrenie, 1940, no. 1, p. 63-64.

Anisimov, I. Posleslovie [Afterword]. *In:* Steinbeck, J. Grozd'ia gneva [The grapes of wrath]. Moscow, 1940. p. 499-503.

Balashov, P. Pevets narodnogo gneva [A singer of the people's wrath]. Novyi mir, 1940, no. 10, p. 200-216.

"Grozd'ia gneva" v kino. 1. Platt, D. Fil'm; 2. Karmon [Carmon], W. Pressa o fil'me ["The grapes of wrath" in the cinema. 1. Platt, D. The film; Carmon, W. The press about the film]. Internatsional'naia literatura, 1940, no. 5-6, p. 331-333.

Miller-Budnitskaia, R. Kniga gneva [A book of wrath]. ("Grozd'ia gneva" ["The grapes of wrath"]). Znamia, 1940, no. 8, p. 191-203.

Miller-Budnitskaia, R. Review of: Grozd'ia gneva [The grapes of wrath]. Leningrad, 1940, no. 11-12, p. 34-35.

Nemerovskaia, O. Kniga o liubvi i nenavisti [A book about love and hate]. (Grozd'ia gneva [The grapes of wrath]). Zvezda, 1940, no. 8-9, p. 271-277.

Roman Steinbeka i ego kritiki [Steinbeck's novel and its critics]. Internatsional'naia literatura, 1940, no. 9-10, p. 220-222.

Sergeev, N. Review of: Grozd'ia gneva [The grapes of wrath]. 1940. Internatsional molodezhi, 1940, no. 11, p. 48.

Khmel'nitskaia, T. "Grozd'ia gneva" Steinbeka [Steinbeck's "The grapes of wrath"]. Literaturnyi sovremennik, 1940, no. 12, p. 156-161.

Chelovekov, F. "Grozd'ia gneva" ["The grapes of wrath"]. Literaturnoe obozrenie, 1940, no. 12, p. 37-40.

1941 Vol'fkovich, S. Kniga potriasaiushchei pravdivosti [A book of unsettling veracity]. Internatsional'naia literatura, 1941, no. 5, p. 186-187.

Pochemu nam nraviatsia "Grozd'ia gneva" [Why we like "The grapes of wrath"]. Internatsional'naia literatura, 1941, no. 5, p. 187-189.

1942 Sergeeva, N. Novaia kniga Dzhona Steinbeka [John Steinbeck's new book]. (*The Moon Is Down.* London, 1942). Pravda, December 21, 1942.

Shneider, I. O novom romane Dzhona Steinbeka [Concerning John Steinbeck's new novel]. (*The Moon Is Down.* London 1942). Internatsional'naia literatura, 1942, no. 12, p. 130-131.

1943 Knipovich, E. Novaia kniga Dzhona Steinbeka [The new book by John Steinbeck]. (*The Moon Is Down.* London, 1942). Znamia, 1943, no. 5-6, p. 238-242.

Motyleva, T. Nepokorennyi narod. [An unconquered people]. (*The Moon Is Down.* London, 1942). Literatura i iskusstvo, September 4, 1943.

1947 Mendel'son, M. Strausovaia utopiia [An ostrich-like Utopia]. (*Cannery Row.* New York, 1945). Literaturnaia gazeta, April 12, 1947.

1954 Romanova, E. "Filosofiia" mistera Steinbeka [Mr. Steinbeck's "philosophy."] (*East of Eden*. New York, 1952). Literaturnaia gazeta, July 10, 1954.

1957 Dmiterko, L. Tragizm obrechennosti. Po povodu odnoi stat'i Dzhona Steinbeka [The tragedy of doom. On the theme of one of John Steinbeck's articles]. Komsomol'skaia pravda, November 17, 1957.

Izakov, B. Predislovie [Foreword]. *In:* Steinbeck, J. Grozd'ia gneva [The grapes of wrath]. Moscow, 1957. p. 5-8.

Makarov, A. Pis'mo v redaktsiiu [A letter to the editor]. ("Zhemchuzhina" ["The pearl"]). Inostrannaia literatura, 1957, no. 2, p. 217-218.

1958 Arkhangel'skaia G. Zreiushchaia nenavist' [A ripening hate]. ["Zhemchuzhina" ["The pearl"]). Don (Rostov n/D.), 1958, no. 3, p. 174-178.

Zhantieva, D. Posleslovie [Afterword]. *In:* Steinbeck, J. Zhemchuzhina [The pearl]. Moscow, 1958. p. 72-74.

1959 Dzhon Steinbek o sebe [John Steinbeck about himself]. Literaturnaia gazeta, December 17, 1959.

Landor, M. Steinbek i ego kritiki [Steinbeck and his critics]. Voprosy literatury, 1959, no. 1, p. 238-244.

1960 Pavlovskaia, A. I. Kolorit i stil' povesti Dzhona Steinbeka "Zhemchuzhina" [The color and style of John Steinbeck's tale "The pearl"]. Sbornik studencheskikh rabot Latviiskogo gosudarstvennogo universiteta. Riga, 1960. no. 3, p. 53-64.

1961 Orlova, R. Chelovek dostig bogatstva... [A man, having acquired riches...]. ("Zima trevogi nashei" ["The winter of our discontent"]). Literaturnaia gazeta, September 16, 1961.

1962 Levidova, I. Poslevoennye knigi Dzhona Steinbeka [John Steinbeck's postwar books]. Voprosy literatury, 1962, no. 8, p. 122-142.

M. T. Grozd'ia liubvi i gneva [The grapes of love and wrath]. Literaturnaia gazeta, March 1, 1962.

Mendel'son, M. Dvazhdy prozvuchavshii vopros. Zametki o tvorchestve Dzhona Steinbeka [A twice-sounded question. Remarks on the work of John Steinbeck]. Zvezda, 1962, no. 8, p. 169-177.

Mendel'son, M. Review of: French, W. *John Steinbeck*. New York, 1961. Sovremennaia khudozhestvennaia literatura za rubezhom, 1962, no. 2, p. 97-99.

Nedelin, V. Padenie Itena Khouli [The fall of Ethan Hawley]. ("Zima trevogi nashei" ["The winter of our discontent"]). Komsomol'skaia pravda, June 26, 1962.

Orlova, R. Den'gi protiv chelovechnosti. (Zametki o tvorchestve Dzhona Steinbeka) [Money against humanity. (Remarks on the work of John Steinbeck)]. Inostrannaia literatura, 1962, no. 3, p. 197-208.

Orlova, R. Pod shutovskoi maskoi. ("Zima trevogi nashei" v tvorchestve Dzhona Steinbeka) [Under a jester's mask. ("The winter of our discontent" in the writings of John Steinbeck)]. *In:* Steinbeck, J. Zima trevogi nashei [The winter of our discontent]. Moscow, 1962. p. 299-312.

Samarin, R. Ponimaem vashu trevogu, Steinbek [We understand your alarm, Steinbeck]. (Zima trevogi nashei [The winter of our discontent]. Moscow, 1962). Izvestiia, November 11, 1962.

Tolchenova, N. Prestuplenie i nakazanie Itena Allena Khouli [The crime and punishment of Ethan Allan Hawley]. Ogonek, 1962, no. 19, p. 25.

1963 Aramian, R. Tri dnia s Dzhonom Steinbekom [Three days with John Steinbeck]. Literaturnaia Armeniia, 1963, no. 11, p. 87-89.

Vishnevetskii, K. Razgovarivaia so Steinbekom [Talking with Steinbeck]. Izvestiia, October 22, 1963. (Moscow evening edition.)

Vstrecha so Steinbekom [A meeting with Steinbeck]. Literaturnaia gazeta, October 24, 1963.

Golenopol'skii, A. and T. Golenopol'skii. Da ne ugasnet ogon' chelovechnosti [And may the flame of humanity never die]. (Zima trevogi nashei [The winter of our discontent]). Sibirskie ogni (Novosibirsk), 1963, no. 2, p. 187-188.

Grozd'ia polny gneva... [The grapes are full of wrath...]. Literaturnaia gazeta, February 12, 1963.

Zlobina, M. Geroi Steinbeka [Steinbeck's heroes]. Novyi mir, 1963, no. 10, p. 262-267.

Mezhelaitis, E. ...Poznavshii "sol' zemli" [Having known the "salt of the earth"]. Literaturnaia gazeta, November 2, 1963.

Mendel'son, M. O Dzhone Steinbeke i dvukh ego povestiakh [Concerning John Steinbeck and two of his works]. *In:* Steinbeck, J. Zhemchuzhina. Kvartal Tortil'ia Flet [The pearl. Tortilla Flat]. Moscow, 1963. p. 3-20.

Ob avtore i ego knige. (Predislovie k publikatsii knigi "Puteshestvie s Charli v poiskakh Ameriki") [Concerning the author and his book. (Foreword to the publication of "Travels with Charley in search of America")]. Inostrannaia literatura, 1963, no. 5, p. 98-99.

Muliarchik, A. S. Tvorchestvo Dzhona Steinbeka [The work of John Steinbeck]. Moscow, Izdatel'stvo Moskovskogo universiteta, 1963. 70 p.

"Nenavizhu populiarnost', boius' ee..." V gostiakh u Dzhona Steinbeka ["I hate popularity, I'm afraid of it..." As guests of John Steinbeck]. Literaturnaia Rossiia, 1963, no. 3, p. 20.

Orlova, R. Ustareli li idealy tridtsatykh godov? [Have the ideals of the '30's become old?]. Inostrannaia literatura, 1963, no. 5, p. 205-206.

D. Steinbek otvechaet zhurnalistam... [John Steinbeck replies to journalists...]. Literaturnaia gazeta, November 5, 1963.

Stoianov, M. Khoziain chudesnogo talismana [The master of a wondrous talisman]. Moskovskaia pravda, October 27, 1963.

Marx, K. and F. Engels. Bicher-Stou [Beecher Stowe]. *In:* K. Marks i
F. Engel's ob iskusstve [K. Marx and F. Engels on art]. v. 1. Moscow, 1957. p. 576.

1856 Suzhdenie gazety Times o novom romane G-zhi Bicher-Stou [The opinion
of *The Times* on Mrs. Beecher Stowe's new novel]. (*Dred.* 1856).
Russkii vestnik, 1856, t. VI, no. 1, p. 143-149.

1857 Serakovskii, S. I. Dred, roman g-zhi Bicher-Stou [Dred, a novel by
Mrs. Beecher Stowe]. Sovremennik, 1857, no. 1, otd. V, p. 140-142.

1872 Likhacheva, E. O. Poslednii roman Bicher-Stou [The latest novel by
Beecher Stowe]. (*My Wife and I*). Otechestvennye zapiski, 1872, no. 8,
otd. II, p. 296-304. (Signed: E. L.)

1874 Likhacheva, E. O. Poslednii roman Bicher-Stou [The latest novel by
Beecher Stowe]. (*Pink and White Tyranny*). Otechestvennye zapiski,
1874, no. 11, otd. II, p. 195-205. (Signed: E. L.)

1882 Kak sozdalsia roman "Khizhina diadi Toma" [How the novel "Uncle
Tom's Cabin" was written]. Zhivopisnoe obozrenie, 1882, no. 36,
p. 576.

1885 G-zha Bicher-Stou v ee domashnei obstanovke [Mrs. Beecher Stowe at
home]. Zhivopisnoe obozrenie, 1885, no. 48, p. 350-351.

1892 Sysoeva, E. A. Zhizn' Garriet Bicher-Stou, avtora "Khizhiny diadi Toma" [The life of Harriet Beecher Stowe, the author of "Uncle Tom's
cabin"]. St. Petersburg, 1892. 151 p. 2nd ed. 1900. *Reviews:* Poznia-
kov, N. I. Obrazovanie, 1892, no. 5, p. 512-513 (Signed: N. P.);
Mir bozhii, 1892, no. 2, p. 19-20; Sever, 1892, no. 2, col. 127.

1893 Bullen, Dzh. Vvedenie [Introduction]. *In:* Stowe, H. B. Khizhina diadi
Toma [Uncle Tom's cabin]. St. Petersburg, 1893. p. 1-43. 2nd ed.
1899. p. 3-45; 3rd ed. 1908. p. 3-45.

E. K. Gospozha Bicher-Stou—zashchitnitsa negrov [Mrs. Beecher
Stowe—a defender of the Negroes]. *In:* E. K. Ocherki iz amerikanskoi zhizni [Sketches from American life]. Khar'kov, 1893. p. 3-21.

1894 Review of: Khizhina diadi Toma [Uncle Tom's cabin]. Moscow, 1893.
Severnyi vestnik, 1894, no. 1, otd. II, p. 139.

1895 Beketova, M. Detstvo i vospitanie Bicher-Stou [Beecher Stowe's childhood and upbringing]. Vestnik vospitaniia, 1895, no. 8, p. 74-97.

1896 Bicher-Stou [Beecher Stowe]. Novoe vremia, July 6/18, 1896. Supplement.
Bicher-Stou. (Nekrolog) [Beecher Stowe. (Obituary)]. Russkii vestnik,
1896, no. 8, p. 360.
Bicher-Stou. (Nekrolog) [Beecher Stowe. (Obituary)]. Sever, 1896, no. 29,
cols. 1006-1007.
Bicher-Stou i istoriia "Khizhiny diadi Toma" [Beecher Stowe and the
story of "Uncle Tom's cabin"]. Severnyi vestnik, 1896, no. 10, otd. II,
p. 72-76.

Garriet Bicher-Stou [Harriet Beecher Stowe]. Vestnik inostrannoi literatury, 1896, no. 8, p. 211-216.

Garriet Bicher-Stou. (Nekrolog) [Harriet Beecher Stowe. (Obituary)]. Zhivopisnoe obozrenie, 1896, no. 29, p. 55.

Garriet Bicher-Stou, avtor "Khizhiny diadi Toma" [Harriet Beecher Stowe, the author of "Uncle Tom's cabin"]. Mir bozhii, 1896, no. 8, p. 271-274.

Garriet Bicher-Stou [Harriet Beecher Stowe]. Niva, 1896, no. 52, p. 1292.

Garriet Bicher-Stou. (Nekrolog) [Harriet Beecher Stowe. (Obituary)]. Russkie vedomosti, June 22, 1896.

Petrov, I. Nevol'niki v Amerike. (Pamiati Garriet Bicher-Stou) [The slaves in America. (In memory of Harriet Beecher Stowe)]. Vskhody, 1896, no. 19, p. 77-124; no. 21, p. 125-160.

1897 Ivanov, I. Uchitel' vzroslykh i drug detei [A teacher of adults and a friend of children]. Detskoe chtenie, 1897, no. 1 (otd. II), p. 47-57; no. 2 (otd. II), p. 119-130; no. 3 (otd. II), p. 247-270; no. 4 (otd. II), p. 47-71. *Also published separately.* Moscow, 1898, 1902, 1907, 1914. *Reviews:* Koltanovskaia, E. Garriet Bicher-Stou. Literaturnyi ocherk [Harriet Beecher Stowe. A literary sketch]. Iunyi chitatel', 1899, no. 8, p. 219-230; Severnyi vestnik, 1898, no. 3 (otd. II), p. 57.

1898 Bicher-Stou [Beecher Stowe]. Russkii vestnik, 1898, no. 10, p. 348-350.

Zhizn' i pis'ma avtora "Khizhiny diadi Toma" [Life and letters of the author of "Uncle Tom's cabin"]. Istoricheskii vestnik, 1898, no. 2, p. 769-770.

Novaia biografiia g-zhi Bicher-Stou [A new biography of Mrs. Beecher Stowe]. Knizhki Nedeli, 1898, no. 9, p. 209-211.

Review of: Khizhina diadi Toma [Uncle Tom's cabin]. St. Petersburg, 1898. Mir bozhii, 1898, no. 10, otd. II, p. 78-79.

1900 Bicher-Stou. Zhenshchiny Novogo Sveta [Beecher Stowe. Women of the New World]. Vestnik inostrannoi literatury, 1900, no. 8, p. 50-56.

Buzkova, E. "Khizhina diadi Toma" i rabstvo negrov v Amerike ["Uncle Tom's cabin" and Negro slavery in America]. Khar'kov, 1900. 63 p.

1901 Murakhina, L. A. Neskol'ko slov ot perevodchitsy [A few words from the translator]. *In:* Stowe, H. B. Khizhina diadi Toma [Uncle Tom's cabin]. Moscow, 1901. p. 3-8. (Signed: L. M.) *Also:* Moscow, 1912. p. 436-443.

1902 Garrietta Bicher-Stou [Harriet Beecher Stowe]. Novyi zhurnal inostrannoi literatury, 1902, no. 2, p. 31-32 (2nd pagination). *Also in:* Plutarkh XIX veka [Plutarch of the 19th century]. v. 2. St. Petersburg, 1903. p. 31-32.

Gorbunov-Posadov, I. Osvoboditeli chernykh rabov. (Prilozhenie k knige "Khizhina diadi Toma") [Liberators of the black slaves. (Supplement to the book "Uncle Tom's cabin")]. Moscow, 1902. p. 402-425. *Also:* 1907, 1910.

Predislovie k novomu amerikanskomu izdaniiu. Bibliograficheskie svede-
niia o "Khizhine diadi Toma" [Foreword to the new American
edition. Bibliographical information about "Uncle Tom's cabin"].
In: Stowe, H. B. Khizhina diadi Toma [Uncle Tom's cabin]. St.
Petersburg, 1902. p. ii-xxxviii, p. 517-531.

Toropov, S. A. Iubilei knigi. ("Khizhina diadi Toma") [The jubilee of a
book. ("Uncle Tom's cabin")]. Sem'ia, 1902, no. 12, p. 11-12.
(Signed: S. T—v.)

1903 Vvedenie [Introduction]. *In:* Stowe, H. B. Khizhina diadi Toma [Uncle
Tom's cabin]. St. Petersburg, 1903. p. 5-101.

1907 Esipova, M. K. Kak iavilas' kniga "Khizhina diadi Toma" i ocherk
zhizni ee avtora [How the book "Uncle Tom's cabin" made its
appearance and a sketch of the life of its author]. *In:* Stowe, H. B.
Khizhina diadi Toma [Uncle Tom's cabin]. Moscow, 1907. p. iii-
xxiii. *Also:* Moscow, 1914.

1909 Peskovskii, M. L. Garrieta Bicher-Stou i ee kniga [Harriet Beecher Stowe
and her book]. *In:* Stowe, H. B. Khizhina diadi Toma [Uncle Tom's
cabin]. St. Petersburg, Moscow, 1909. p. i-iv.

1911 Garriet Bicher-Stou [Harriet Beecher Stowe]. Niva, 1911, no. 25, p. 465-466.

Noskov, N. Drug unizhennykh. Pamiati Bicher-Stou [A friend of the
oppressed. In memory of Beecher Stowe]. Vskhody, 1911, no. 9,
p. 682-691. (Signed: N. N-v.)

1914 Annenskaia, A. N. Vvedenie [Introduction]. *In:* Stowe, H. B. Khizhina
diadi Toma [Uncle Tom's cabin]. Petrograd, 1914. p. v-xxvii.

1941 Petrovskaia, T. Review of: Khizhina diadi Toma [Uncle Tom's cabin].
Moscow, Leningrad, 1941. Literaturnaia gazeta, February 4, 1941.

Sinel'nikov, Ia. Review of: Khizhina diadi Toma [Uncle Tom's cabin].
Moscow, Leningrad, 1941. Leningrad, 1941, no. 5, p. 24.

Khalturin, I. Review of: Khizhina diadi Toma [Uncle Tom's cabin].
Moscow, Leningrad, 1941. Detskaia literatura, 1941, no. 5, p. 33-36.

Khalturin, I. Review of: Khizhina diadi Toma [Uncle Tom's cabin].
Moscow, Leningrad, 1941. Literaturnoe obozrenie, 1941, no. 12,
p. 82-84.

Chukovskii, K. Bicher-Stou i ee kniga [Beecher Stowe and her book]. *In:*
Stowe, H. B. Khizhina diadi Toma [Uncle Tom's cabin]. Moscow,
Leningrad, 1941. p. 3-16.

1949 Etkind, E. Garriet Bicher-Stou i ee roman [Harriet Beecher Stowe and
her book]. *In:* Stowe, H. B. Khizhina diadi Toma ili Zhizn' negrov v
Amerike [Uncle Tom's cabin, or, Life of the Negroes in America].
Leningrad, 1949. p. 416-422.

1950 Erofeev, P. P. Posleslovie. Bicher-Stou i ee roman "Khizhina diadi
Toma" [Afterword. Beecher Stowe and her novel "Uncle Tom's
cabin"]. *In:* Stowe, H. B. Khizhina diadi Toma [Uncle Tom's cabin].
Krasnoyarsk, 1950. p. 375-379.

Sergeeva, N. Garriet Bicher-Stou i ee kniga [Harriet Beecher Stowe and her book]. *In:* Stowe, H. B. Khizhina diadi Toma [Uncle Tom's cabin]. Moscow, Leningrad, 1950. p. 3-12. *Also:* Moscow, 1955. p. 3-10; Moscow, 1956.

1953 Shor, V. Predislovie [Foreword]. *In:* Stowe, H. B. Khizhina diadi Toma [Uncle Tom's cabin]. Moscow, Leningrad, 1953. p. 4-6.

1955 Polonskaia, N. K. Tvorchestvo Garriet Bicher-Stou [The work of Harriet Beecher Stowe]. Abstract of dissertation presented for the degree of Candidate of Philological Sciences. Leningrad, 1955. 13 p.

Stepanov, A. Kniga o chernykh godakh rabstva [A book about the black years of slavery]. *In:* Stowe, H. B. Khizhina diadi Toma [Uncle Tom's cabin]. Khabarovsk, 1955. p. 3-20.

1957 Alekseev, N. Avtografy znamenitykh pisatelei: Garriet Bicher-Stou — O. A. Novikovoi (Kireevoi). (S publikatsiei pisem) [Autographs of noted writers: Harriet Beecher Stowe to O. A. Novikova (Kireeva). (With publication of letters)]. Kul'tura i zhizn', 1957, no. 5, p. 38-41.

1958 Svetlanov, Iu. Garriet Bicher-Stou [Harriet Beecher Stowe]. *In:* Stowe, H. B. Khizhina diadi Toma [Uncle Tom's cabin]. Moscow, 1958. p. 428-434.

1960 Ermolaeva, V. Garriet Bicher-Stou i ee roman "Khizhina diadi Toma" [Harriet Beecher Stowe and her novel "Uncle Tom's cabin"]. *In:* Stowe, H. B. *Uncle Tom's Cabin. A Key to Uncle Tom's Cabin*[1] (Extracts). Moscow, 1960. p. 3-21.

Nikulin, L. Oblichenie rasizma [An unmasking of racism]. Pravda, June 14, 1960.

1961 Brushtein, A. Bicher-Stou [Beecher Stowe]. V mire knig, 1961, no. 6, p. 31-32.

Vladimirov, V. Malen'kaia zhenshchina i bol'shaia voina [A little woman and a great war]. Nedelia, 1961, no. 24, p. 19.

Kogan, S. Oblichitel' rabstva i rasizma [A foe of slavery and racism]. Narodnoe obrazovanie, 1961, no. 7, p. 96-97.

Urnov, D. M. Garriet Bicher-Stou [Harriet Beecher Stowe]. Literatura v shkole, 1961, no. 3, p. 84-86.

Ustenko, G. A. Abolitsionistskie romany Bicher-Stou. ("Khizhina diadi Toma," "Dred") [The abolitionist novels of Beecher Stowe. ("Uncle Tom's cabin," "Dred")]. Odessa, 1961. 71 p.

1963 Fialkovskii, E. E. Bicher-Stou v sovetskoi i amerikanskoi kritike [Beecher Stowe in Soviet and American criticism]. Uchenye zapiski Adygeis-kogo pedagogicheskogo instituta. Seriia filologicheskikh nauk. Maykop, 1963, vyp. 4. p. 91-107.

[1] A work in the English language published in the Soviet Union.

STRIBLING Tomas Sigizmund   STRIBLING Thomas Sigismund

1925 V. K. Predislovie k russkomu izdaniiu [Foreword to the Russian edition]. *In:* Stribling, T. General Fombombo [General Fombombo]. Moscow, Leningrad, 1925. p. 7.
1927 S. K. Review of: Drama krovi [The drama of blood—i.e. *Birthright*]. Moscow, 1927. Na literaturnom postu, 1927, no. 17-18, p. 91-92.
1930 Review of: Iarkii metall [Bright metal]. Moscow, Leningrad, 1929. Vestnik inostrannoi literatury, 1930, no. 4, p. 166.
1940 Abramov, A. Review of: Megafon [The megaphone—i.e. *The Sound Wagon*]. Internatsional'naia literatura, 1940, no. 11-12, p. 148-149.
1948 Viktorov, Ia. Predislovie [Foreword]. *In:* Stribling, T. S. Megafon [The megaphone—i.e. *The Sound Wagon?*]. Moscow, 1948. p. 5-15.
      Marvich, S. Pod maskoi burzhuaznoi demokratii [Under the mask of bourgeois democracy]. ("Megafon" [The" megaphone"—i.e. *The Sound Wagon*]). Zvezda, 1948, no. 11, p. 164-165.

SILVESTR Robert   SYLVESTER Robert

1956 Zaslavskii, D. Byt i nravy sovremennoi burzhuaznoi pechati [The life and morals of the contemporary bourgeois press]. *In:* Sylvester, R. Vtoraia drevneishaia professiia [The second oldest profession]. Moscow, 1956. p. 310-328. 2nd ed., 1957.
1957 Arkad'ev, M. Raby dollara [Slaves of the dollar]. (Vtoraia drevneishaia professiia [The second oldest profession]. Moscow, 1956). Sovetskaia pechat', 1957, no. 1, p. 54-55.
      Dmitriev, S. Kogda v cheloveke umiraet chelovek... [When humanity dies in a person...]. (Vtoraia drevneishaia professiia [The second oldest profession]. Moscow, 1956,). Znamia, 1957, no. 2, p. 215-217.
      Smirnov, B. Chelovek i sensatsiia [Man and sensation]. (Vtoraia drevneishaia professiia [The second oldest profession]). Zvezda, 1957, no. 2, p. 207-208.

TEGGARD Dzhenev'ev   TAGGARD Genevieve

1939 Zenkevich, M. Review of: *Collected Poems.* New York, 1939. Internatsional'naia literatura, 1939, no. 7-8 (first printing), p. 351. *Also:* Internatsional'naia literatura, 1939, no. 11, p. 218.

TENK Gerb   TANK Herb

1953 Gribanov, B. Predislovie [Foreword]. *In:* Tank, H. 49-i—i.e. Sorokdeviatyi—meridian [The forty-ninth meridian]. Moscow, 1953. p. 3-5.

TENNER Dzhon   TANNER John

1836 Pushkin, A. S. Dzhon Tenner [John Tanner]. Sovremennik, 1836, no. 3, p. 205-256. (Signed: The Reviewer [In English].) *Also in:* Pushkin, A. S. Polnoe sobranie sochinenii [Complete collected works]. v. 12. Moscow, Leningrad, 1949. p. 104-132.

1937 Feinberg, I. Dzhon Tenner [John Tanner]. Literaturnaia gazeta, February 5, 1937.

1949 Tamakhin, V. M. Pushkin o "Zapiskakh Dzhona Tennera" [Pushkin on the "Notes of John Tanner"]. *In:* Pushkinskii sbornik [A Pushkin collection]. Stavropol', 1949. p. 47-51.

1962 Mar'ianov, B. Ob odnom primechanii k stat'e A. S. Pushkina "Dzhon Tenner" [Concerning a note to the article "John Tanner" by A. S. Pushkin]. Russkaia literatura, 1962, no. 1, p. 64-67.

1963 Averkieva, Iu. P. Predislovie k russkomu izdaniiu. [Foreword to the Russian edition]. Dzhems, Edvin. [James, Edwin]. Vvedenie d-ra Edvina Dzhemsa k zhizneopisaniiu Tennera [Dr. Edwin James's introduction to the biography of Tanner]. *In:* Tanner, John. Tridtsat' let sredi indeitsev [Thirty years among the Indians[1]]. Moscow, 1963. p. 5-24; 25-44.

TEILOR Beiiard   TAYLOR Bayard

1865 Pypin, A. N. Amerikanskie nravy. "Khanna Torston" [American customs. "Hannah Thurston"]. Sovremennik, 1865, no. 1, otd. 1, p. 73-108. (Signed: A.)

1878 Nekrolog Baiiarda Teilora [An obituary of Bayard Taylor]. Severnaia zvezda, 1878, no. 33, p. 522-523.

1879 B. Teilor. (Nekrolog) [B. Taylor. (Obituary)]. Zhivopisnoe obozrenie, 1879, no. 8, p. 178-179.

TORO Genri Devid   THOREAU Henry David

1900 Review of: Opyt uproshcheniia zhizni. (U Val'denskogo ozera v Amerike) [An effort toward the simplification of life. (By Walden Lake in America—i.e. *Walden*)]. Moscow, 1900. Russkoe bogatstvo, 1900, no. 2, otd. II, p. 65-68.

1902 Genri Toro [Henry Thoreau]. Novyi zhurnal inostrannoi literatury, iskusstva i nauki, 1902, no. 9 (2nd pagination), p. 130. *Also in:* Plutarkh XIX veka [Plutarch of the 19th century]. v. 2. St. Petersburg, 1903. p. 130.

---

[1] *Narrative of the Captivity and Adventures of John Tanner During Thirty Years' Residence Among the Indians*, ed. Edwin James (New York, 1830).

1903 Chunosov, M. Vragi progressa [Enemies of progress]. Beseda (St. Petersburg), 1903, no. 7, cols. 363-372.
1910 Emerson, R. Toro. Biograficheskii ocherk [Thoreau. A biographical
sketch]. *In:* Thoreau, H. D. Val'den [Walden]. Moscow, 1910.
p. 5-28.
1944 Chukovskii, K. Genri Toro [Henry Thoreau]. *In:* Whitman, W. Izbrannye stikhotvoreniia i proza [Selected poetry and prose]. Moscow,
1944. p. 196-197.
1961 Elistratova, A. Review of: *Approaches to Walden.* San Francisco, 1961.
Sovremennaia khudozhestvennaia literatura za rubezhom, 1961,
no. 7, p. 106-108.
1962 Elistratova, A. Robinzon iz Konkorda [A Robinson—i.e. Robinson
Crusoe—from Concord]. Literaturnaia gazeta, May 12, 1962.
Sokolov-Mikitov, I. Zhizn' v lesu. ("Uolden, ili, Zhizn' v lesu") [Life in
the woods. ("Walden, or, Life in the woods")]. Moscow, 1962.
Novyi mir, 1962, no. 9, p. 266-268.
Startsev, A. Posleslovie [Afterword]. *In:* Thoreau, H. D. Uolden, ili
Zhizn' v lesu [Walden, or, Life in the woods]. Moscow, 1962. p. 213-
230.

TIKNOR Dzhordzh   TICKNOR George

1883 Storozhenko, N. Dzhordzh Tiknor. (Biograficheskii ocherk) [George
Ticknor. (Biographic sketch)]. *In:* Ticknor, G. Istoriia ispanskoi
literatury [History of Spanish literature]. v. 1. Moscow, 1883. p. ii-
xliv.

TRAMBO Dal'ton   TRUMBO Dalton

1940 Grou [Growe?], M. Review of: *Johnny Got His Gun.* New York, 1939.
Literaturnaia gazeta, July 5, 1940.
Gus, M. Golos neizvestnogo soldata [The voice of an unknown soldier].
(*Johnny Got His Gun.* New York, 1939). Internatsional'naia literatura, 1940, no. 9-10, p. 212-218.
Romanova, E. Otkliki amerikanskoi pressy na knigu D. Trambo "Dzhon-
ni poluchil vintovku" [The views of the American press of D. Trumbo's book "Johnny got a gun"]. Internatsional'naia literatura, 1940,
no. 9-10, p. 261-262.

TVEN Mark   TWAIN Mark (CLEMENS Samuel Langhorne)

1883 Review of: Prints i nishchii [The prince and the pauper]. St. Petersburg,
1883. Delo, 1883, no. 7, otd. II, p. 75-76.
Review of: Prints i nishchii [The prince and the pauper]. St. Petersburg,
1883. Otechestvennye zapiski, 1883, no. 8, otd. II, p. 212-213.

1888 Ot izdatelia. [From the publisher]. *In*: Twain, M. Ocherki i rasskazy [Sketches and stories]. Moscow, 1888. p. 1-2.

1891 Engel'gardt, A. Beseda Marka Tvena s reporterom [Mark Twain's conversation with a reporter]. Vestnik inostrannoi literatury, 1891, no. 3, p. 375-378. (Signed: A. E.)

1894 Eizen, I. M. Mark Tven [Mark Twain]. Niva, 1894, no. 10, p. 234. (Signed: E.)

1896 K biografii Marka Tvena [About Mark Twain's biography]. Knizhki Nedeli, 1896, no. 9, p. 295-296.

1897 Mark Tven. Biograficheskii ocherk [Mark Twain. Biographical sketch]. Nov', 1897, no. 9, p. 230-236.

Mark Tven v Vene [Mark Twain in Vienna]. Vestnik inostrannoi literatury, 1897, no. 11, p. 316-317.

Mark Tven i nemetskii iazyk [Mark Twain and the German language]. Vestnik inostrannoi literatury, 1897, no. 12, p. 281-282.

Novoe proizvedenie Marka Tvena [A new work by Mark Twain]. ("Vdol' ekvatora" ["Along the equator"—i.e. *Following the Equator*]). Vestnik inostrannoi literatury, 1897, no. 10, p. 381-382.

Review of: Vospominaniia o Ioanne d'Ark [Memoirs of Joan of Arc—i.e. *Personal Recollections of Joan of Arc*]. St. Petersburg, 1897. Severnyi vestnik, 1897, no. 4, otd. II, p. 70-71.

1898 Predislovie: Avtobiografiia Marka Tvena [Foreword: the autobiography of Mark Twain]. *In:* Twain, M. Izbrannye sochineniia. Eskizy [Selected works. Sketches]. v. 1. St. Petersburg, 1898. p. 5-15.

Smythe, Carlyle. Mark Tven [Mark Twain]. Zhurnal zhurnalov, 1898, no. 22, p. 351-357.

1899 Bruks [Brooks?], N. Mark Tven v Kalifornii [Mark Twain in California]. Literaturnye vechera "Novogo mira," 1899, no. 9, p. 548-552.

Kniga, kotoraia vyidet v svet cherez 100 let posle smerti avtora ee [A book which will appear 100 years after its author's death]. Literaturnye vechera "Novogo mira," 1899. no, 9, p. 559-560.

Krasnov, P. Bezobidnyi iumor. Sochineniia Dzheroma K. Dzheroma i Marka Tvena [Inoffensive humor. The works of Jerome K. Jerome and Mark Twain]. Knizhki Nedeli, 1899, no. 10, p. 167-177.

Mark Tven o vseobshchem mire [Mark Twain about universal peace]. Novoe vremia, January 23/February 4, 1899. Illustrated supplement.

Pereferkovich, I. Mark Tven o evreiakh [Mark Twain about the Jews]. Voskhod, 1899, no. 10, otd. II, p. 24-28.

1901 Nikol'skii, M. N. Predislovie [Foreword]. *In:* Twain, M. Prints i nishchii [The prince and the pauper]. 3rd ed. St. Petersburg, Moscow, 1901. p. i-iv.

1902 Lavrova, E. V. Predislovie [Foreword]. *In:* Twain, M. Lichnye vospominaniia o Zhanne d'Ark... [Personal recollections of Joan of Arc...]. St. Petersburg, 1902. p. 5-7. (Signed: E. L.)

Morozov, P. Review of: Zhanna d'Ark [Joan of Arc—i.e. *Personal Recollections of Joan of Arc*]. St. Petersburg, 1902. Obrazovanie, 1902, no. 1, otd. III, p. 77-78.

Nortrop [Northrop?], B. Odin den' v obshchestve Marka Tvena. Ocherk. [One day in Mark Twain's company. An essay]. Vestnik inostrannoi literatury, 1902, no. 11, p. 241-247.

Faresov, A. Review of: Zhanna d'Ark [Joan of Arc—i.e. *Personal Recollections of Joan of Arc*]. St. Petersburg, 1902. Istoricheskii vestnik, 1902, no. 2, p. 708-709.

1905 Mark Tven o prave literaturnoi sobstvennosti [Mark Twain about the copyright problem]. Novyi zhurnal literatury, iskusstva i nauki, 1905, no. 4, p. 112-113.

Toropov, S. A. Znamenityi iumorist [A noted humorist]. Sem'ia, 1905, no. 47, p. 10. (Signed: S. T-v.)

1906 Glinka, S. Review of: Sochineniia [Works]. 2nd ed. n.p., n.d. Zhurnal Ministerstva narodnogo prosveshcheniia, 1906, no. 6, otd. II, p. 216-222.

Mark Tven [Mark Twain]. Vestnik inostrannoi literatury, 1906, no. 1, p. 274-277.

Po povodu M. Gor'kogo i Marka Tvena [Concerning M. Gor'kii and Mark Twain]. St. Petersburg, "Kliuch," 1906, 18 p.

1907 Iz avtobiografii Marka Tvena [From Mark Twain's autobiography]. Novyi zhurnal literatury, iskusstva i nauki, 1907, no. 1, p. 90-91.

1908 Chumak, A. Review of: Dnevnik Adama [Adam's diary]. St. Petersburg, 1908. Dnevnik pisatelia, 1908, no. 7-8, p. 79.

1910 Anekdoty o Marke Tvene [Anecdotes about Mark Twain]. Vsemirnaia panorama, 1910, no. 55, p. 15-16.

Zhizn' Marka Tvena (po biograficheskim ocherkam Dzh. K. Gottena i S. E. Moffeta) [The life of Mark Twain (according to the biographical sketches of J. C. Hotten and S. E. Moffett)]; Averchenko, A. Pevets zdravogo smysla. (Neskol'ko slov o Marke Tvene) [The bard of common sense. (A few words about Mark Twain)]. *In:* Twain, M. Sobranie sochinenii [Collected works]. v. 1. St. Petersburg, 1910. p. v-xxiii, xxv-xxxv.

Kozlovskii, L. Iz zapadnoi literatury. Dve smerti (B'ernsterne B'ernson i Mark Tven) [From Western literature. Two deaths. (Björnstjerne Björnson and Mark Twain)]. Vestnik znaniia, 1910, no. 5, p. 251-256. *Also, titled* "Mark Tven" ["Mark Twain"], *in:* Literaturnyi al'manakh "Vestnika znaniia," 1911, al'm. 2, p. 118-122.

Korol' smekha. (Pamiati Marka Tvena). (Nekrolog) [The king of laughter. (In memory of Mark Twain). (Obituary)]. Priroda i Liudi, 1910, no. 27, p. 418-420.

Kuprin, A. Umer smekh [Laughter has died]. Odesskie novosti, April 10/23, 1910. *Also in:* Kuprin, A. Sobranie sochinenii [Collected works]. 2nd ed. v. 11. Moscow, 1916. p. 270-272.

Lorie, S. Predislovie [Foreword]. *In:* Twain, M. Zhizn' na Missisipi [Life on the Mississippi]. Moscow, 1910. p. 1-4.

Mark Tven. (Nekrolog) [Mark Twain. (Obituary)]. Baian, 1910, no. 6, p. 110.

Mark Tven [Mark Twain]. Vestnik inostrannoi literatury, 1910, no. 6, p. 136-137.

Mark Tven. (Nekrolog) [Mark Twain. (Obituary)]. Niva, 1910, no. 21, p. 393-394.

Noskov, N. D. Mark Tven. Nekrolog [Mark Twain. An obituary]. Mir, 1910, no. 7-8, p. 587-588. (Signed: N. N.)

Sil'vio. Mark Tven [Mark Twain]. Teatr i iskusstvo, 1910, no. 15, p. 321-322.

Mark Tven. Nekrolog [Mark Twain. An obituary]. Istoricheskii vestnik, 1910, no. 7, p. 319-320.

Tverskoi, P. Smert' Marka Tvena [The death of Mark Twain]. Vestnik Evropy, 1910, no. 7, p. 323-325.

Chukovskii, K. Mark Tven [Mark Twain]. Sovremennoe slovo, April 10/23, 1910.

1911 Iasinskii, I. I. (Maksim Belinskii). Mark Tven. Kritiko-biograficheskii ocherk [Mark Twain. Critico-biographic essay]. *In:* Twain, M. Polnoe sobranie sochinenii [Complete collected works]. v. 1. St. Petersburg, 1911. p. 3-28. *Also:* St. Petersburg [*sic*], 1918.

1912 Gnedich, P. Mark Tven, Satana i Shekspir [Mark Twain, Satan and Shakespeare]. *In:* Ezhegodnik imperatorskikh teatrov. vyp. III. St. Petersburg, 1912. p. 14-29.

1914 Vospominaniia o Marke Tvene. (Neizdannye dokumenty) [Reminiscences about Mark Twain. (Unpublished documents)]. Vestnik inostrannoi literatury, 1914, no. 3, p. 34-37.

1919 Chukovskii, K. Predislovie [Foreword]. *In:* Twain, M. Prikliucheniia Toma [The adventures of Tom]. Peterburg, 1919. p. 5-9. *Also:* Petrograd, Moscow, 1923. p. 7-8.

1922 Oksenov, I. A. Review of: Prints i nishchii [The prince and the pauper]. Petrograd, 1922. Kniga i revoliutsiia, 1922, no. 9-10, p. 71. (Signed: I. O.)

Chukovskii, K. Predislovie [Foreword]. *In:* Twain, M. Prints i nishchii [The prince and the pauper]. Petrograd, 1922. p. 5-7.

1925 Men'shoi, A. Doloi chestnost'! ("Chelovek, kotoryi razoblachil Gedliburg") [Away with honor! ("The man that corrupted Hadleyburg")]. Zhizn' iskusstva, 1925, no. 14, p. 4-5.

Sinclair, U. Nekoronovannyi korol' [The uncrowned king]. Ogonek, 1925, no. 39, p. 7. *Also in:* Sinclair, U. Sobranie sochinenii [Collected works]. v. 7. Moscow, 1926. p. 437-444.

1927 Kozyrev, M. Predislovie redaktora [Editor's foreword]. *In:* Twain, M. Ianki pri dvore korolia Artura [A Yankee in King Arthur's court —

189

i.e. *A Connecticut Yankee in King Arthur's Court*]. Khar'kov, 1927. p. 3-6.

1928 Griuntal', S. Review of: Prostaki za granitsei [The innocents abroad]. Moscow, Leningrad, 1928. Kniga i profsoiuzy, 1928, no. 9, p. 36.

Guber, P. K. Posleslovie k russkomu izdaniiu [Afterword to the Russian edition]. *In:* Twain, M. Sobranie sochinenii. T. 4. Prostaki za granitsei [Collected works. V. 4. The innocents abroad]. Moscow, Leningrad, 1928. p. 497-503. (Signed: P. G.)

Guber, P. K. Predislovie k russkomu izdaniiu [Foreword to the Russian edition]. *In:* Twain, M. Sobranie sochinenii. T. 5. Prints i nishchii [Collected works. V. 5. The prince and the pauper]. Moscow, Leningrad, 1929. p. v-viii. (Signed: G.)

Tsingovatov, A. Predislovie [Foreword]. *In:* Twain, M. Ianki pri dvore korolia Artura [A Yankee at King Arthur's court—i.e. *A Connecticut Yankee in King Arthur's Court*]. Moscow, 1928. p. 3-6.

1929 A. D. Predislovie [Foreword]. *In:* Twain, M. Moi chasy [My watch— original English title not determined]. Moscow, 1929. p. 3-6.

Vygodskii, D. Predislovie k russkomu izdaniiu [Foreword to the Russian edition]. *In:* Twain, M. Pustogolovyi Uil'son [Pudd'nhead Wilson]. Leningrad, 1929. p. 3-6.

Guber, P. K. Predislovie k russkomu izdaniiu [Foreword to the Russian edition]. *In:* Twain, M. Sobranie sochinenii. T. 5: Prints i nishchii [Collected works. V. 5: The prince and the pauper]. Moscow, Leningrad, 1929. p. v-viii. (Signed: G.)

1930 Dinamov, S. Predislovie [Foreword]. *In:* Twain, M. Amerikanskii pretendent [The American claimant]. Moscow, 1930. p. 3-8.

1932 L. G. S Tomom Soierom pioneru ne po puti [A member of the "Pioneers" has no common ground with Tom Sawyer]. Kniga i proletarskaia revoliutsiia, 1932, no. 2-3, p. 194-196.

1934 Knipovich, E. Prikliucheniia malen'kogo liumpena [The adventures of a small member of the Lumpen-proletariat]. (Prikliucheniia Gekl'beri Finna [The adventures of Huckleberry Finn]. Moscow, 1933). Detskaia i iunosheskaia literatura, 1934, no. 2, p. 1-2.

Kogan, M. Prikliuchenchesko-psikhologicheskaia povest' Tvena [Twain's psychological-adventure tale]. Detskaia i iunosheskaia literatura, 1934, no. 7, p. 4-11.

1935 Dinamov, S. Satira i iumor Marka Tvena [Mark Twain's satire and humor]. Za rubezhom, 1935, no. 32, p. 723.

Dinamov, S. Smeshoe i strashnoe u Marka Tvena [Joy and horror in Mark Twain]. Izvestiia, April 21, 1935. *Also, enlarged, in:* Twain, M. Izbrannye rasskazy [Selected stories]. Moscow, 1936, p. 7-13.

Dreiser, T. Dva Marka Tvena [Two Mark Twains]. Internatsional'naia literatura, 1935, no. 11, p. 3-10. *Also in:* Dreiser, T. Polnoe sobranie sochinenii [Complete collected works]. v.11. Moscow,1954. p.581-595.

Startsev, A. Mark Tven [Mark Twain]. Izvestiia, December 3, 1935.

Sto let so dnia rozhdeniia Marka Tvena [A hundred years since the birth of Mark Twain]. Literaturnaia gazeta, November 11, 1935.

Twain, M. Avtobiografiia. (Otryvki iz knigi) [Autobiography. (Selections from the book)]. Internatsional'naia literatura, 1935, no. 11, p. 85-97.

1936 Brooks, V. W. Iumor Marka Tvena [Mark Twain's humor]. Internatsional'naia literatura, 1936, no. 6, p. 143-152.

Gor'kii, M. Mark Tven [Mark Twain]. In: Opisanie rukopisei M. Gor'-kogo [Description of the manuscripts of M. Gor'kii]. vyp. I. Moscow, Leningrad, 1936. p. 124-125. Also in: Gor'kii, M. Sobranie sochinenii [Collected works]. v. 10. Moscow, 1951. p. 309.

Margolin, B. Mark Tven [Mark Twain]. In: Twain, M. Prostaki za granitsei [The innocents abroad]. Moscow, 1936. p. 4-6.

Startsev, A. "Zapisnye knizhki" Marka Tvena [Mark Twain's "Notebooks"]. Krasnaia nov', 1936, no. 2, p. 276-278.

Startsev, A. Mark Tven i Amerika [Mark Twain and America]. Literaturnaia ucheba, 1936, no. 10 (second printing), p. 73-104. Also in: Twain, M. Izbrannye proizvedeniia [Selected works]. Moscow, 1937. p. 5-27.

1937 A. D. Mark Tven [Mark Twain]. Detskaia literatura, 1937, no.16, p.41-42.

Balashov, P. "Izbrannye rasskazy" Marka Tvena ["Selected stories" by Mark Twain]. Literaturnoe obozrenie, 1937, no. 12, p. 38-41.

Kon, L. Review of: Prints i nishchii [The prince and the pauper]. Moscow, 1936. Detskaia literatura, 1937, no. 7, p. 39-43.

1938 Zamotin, N. Odnotomnik Marka Tvena [A one-volume edition of Mark Twain]. Knizhnye novinki, 1938, no. 9, p. 32-33.

Meierovich, E. Izbrannye proizvedeniia Marka Tvena [Selected works by Mark Twain]. Moscow, 1937. Literaturnoe obozrenie, 1938, no. 7, p. 57-65.

O "Pokhozhdeniiakh Toma Soiera." Sbornik statei [Concerning "The Adventures of Tom Sawyer." A collection of articles]. Leningrad, 1937, 111 p. Contents: Derzhavin, K. Zhizn' i tvorchestvo Marka Tvena, 1835-1910 [Life and work of Mark Twain, 1835-1910]. p. 7-30. (Signed: K. D.); Derzhavin, K. Tom Soier i ego druz'ia [Tom Sawyer and his friends]. p. 31-76; Zon, B. V. Spektakl' "Pokhozhdeniia Toma Soiera" v TIuZ'e [The play "The Adventures of Tom Sawyer" in the Youth Theater]. p. 77-110.

Semenov, S. Review of: Vizit kapitana Stormfil'da na nebesa [Captain Stormfield's visit to heaven]. Detskaia literatura, 1938, no. 17, p. 66.

Silman, T. Predislovie [Foreword]. In: Twain, M. Amerikanskie russkazy [American tales]. Leningrad, 1938, p. 3-10.

Startsev, A. Predislovie [Foreword]. In: Twain, M. Vizit kapitana Stormfil'da na nebesa [Captain Stormfield's visit to heaven]. Moscow, 1938. p. 3-8.

Shklovskii, V. O Marke Tvene i o tom, kto emu blizok [About Mark Twain and the one who resembles him]. Detskaia literatura, 1938, no. 20, p. 21-27.

1939 A. E. Razoblachennyi Mark Tven [Mark Twain unmasked]. Literaturnyi kritik, 1939, no. 5-6, p. 295-296.

Gershenzon, M. Istoriia Toma i Geka [The story of Tom and Huck]. Detskaia literatura, 1939, no. 1, p. 75-79.

Inber, V. Mark Tven i Maksim Gor'kii [Mark Twain and Maxim Gor'kii]. Internatsional'naia literatura, 1939, no. 7-8 (first printing), p. 314.

Mendel'son, M. Mark Tven [Mark Twain]. Moscow, "Molodaia gvardiia," 1939. 271 p. *Reviews:* Novinskii, B. Ogonek, 1940, no. 12, p. 23; Fomenko, V. Nezakonchennyi portret [An unfinished portrait]. Literaturnaia gazeta, April 26, 1940; Shklovskii, V. Sud'ba i schast'e [Fate and happiness]. Detskaia literatura, 1940, no. 3, p. 8-11.

Mendel'son, M. Rasskazy Marka Tvena [Mark Twain's stories]. (Izbrannye rasskazy [Selected stories]. Moscow, Leningrad, 1939). Detskaia literatura, 1939, no. 8, p. 25-28.

Startsev, A. Predislovie k publikatsii "Zapisnykh knizhek" Marka Tvena [Foreword to the publication of Mark Twain's "Notebooks"]. Internatsional'naia literatura, 1939, no. 7-8 (first printing), p. 219. *Also:* second printing, p. 205.

Shklovskii, V. O Marke Tvene [Concerning Mark Twain]. Internatsional'naia literatura, 1939, no. 7-8 (first printing), p. 218.

1940 Berkutov, E. "Zapisnaia knizhka" Marka Tvena [Mark Twain's "Notebook"]. Literaturnoe obozrenie, 1940, no. 5, p. 38-40.

Koziura, N. Mark Tven, 1835-1910 [Mark Twain, 1835-1910]. Chto chitat'?, 1940, no. 10, p. 60-63.

Koziura, N. Rasskazy Marka Tvena [The stories of Mark Twain]. Literaturnoe obozrenie, 1940, no. 4, p. 40-42.

Mendel'son, M. Amerikanskii imperializm i Mark Tven [American imperialism and Mark Twain]. Literaturnaia gazeta, January 10, 1940.

Mendel'son, M. Antireligioznye elementy v tvorchestve Marka Tvena [Antireligious elements in the works of Mark Twain]. Antireligioznik, 1940, no. 7, p. 25-29.

Mendel'son, M. Mark Tven [Mark Twain]. 30—i.e. Tridtsat'—dnei, 1940, no. 3-4, p. 35-36.

Neopublikovannye pis'ma Marka Tvena [Unpublished letters by Mark Twain]. Literaturnoe obozrenie, 1940, no. 5, p. 62.

1941 Abramov, A. Mark Tven govorit [Mark Twain speaks]. Foreword to the publication of selections from his diary. Internatsional'naia literatura, 1941, no. 11-12, p. 239-279.

1942 Bobrova, M. N. Fol'klornye traditsii u Marka Tvena [Mark Twain's folklore traditions]. Uchenye zapiski Kuybyshevskogo pedagogicheskogo i uchitel'skogo instituta, 1942, vyp. 6, p. 153-179.

Startsev, A. Sem'desiat piat' let tomu nazad [Seventy-five years ago]. Oktiabr', 1942, no. 7, p. 117-127. *Also, with title:* Molodoi Tven v Rossii [The young Twain in Russia], *in:* Twain, M. Znamenitaia skachushchaia liagushka i drugie rasskazy [The celebrated jumping frog and other stories]. Moscow, 1943. p. 128-136.

1943 Startsev, A. Predislovie [Foreword]. *In:* Twain, M. Znamenitaia skachushchaia liagushka i drugie rasskazy [The celebrated jumping frog and other stories]. Moscow, 1943. p. 3-6. *Also, with changes, in:* Twain, M. Rasskazy [Stories]. Moscow, Leningrad, 1947. p. 3-7.

1945 Alekseev, M. P. O romane "Ianki pri dvore korolia Artura" [Concerning the novel "A Yankee at the court of King Arthur"]. *In:* Twain, M. Ianki pri dvore korolia Artura [A Yankee at the court of King Arthur—i.e. *A Connecticut Yankee in King Arthur's Court*]. Moscow, Leningrad, 1945. p. 325-337.

1946 Mendel'son, M. Review of: Ianki pri dvore Korolia Artura [A Yankee at the court of King Arthur]. Sovetskaia kniga, 1946, no. 6, p. 112-115.

1947 Mendel'son, M. Tven, amerikanskie imperialisty i "liudi, nakhodiashchiesia vo t'me" [Twain, American imperialists and "the people sitting in darkness"]. Literaturnaia gazeta, July 26, 1947.

1948 Mendel'son, M. Posleslovie [Afterword]. *In:* Mark Tven ob amerikanskom imperializme [Mark Twain about American imperialism]. Znamia, 1948, no. 4, p. 150-155.

Startsev, A. Mark Tven [Mark Twain]. *In:* Twain, M. Prikliucheniia Toma Soiera [The adventures of Tom Sawyer]. Moscow, Leningrad, 1948, p. 5-8.

1949 Bobrova, M. Amerikanskaia "demokratiia" v otsenke satirika Marka Tvena. Stenogramma publichnoi lektsii [American "democracy" in the eyes of the satirist Mark Twain. Stenographic report of a public lecture]. Saratov, 1949. 36 p.

Bobrova M. Mark Tven i "demokratiia" dollara [Mark Twain and the "democracy" of the dollar]. *In:* Twain, M. Izbrannoe [Selected works]. v. 1. Moscow, 1949. p. 3-10.

1950 Kataev, V. Mark Tven i Amerika [Mark Twain and America]. Novyi mir, 1950, no. 5, p. 229-233.

Kashkin, I. O knige M. Tvena "Prikliucheniia Gekl'berri Finna" [Concerning M. Twain's book "The adventures of Huckleberry Finn"]. *In:* Twain, M. Prikliucheniia Gekl'berri Finna [The adventures of Huckleberry Finn]. Moscow, Leningrad, 1950. p. 283-287. *Also:* Moscow, 1955. p. 285-288.

1951 Samokhvalov, N. Posleslovie [Afterword]. *In:* Twain, M. Izbrannye rasskazy i pamflety [Selected stories and pamphlets]. Moscow, 1951. p. 240-245.

Soboleva, A. Predislovie [Foreword]. *In:* Twain, M. Rasskazy i pamflety [Stories and pamphlets]. Leningrad, 1951. p. 3-8.

1952 Bobrova, M. N. Mark Tven. Kritiko-biograficheskii ocherk [Mark Twain. A critico-biographic study]. Moscow, Goslitizdat, 1952. 156 p. *Reviews:* Elistratova, A. Kniga o velikom amerikanskom satirike [A book about a great American satirist]. Literaturnaia gazeta, November 11, 1952; Narkevich, A. Iu. Sovetskaia kniga, 1952, no. 12, p. 98-101.

Galinskaia, M. M. Predislovie [Foreword]. *In:* Twain, M. Rasskazy i pamflety [Stories and pamphlets]. Moscow, 1952. p. 3-13.

1953 Bobrova, M. Posleslovie [Afterword]. *In:* Twain, M. Ianki pri dvore korolia Artura [A Yankee in the court of King Arthur]. Moscow, 1953. p. 296-307.

Lanina, T. O knige i o pisatele [About the book and the writer]. *In:* Twain, M. Prikliucheniia Toma Soiera [The adventures of Tom Sawyer]. Moscow, Leningrad, 1953. p. 3-10.

Orlova, R. Posleslovie [Afterword]. *In:* Twain, M. Izbrannye proizvedeniia [Selected works]. v. 2. Moscow, 1953. p. 567-578.

Semenov, M. Tom Soier v naruchnikakh [Tom Sawyer in handcuffs]. Izvestiia, May 17, 1953.

1954 Lanina, T. Posleslovie [Afterword]. *In:* Twain, M. Prints i nishchii [The prince and the pauper]. Moscow, 1954. p. 262-270.

Lanina, T. V. Roman M. Tvena "Ianki pri dvore korolia Artura" i ego mesto v evoliutsii Tvena-romanista [M. Twain's novel "A Yankee at the court of King Arthur" and its place in the evolution of Twain the novelist]. Abstract of dissertation presented for the degree of Candidate of Philological Sciences. Moscow, 1954. 16 p.

Orlova, R. Mark Tven, 1835-1910 [Mark Twain, 1835-1910]. *In:* Twain, M. Izbrannoe [Selections]. Moscow, 1954. p. 544-550. *Also:* Moscow, 1958.

1955 Adzhubei, A. "Derzhite put' k gazete Marka Tvena" ["Hold to Mark Twain's path to journalism"]. Komsomol'skaia pravda, December 18, 1955.

Lanina, T. Predislovie [Foreword]. *In:* Twain, M. *A Connecticut Yankee in King Arthur's Court.*[1] Moscow, 1955. p. 3-18.

Mark Tven, 1835-1910. Materialy k vecheru, posviashchennomu 120-letiiu so dnia rozhdeniia [Mark Twain, 1835-1910. Materials for an evening in commemoration of the 120th anniversary of his birth]. Moscow, 1955. 19 p.

1956 Bobrova, M. Predislovie [Foreword]. *In:* Twain, M. *The Adventures of*

---

[1] A book in the English language published in the Soviet Union.

Tom Sawyer. The Adventures of Huckleberry Finn.[1] Moscow, 1956. p. 3-17.

Lanina, T. Posleslovie [Afterword]. *In:* Twain, M. Prints i nishchii [The prince and the pauper]. Moscow, 1956. p. 286-295. *Also:* Moscow, 1961. p. 212-219.

Naer, V. L. O nekotorykh osobennostiakh ispol'zovaniia leksikografiko-frazeologicheskikh sredstv gazetno-publitsisticheskogo stilia v proizvedeniiakh Marka Tvena [Concerning some features of the use of lexico-phraseological means of the newspaper and publicist style in the works of Mark Twain]. Abstract of dissertation presented for the degree of Candidate of Philological Sciences. Moscow, 1956, 16 p.

Romm, A. S. Rannie iumoristicheskie rasskazy Marka Tvena. (K voprosu o iumore Tvena) [The early humorous stories of Mark Twain. (On the problem of Twain's humor)]. Uchenye zapiski Leningradskogo pedagogicheskogo instituta, 1956, t. 18. Fakul'tet iazyka i literatury. vyp. 5, p. 125-139.

1957 Bobrova, M. N. Literaturnye parodii v tvorchestve Marka Tvena rannego perioda [Literary parodies in the work of Mark Twain in the early period]. Uchenye zapiski Saratovskogo universiteta, 1957, t. 56, vyp. filol. p. 331-349.

Bobrova, M. N. Tvorchestvo Marka Tvena [The works of Mark Twain]. Abstract of dissertation presented for the degree of Doctor of Philological Sciences. Saratov, 1957. 34 p.

Il'ina, E. Nekotorye osobennosti masterstva Marka Tvena v "Prikliucheniiakh Toma Soiera" [Some features of the talent of Mark Twain in "The adventures of Tom Sawyer"]. *In:* O literature dlia detei [Concerning literature for children]. vyp. 2. Leningrad, 1957. p. 158-170.

Korshunova, V. and M. Sitkovetskaia. Novoe o Marke Tvene [New information about Mark Twain]. (With publication of a letter from Twain to Stepniak-Kravchinskii). Ogonek, 1957, no. 24, p. 24.

Okov, Iu. Mark Tven i "zhalkie umy" [Mark Twain and the "petty minds"]. Sovetskaia kul'tura, December 17, 1957.

Romm, A. O "Prikliucheniiakh Toma Soiera" Marka Tvena [Concerning Mark Twain's "The adventures of Tom Sawyer"]. *In:* O literature dlia detei [Concerning literature for children]. vyp. 2. Leningrad, 1957. p. 130-157.

Startsev, A. Nesobrannye stroki Marka Tvena [Uncollected lines by Mark Twain]. (With publication of materials). Inostrannaia literatura, 1957, no. 6, p. 256-259.

1958 Lanina, T. Posleslovie [Afterword]. *In:* Twain, M. Prikliucheniia Toma Soiera. Prikliucheniia Gekl'berri Finna [The adventures of Tom

---

[1] A book in the English language published in the Soviet Union.

Sawyer. The adventures of Huckleberry Finn]. Moscow, 1958. p. 561-576.

Mendel'son, M. O. Mark Tven [Mark Twain]. Moscow, Molodaia gvardiia, 1958. 384 p.

Novitskaia, E. V. K voprosu o stilisticheskikh funktsiiakh rechevykh sredstv komicheskogo u Marka Tvena [On the problem of the stylistic functions of the oral form of comedy in Mark Twain]. Uchenye zapiski Ukrainskoi akademii sel'skokhoziaistvennykh nauk [sic]. Kafedra inostrannykh iazykov. Kiev, 1958. t. 1. p. 23-61.

Petrova, E. N. Mark Tven i kritiki "bostonskoi shkoly." (Iz istorii literaturnoi kritiki v SShA vtoroi poloviny XIX veka) [Mark Twain and the critics of the "Boston School." (From the history of literary criticism in the USA in the second half of the 19th century)]. Uchenye zapiski Leningradskogo pedagogicheskogo instituta, 1958, t. 158. Kafedra zarubezhnoi literatury, p. 193-217.

Romm, A. S. Demokraticheskii geroi v romane Tvena "Prikliucheniia Gekl'berri Finna" [The democratic hero in Twain's novel "The adventures of Huckleberry Finn"]. Uchenye zapiski Leningradskogo pedagogicheskogo instituta, 1958, t. 170. Kafedra russkoi literatury, p. 379-405.

Romm, A. Mark Tven i ego knigi o detiakh [Mark Twain and his books about children]. Leningrad, Detgiz, 1958. 136 p. *Review:* Pogorelaia, E. Zvezda, 1959, no. 8, p. 222.

Startsev, A. Novoe o molodom Tvene [New information about the young Twain]. Inostrannaia literatura, 1958, no. 4, p. 261-263.

1959 Tven, M. Sobranie sochinenii [Collected works]. v. 1-12. Moscow, Goslitizdat, 1959-1961.

v. 1: Prostaki za granitsei [The innocents abroad]. Mendel'son, M. Mark Tven, 1835-1910 [Mark Twain, 1835-1910]. p. 5-58. *Commentary:* Aleksandrova, Z. p. 607-633.

v. 2: Nalegke [Free and easy—i.e. *Roughing It*]. *Commentary:* Mendel'son, M. p. 483-487; Lorie, M. F. p. 488-495.

v. 3: Pozolochennyi vek [The gilded age]. *Commentary:* Startsev, A. p. 553-557; Khvostenko, L. p. 558-579.

v. 4: Prikliucheniia Toma Soiera. Zhizn' na Missisipi [The adventures of Tom Sawyer. Life on the Mississippi]. *Commentary:* Lanina, T. p. 667-671; Dynnik, N. p. 672-678.

v. 5: Peshkom po Evrope. Prints i nishchii [On foot in Europe—i.e. *A Tramp Abroad*. The prince and the pauper]. *Commentary:* Elistratova, A. p. 647-652; Nikoliukin, A. N. and Z. E. Aleksandrova. p. 653-664.

v. 6: Prikliucheniia Gekl'berri Finna. Ianki iz Konnektikuta pri dvore korolia Artura [The adventures of Huckleberry Finn. A

Connecticut Yankee in King Arthur's court]. *Commentary:*
Startsev, A. p. 631-637; Brakhman, S. R. p. 638-652.

v. 7: Amerikanskii pretendent. Tom Soier za granitsei. Prostofilia
Vil'son [The American claimant. Tom Sawyer abroad. Pudd'nhead
Wilson]. *Commentary:* Narkevich, A. p. 493-508.

v. 8: Lichnye vospominaniia o Zhanne d'Ark [Personal recollections of Joan of Arc]. *Commentary:* Elistratova, A. p. 469-475;
Aleksandrova, Z. p. 476-484.

v. 9: Po ekvatoru. Tainstvennyi neznakomets [Following the
equator. The mysterious stranger]. *Commentary:* Startsev, A.
p. 677-682; 700-701; Antonova, K. p. 683-700.

v. 10: Rasskazy. Ocherki. Publitsistika [Stories. Sketches. Articles].
Commentary: Mendel'son, M. p. 693-701; Nikoliukin, A. p. 702-
729.

v. 11: Rasskazy. Ocherki. Publitsistika [Stories. Sketches. Articles].
Commentary: Elistratova, A. p. 593-599; Lorie, M. F. p. 600-612.

v. 12: Iz "Avtobiografii." Iz "Zapisnykh knizhek" Izbrannye
pis'ma. [From the "Autobiography." From the "Notebooks."
Selected letters]. *Commentary:* Startsev, A. p. 689-697; Gilenson,
B. p. 698-731.

Bobrova, M. N. Literaturno-kriticheskie stat'i Marka Tvena 90-kh
godov [The literary-critical articles of Mark Twain of the '90's].
Uchenye zapiski Saratovskogo universiteta, 1959, t. 67. vyp. filol.,
p. 169-178.

Discussion between "Literaturnaia gazeta" and the *New York Times* about
the edition of Mark Twain's *Autobiography* prepared by Ch. Neider:
Bereznitskii, Ia. Mark Tven na prokrustovom lozhe [Mark Twain on
the bed of Procrustes]. Literaturnaia gazeta, August 18, 1959;
Neider, Ch. "My ne sovershili prestupleniia protiv Marka Tvena"
["We have not committed a crime against Mark Twain"]. Literaturnaia gazeta, December 12, 1959; Bereznitskii, Ia. Vopros znachi-
tel'no glubzhe. Pis'mo Charl'zu Naideru [The problem is much deep-
er. A letter to Charles Neider]. Literaturnaia gazeta, December 12,
1959.

Lanina, T. Da, Mark Tven—"master anekdota", no... [Yes, Mark Twain
is a "master of the anecdote," but...]. Inostrannaia literatura, 1960,
no. 5, p. 233-235.

Kustov, V. Neizvestnye pis'ma Marka Tvena [Unknown letters of Mark
Twain]. Vecherniaia Moskva, November 13, 1959.

Leont'eva, O. S. Antivoennye pamphlety Marka Tvena (1898-1910 gg.)
[Mark Twain's antiwar pamphlets (1898-1910)]. Uchenye zapiski
Moskovskogo gosudarstvennogo pedagogicheskogo instituta, 1959,
t. 137, vyp. 4. Kafedra zarubezhnoi literatury. Sbornik statei po
zarubezhnoi literature (srednie veka, XIX, XX vek), p. 67-79.

Mendel'son, M. "Novaia dinastiia" Marka Tvena. (Eshche odna publi-katsiia iz arkhiva pisatelia) ["The new dynasty" of Mark Twain. (Yet another publication from the writer's archive)]. Voprosy literatury, 1959, no. 7, p. 156-167.

Orlova, R. Mark Tven—pisatel'-grazhdanin [Mark Twain—writer-citizen]. (Foner, P. *Mark Twain: Social Critic.* New York, 1958). Voprosy literatury, 1959, no. 5, p. 227-231.

1960 Anikst, A. Umer li Mark Tven? [Is Mark Twain dead?]. Literaturnaia gazeta, April 26, 1960.

Bobrova, M. Velikii amerikanskii pisatel' [The great American writer]. Pravda, April 20, 1960.

B'iukenen, T. Dzh. [Buchanan, T. J.?]. Samyi pronitsatel'nyi iz ameri-kantsev [The most perspicacious of Americans]. V zashchitu mira, 1960, no. 2, p. 34-40.

Vostokova, S. Ateisticheskoe zaveshchanie Marka Tvena [Mark Twain's atheistic will]. Nauka i religiia, 1960, no. 4, p. 90-93.

Gilenson, B. Smekh i slezy Marka Tvena [Mark Twain's laughter and tears]. Moskva, 1960, no. 5, p. 205-214.

Dodd, M. Linkol'n amerikanskoi literatury [The Lincoln of American literature]. Izvestiia, April 20, 1960.

Zagraevskaia, Z. Mark Tven v Ialte [Mark Twain in Yalta]. Krym (Simferopol'), 1960, no. 25, p. 131-133.

Kamenskii, Iu. Nash drug [Our friend]. Komsomol'skaia pravda, November 30, 1960.

Kokovin, E. Tom Soier i sovetskie rebiata. Segodnia—125 let so dnia rozhdeniia Marka Tvena [Tom Sawyer and Soviet children. Today is 125 years since the birth of Mark Twain]. Literatura i zhizn', November 30, 1960.

Kuleshov, A. Tam gde S. Klemens stal Markom Tvenom [There where S. Clemens became Mark Twain]. Iunost', 1960, no. 7, p. 100-102.

Lanina, T. Mark Tven [Mark Twain]. Kul'tura i zhizn', 1960, no. 4, p. 60.

Mendel'son, M. O. Mark Tven, 1835-1910 [Mark Twain, 1835-1910]. Moscow, Znanie, 1960. 48 p.

Olesha, Iu. Mark Tven [Mark Twain]. Literatura i zhizn', April 24, 1960.

50-letie—i.e. Piatidesiatiletie—so dnia smerti Marka Tvena [The fiftieth anniversary of the death of Mark Twain]. Vestnik Akademii nauk SSSR, 1960, no. 7, p. 114-115.

Savurenok, A. K. Mark Tven [Mark Twain]. Leningrad, 1960. 50 p.

Savurenok, A. K. Roman M. Tvena "Ianki iz Konnektikuta pri dvore korolia Artura." (K voprosu o literaturno-esteticheskikh pozitsiiakh pisatelia) [Mark Twain's novel "A Connecticut Yankee in King Arthur's court." (On the problem of the literary-esthetic positions of the writer)]. *In:* Literatura i estetika [Literature and esthetics]. Leningrad, 1960. p. 262-277.

Samarin, R. Mark Tven [Mark Twain]. Sovetskii Soiuz, 1960, no. 4, p. 20.

Foner, M. [*sic*]. Mark Tven i rabochii klass [Mark Twain and the working class]. Introduction and notes by A. Startsev. Inostrannaia literatura, 1960, no. 4, p. 191-203. *Complete translation in the following item.*

1961 Foner, Ph. S. Mark Tven — sotsial'nyi kritik [Mark Twain — social critic]. Afterword by Ia. N. Zasurskii. Commentary by Iu. I. Kagarlitskii. Moscow, 1961. 416 p.

Mendel'son, M. Knigi Marka Tvena o Tome i Geke [Mark Twain's books about Tom and Huck]. *In:* Twain, M. Prikliucheniia Toma Soiera. Prikliucheniia Gekl'berri Finna. Tom Soier za granitsei. Tom Soier-syshchik [The adventures of Tom Sawyer. The adventures of Huckleberry Finn. Tom Sawyer abroad. Tom Sawyer detective]. Moscow, 1961. p. 635-643.

Mendel'son, M. O. Problema neizdannogo literaturnogo naslediia Marka Tvena [The problem of the unpublished literary heritage of Mark Twain]. Izvestiia Akademii nauk SSSR. Otdelenie literatury i iazyka. 1961, t. 20, vyp. 1, p. 27-43.

Faktorovich, D. Mark Tven i ego kniga o Zhanne d'Ark [Mark Twain and his book about Joan of Arc]. *In:* Twain, M. Zhanna d'Ark [Joan of Arc]. Minsk, 1961. p. 5-15.

Shprink, V. Maloizvestnyi roman Marka Tvena [A little-known novel of Mark Twain's]. Nauka i religiia, 1961, no. 10, p. 94.

1962 Bobrova, M. Mark Tven. Ocherk tvorchestva. [Mark Twain. An essay on his works]. Moscow, Goslitizdat, 1962. 504 p.

"Kamennaia poema" Marka Tvena [The "stone poem" of Mark Twain]. Za rubezhom, 1962, no. 52, p. 30.

Nekhai, O. and A. Prokof'eva. Iz glubiny vekov [Out of the depth of the centuries]. (Zhanna d'Ark [Joan of Arc]. Minsk. 1961). Neman (Minsk), 1962, no. 4, p. 155-156.

Novitskaia, Z. V. Traditsii amerikanskogo iumora XIX st. i rechevye sredstva komicheskogo u Marka Tvena [The traditions of American humor of the 19th century and the oral form of comedy in Mark Twain]. Abstract of dissertation presented for the degree of Candidate of Philological Sciences. Moscow, 1962. 28 p.

Startsev, A. Mark Tven i amerikanskie tekstologi [Mark Twain and American textologists]. Voprosy literatury, 1962, no. 6, p. 136-139.

Startsev, A. Problema pozdnego Tvena [The problem of the later Twain]. Voprosy literatury, 1962, no. 11, p. 138-159.

1963 Belov, A. Velikii satirik Mark Tven [Mark Twain, the great satirist]. *In:* Twain, M. Puteshestvie kapitana Stormfilda v rai [Captain Stormfield's visit to heaven]. Moscow, 1963. p. 67-70.

Garkavenko, F. I. Posleslovie [Afterword]. *In:* Twain, M. Pis'ma s zemli [Letters from the earth]. Moscow, 1963. p. 304-308.

Marti, Kh. [Jose]. Teatral'nyi sezon v N'iu-Iorke. Mark Tven [The theatrical season in New York. Mark Twain]. *In:* Marti, Kh. [Jose]. Severoamerikanskie stseny [North American scenes]. Moscow, 1963. p. 98-106.

Mendel'son, M. Tveniana [Twainiana]. Literaturnaia Rossiia, December 13, 1963, p. 20.

Startsev, A. Mark Tven i Amerika [Mark Twain and America]. Moscow, Sovetskii pisatel', 1963. 307 p. *Reviews:* Vil'mont, N. Nepotukhshii vulkan [The non-quiescent volcano]. Inostrannaia literatura, 1963, no. 9, p. 264-266; Elistratova, A. "Mark Tven—nepotukhshii vulkan!" ["Mark Twain—an erupting volcano!"]. Voprosy literatury, 1963, no. 8, p. 224-228; T. M. Novyi mir, 1963, no. 7, p. 284-285.

Startsev, A. "Mark Tven i russkie" ["Mark Twain and the Russians"]. (Neider, Ch. *Mark Twain and the Russians.* New York, 1960). Voprosy literatury, 1963, no. 12, p. 116-121.

APDAIK Dzhon   UPDIKE John

1963 Anastas'ev, N. "Pravdivaia i bezzhalostnaia" ["True and pitiless"]. (*Rabbit, Run.* New York, 1962). Molodaia gvardiia, 1963, no. 5, p. 296-299.

Elistratova, A. Review of: *The Centaur.* Sovremennaia khudozhestvennaia literatura za rubezhom, 1963, no. 5, p. 48-51.

Elistratova, A. "Tragicheskoe zhivotnoe—chelovek." O dvukh romanakh Dzhona Apdaika ["Man—a tragic animal." Concerning the two novels of John Updike]. (*Rabbit, Run* and *The Centaur*). Inostrannaia literatura, 1963, no. 12, p. 220-226.

VAN-VEKHTEN Karl   VAN VECHTEN Carl

1928 Lann, E. Review of: Negritianskii rai [Nigger heaven]. Leningrad, 1928. Pechat' i revoliutsiia, 1928, no. 6, p. 217-219.

VORS Meri Khiton   VORSE Mary Heaton

1931 L. F. Review of: *Strike.* New York, 1930. Inostrannaia kniga, literaturno-khudozhestvennaia seriia, 1931, no. 1, p. 4-5.

1932 Gendriks, K. Predislovie [Foreword]. *In:* Vorse, M. H. Stachka [Strike]. Moscow, Leningrad, 1932. p. 3-8.

Zapadnyi, Ia. Roman o gastonskoi stachke [A novel about the Gastonia strike]. LOKAF, 1932, no. 8-9, p. 219-221.

Mingulina, A. Na revoliutsionnom pod"eme [On the upswing of the revolution]. Kniga stroiteliam sotsializma (Khudozhestvennaia literatura), 1932, no. 11-12, p. 14-15.

Nikolaeva, T. S pozitsii nabliudatelia [From the point of view of an observer]. Literaturnaia gazeta, May 12, 1932.

Filatova, L. Review of: Stachka [Strike]. Na literaturnom postu, 1932, no. 12, p. 28-30.

1936 Mendel'son, N. Zametki o godakh bezumiia [Notes on the years of folly]. (*A Footnote to Folly*, 1935). Za rubezhom, 1936, no. 32, p. 726.

UIVER Dzhon   WEAVER John D.

1950 Gus, M. Pirrovy pobedy generala Makartura [The pyrrhic victories of General MacArthur]. (Pirrova pobeda [A pyrrhic victory[1]]. Moscow, 1950). Ogonek, 1950, no. 36, p. 24.

Lagin, L. Review of: Pirrova pobeda [A pyrrhic victory]. Moscow, 1950. Novoe vremia, 1950, no. 36, p. 24-29.

Mendel'son, M. Predislovie [Foreword]. *In:* Weaver, J. Pirrova pobeda [A pyrrhic victory]. Moscow, 1950. p. 5-16.

Moiseev, K. Review of: Pirrova pobeda [A pyrrhic victory]. Moscow, 1950. Voennyi vestnik, 1950, no. 20, p. 60-63.

Razgovorov, N. Pod sen'iu Belogo Doma [Under the shadow of the White House]. Literaturnaia gazeta, October 28, 1950.

1951 Maksimov, P. Review of: Pirrova pobeda [A pyrrhic victory]. Moscow, 1950. Novyi mir, 1951, no. 2, p. 258-261.

UITMEN Uolt   WHITMAN Walt

1861 "List'ia travy" Uaitmena [Whitman's "Leaves of grass"]. Otechestvennye zapiski, 1861, no. 1, otd. IV, p. 61.

1883 Popov, P. Uolt Guitman [Walt Whitman]. Zagranichnyi vestnik, 1883, no. 3, p. 567-580.

1892 Amerikanskii Tolstoi [An American Tolstoi]. Knizhki nedeli, 1892, no. 5, p. 167-171.

Zotov, V. Severo-amerikanskii poet i gumanist [A North American poet and humanist]. Nabliudatel', 1892, no. 6, otd. II, p. 15-16.

Uitmen. Nekrolog [Whitman. An obituary]. Bibliograficheskie zapiski, 1892, no. 5, p. 390.

1898 Shklovskii, I. V. Iz Anglii. IV. (Uot Uitmen) [From England. IV (Walt Whitman)]. Russkoe bogatstvo, 1898, no. 8, otd. II, p. 207-214. (Signed: Dioneo.) *Also, with title:* "Oskar Uail'd i Uot Uitmen" ["Oscar Wilde and Walt Whitman"], *in:* Dioneo (pseud. of I. Shklovskii). Ocherki sovremennoi Anglii [Sketches of contemporary England]. St. Petersburg, 1903. p. 392-423.

Shklovskii, I. Uot Uitmen [Walt Whitman]. Russkie vedomosti, Jan. 10, 1898. (Signed: S.)

[1] *Another Such Victory.*

1902 Ual't Vitman [Walt Whitman]. Novyi zhurnal inostrannoi literatury, iskusstva i nauki, 1902, no. 10. (2nd pagination), p. 153-154. *Also in:* Plutarkh XIX veka [Plutarch of the 19th century]. v. 2. St. Petersburg, 1903. p. 153-154.

1903 Friche, V. Ocherki inostrannoi literatury. Vozrozhdenie pervobytnoi poezii [Sketches of foreign literature. The renascence of primeval poetry]. Kur'er, September 27, 1903.

1904 Bal'mont, K. Pevets lichnosti i zhizni. Uol't Uitman [The singer of personality and life. Walt Whitman]. Vesy, 1904, no. 7, p. 9-32. *Also in:* Bal'mont, K. Belye zarnitsy [White sheet-lightning]. St. Petersburg, 1908. p. 59-84.

1906 Chukovskii, K. Russkaia Whitmaniana [Russian Whitmaniana]. Vesy, 1906, no. 10, p. 43-45. *Review:* Ts. E. Ob Uitmane, Bal'monte, narekaniiakh i dobrosovestnosti. Zametka dokazatel'naia [Concerning Whitman, Balmont, words of blame, and good intentions. A convincing remark]. Vesy, 1906, no. 12, p. 46-51.

Chukovskii, K. O pol'ze broma. Po povodu g-zhi Eleny Ts (Concerning the uses of bromide. On the theme of Mme. Elena Ts]. Vesy, 1906, no. 12, p. 52-60.

Chukovskii, K. Uot Uitman. (Lichnost' i demokratiia ego poezii) [Walt Whitman. (The individuality and democracy of his poetry)]. *In:* Maiak, vyp. 1. St. Petersburg, 1906. p. 240-256.

1907 Bal'mont, K. Poeziia bor'by. (Idealizovannaia demokratiia) [The poetry of struggle. (Idealized democracy)]. Pereval, 1907, no. 3, p. 37-48. *Also in:* Bal'mont, K. Belye zarnitsy [White sheet-lightning]. St. Petersburg, 1908. p. 85-134.

Chukovskii, K. I. Poet anarkhist Uot Uitman. Perevod v stikhakh i kharakteristika. [The anarchist poet Walt Whitman. A translation in verse and a character sketch]. St. Petersburg, Kruzhok molodykh, 1907. 82 p. *Also, revised and enlarged, under titles:* Poeziia griadushchei demokratii. Uot Uitmen [The poetry of dawning democracy. Walt Whitman]; *and:* Uot Uitmen. Poeziia griadushchei demokratii [Walt Whitman. The poetry of dawning democracy]. Moscow, 1914. 126 p.; Petrograd, 1918. 155 p.; 4th ed. Petrograd, 1919. 120 p.; 5th ed., *supplement to:* List'ia travy [Leaves of grass]. Peterburg, 1922; 6th ed. Moscow, Petrograd, 1923. 165 p. *Reviews:* A—vich, N. Ia. Novaia kniga, 1907, no. 5, p. 16-17. Aikhenval'd, Iu. Russkaia mysl', 1907, no. 8, p. 145-147. *Also in:* Aikhenval'd, Iu. Otdel'nye stranitsy [Separate pages]. 2. Moscow, 1910. p. 160-164. Niva, ezhemesiachnoe literaturnoe prilozhenie, 1907, no. 6, p. 303; N. V. Knizhnyi ugol, 1918, no. 1, p. 11-12; V. L. Zhizn' iskusstva, 1923, no. 41, p. 25.

Chukovskii, K. Review of: Carpenter, Ed. *Days with Walt Whitman.* London, 1906. Vesy, 1907, no. 2, p. 95-96.

1908 A. Review of: Bazalgette, L. *Walt Whitman*. Vesy, 1908, no. 7, p. 96.
Bal'mont, K. O vragakh i vrazhde. (Uolt Uitmen) [Concerning enemies
and enmity. (Walt Whitman)]. *In:* Bal'mont, K. Morskoe svechenie
[Sea-fire]. St. Petersburg, Moscow, 1910. p. 165-172.
1909 Bal'mont, K. Pevets pobegov travy [The singer of the leaves of grass].
Zolotoe runo, 1909, no. 1, p. 67-77.
1910 Bal'mont, K. Poliarnost'. (O tvorchestve Uol'ta Uitmana) [Polarity.
(On the work of Walt Whitman)]. Sovremennyi mir, 1910, no. 8,
p. 135-139. *Also in:* Whitman, W. Pobegi travy [Leaves of grass].
Moscow, 1911. p. 5-8.
Dzhems, V. [James, W.]. Pragmatizm i religii. (Uot Uitmen) [Pragmatism
and religion. (Walt Whitman)]. *In:* James, W. Pragmatism. 2nd ed.
St. Petersburg, 1910. p. 166-170.
Dzhems, V. [James, W.]. Uot Uitman [Walt Whitman]. *In:* James, W.
Mnogoobrazie religioznogo opyta [The varieties of religious expe-
rience]. Moscow, 1910. p. 75-77.
1912 Sorokin, P. A. Bard zhizni. (Uot Uitman, 1819-1892) [The bard of life.
(Walt Whitman, 1819-1892)]. Vseobshchii zhurnal literatury, iskusstva, nauki i obshchestvennoi zhizni, 1912, no. 2, p. 105-130.
1918 Lunacharskii, A. Uitmen i demokratiia [Whitman and democracy]. *In:*
Chukovskii, K. Poeziia griadushchei demokratii [The poetry of
dawning democracy]. Petrograd, 1918. p. 150-153. *Also, revised, in:*
Whitman, W. Izbrannye stikhotvoreniia [Selected poetry]. Moscow,
1932. p. 3-6; *and:* Lunacharskii, A. Stat'i o literature [Articles about
literature]. Moscow, 1957. p. 617-619.
P. Chelovek s raskrytym serdtsem (Uot Uitmen) [A man with an open
heart (Walt Whitman)]. Plamia, 1918, no. 21, p. 13-14.
1919 Friche, V. Uot Uitmen [Walt Whitman]. Vestnik zhizni, 1919, no. 3-4,
p. 67-70.
1920 F. Neskol'ko slov o proze Uota Uitmena [Some words about Walt
Whitman's prose]. Zhizn' iskusstva, January 27-30, 1920.
1922 Aksenov, I. A. Review of: Izbrannye sochineniia [Selected works].
Petersburg, 1922. Pechat' i revoliutsiia, 1922, no. 7, p. 310-311.
Bal'mont, K. Predislovie [Foreword]. *In:* Bal'mont, K. Revoliutsion-
naia poeziia Evropy i Ameriki. Uitman [The revolutionary poetry of
Europe and America. Whitman]. Moscow, 1922. p. 3-4.
Borodin, A. Uot Uitmen [Walt Whitman]. Baku, "Rubiny," 1922. 28 p.
Tugenkhol'd, Ia. Pamiati Uota Uitmena (1819-1892) [In memory of
Walt Whitman (1819-1892)]. *In:* Pomoshch', sbornik no. 1. Sim-
feropol', 1922. p. 30-34.
Uolles, Dzh. [Wallace, J.?]. Uot Uitmen i mirovoi krizis [Walt Whitman
and the world crisis]. Moscow, Petrograd, Gosizdat, 1922. 32 p.
Review: Aksenov, I. A. Pechat' i revoliutsiia, 1923, no. 2, p. 223.
Friche, V. Uitman [Whitman]. *In:* Friche, V. Ocherk razvitiia zapadno-

evropeiskoi literatury [Outline of the development of Western European literature]. Moscow, 1922. p. 255-257. *Also, with title:* "Poeziia U. Uitmena" ["The poetry of Walt Whitman"], *in:* Sotsial'naia i revoliutsionnaia poeziia Ameriki i Evropy [The social and revolutionary poetry of America and Europe]. Moscow, 1927. p. 17-21.

Chukovskii, K. Predislovie [Foreword]. *In:* Whitman, W. List'ia travy [Leaves of grass]. Petrograd, 1922. p. 157-158.

1923 Tiniakov, A. Indiia v Amerike ("List'ia travy") [India in America ("Leaves of grass")]. *In:* Petrograd, Al'manakh 1. Moscow, Petrograd, 1923. p. 217-223.

1926 G. Ia. Uot Uitmen (1819-1892) [Walt Whitman (1819-1892)]. Ekran, 1926, no. 20, p. 11.

Friche, V. M. Predshestvenniki literatury XX veka. Uot Uitmen [The predecessors of the literature of the 20th century. Walt Whitman]. *In:* Friche, V. M. Zapadnoevropeiskaia literatura XX veka v ee glavneishikh proiavleniiakh [Western European literature of the 20th century in its chief characteristics]. Moscow, Leningrad, 1926. p. 9-17.

1928 Bruks, V. V. [Brooks, V. W.?]. Uot Uitmen v dialogakh [Walt Whitman in dialogues]. Na literaturnom postu, 1928, no. 11-12, p. 81-82.

1931 Chukovskii, K. Predtecha revoliutsionnykh poetov. K 75-letiiu "List'ev travy" Uota Uitmena [A forerunner of revolutionary poets. On the 75th anniversary of "Leaves of grass" by Walt Whitman]. Ogonek, 1931, no. 7, p. 14. *Also, with additions, in:* Whitman, W. List'ia travy [Leaves of grass]. Moscow, 1931. p. 3-6.

1932 Mgebrow, A. A. Uolt Uitmen [Walt Whitman]. *In:* Mgebrov, A. A. Zhizn' v teatre [Life in the theater]. Moscow, Leningrad, 1932, v. 2, p. 335-360.

Chukovskii, K. Predislovie [Foreword]. Uot Uitmen, ego zhizn' i kniga [Walt Whitman, his life and his book]. *In:* Whitman, W. Izbrannye stikhotvoreniia [Selected works]. Moscow, Leningrad, 1932. p. 7-49. *Also in:* Whitman, W. List'ia travy [Leaves of grass]. Moscow, Leningrad, 1935. p. 5-68.

1933 Startsev, A. Grazhdanin mira [A citizen of the world]. Khudozhestvennaia literatura, 1933, no. 4, p. 26-28.

1935 Maizel', D. Uot Uitmen [Walt Whitman]. Molodaia gvardiia, 1935, no. 7, p. 25-26.

Mirskii, D. Poet amerikanskoi demokratii [A poet of American democracy]. Chukovskii, K. Uolt Uitman; ego zhizn' i kniga [Walt Whitman; his life and his book]. Chukovskii, K. Primechaniia [Notes]. *In:* Whitman, W. List'ia travy [Leaves of grass]. Leningrad, 1935. p. 5-68, 221-230.

Spir [Speare?], L. Uolt Uitmen [Walt Whitman]. Internatsional'naia literatura, 1935, no. 12, p. 105-112.

1936 Startsev, A. Stikhi Uitmena [Whitman's poetry]. Literaturnaia gazeta, January 10, 1936.
Stepanov, N. Review of: List'ia travy [Leaves of grass]. Leningrad, 1935. Literaturnyi sovremennik, 1936, no. 6, p. 223-225.
1937 Dinamov, S. Pevets demokratii [A singer of democracy]. Pravda, March 26, 1937.
1938 Maikl Gold ob Uote Uitmene [Michael Gold on Walt Whitman]. Literaturnaia gazeta, August 26, 1938.
1939 Chukovskii, K. Uolt Uitman [Walt Whitman]. Literaturnaia gazeta, June 10, 1939.
1940 Chukovskii, K. L. Tolstoi ob Uolte Uitmane [L. Tolstoi on Walt Whitman]. Literaturnaia gazeta, August 25, 1940.
1941 Chukovskii, K. Maiakovskii i Uitman [Maiakovskii and Whitman]. Leningrad, 1941, no. 2, p. 18-19.
Chukovskii, K. Uolt Uitmen [Walt Whitman]. Internatsional'naia literatura, 1941, no. 2, p. 176-178.
1942 Gorbov, D. Velikii poet demokratii [A great poet of democracy]. Internatsional'naia literatura, 1942, no. 1-2, p. 201-202.
Chukovskii, K. Uolt Uitmen v SSSR. Bibliograficheskie zametki [Walt Whitman in the USSR. Bibliographical notes]. Internatsional'naia literatura, 1942, no. 1-2, p. 204-206.
1944 Chukovskii, K. Uolt Uitman, ego zhizn' i tvorchestvo. Iz anglo-amerikanskikh materialov ob Uitmene. Turgenev i Lev Tolstoi o "List'iakh travy." Uitman i Maiakovskii. Bibliografiia [Walt Whitman, his life and works. From Anglo-American materials about Whitman. Turgenev and Leo Tolstoi about "Leaves of grass." Whitman and Maiakovskii. Bibliography]. *In:* Whitman, W. Izbrannye stikhotvoreniia i proza [Selected poetry and prose]. Moscow, 1944. p. 5-42, 194-214.
1945 Mendel'son, M. Uolt Uitmen [Walt Whitman]. Novyi mir, 1945, no. 5-6, p. 183-188.
Review of: Izbrannye stikhotvoreniia i proza [Selected poetry and prose]. Moscow, 1944. Oktiabr', 1945, no. 5-6, p. 264-265.
1946 Startsev, A. Review of: Izbrannye stikhotvoreniia i proza [Selected poetry and prose]. Moscow, 1944. Sovetskaia kniga, 1946, no. 1, p. 117-119.
1951 Mendel'son, M. Uolt Uitmen i bor'ba za mir i demokratiiu [Walt Whitman and the struggle for peace and democracy]. Znamia, 1951, no. 5, p. 170-182.
1952 Mendel'son, M. Uolt Uitmen [Walt Whitman]. Ogonek, 1952, no. 13, p. 15.
1954 Gogoberidze, L. L. Kritika amerikanskoi deistvitel'nosti v tvorchestve Uolta Uitmena [Criticism of American reality in the work of Walt Whitman]. Abstract of dissertation presented for the degree of Candidate of Philological Sciences. Tbilisi, 1954. 18 p.

Mendel'son, M. Uolt Uitmen. Kritiko-biograficheskii ocherk [Walt Whitman. Critico-biographic sketch]. Moscow, Goslitizdat, 1954. 256 p. *Reviews:* Gaziev, Iu. Narodnyi poet Ameriki [A people's poet of America]. Inostrannaia literatura, 1955, no. 1, p. 206-209; Zasurskii, Ia. Obraz poeta-demokrata [The image of a poet-democrat]. Oktiabr', 1956, no. 3, p. 189-191.

Mendel'son, M. Uolt Uitmen [Walt Whitman]. *In:* Whitman, W. Izbrannoe [Selections]. Moscow, 1954. p. 3-34.

Toper, P. Gordye pesni Uitmena [The proud songs of Whitman]. Ogonek, 1954, no. 33, p. 25.

1955 Anikst, A. Vydaiushchiisia amerikanskii poet-demokrat [An outstanding American poet-democrat]. Mezhdunarodnaia zhizn', 1955, no. 7, p. 88-95.

Bannikov, N. Uolt Uitmen (1819-1892) [Walt Whitman (1819-1892)]. *In:* Whitman, W. Iz knigi "List'ia travy" [From the book "Leaves of grass"]. Moscow, 1955. p. 3-6.

Gogoberidze, L. L. Uitmen—pevets prostogo naroda Ameriki [Whitman—a singer of the common people of America]. Izvestiia Akademii nauk SSSR, otdelenie literatury i iazyka, 1955, t. 14, vyp. 3, p. 255-266.

Zhamagi, P. Uot Uitmen. "Slavnyi sedovlasyi poet" [Walt Whitman. The "good gray poet"]. V zashchitu mira, 1955, no. 50, p. 123-129.

Zasurskii, Ia. N. Zhizn' i tvorchestvo U. Uitmena. (K stoletiiu so dnia vykhoda v svet pervogo izdaniia "List'ev travy") [The life and work of Walt Whitman. (On the centennial of the publication of the first edition of "Leaves of grass")]. Moscow, "Znanie," 1955. 32 p.

Zasurskii, Ia. Poeziia zhizni [The poetry of life]. Smena, 1955, no. 10, p. 18.

Zasurskii, Ia. Uitmen na stranitsakh "Ordine nuovo" [Whitman on the pages of "Ordine nuovo"]. Ogonek, 1955, no. 27, p. 23.

Kemenova, A. B. Uolt Uitmen (1819-1892) [Walt Whitman (1819-1892)]. *In:* Kemenova, A. B. Velikie predstaviteli mirovoi kul'tury. Bibliograficheskie i metodicheskie materialy v pomoshch' massovym bibliotekam [Great representatives of world culture. Bibliographic and program materials for the assistance of mass libraries]. vyp. 6. Moscow, 1955. p. 1-13.

Kornilova, E. Pevets svobody i progressa. Uolt Uitmen i ego kniga "List'ia travy" [A bard of freedom and progress. Walt Whitman and his book "Leaves of grass"]. Sovetskaia kul'tura, July 2, 1955.

Mendel'son, M. Neumiraiushchaia kniga. K. 100-letiiu vykhoda knigi U Uitmena "List'ia travy" [An undying book. On the centennial of the appearance of W. Whitman's book "Leaves of grass"]. Pravda, June 13, 1955.

Mendel'son, M. Stoletie "List'ev travy" [The centennial of "Leaves of grass"]. Oktiabr', 1955, no. 7, p. 151-159. *Also, with title:* "Stoletie velikoi knigi" ["The centennial of a great book"], *in:* Whitman, W. List'ia travy [Leaves of grass]. Moscow, 1955. p. 19-34.

Mendel'son, M. Uolt Uitmen i lilliputy [Walt Whitman and the Lilliputians]. Sovetskaia kul'tura, July 5, 1955.

Orlova, R. Poeziia Uolta Uitmena [The poetry of Walt Whitman]. Nauka i zhizn', 1955, no. 6, p. 54.

Sillen, S. Zametki ob Uitmene. K 100-letiiu so dnia vykhoda "List'ev travy" [Remarks on Whitman. On the centennial of the publication of "Leaves of grass"]. Literaturnaia gazeta, July 14, 1955.

Chapek, A. Uolt Uitmen (1819-1892) [Walt Whitman (1819-1892)]. Vsemirnye studencheskie novosti, 1955, no. 5, p. 4-5.

Chukovskii, K. Pevets druzhby narodov [A singer of the friendship of nations]. Izvestiia, June 12, 1955.

Chukovskii, K. Uolt Uitmen [Walt Whitman]. *In:* Whitman, W. Stikhotvoreniia i proza [Poetry and prose]. Moscow, 1955. p. 3-5.

1956 Mendel'son, M. O. Amerikanskii poet-demokrat. Uolt Uitmen [An American poet-democrat. Walt Whitman]. Abstract of dissertation presented for the degree of Doctor of Philological Sciences. Moscow, 1956. 23 p.

1957 Mendel'son, M. Kak dokazyvaiut nedokazuemoe [How they demonstrate the undemonstrable]. (Clark, L. M. *Walt Whitman's Concept of the American Common Man.* New York, 1955). Inostrannaia literatura, 1957, no. 10, p. 216-222.

Savurenok, A. K. Uolt Uitmen i abolitsionistskoe dvizhenie 1840-1850kh godov [Walt Whitman and the abolitionist movement of the 1840's and 1850's]. Uchenye zapiski Leningradskogo universiteta, 1957, no. 234. Seriia filologicheskikh nauk, vyp. 37, p. 159-173.

1958 Mendel'son, M. O. Bor'ba za Uitmena v SShA [The struggle for Whitman in the USA]. Uchenye zapiski Pervogo Moskovskogo pedagogicheskogo instituta inostrannykh iazykov, 1958. t. 21. Kafedra literatury, p. 71-110.

1959 Uolt Uitmen (1819-1892). Metodicheskie materialy k vecheru, posviashchennomu 140-letiiu so dnia rozhdeniia [Walt Whitman (1819-1892). Program materials for an evening in commemoration of the 140th anniversary of his birth]. Moscow, 1959. 8 p.

1960 Dicharov, Z. Zametki o Rossii [Notes on Russia]. Nedelia, May 8-14, 1960, p. 10.

Chukovskii, K. Uolt Uitmen [Walt Whitman]. *In:* Chukovskii, K. Liudi i knigi [People and books]. Moscow, 1960. p. 607-624. Also, 2nd edition, 1962.

1962 Dicharov, Z. L. "Zametki o Rossii" Uolta Uitmena ["Notes about Russia" by Walt Whitman]. (With publication of the text). Izvestiia Akademii nauk SSSR, otdelenie literatury i iazyka, 1962, t. 21. vyp. 3, p. 245-251.

207

1963 Marti, Kh. [Marti, Jose]. Poet Uolt Uitmen [The poet Walt Whitman]. *In:* Marti, J. Severo-amerikanskie stseny [North American scenes]. Moscow, 1963. p. 314-330.

UITT'ER Dzhon Grinlif   WHITTIER John Greenleaf

1892 V. T. Literaturnye poteri. (...Smert' Vittiera) [Literary losses. (...The death of Whittier)]. Russkoe bogatstvo, 1892, no. 10, p. 77, 80-81.
1893 V. L. T. Dzhon Grinlif Vittier [John Greenleaf Whittier]. Istoricheskii vestnik, 1893, no. 1, Supplement, p. 1-12.
1908 Stoletie Vittiera [Whittier's centennial]. Istoricheskii vestnik, 1908, no. 2, p. 723-724.
1936 Dzhon Uittier [John Whittier]. Literaturnaia gazeta, July 26, 1936.

VIL'IAMS Al'bert Ris   WILLIAMS Albert Rhys

1925 Bocharov, Iu. Amerikanskii zhurnalist o proletarskoi revoliutsii [An American journalist on the proletarian revolution]. (Narodnye massy v russkoi revoliutsii [The masses in the Russian Revolution]. Moscow, Leningrad, 1925). Knigonosha, 1925, no. 30, p. 10-11.
1958 Nash staryi vernyi drug [Our old and true friend]. Literaturnaia gazeta, September 27, 1958.
Chumak, P. Nash bol'shoi drug. 75 — i.e. Sem'desiatipiati — letie pisatelia Al'berta Risa Vil'iamsa [Our great friend. The seventy-fifth anniversary of the writer Albert Rhys Williams]. Pravda, September 28, 1958.
1959 Mar, N. Al'bert Ris Vil'iams: "Moskva chudesno izmenilas'..." [Albert Rhys Williams: "Moscow has been wondrously transformed...". Literaturnaia gazeta, April 23, 1959.
1960 Levitskii, V. Al'bert Ris Vil'iams na Dal'nem Vostoke [Albert Rhys Williams in the Far East]. Dal'nyi Vostok, 1960, no. 6, p. 143-148.
Penkin, M. Pravda svetlee solntsa. (O Lenine i Oktiabr'skoi revoliutsii [Truth brighter than the sun. (On Lenin and the October Revolution)] Kommunist, 1960, no. 6, p. 153-156.
1961 Polevoi, B. Lafaiet russkoi revoliutsii? [The Lafayette of the Russian Revolution?]. *In:* Polevoi, B. Vstrechi na perekrestkakh [Meetings at the crossroads]. Moscow, 1961. p. 80-106.
1962 Dvorkin, Ia. Poslednii privet druga [The last greeting of a friend]. Literaturnaia gazeta, March 6, 1962.
Pamiati Al'berta Risa Uil'iamsa [To the memory of Albert Rhys Williams]. Pravda, March 17, 1962.
Sekretareva, Z. Tovarishch Ris Vil'iams [Comrade Rhys Williams]. Neva, 1962, no. 6, p. 177-187.

Strel'nikov, B. On zval k miru i druzhbe [He called for peace and friendship]. Pravda, March 2, 1962.

Frimen, G. [Freeman, H.]. Umer Al'bert Ris Vil'iams [Albert Rhys Williams is dead]. Literaturnaia gazeta, March 1, 1962.

Chakovskii, A. Muzhestvennyi borets [A courageous fighter]. Pravda, March 1, 1962.

Chumak, P. Velikii amerikanets [A great American]. Literatura i zhizn', March 2, 1962.

1963 Dangulov, S. Drug Oktiabria [A friend of October]. Izvestiia, September 28, 1963. (Moscow evening edition).

Dvorkin, Ia. Poslednie pis'ma [Last letters]. Literaturnaia gazeta, September 28, 1963.

Petrov, P. Dal'novidnyi drug [A farsighted friend]. Pravda, September 28, 1963.

Petrov, P. Nash bol'shoi drug. Predislovie k publikatsii otryvka iz knigi "Sovety" [Our great friend. Foreword to the publication of a selection from the book "The Soviets"]. Literaturnaia gazeta, September 28, 1963.

Polevoi, B. Pamiati slavnogo druga [To the memory of a glorious friend]. Inostrannaia literatura, 1963, no. 9, p. 240.

Chumak, P. Po zovu Lenina [At Lenin's call]. Ogonek, 1963, no. 41, p. 25.

UIL'IAMS Tennessi WILLIAMS Tennessee (WILLIAMS Thomas L.)

1958 Gaevskii, V. Tenessi Vil'iams—dramaturg "bez predrassudkov" [Tennessee Williams, a dramatist "without prejudices"]. Teatr, 1958, no. 4, p. 181-183.

1959 Zlobin, G. Orfei s Missisipi [Orpheus from Mississippi]. (*Orpheus Descending*). Inostrannaia literatura, 1959, no. 5, p. 258-260.

1960 Zlobin, G. Na stsene i za stsenoi. (P'esy Tennessi Uil'iamsa) [On stage and off stage. (The plays of Tennessee Williams)]. Inostrannaia literatura, 1960, no. 7, p. 199-210.

1961 Solov'eva, I. "Orfei spuskaetsia v ad" ["Orpheus descends into hell"]. Teatr, 1961, no. 12, p. 83-85.

1962 Tenessi Uil'iams o sebe [Tennessee Williams about himself]. Inostrannaia literatura, 1962, no. 8, p. 205-206.

1963 G. Z. Review of: *The Night of the Iguana*. New York, 1962. Sovremennaia khudozhestvennaia literatura za rubezhom, 1963, no. 12, p. 73-75.

UILSON Mitchell   WILSON Mitchell

1951 Pisarzhevskii, O. Predislovie [Foreword]. *In:* Wilson, M. Zhizn' vo mgle [Life in the shadows—i.e. *Live with Lightning*]. Moscow, 1951. p. 3-20. *Also, abridged:* Moscow, 1954. p. 3-18.

1952 Vetoshkina, N. Zhizn' vo mgle [Life in the shadows—i.e. *Live with Lightning*]. Smena, 1952, no. 18, p. 22-23.

Vetoshkina, N. Talantlivaia kniga [A talented book]. (Zhizn' vo mgle [Life in the shadows—i.e. *Live with Lightning*]. Moscow, 1951). Literaturnaia gazeta, August 7, 1952.

Galanov, B. Sila pravdivoi knigi [The strength of a truthful book]. (Zhizn' vo megle [Life in the shadows—i.e. *Live with Lightning*]. Moscow, 1952). Pravda, November 25, 1952.

Zaslavskii, D. Iarkii roman ob amerikanskikh uchenykh [A bright novel about American scholars]. Novyi mir, 1952, no. 9, p. 268-272.

Kovalev, Iu. Review of: Zhizn' vo mgle [Life in the shadows—i.e. *Live with Lightning*]. Moscow, 1951. Zvezda, 1952, no. 8, p. 185-186.

Mendel'son, M. Pod piatoi imperializma [Under the heel of imperialism]. (Zhizn' vo mgle [Life in the shadows—i.e. *Live with Lightning*]. Moscow, 1951). Znamia, 1952, no. 9, p. 188-192.

Rogal', N. Sud'ba uchenogo v strane atomshchikov [The fate of a scholar in the country of the wielders of the atom]. Dal'nii Vostok, 1952, no. 6, p. 147-151.

Ryklin, G. E. Review of: Zhizn' vo mgle [Life in the shadows—i.e. *Live with Lightning*]. Moscow, 1952. Nauka i zhizn', 1952, no. 9, p. 44-46.

Toper, P. V strane atomshchikov [In the country of the wielders of the atom]. Ogonek, 1952, no. 33, p. 24.

1953 Guseva, E. Roman ob amerikanskikh uchenykh [A novel about American scholars]. (Zhizn' vo mgle [Life in the shadows—i.e. *Live with Lightning*]. Moscow, 1951). Oktiabr', 1953, no. 1, p. 179-182.

Dubashinskii, I. Zhizn' v SShA—zhizn' bez sveta. (O knige Mitchela Uilsona [Zhizn' vo mgle"]) ("Life in the US is life without light. (About Mitchell Wilson's book "Life in the shadows"—i.e. *Live with Lightning*)]. Molodoi kommunist, 1953, no. 1, p. 126-128.

Podobedov, M. V dzhungliakh sovremennoi Ameriki. Dve knigi o SShA [In the jungles of contemporary America. Two books about the US]. Literaturnyi Voronezh, Almanakh. 1953, no. 32, p. 192-203.

1956 Vetoshkina, N. Talant v mire biznesa. ("Brat moi, vrag moi") [Talent in the world of business. ("My brother, my enemy")]. Literaturnaia gazeta, July 12, 1956.

Galanov, B. Brat moi, vrag moi [My brother, my enemy]. Iunost', 1956, no. 8, p. 78-79.

Granin, D. Roman Uilsona ["Brat moi, vrag moi" [Wilson's novel "My brother, my enemy"]. Novyi mir, 1956, no. 6, p. 254-258.

Druzina, M. Riadom, no ne vmeste [Side by side, but not together]. (Brat moi, vrag moi [My brother, my enemy]). Neva, 1956, no. 9, p. 193-194.

210

Dubinskaia, A. Sud'ba brat'ev Mellori [The fate of the Mallory brothers]. Oktiabr', 1956, no. 8, p. 188-191.

Rubin, V. and P. Toper. Posleslovie [Afterword]. *In:* Wilson, M. Brat moi, vrag moi [My brother, my enemy]. Moscow, 1956, p. 420-431.

Ryklin, G. Nauka v mire dollara [Science in the world of the dollar]. Nauka i zhizn', 1956, no. 10, p. 59-60.

Tolchenova, N. Truzhenik nauki Devi Mellori [The worker in science, Davy Mallory]. Ogonek, 1956, no. 40, p. 29.

Wilson, M. Zametki o romane "Brat moi, vrag moi" [Remarks about the novel "My brother, my enemy"]. Inostrannaia literatura, 1956, no. 5, p. 187-190.

1957 Iezuitov, A. Dva mira — dva cheloveka. ("Zhizn' vo mgle" v sopostavlenii s romanom D. Granina "Iskateli") [Two worlds — two men. ("Life in the Shadows" — i.e. *Live with Lightning* — in comparison with D. Granin's novel "Iskateli" — "The searchers")]. *In:* Molodoi Leningrad, Al'manakh. Leningrad, 1957. p. 374-385.

Kornilova, E. Predislovie [Foreword]. *In:* Wilson, M. *Live with Lightning.*[1] Moscow, 1957. p. iii-xiv.

Mikhailov, R. Torzhestvo i tragediia brat'ev Mellori [The triumph and tragedy of the Mallory brothers]. Zvezda, 1957, no. 5, p. 211-213.

Poletika, Iu. Geroi, kotoryi osmelivaetsia [A hero who dares]. (Brat moi, vrag moi [My brother, my enemy]). Sovetskaia Ukraina, 1957, no. 4, p. 182-184.

Toper, P. Dve knigi Mitchela Uilsona [The two books of Mitchell Wilson]. Inostrannaia literatura, 1957, no. 7, p. 197-206.

1958 Vstrecha s Mitchelom Uilsonom [A meeting with Mitchell Wilson]. Literaturnaia gazeta, July 3, 1958.

Ryzhikov, V. Vstrecha s Mitchelom Uilsonom [A meeting with Mitchell Wilson]. Literatura i zhizn', November 16, 1958.

Wilson, M. Moi knigi, moi plany [My books, my plans]. Druzhba narodov, 1958, no. 10, p. 215-216.

1960 Mar, N. Spustia dva goda... [After two years...]. Literaturnaia gazeta, July 12, 1960.

1961 Kantorovich, I. Cheloveku dolzhen prinadlezhat' ves' mir! [The whole world should belong to man!]. (Vstrecha na dalekom meridiane [Meeting at a far meridian]). Ural (Sverdlovsk), 1961, no. 9, p. 158-166.

Leont'ev, B. Podvig khudozhnika. O novom romane Mitchela Uilsona [The deed of an artist. About Mitchell Wilson's new novel]. *In:* Wilson, M. Vstrecha na dalekom meridiane [Meeting at a far meridian]. Moscow, 1961. p. 5-14.

O romane "Vstrecha na dalekom meridiane" [Concerning the novel "Meet-

---

[1] A book in the English language published in the Soviet Union.

ing at a far meridian"]. Simonov, K. V interesakh vsego naroda [In the interests of the whole people]; Leont'ev, B. "Bystree, bystree idti vpered!... [Faster, ever faster, go forward!...]. Inostrannaia literatura, 1961, no. 5, p. 187-193.

Wilson, M. Posle pervykh chitatel'skikh otklikov [After the first responses from readers]. Inostrannaia literatura, 1961, no. 9, p. 196-198.

Samarin, R. Uilson o nas [Wilson about us]. (Vstrecha na dalekom meridiane [Meeting at a far meridian]). Izvestiia, June 21, 1961.

Wilson, M. Otvet kritikam [An answer to critics]. Izvestiia, August 29, 1961.

1962 Interv'iu s neozhidannostiami [An interview with the unexpected]. Literaturnaia gazeta, March 27, 1962.

Levitin, K. and A. Melamed. On pishet ob uchenykh. (Besada s Mitchelom Uilsonom) [He writes about scholars. (A conversation with Mitchell Wilson)]. Nauka i zhizn', 1962, no. 5, p. 44-47.

UINTROP TEODOR   WINTHROP Theodore

1865 Pypin, A. N. Teodor Vintrop [Theodore Winthrop]. Sovremennik, 1865, no. 11-12, otd. II, p. 47-55.

VULF Tomas   WOLFE Thomas

1937 Review of: *The Story of a Novel*. 1936. Internatsional'naia literatura, 1937, no. 2, p. 269-270.

1938 Maikl Gold o Tomase Volfe [Michael Gold on Thomas Wolfe]. Internatsional'naia literatura, 1938, no. 12, p. 243.

1940 Gan, Z. Tomas Uolf [Thomas Wolfe]. Internatsional'naia literatura, 1940, no. 11-12, p. 298-301.

1960 Levidova, I. Syn Ameriki. K 60-letiiu so dnia rozhdeniia T. Vulfa [A son of America. On the sixtieth anniversary of the birth of T. Wolfe]. Literaturnaia gazeta, October 11, 1960.

UOLFERT Aira   WOLFERT Ira

1947 Zaslavskii, D. Predislovie [Foreword]. *In:* Wolfert, A. Banda Tekkera [Tucker's band—i.e. *Tucker's People*]. Moscow, 1947. p. 5-17.

1948 Berkovskii, N. "Amerikanskii obraz zhizni" ["The American way of life"]. (Banda Tekkera [Tucker's band—i.e. *Tucker's People*]. Moscow, 1947). Leningradskaia pravda, March 20, 1948.

Viktorov, K. Kniga o banditizme v SShA [A book about banditry in the US]. (Banda Tekkera [Tucker's band—i.e. *Tucker's People*]. Moscow, 1947). Pravda, February 7, 1948.

Voronov, N. V dzhungliakh biznesa [In the jungles of business]. [Banda

Tekkera [Tucker's band—i.e. *Tucker's People*]. Moscow, 1947). Vechernii Leningrad, May 30, 1948.

Koziura, N. Vlast' strakha [The power of fear]. (Banda Tekkera [Tucker's band—i.e. *Tucker's People*]. Moscow, 1947). Znamia, 1948, no. 5, p. 180-184.

Rubin, V. Ben Tekker i drugie [Ben Tucker and the others]. (Banda Tekkera [Tucker's band—i.e. *Tucker's People*]. Moscow, 1947). Literaturnaia gazeta, January 3, 1948.

Smolian, A. Roman o "biznesmenakh." Kniga Uolferta "Banda Tekkera." [A novel about "businessmen." Wolfert's book "Tucker's band"—i.e. *Tucker's People*]. Smena, March 3, 1948.

Shereshevskaia, M. Tekker i drugie [Tucker and the others]. (Banda Tekkera [Tucker's band—i.e. *Tucker's People*]. Moscow, 1947). Zvezda, 1948, no. 6, p. 194-195.

RAIT RICHARD   WRIGHT RICHARD

1938 Barsov, V. Review of: Deti diadi Toma [Uncle Tom's children]. Literaturnyi kritik, 1938, no. 11, p. 196-198.

Beilin, I. Review of: Deti diadi Toma [Uncle Tom's children]. Literaturnoe obozrenie, 1938, no. 22, p. 42-46.

Vostokova, S. Review of: Deti diadi Toma [Uncle Tom's children]. Novyi mir, 1938, no. 11, p. 281-283.

Grigor'ev, V. Rasskazy o negritianskom proletariate [Stories about the Negro proletariat]. (Deti diadi Toma [Uncle Tom's children]). Kniga i proletarskaia revoliutsiia, 1938, no. 12, p. 125-127.

Elistratova, A. Review of: Deti diadi Toma [Uncle Tom's children]. Pravda, October 21, 1938.

Shneider, A. Richard Rait [Richard Wright]. Internatsional'naia literatura, 1938, no. 7, p. 175-177. *Also, abridged, in:* Wright, R. Deti diadi Toma [Uncle Tom's children]. Moscow, 1939. p. 5-9.

1939 Nevel'skii, V. Review of: Deti diadi Toma [Uncle Tom's children]. Oktiabr', 1939, no. 10-11, p. 326-328.

1940 A. K. Review of: Deti diadi Toma [Uncle Tom's children]. Moscow, 1939. Leningrad, 1940, no. 2, p. 25.

Abramov, A. Syn diadi Toma [The son of Uncle Tom]. (Deti diadi Toma [Uncle Tom's children]. Moscow, 1939). Literaturnaia gazeta, September 8, 1940.

Romanova, E. Amerikanskaia pressa o novom romane Richarda Raita [The American press about Richard Wright's new novel]. (*Native Son*). Internatsional'naia literatura, 1940, no. 7-8, p. 314-315.

Startsev, A. Amerikanskaia tragediia. ("Syn Ameriki") [An American tragedy. ("A son of America"—i.e. *Native Son*)]. Internatsional'naia literatura, 1940, no. 9-10, p. 207-212.

1941 Mendel'son, M. Chernokozhii pasynok. ("Syn Ameriki") [A blackskin-ned stepson. ("A son of America"—i.e. *Native Son*)]. Novyi mir, 1941, no. 6, p. 238-241.

Nikulin, L. Prestuplenie i nakazanie Tomasa Biggera [The crime and punishment of Thomas Bigger]. ("Syn Ameriki" ["A son of America" —i.e. *Native Son*]). Internatsional'naia literatura, 1941, no. 5, p. 182-185.

Nikulin, L. Review of: Syn Ameriki [A son of America—i.e. *Native Son*]. Pravda, April 13, 1941.

Wright, R. Zhiznennyi kodeks Dzhima Krou. Avtobiograficheskii ocherk [The rules of life of Jim Crow. An autobiographic sketch]. Inter-natsional'naia literatura, 1941, no. 5, p. 119-125.

Wright, R. Kak rodilsia "Bigger" [How Bigger was born]. ("Syn Ameriki" ["A son of America"—i.e. *Native Son*]). Internatsional'naia litera-tura, 1941, no. 1, p. 145-156.

Rokotov, T. Tvorcheskii rost Richarda Raita [The creative growth of Richard Wright]. Internatsional'naia literatura, 1941, no. 2, p. 154-157.

Sergeev, N. Review of: Syn Ameriki [A son of America—i.e. *Native Son*]. Internatsional molodezhi, 1941, no. 6, p. 48-49.

Sillen, S. Bigger Tomas na stsene [Bigger Thomas on the stage]. ("Syn Ameriki" ["A son of America"—i.e. *Native Son*]). Literaturnaia gazeta, June 1, 1941.

1961 Zhukov, D. Review of: *Eight Men*. New York, 1961. Sovremennaia khudozhestvennaia literatura za rubezhom, 1961, no. 1, p. 81-82.

1962 Zhukov, D. Richard Rait [Richard Wright]. Molodaia gvardiia, 1962, no. 6, p. 113-114.

ZUGSMIT Lin   ZUGSMITH Leane

1937 Rubin, V. Povest' o "liudiakh v belykh vorotnichkakh" [A story about "people in white collars"]. (*A Time to Remember*. New York, 1936). Internatsional'naia literatura, 1937, no. 10, p. 222-225.

1938 Rubin, V. Review of: *Home is Where You Hang Your Childhood*. New York, 1937. Internatsional'naia literatura, 1938, no. 4, p. 189-190.

1939 Lina, A. Review of: *The Summer Soldier*. New York, 1938. Internatsio-nal'naia literatura, 1939, no. 9-10, p. 254-255.

Mingulina, A. Review of: *The Summer Soldier*. New York, 1938. Inter-natsional'naia literatura, 1939, no. 7-8 (first printing), p. 344-345.

INDEX OF AMERICAN AUTHORS

216

217

REPRINTS FROM OUR COMPARATIVE LITERATURE STUDIES

Through the University of North Carolina Press
Chapel Hill, North Carolina 27514

2. Werner P. Friederich. DANTE'S FAME ABROAD, 1350-1850. The Influence of Dante Alighieri on the Poets and Scholars of Spain, France, England, Germany, Switzerland and the United States. Rome, 1950; Third Printing 1966. Pp. 584. Paper, $ 10.00.

10. Charles E. Passage. DOSTOEVSKI THE ADAPTER. A Study in Dostoevski's Use of the Tales of Hoffmann. 1954. Reprinted 1963. Pp. x, 205. Paper, $ 3.50. Cloth, $ 4.50.

11. Werner P. Friederich and David H. Malone. OUTLINE OF COMPARATIVE LITERATURE. From Dante Alighieri to Eugene O'Neill. 1954. Fourth Printing, 1967. Pp. 460. Paper, $ 6.50.

Through Russell and Russell, Inc.
Publishers, 122 East 42nd Street
New York, New York 10010

1. Fernand Baldensperger and Werner P. Friederich. BIBLIOGRAPHY OF COMPARATIVE LITERATURE. 1950. Pp. 729. Cloth, $ 15.00.

6. 7, 9, 14, 16, 18, 21, 25 and 27. W. P. Friederich and H. Frenz (eds): YEARBOOKS OF COMPARATIVE AND GENERAL LITERATURE. Vols. I (1952) to IX (1960). Cloth, $ 6.50 per volume.

Through Johnson Reprint Corporation
111 Fifth Avenue
New York, New York 10003

3. R. C. Simonini, Jr. ITALIAN SCHOLARSHIP IN RENAISSANCE ENGLAND. Cloth, $ 12.50.

4. GOETHE'S SORROWS OF YOUNG WERTER, TRANSLATED BY GEORGE TICKNOR. Edited with Introduction and Critical Analysis by Frank G. Ryder. Cloth, $ 8.00.

5. Helmut A. Hatzfeld. A CRITICAL BIBLIOGRAPHY OF THE NEW STYLISTICS APPLIED TO THE ROMANCE LITERATURES, 1900-1952. Cloth, $ 12.00.

13. Horst Frenz and G. L. Anderson, eds INDIANA UNIVERSITY CONFERENCE ON ORIENTAL-WESTERN LITERARY RELATIONS. Cloth, $ 15.00.

15. Dorothy B. Schlegel. SHAFTESBURY AND THE FRENCH DEISTS. Cloth, $ 12.50.

19. P. A. Shelley, A. O. Lewis Jr. and W. W. Betts Jr., eds. ANGLO-GERMAN AND AMERICAN-GERMAN CROSSCURRENTS, Volume One. Cloth, $ 15.00.

22. Harvey W. Hewett-Thayer. AMERICAN LITERATURE AS VIEWED IN GERMANY, 1818-1861. Cloth $ 8.50.

23-24. Werner P. Friederich, ed. COMPARATIVE LITERATURE: PROCEEDINGS OF THE SEDOND CONGRESS OF THE INTERNATIONAL COMPARATIVE LITERATURE ASSOCIATION, 2 vols. Cloth $ 45.00.

26. DANTE'S LA VITA NUOVA, TRANSLATED BY RALPH WALDO EMERSON. Edited and annotated by J. Chesley Mathews. Cloth, $ 8.00.

28. Haskell M. Block, ed. THE TEACHING OF WORLD LITERATURE. Cloth, $ 6.00.

30. Oskar Seidlin. ESSAYS IN GERMAN AND COMPARATIVE LITERATURE. Cloth, $ 10.00.

34. William A. McQueen and Kiffin A. Rockwell. THE LATIN POETRY OF ANDREW MARVELL. Introduction, Original Text and Translation. Cloth, $ 8.50.